WITHDRAWN
UTSA Libraries

DICKINSON'S NERVES, FROST'S WOODS

WILLIAM LOGAN

Dickinson's Nerves, Frost's Woods

Poetry in the Shadow of the Past

COLUMBIA UNIVERSITY PRESS   New York

COLUMBIA UNIVERSITY PRESS

Publishers Since 1893

NEW YORK   CHICHESTER, WEST SUSSEX

cup .columbia.edu

Copyright © 2018 William Logan

All rights reserved

Library of Congress Cataloging-in-Publication Data

Names: Logan, William, 1950 November 16– author.

Title: Dickinson's nerves, Frost's woods : poetry in the shadow of the past / William Logan.

Description: New York : Columbia University Press, [2018] |
Includes bibliographical references and index.

Identifiers: LCCN 2017055936 (print) | LCCN 2017056235 (ebook) |
ISBN 9780231546515 (e-book) | ISBN 9780231186148 (cloth)

Subjects: LCSH: English poetry—History and criticism. | American poetry—History
and criticism. | Poetry—Psychological aspects. | Poetics.

Classification: LCC PR503 (ebook) | LCC PR503 .L59 2018 (print) | DDC 821.009—dc23

LC record available at https://lccn.loc.gov/2017055936

Cover image: Debora Greger

Library
University of Texas
at San Antonio

For Debora Greger

What you look hard at seems to look hard at you.
—Gerard Manley Hopkins, *Journals and Papers*

This evening at the ball given by the . . . Marchioness of Londonderry, I had my first glimpse here of the *polonaise* and the mazurka, both danced very badly. We ate in the sculpture gallery, where many of the statues had been topped and draped by the ladies' hats and shawls, something that really sparked one's artistic sensibilities!
—Prince Hermann von Pückler-Muskau, *Letters of a Dead Man*

He was the elected Xerxes of vast herds of wild horses. . . . At their flaming head he westward trooped it like that chosen star which every evening leads on the hosts of light.
—Herman Melville, *Moby-Dick*

Contents

Illustrations

Acknowledgments

These essays, with the exception of "Frost's Woods," were first published in the following journals. To their editors I owe a debt.

Hopkins Review: "Longfellow's Hiawatha, Carroll's Hiawatha: The Name and Nature of Parody"; *Hudson Review*: "Dickinson's Nerves"; *New Criterion*: "Frost's Horse, Wilbur's Ride," "Justice's Henry James," "Pound's Metro," "Shakespeare's Rotten Weeds, Shakespeare's Deep Trenches"; *Parnassus*: "Williams's Wheelbarrow," "Shelley's Wrinkled Lip, Smith's Gigantic Leg"; *Salmagundi*: "Lowell's Skunk, Heaney's Skunk"; *Yale Review*: "Keats's Chapman's Homer."

I owe thanks to many people who went out of their way to answer obscure questions: [Shelley] Alex Chanter (Victoria and Albert Museum), June Holmes (Bewick Society); [Lowell] Stephen Axelrod, Henry Erhard, Grzegorz Kosc; [Keats] Duncan Wu; [Shakespeare] John Kerrigan, Christopher Ricks, Gary Taylor; [Pound] Melanie Brkich, Julian Pepinster; [Williams] Sharon Dunn, Reverend Ray Frazier, Rod Leith, Lauren Puchowski; [Dickinson] Richard Brantley, John Cech, Marianne Curling (Amherst Historical Society), Tim Engels (Brown University Library), Kenneth Kidd, U. C. Knoepflmacher, Ruslyn Vear (Amherst Town Library), Jack Zipes; [Frost] Karen Bennett (University of New Hampshire Cooperative Extension), Richard Holmes (Derry Town Historian), Mark Richardson, Barbara Rimkunas (Exeter Historical Society), Suzanne Stillman, Trudy Van Houten. I have depended, not just on the kindness of strangers, but on the kindness of friends.

DICKINSON'S NERVES, FROST'S WOODS

Notes Toward an Introduction

One knows ahead of time how the machine will grind.
—Robert Lowell, on interpretation

Fashions in criticism rise like hemlines and fall like stocks, but the burden of criticism remains. The biographical interpretations a century ago, psychological readings a generation back, poststructuralist readings of the day before yesterday—all had their day. Many of the claustrophobia-inducing methods of the moment will soon be old hat, perhaps to be replaced by methods even worse. There's no Whig history of criticism, at least to the cynic, only small successes in a landscape strewn with pitfalls and bear traps.

The critic's job of work is to drag poems back to the world in which they were made, to restore the lost background of their creation, while knowing that history has sometimes been used to bully poems and their authors. Wordsworth had a child out of wedlock. Coleridge was an opium addict. Ben Jonson killed a man in a duel. Shakespeare may have been in favor of enclosure (or maybe not—the evidence is ambiguous). You don't have to scratch the great modernists very deeply to find something unhappy in their makeup, whether anti-Semitism or the casual racist slurs of which all were guilty. We cannot blame the past for being the past, for having attitudes that strike us as unfortunate or even horrifying. None has much influence on the poetry—it has effect only when critics decide that all authors should be taken to the pillory, if not the gallows.

Such uses of the past condescend to the poet for failing to anticipate, within the roil of his life, what our advanced age would think, not of his poetry, but of his prejudices. We're allowed to shake our heads a little at what previous ages thought (or more usually failed to think), but we cannot escape the knowledge that the future may look askance at moral failings to which we are blind. Meanwhile, we patronize the past only at the risk of becoming a mob of Mrs. Grundys.

Poetry is written in a world that richly impinges on the words, the images, the culture of the poem. To look at what surrounded the poem's birth does not suggest that the artist is merely an empty suit, a medium for culture. Authors rarely believe in the death of the author. Ignorance of a poem's inner history, however, amounts to willful neglect. A poem is a historical artifact, no less an artifact than a Renaissance slipper or a marble fragment of the Acropolis. History interprets the artifact, and on occasion the artifact interprets history.

The critic must reconcile history and poetry. A poem is a product of its time just as much—if the poem's any good—as a triumph over its time. I don't claim any originality to the insight. Perhaps I have pushed the methods of analysis a little further, once or twice. Most of the poems discussed here are so familiar we have forgotten how to read them. We see the words but paper over the cracks in our understanding. Criticism should try to see poems from the inside, to get down into the muck of the poem's invention—and, of course, into the muck of its language.

Readers of poetry owe the deepest debt to the New Critics, who showed how much the discussion of poetry had ignored what poems actually said, ambiguously, ambivalently. For nearly a century, those critics have set the standard for the way we talk about poetry. Taken to extremes, New Criticism had vices among its many virtues, since every scrap of attention given to one part of a poem takes away attention from the rest. Just as there is no perfect critic, there can be no perfect criticism.

The New Critics, unfortunately, often removed the poem from its setting. Poems, in the end, have only their words; we're unlikely to recover much else about poets long dead. What we can rescue, even from the distant past, is something of the world in which the poems were written, guideposts like wooden stakes marking a road through heavy snow. Such context has long been part of literary history, and even New Criticism was not immune to glimpses of the historical and biographical that buttressed meaning. In the 1950 revision of *Understanding Poetry*, the classic text of New Criticism, Cleanth Brooks and Robert Penn Warren added sections on biography, history, even intention—courses of meaning beyond verbal assay or diagnosis. In his posthumous collection

Using Biography, William Empson, the deepest analyst of poetic language, also tried to restore some of the balance missing. I want to argue that facts lying outside the poem are often crucial to its inner working and that we might look a little deeper when a poem like "The Red Wheelbarrow" is allowed to exist only on its miniature islet of words.

Perhaps too much New Criticism lies between hagiography (every word a saint) and Gnosticism—or hagiography practiced by Gnostics. I'm as eager as those critics to take apart the gummed-up watchworks or faulty transmission to see what's going on and to draw with compass and French curve an exploded diagram of a sonnet. There are critics who do this very well, but two decades ago I began to feel that the old approaches had become perfect within their limitations and perfect because of their limitations. I found myself more interested in the footnotes that litter anthologies, fallen into mouse print at the bottom of the page.

Poems can absorb a lot of close reading in service of the meaning the author apparently sought. There's a fine line between trying to detect the undetectable—resurrecting the long-dead arguments about intention— and suggesting what the author could reasonably have known and might reasonably have meant (using backdrop and atmosphere, the practical surroundings that bear). I want to recognize what art criticism always has: that art is embedded in the world from which it is made.

A critic should be aware of the many ways—through etymology, grammar, the whims of private life, stray evidence of drafts and notes, the corruptions of history, and weather reports—that the reader may peer beneath the blank face of the poem. Some may be more useful than others, but all have purpose. Hints and whispers lie at the margins of the poem; and I haven't been shy about seeking whatever evidence, however buried, might help. The germ of imagination may forever remain unknown, and even known it can tell us only so much. Still, by such knowledge, the knowledge of the rude beginnings, of the autobiographical touch, among other things, some interpretations might at least be eliminated or made less likely.

A poem long settled in anthologies, memorized by many, read by almost everyone, can become so encrusted with criticism it can no longer be seen plain. It lives in its own shadow. The poems considered here are mostly poems I've talked about for many years, read more often than taught, and puzzled over as often as read. The genesis of this book was my slightly cracked notion that standard criticism has often ignored the practical aspects of the poem—call them material culture, local bearings, or the unseemly logic of argument.

When I try to dissect a poem for others or for my own amusement, I usually end with a copy scribbled with notes. Over the years, the margins have become dense with loose thought, sometimes leaking onto a second or third page. Beginning these essays, I thought I'd merely write up my notes. That proved a delusion. As I read more and more slowly, reconsidering the lines before me, I found my thought wandering off in unexpected directions. Nothing in these essays is meant as the template of a method, though some lines of analysis might be considered private maps, back roads toward meaning.

The main problem new readers wrestle with is not so much what the poem is trying to say—though that, that too, offers its difficulties—but what the things said meant in the world for which they were written. This requires, not encyclopedic knowledge (we have knowledge enough now at our fingertips), merely encyclopedic attention, and the curiosity necessary to attention. It helps to know, for example, in Donald Justice's "Henry James by the Pacific," how James made his way west. When Emily Dickinson invokes the locomotive in "I like to see it lap the Miles,"[1] it's relevant to recall that her father promoted the branch railway line to Amherst and that she traveled by train herself.[2] Such knowledge is not the end all, but for certain questions of meaning it is the be all.

I'm all for teasing out the history of a poem, the gravity in which it abided when written. "Skunk Hour" contains secrets that close reading of Robert Lowell's biography and correspondence reveals—such a case lies at the border of what a reader can be expected to know, probably just to the wrong side. Knowledge of the circumstance is not ipso facto knowledge of the poem. If we discovered a document proving that Shakespeare had once been a soldier, or a scrivener, or a tutor—or any of the occupations that, as various critics and cranks have argued, may have occupied him before he became a playwright—it would tell us much about the man but little about the plays. The coroner's report that surfaced only in 1925,[3] recording the circumstances of Marlowe's death (fight over an inn bill, dagger), illuminates almost nothing in his work. Still, more than five centuries after the publication of Dante's *Commedia*, a scholar has shown how much the poem benefits from knowledge of medieval jurisprudence.[4] It's late news—news, indeed, that many who read the poem in its first century might not have needed, because they already knew.

Much criticism focuses on what the poet does subconsciously or unconsciously, yet very few working poets would lay claim to the strange devices and rattletrap artifice some critics discover. In a now infamous example, a critic convinced herself that the name of the ship *Berengaria* in Willa Cather's *The Professor's House* was some "nonsense word," a cipher whose meaning could be teased out only in a series of increasingly ludicrous anagrams:

> Berengaria, ship of women: the {green} {aria}, the {eager} {brain}, the {bearing} and the {bairn}, the {raring} {engine}, the {bargain} {binge}, the {ban} and {bar}, the {garbage}, the {barrage} of {anger}, the {bare} {grin}, the {rage} to {err}, the {rare} {grab} for {being}, the {begin} and {rebegin} {again}.[5]

This bit of Beckettian fireworks might have seemed a scholar's joke had she not prefaced it by saying, *"Berengaria*—a very mother-lode of anagrammatic *energia*."* Unfortunately, *Berengaria* was just the name of a Cunard liner. The lesson on method is that a hammer may be a pretty good hammer, but it makes a lousy drill.

Criticism is the guesswork of meaning. I haven't tried to exhaust all the things to be said about these poems, though some readers may feel that for the essays on "After great pain, a formal feeling comes" and "Stopping by Woods" I've thrown in everything but the kitchen sink—then the sink, too. Nor can I pretend that all poems can best be analyzed in this historical-biographical-archeological way—even for the archeologist, different landscapes require different tools: field walking or core samples, say. Competing methods are the devil's playground, for any devil of a critic. About such poems, there is always more to be said.

The poems have been paired off to show how poems sometimes speak to each other. The essays imagine that certain poems live in relation, not exactly collaborative and not exactly in opposition, but mysteriously linked by who wrote them, by theme or subject, linked by the "spooky action at a distance" quantum physicists adore. Shelley and Smith wrote in competition, Pound and Williams influenced by modern art, Justice perhaps with subconscious memory of Keats, Frost and Dickinson touching on the same American fear.

Some of what these essays dredge up is certainly trivial—but in trivia we often find a clue to what the author was after. To take an example distant from poetry, musicologists now argue that the French taxi horns in Gershwin's *An American in Paris* have been at the wrong pitch for seventy years. Instead of A, B, C, and D, they should be tuned, as they were in an early recording, to A-flat, B-flat, higher D, and lower A.[6] The older notes are more dissonant. From such stray facts, brought again to bear, we learn something about Gershwin's intentions, harmonics, and . . . and taxi horns. The recent linking of Marvell's "Bermudas" to specific events in the fraught history of the islands during the English Civil War, on the other hand, has explained many obscure references.[7]

The critic must be careful not to turn an interest in the past into corrosive nostalgia (or the poem into some seedy adjunct of a lecture on power and class, as so often happens in New Historicism and cultural studies). The discovery of the Derry, New Hampshire, phone directory for a year Frost lived in his farmhouse brings us little closer to the poet's world; but to know that he was the only farmer in the neighborhood with a telephone tells us something about the poet—about his income, or his expectations, or his sense of standing.[8] It may have been a gesture to relieve the isolation of his wife. Van Gogh's mustard-colored bed, portrayed in the various versions of *Bedroom in Arles*, apparently survived at least through the end of the Second World War. Even if the search is sentimental, finding it might tell us how far his painting transformed the ordinary ruck of his life.[9] To learn, however, that the hare in Turner's *Rain, Steam and Speed* could outrun the locomotive is more telling.[10] Something in the painting is released from the amnesia of history. Critics, alas, must be omnivorous, if they are to be critics.

Think of the scrap of a bookseller's list taken from the spine of a seventeenth-century binding, confirming that there actually was a quarto of *Love's Labour's Won*.[11] Two of Milton's sonnets change when we know that the former pupil for whom he wrote them was heavily in debt.[12] Or, more simply, considering how often flowers appear in her work, we come closer to her art by recalling that Emily Dickinson kept an orchard and a small greenhouse. The remains of the latter were recently discovered.[13]

Reading poems even of recent decades, readers tend to impose their own experiences upon them, to introduce their own lives into those lives past. The longing for the universal lets readers suppress phrases and gestures that no longer answer to experience—those that require footnotes become easiest to ignore. Though such a desire is mostly harmless, part of a poem's meaning lies in its limitation in time rather than its triumph over it. The poem that has no echo in the future is illegible, but that does not license the reflexive updating that is a footnote to the psychology of reading. The private and emollient gestures of readers, often the icing of sentiment, may be crucial to the study of a poem's reception; but they are more or less useless to its interpretation, perverse to the extent they distort or corrupt the poem's meaning. I'm not asking for some impossibly pure criticism that would trap the poem in amber, only a recognition of the subtle ways the past of a poem lies within the present.

Poetry is an atavistic force thrust against modern ignorance. I want to call the method of these essays, insofar as it is a method, reading the margins. Poems are stained with history, their making rooted in history; and it does them no favors to suppress history or pretend it doesn't exist. To say that poems are only history, however, cobbled from the time and its transient conventions or prejudices, is an ugly simplification. Poems are a language already penetrated by centuries of use, a language particular to the quirks, happenstance, and defective personality of the poet. Poems are not mirrors, no matter how reflective they seem. They're black pools—tarns, in Frost's word. As the reader often senses, something moves within or beneath a poem, the shadow of a great fish, or an invisible hand.

1. Shelley's Wrinkled Lip, Smith's Gigantic Leg

PERCY BYSSHE SHELLEY, "OZYMANDIAS"

The younger Romantics were the first generation of British poets—perhaps the first generation of poets anywhere—to write poems contemplating remnants of the ancient world. This interest in the past, in the pastness of the past, infused the Romantic sublime, for there is no more useful reminder of mortality than a vine-covered ruin. If you wanted your own ruin and had the means, local masons could build what was called a folly, the make-believe remains of abbey or castle. (Byron might have indulged himself had he not been Byron—in any case, his ancestral home had been built next to the ruins of an ancient abbey.) If you were without means, if you could not afford the Grand Tour, you had to take your inspiration from books, as Keats did in "On First Looking Into Chapman's Homer." Or you had to visit museums.

England was not always the warehouse of empire. When the British Museum opened in 1759, it contained few antiquities amid the thousands of books, stuffed animals, and dried plants. Not until the 1780s did the museum begin to acquire Brobdingnagian fragments, like the colossal sandaled foot found near Naples and purchased from William Hamilton. Among the wrack of vanished civilizations were prodigious buildings (the Great Pyramid at Giza covered more ground than St. Paul's and St. Peter's combined), as well as sky-scraping heroic statues, often preserved in mutilated form. These statues were a particular curiosity to the British, who could offer, as massive fragments of antique civilization, not much more than an earthen dike or two, some lengths of Roman wall, and Stonehenge. Articles about statues and other objects from the Near East filled the reviews of the day and drove the public to the museum, sometimes in eager anticipation of objects to come.

The older Romantics, however much they loved books (we owe our deepest knowledge of Coleridge's imagination to his marginal scrawls—if he ever returned a borrowed book, it was defaced with his genius), depended on the close observation of nature. Wordsworth hated the city and couldn't wait to escape it—in his devious sonnet "Composed Upon Westminster Bridge," he looked upon London as if it were another landscape. When he hiked above Tintern Abbey, he was more interested in the hills and cataracts than in the abbey's lost majesties—the roofless stones famously make no direct appearance in the poem. This is not to say that Wordsworth and Coleridge failed to hold ruins in due Romantic reverence—fallen walls litter their work, but they are largely local.[1] The second generation of Romantics, who in the main preferred city life, were drawn to ruins far flung—perhaps their fascination derived partly from discoveries made during the Napoleonic wars. (Byron's use of Greek ruins in the early cantos of *Childe Harold's Pilgrimage* [1812] may have been crucial for thinking of ruins in political terms.) These late Romantics were not counterfeiting antique poetry, like Thomas Chatterton or James Macpherson, or like the Elizabethans dramatizing twice-told tales of Caesar, or Sejanus, or Tamburlaine. The monumental past was newly available in journal and book and museum, as well as by travel—and poets were quick to make use of it.

The awe these artifacts instilled in viewers should not be understated. The illiterate souls who came across the mammoth ruins, long after the civilizations had collapsed, were dumbfounded by what they saw—some of the secrets of building the pyramids are secrets still. The world that emerged from the Dark Ages had been staggered by the achievements of its distant ancestors. It did seem, especially to peoples without history, that in those days Titans ruled.

We think of the Romantics as the embodiment of imagination, not fancy; of the "spontaneous overflow of powerful feelings," as Wordsworth had it, not cautious artifice; of "incidents and situations from common life," not gossip of dead kings.[2] Yet in some ways the Romantics were just as much in love with artifice as the Augustans before them. Inspiration cannot derive mystically from nature if it can be poured out on demand, from a tap; but some of the Romantics, as a kind of parlor trick, loved to write when inspiration was forced. Think of that gloomy

June evening on Lake Geneva during the summer of 1816—the notorious Year Without a Summer. The company having diverted itself with a book of supernatural tales, Byron (for he was the host) proposed that each write a ghost story.[3] They pottered about in prose—John William Polidori supposedly writing of a "skull-headed lady"[4]—but eventually gave up the task. All but one, that is: Shelley's eighteen-year-old lover Mary Godwin, who had been listening when talk during the previous weeks had strayed to galvanism and the reanimation of corpses, wrote the first draft of *Frankenstein*. (By the end of the year, she was Mary Shelley.) The discarded germ of Byron's own idea, published at the end of *Mazeppa* (1819), is the grandfather of all vampire tales in our literature.

One of the many ways to pass a London evening with Leigh Hunt was to accept his challenge to write a poem in fifteen minutes. He would prescribe the theme, usually choosing a sonnet as the frame. (The sonnet-mad decade of the 1590s was almost matched when the Romantics revived the form.) We have at least four poems Keats wrote in Hunt's verse duels,[5] as well as one by Shelley, whose sonnet on the Nile, written one evening in February 1818, was not discovered among Hunt's papers until half a century after Shelley's death.[6] Hunt comes off rather well in these competitions (*his* sonnet on the Nile is one of his better),[7] Keats rather poorly. Shelley's Nile poem is workmanlike, but the one he had written on an Egyptian theme a few weeks earlier, at home in Marlow after Christmas, is a different matter. Having read about the ruin of a colossal granite statue in Egypt, most critics believe, he and his friend Horace Smith provoked each other to sonnets. It remains Shelley's best-known poem.

OZYMANDIAS

I met a traveller from an antique land,
Who said—"Two vast and trunkless legs of stone
Stand in the desert. Near them, on the sand,
Half sunk a shattered visage lies, whose frown,
And wrinkled lip, and sneer of cold command,
Tell that its sculptor well those passions read
Which yet survive, stamped on these lifeless things,
The hand that mocked them, and the heart that fed;

And on the pedestal these words appear:
'My name is Ozymandias, King of Kings,
Look on my Works ye Mighty, and despair!'
No thing beside remains. Round the decay
Of that colossal Wreck, boundless and bare
The lone and level sands stretch far away."[8]

The first pleasure of this traveler's tale is the artless contrivance of the traveler himself. This nameless and faceless creature, who exists only to spin his thirteen lines, is not compelled, like the Ancient Mariner, to seek absolution by constantly rehearsing his story. The traveler doesn't even provide a proper introduction, launching into his lines in medias res. If character can be read in such things, it should be read in the sudden outburst, as well as in the scene described—yet we have no context in which a psychology can be enacted, as in "My Last Duchess" or "Resolution and Independence" (or even in Carroll's wicked parody of the latter). If you want to know this character's character, the poem offers nothing more than his expedient appearance.

The traveler, however, relieves the speaker of the moral burden of the tale, which is charged to someone else's account—however much we are aware that this Marco Polo is imaginary, his is the moral judgment and his the *topos* almost as ancient as Ozymandias himself: the transience of earthly things, the transience of earthly kings. "How are the mighty fallen!" 2 Samuel has it. (The traveler's absence in Shelley's raw early draft proves him a tactical second thought.) This removes the poem just beyond Keats's condemnation, when he remarked that "we hate poetry that has a palpable design upon us" and asked whether the reader was "to be bullied into a certain Philosophy."[9] All poems have such designs; but in the successful poem we don't particularly notice them, or we come to believe the designs our own.

Ozymandias was the Greek name for the greatest pharaoh of Egypt's Nineteenth Dynasty, Rameses II. Rameses is a peculiar choice for Shelley's poem because he was one of the few pharaohs whose temples have survived three millennia more or less intact—the triumphal architecture of his long kingship includes some of the ruins at Abu Simbel, Luxor, and Karnak. Shelley did not intend to write history; even had he wanted to, detailed knowledge of the Egyptian dynasties had to wait for

Champollion's decipherment of hieroglyphics. However accidental, the irony of Shelley's choice confirms the rupture between past and present that dominates the poem.

The ruins so central to the Romantic age have a curious pathos the action of the poem must tease out and modify. The following November, Shelley was strolling amid the overgrown stones of the Colosseum. As he wrote in an unfinished fragment:

> The great wrecked arches, the shattered masses of precipitous ruin, overgrown with the younglings of the forest, and more like chasms rent by an earthquake among the mountains than like the vestige of what was human workmanship—what are they? . . . It is because we enter into the meditations, designs, and destinies of something beyond ourselves that the contemplation of the ruins of human power excites an elevating sense of awfulness and beauty.[10]

There is perhaps a pathos to all broken things (rusty mine-machinery proved seductive to Auden), but the sonnet's initial grand vision of amputated legs and mutilated head is destroyed by the ugliness of the sculpted face. The traveler could see this sneering face only if certain conditions were met: it must have been "half sunk" in the sands, with the mouth left visible.[11] The head must therefore be lying on its side or perhaps partly upside-down. That would not be an image far from Shelley's radical mind when he thought of tyrants. The disembodied head would look as if Pharaoh had been executed by guillotine.

After five lines, Shelley has a formal problem. The rhyme scheme, odd lines rhyming on -*and*, the even on -*own* or some variant (in British English, *stone* and *frown* are near neighbors in rhyme but not identical), requires another rhyme on the latter—but here the Petrarchan scheme breaks down. This is not beyond the liberties the Romantics took with the sonnet, though the effect is a mild breach of expectation, a small but sharp deceit in harmony. Perhaps only by chance has the poet placed here the betrayal of the king:

> "Half sunk a shattered visage lies, whose frown,
> And wrinkled lip, and sneer of cold command,
> Tell that its sculptor well those passions read

Which yet survive, stamped on these lifeless things,
The hand that mocked them, and the heart that fed."

The poet did not lack rhymes: "alone," "bemoan," "condone," "disown,"
"dethrone," and even "overthrown" are near to the theme. He must have
seen greater advantage in a different line of thought.

Forming this indictment of the king in the very art that is his legacy,
his sole legacy, Shelley finds himself in a syntactical thicket. The sculptor
read certain passions in the king's expression—the synecdoche is strongly
willed. The statue offers two readings (two texts, as it were): what is
carved at the king's feet and what, as we say metaphorically, is written
on his face. The syntax here might first seem a list: the series composing
the subject of the relative clause ("whose frown, / And wrinkled lip, and
sneer") could have been balanced by objects in the "that" clause—the
sculptor read (1) those passions, (2) the hand, and (3) the heart. Unhappily, this makes no sense. Because of the interrupting participial phrase,
we don't immediately register that "survive" is a transitive verb—the
passions don't simply survive; they survive "the hand that mocked
them" as well as "the heart that fed [them]." The hand is the sculptor's;
the heart, the pharaoh's. The pronoun is problematic, too, but the poet
cannot have meant "the hand that mocked [these lifeless things]" unless
the king was mocking his own sculpture. Similar superficially plausible
readings (the "passions" can't be "stamped" on the "hand that mocked
them," because Shelley's statue no longer has a sculpted hand) would
require a greater degree of ingenuity than the poem can probably bear.
Shelley's syntax in this long crowded sentence is troublesome enough
(there are four relative clauses and one subordinate clause) without being
monstrous. A grammar teacher could do worse than have his students
parse the sentence—and all its false variants.

Shelley has exceeded the grace of his means, but the thought is elegant—the sculptor is gone, the king is gone, but the passions that chill
the viewer have survived the intervening centuries. (It is doubtful that
the poet had learned enough about the early excavations of the tombs to
realize that the king's salted liver or lungs might have been preserved in
what was later called a Canopic jar. If Rameses possessed a heart, it would
have been left in his mummified body.) Neither the traveler nor Shelley
could be certain that the passions ("its sculptor well those passions read")

had been rendered accurately—the traveler no doubt judged them by the inscription. If such emotions could be read in the face, Shelley might be intimating that hieroglyphs tell us no more than can be deciphered in the statues. Not every passing traveler would be literate: Shelley's imagined statue offers an alternate text—that of the face—for those who cannot read. Had he known anything about the conventional art of the pharaohs, however, he would not have invented so grim an expression—pharaohs ruled their temples with lofty impersonality, their expression no less impassive than the plaster or stone that bore them. To the Egyptian sculptor of that period, one pharaoh looked pretty much like another—personality came much later.

It's easy to lose the subtlety of Shelley's thought in the coils of syntax. The tyrant's power is corrupt from the start, if he cannot command basic loyalty from the sculptor. Artists have been murdered for less. The pharaoh is not blind to the sneer or frown—they are exactly what he wants. It is only time that has forced judgment upon them. Time has done a better job than the sculptor at providing a comeuppance. Shelley hated tyrants (few poets put in a good word for them); but his pleasure in this broken sneer, this ruined frown, must lie in the schadenfreude difficult to avoid when any high figure is brought low by his own hand. We love an art that shows us the self-delusion of the sitter, just as we despise one that reveals the self-delusion of the artist. Having seen through someone else's deceptions, no doubt we feel immune to our own.

The poem's sestet is almost an afterthought, but few afterthoughts have been more cunning:

"And on the pedestal these words appear:
'My name is Ozymandias, King of Kings,
Look on my Works ye Mighty, and despair!'
No thing beside remains. Round the decay
Of that colossal Wreck, boundless and bare
The lone and level sands stretch far away."

Some critics mark the turn only in the last three lines, which are taken as an abrupt break of thought. However tied into the preceding sentence, the pedestal's words read like a summary caption or museum label (or a caricature's speech balloon), observation becoming interpretation. The shift in gaze from head to pedestal is part of this summation—it prepares the final vision, where the dead king's words do not echo amid the resounding stones of his great works but are lost in the vacancy of nowhere. Lines 9–11 act like a hinge. This is another way of toppling a tyrant—in the poem, the head is mounted above the inscription only because the lines follow the traveler's eye. The pharaoh's head really lies at his feet.

It's a minor point of construction, but Shelley must have felt *some* rupture after the eighth line, even as his rhymes knitted the divided sonnet together. The scheme, in the end, is *ababacdc/edefef*—some rhymes are over- or underrepresented. If "these lifeless things" bridges the gap by rhyming with "King of Kings," only a half-deaf critic would fail to detect a thematic rhyme and a thematic criticism—the great king *is* now reduced to lifeless art. Art, in the end, is what has remained. No doubt this is some comfort to artists, or was at least to Shelley.

Hubris is an act of insolence or presumption, not, as we sometimes take it, pride. We know that "pride goes before a fall," though folk editing has reduced the force of Proverbs 18, which reads, "Pride goeth before destruction, and an haughty spirit before a fall." Insolence must be directed at someone greater. Shelley would not have seen it this way, as he was an atheist. Neither would Rameses the Great, as he was a god. To Shelley, the gesture would have been empty—we are humbled by time, not gods. Time is the only god the atheist acknowledges.

The idea beneath the poem was no doubt current. One of Thomas Bewick's "vignettes" in *History of British Birds* (1797) shows a donkey rubbing its hindquarters against a leaning and partly legible memorial-stone that reads "Battle . . . Splendid Victory . . . Immortal."[12] Bewick later remarked that this was the "proper use, at last, of all warlike monuments."[13] Another vignette showed a man pissing against a fragment of what may be Hadrian's Wall.[14]

To feel small before the immensity of the universe is one thing; to feel insignificant before the work of man quite another—the glory of the achievement is embodied more in the face of Ozymandias than in the inscription. It is the face that makes him disconcertingly human, a man and more than a man. That "passions" survive animates the devastation. (Museums love statues or mummies, the human remnants—we long for the anthropomorphic. Curators are never much interested in bare blocks of granite.)

The sonnet's final lines open outward to a view, and there perhaps lies the secret of the poem's power. Such unexpected vistas, onto unseen valley or snow-capped mountain, usually mark sudden access of the sublime; but here the lift in spirit before nature's grandeur, as the poem abandons the arrogant, sneering king, is immediately crushed—the view has breadth and depth, but the breadth and depth of a vast waste. That is a more eloquent judgment on ambition than anything Shelley might say, and he benefits from a second drama of opposition: the contrast between the king's vaunted works and their absolute erasure.

"Decay" may refer only to the gargantuan fragments, but perhaps in Shelley's mind shards of the vanished whole litter the sands. "Level" suggests the amplitude of destruction—in this imaginary Egypt, there are no dusty tells to betray a lost city. The land has been washed clean as the Margate sands, as if after the Flood. The most vigorous word in these closing lines, however, is "wreck," which originally referred to something cast ashore by the tide, later the wreck of a ship. Only in the day of Pope did it begin to refer to the shattered remains *of* something demolished, and only in the hour of the Romantics to anything in a state of ruin.

Shelley used the word some thirty times, perhaps most hauntingly in his curious lyric-drama *Hellas* (1822): "If Greece must be / A wreck, yet shall its fragments reassemble."[15] He is alluding to the myth of Osiris, one of the most ancient Egyptian gods. "Colossal" comes down to us through Herodotus, who first used it to describe these very Egyptian statues. But just as "colossal" holds within it memory of the Colossus of Rhodes, that later wonder (for it postdates the ruin of Thebes), is it far fetched to suggest that "colossal Wreck" did not quite conceal from Shelley its nautical origins? British knowledge of the East, and the public inheritance of the rubble of Egypt, came after the Battle of the Nile, which left the burnt or sunken wreckage of the *Orient* (Napoleon's flagship), the *Mercure*, the *Hercule*, and many another, names redolent of failed conquest and half-forgotten gods.

What is most remarkable about this coda, however, is that it refuses to point a moral. The results of the pharaoh's hubris are so devastating, there is no need to comment upon them. Shelley knows how much he has to say, but he also knows how much he doesn't—the ending falls like a trip-hammer. The long tail to his poem goes unremarked. We must read his lines remembering where they were written: in a country lush with greenery, and without deserts. (The poet wrote at a time when many men never left their home villages. Tales of Egypt were tales of the moon.) The implication is that once, long ago, the sands had held a vast and thriving civilization. The extent of the loss is as terrifying as the sparsity of the material remains and their giant size. In the early dynastic period, great reaches of Egypt still possessed sweeping savannahs; but by the hour of the New Kingdom, fifteen hundred years later, much of this landscape had already turned to sand. (The Sahara is now forty times larger than all Britain.) The poem shrewdly—no doubt luckily more than uncannily—records the devastation of a natural world.

Leigh Hunt published the sonnet in the *Examiner* of January 11, 1818,[16] two weeks after it was written—the poem lay beneath the heading "Original Poetry," in an issue that included articles on distressed seamen, the Poor Laws, and a painting by Benjamin West, as well as police reports (a "celebrated comedian" had been charged with using "threatening language," a gang of robbers infested Hyde Park) and a bit of scandal involving a "young Gentleman" who had resolved "to quit the country for ever."[17] Shelley used the pseudonym Glirastes, a macaronic compound probably meaning "Dormouse lover." ("Dormouse" was Shelley's pet name for Mary.)[18] He had made a few changes to his fair copy before publishing the poem, sharpening "wrinkled lips" to "wrinkled lip" ("wrinkled lips" might have suggested age) and reversing "remains beside" to the poetic "beside remains." More importantly, "And on the pedestal these words appear" was originally the flatter, verb-deprived "And on the pedestal, this legend clear."[19] "Appear" lets the words rise out of the concealing sands, almost a quiet acknowledgment that they could not have been deciphered in Shelley's day, had they still existed.[20]

In the version I have printed, I have retained the antique spelling of "desart" and the separation of "nothing" into "no thing" on the authority of Shelley's fair copy, which lies in one of his notebooks on a page that also contains a small faint sketch of some trees. Bound in boards and trimmed with red leather, the volume was likely sold as an artist's sketch-book. On the reverse of the elegantly inscribed fair copy, there's a

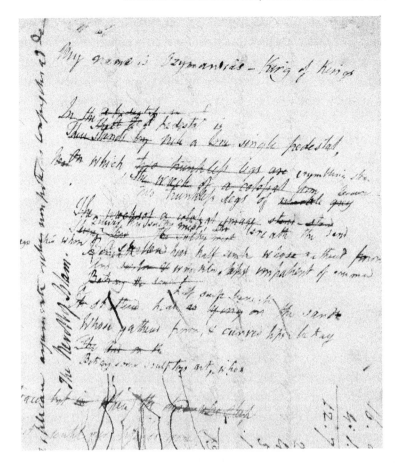

Draft of Percy Bysshe Shelley, "Ozymandias."
Source: MS. Shelley e. 4, fol. 85v, Bodleian Libraries, University of Oxford.
Used by permission.

clumsy sketch of a mountain reflected in a lake, as well as calculations on account, some Cicero, and drafts of various poems (crossed to conserve space), including the false start of "Ozymandias," some two dozen lines that reveal the poem's crude beginnings.

At the top of the draft page, Shelley wrote the crucial line, "My name is Ozymandias—King of Kings," the axle on which the poem turns. He made five attempts at a line about the pedestal, the last stating that the ruined statue "stands by Nile," probably placing it in the necropolis across from Luxor. Though he hasn't started to shape the poem, Shelley was already trying to tie the lines into rhyme: "The wrecks of a colossal image stand" lies canceled above "Quiver thro sultry mist, thr beneath the sand." The mist is a nice touch, but it is atmospheric filler that doesn't fit the later idea of a desert. (The plural "wrecks" suggests the scattered fragments slyly omitted from the finished poem.) Shelley must have thought the statue marble, as he wrote, "two trunkless legs of marble grey."

The drafts of every poem are the wreckage from which it is built, and these halting lines remain the ghostly predecessor. The brilliance came after the wreckage, including the chain of hearsay that serves, like the final line ("The lone and level sands stretch far away"), as an act of perspective in which the view fades into the distance—the poet relates what a traveler said about what a ruined statue recorded of the boast of a dead king. The very rough lines are the fragments of something yet to be made whole—the limbs, in other words, of Osiris.

Horace Smith, "Ozymandias"

What of Shelley's rival in sonnet writing, the indefatigable Horace Smith, stockbroker poet? Shelley once said of his friend, according to Leigh Hunt, "He writes poetry and pastoral dramas, and yet knows how to make money, and does make it, and is still generous!"[21] (You can hear the wonder still.) The *Examiner* published Smith's poem a few weeks after Shelley's, and under the same title; but that may have been an editorial intervention to emphasize that the poems, as a note from the author explained, shared the same source of inspiration: "The subject which suggested the beautiful Sonnet, in a late number, signed 'Glirastes,' produced also the enclosed from another pen."[22] When Smith collected the sonnet in his book of miscellaneous verse, *Amarynthus, the Nympholept* (1821), his title was slightly longer:

On a Stupendous Leg of Granite, Discovered
Standing by Itself in the Deserts of Egypt,
with the Inscription Inserted Below

In Egypt's sandy silence, all alone,
  Stands a gigantic leg, which far off throws
  The only shadow that the desert knows.

"I am great Ozymandias," saith the stone,
  "The king of kings: this mighty city shows
The wonders of my hand." The city's gone!
  Nought but the leg remaining to disclose
The site of that forgotten Babylon.

We wonder, and some hunter may express
Wonder like ours, when thro' the wilderness,
  Where London *stood*, holding the wolf in chace,
He meets some fragment huge, and stops to guess
  What powerful, but unrecorded, race,
  Once dwelt in that annihilated place.[23]

This was followed by a sonnet to Shelley. However the two friends came to write these sonnets, not only did they use versions of the same inscription, but their lines contained certain echoes—Shelley's "lone and level sands" lies close to "Egypt's sandy silence, all alone," and Smith's "The only shadow that the desert knows" (like the gnomon of a gigantic sundial) is visually more arresting than the dramatic "Nothing beside remains." (In the *Examiner* text, which differs only trivially, Smith had spelled the word "desart," like Shelley.) Smith's London is Cato's Carthage, a starker figure than Shelley's vague "works." A poem consists not simply of images, however, but images set in the context of argument; and here the stockbroker is at a disadvantage.

Smith did not have the judgment a better poet requires. The longer title makes the poem almost redundant. (The title isn't a hint or a fingerpost so much as a movie preview.) The title also unhappily emphasizes Smith's major poetic mishap—that poor leg! A disembodied granite arm has pathos, a granite leg nothing but bathos. Shelley mitigates the potential farce in part by emphasizing the once-complete sculpture (he follows with immediate reference to the shattered head), in part by insisting on a *pair* of legs and finally by placing the verb after the legs—"stand" is forcefully lodged at the beginning of the following line. Yet where those "legs of stone" seem oddly majestic, Smith's solitary "gigantic leg" is anticlimactic and ridiculous. In Shelley's draft, though he had written "two trunkless legs," further down he canceled a "shattered leg"—perhaps his notion briefly coincided with Smith's.

No doubt Smith felt that the mighty leg alone would be enough to awe his reader, but perhaps he didn't reckon with the unintended suggestion of war amputation (London was rife with King George's mutilated soldiers, reduced to beggary) or, worse, of a king reduced to hopping. Even his positioning of the verb (identical to Shelley's) doesn't save him, because he has unhappily reversed the syntax—a standard poetic technique then, to be sure, but one that backfires here.

Smith's second mistake is to make his stone speak. The metonymy is precious and artful, catching the rhyme at cost, where Shelley gives the words directly to the pharaoh. Too, Shelley has placed the inscription as a climax of hubris; Smith needs to get it out of the way because he has another end in view. ("The city's gone!" is too eager to shock—Shelley's lingering, paced revelation is far subtler.) Apart from their clownish whimsy, the first half-dozen lines of Smith's poem are forgettable—but then something unexpected occurs. The lines "Nought but the leg remaining to disclose / The site of that forgotten Babylon" place that amputated leg in the vast city that once surrounded it. That a city the equal of Babylon could vanish without trace is a conceit with theatrical flair. (The rhyme "gone" and "Babylon" deepens the loss.) In the sestet, the stockbroker comes into his own:

> We wonder, and some hunter may express
> Wonder like ours, when thro' the wilderness,
>   Where London *stood*, holding the wolf in chace,
> He meets some fragment huge, and stops to guess
>   What powerful, but unrecorded, race,
>   Once dwelt in that annihilated place.

We move from the present to some impossibly future day when even London shall be waste ground, overgrown like the Roman Forum with shrubs and vines. (Through most of the nineteenth century, the Forum was not the "long, clean, livid trench" Zola later called it but a great woodsy meadow filled with cattle and churches ancient as well as Baroque, the last now long since razed.)[24] The absoluteness of "annihilated" is total; but the Latin, embedded here, offers not just an elevated diction, full of a stateliness now dead, but a terrible vision of the Roman Empire brought low, reduced to the scraps of its tongue in those lands it once conquered. "Stood" is emphasized like no other word in the poem, and the implicit "fell" rises in ghostly partnership. Gibbon's *Decline and Fall* had been published a few decades before.

The wolf would have been an image more highly charged in Smith's day; though the last English wolf had been killed probably early in the previous century, the wolves of Scotland and Ireland had been hunted to extinction within living memory. We must imagine the hunter, headlong in his career through brush and thicket, suddenly arrested by this sight—"wilderness" implies savage and unchecked growth. The lines may be a memory of *Henry IV, Part II*: "O my poor kingdom . . . ! / . . . Thou wilt be a wilderness again, / Peopled with wolves, thy old inhabitants!"[25] The wild and rank verdure stands in florid contrast to Shelley's stark wastes. Finding some immense stone fragment of a lost city, the hunter is so stunned he stops cold. (Here was exactly the power of the sublime to halt a man in the blind course of his existence, to make him contemplate and reflect.) The hunter is Shelley's traveler hurled into the future, but he serves a more subtle purpose as the reader's filtering consciousness. He's no archeologist (a term that appeared only a few years after the poem); any conclusion he derives about the makers of this fragment must be only a guess.

Perhaps Smith had read *Eighteen Hundred and Eleven*, where Anna Laeticia Barbauld saw a future where all Europe would be laid waste and "England, the seat of arts, be only known / By the gray ruin and the mouldering stone." Strangers, "when midst fallen London, they survey / The stone where Alexander's ashes lay, / Shall own with humbled pride the lesson just / By Time's slow finger written in the dust."[26] Shelley was certainly reading her two years later.[27] Less than a generation after, a similar trope animated a famous passage by Thomas Babington Macaulay, who in 1840, reviewing a work by his great rival von Ranke, was moved to say of the Catholic Church:

> She was great and respected before the Saxon had set foot on Britain—before the Frank had passed the Rhine—when Grecian eloquence still flourished at Antioch—when idols were still worshipped in the temple of Mecca. And she may still exist in undiminished vigour

when some traveller from New Zealand shall, in the midst of a vast
solitude, take his stand on a broken arch of London Bridge to sketch
the ruins of St. Paul's.[28]

It's a haunting thought, London destroyed. (The idea, usually applied
to New York or Los Angeles, has become a Hollywood commonplace.)
It proves equally disturbing that in Smith's poem no living man recalls
the city, that even the name of that distant people has been effaced. By
"unrecorded," the poet must mean not just in the hunter's own literature and history, if he had them—the race itself has left no record. No
inscription survives, at least none seen. Which ruin in London did the
poet have in mind? What great lump would be equal to the oppressive
wreck of Ozymandias? Presumably Smith meant a fragment of Westminster Abbey, St. Paul's, or the Tower. This future devastated London lies
in contrast to the ancient Egypt revealed by the maimed statue of the
great pharaoh—but are we to imagine all that remains is a hulking fragment or a landscape hillocky with viny wreckage half concealed?

That awe felt by the hunter is reminiscent of a poem that had appeared
in the *Examiner* (Hunt's journal, recall) scarcely a year before. That poem
ended:

Or like stout Cortez when with eagle eyes
   He stared at the Pacific, and all his men
Looked at each other with a wild surmise —
   Silent, upon a peak in Darien.[29]

There is the closing view whose expectation Shelley toys with—the sense
of epic nature that dwarfed a man. The conquistador (Balboa, of course,
not Cortez) would have just emerged after a long trek through the thick
malarial jungle of the Isthmus. (A similar figure stands upon a moun-
taintop in Caspar David Friedrich's *Wanderer Above the Sea of Fog* [1817].)
The fragment the hunter discovers, along his jungly Thames, induces a
similar sense of wonder before a majesty previously unknown.

Shelley's poem is a masterpiece, Smith's merely a curiosity. Though
Shelley has managed his effects with greater tactical skill—not just
the movement of detail but of emotion behind detail—we must not
ignore that Smith, at least this once, was no mean poet. His vision is

horrifically bleak. How disquieting it must have been, for this stockbroker in London and of London, to think of that distant day when his own civilized home would be rank wilderness. Disquieting, or perhaps thrilling.

CODA

We know nearly the hour these poems were written, but what was the source that so inflamed the imaginations of Shelley and Smith? The question has been as popular with scholars as the source of the Nile was once to explorers. According to the biographer Richard Holmes, the poets had been to the British Museum and seen the massive granite bust of Rameses II; but this can't be true, as that sculpture, called the Younger Memnon, was not exhibited until 1820.[30]

One possible influence, perhaps insufficiently recognized, may have been Coleridge's "dramatic fragment" "The Night-Scene," which ends,

The whirl-blast comes, the desert-sands rise up
And shape themselves: from earth to heaven they stand,
As thought they were the pillars of a temple,
Built by Omnipotence in its own honour!
But the blast pauses, and their shaping spirit
Is fled: the mighty columns were but sand,
And lazy snakes trail o'er the level ruins![31]

Here writ small are the desert sands, the majestic ruins (made of sand), the omnipotence that has built a monument to itself, the notion of vanity, and the colossal wreck of the colossal, leaving only Coleridge's "level ruins" and Shelley's "level sands." Though an early draft had been composed in 1801, Coleridge did not collect this fragment until *Sibylline Leaves*, published in July 1817, six months before Shelley and Smith composed their poems. Shelley ordered the book in the month of publication.[32] He was at the time particularly influenced by Coleridge.[33]

Shelley and Smith owed a debt to the universal history of Diodorus Siculus, whose *Bibliotheca Historica* was written about the time of Caesar.[34] (Poets stand like beggars before a long line of ancient librarians.) Paraphrasing an even more ancient historian, Diodorus describes the monstrous statue, which then still possessed its legs and the hieroglyphic inscription. Usually spelled "Osymandyas" or "Osymandias," the Greek name was an attempted transliteration of the inscription's royal cartouche. In George Booth's translation of 1814, the place Shelley probably came across Diodorus (that Shelley knew Greek does not mean he found it in Greek), the inscription reads: "I am Osymandyas, king of kings; if any would know how great I am, and where I lie, let him excel me in any of my works."[35] This is telling on two counts. First, Ozymandias says that no one can judge his greatness except the man who has surpassed him. Second, only such a man can know where the king is buried—it's a riddle; but perhaps the burden is, "If you're clever enough to overshadow me, you're clever enough to find my tomb."

It will be no comfort to those who believe that inspiration must be immediate and direct to know that, in all likelihood, Shelley took his ideas, not from secondhand sources, but thirdhand at best, specifically from a review in the *Quarterly Review* of a travel book by the aptly named Thomas Legh.[36] (That in "Ozymandias" the tale is the secondhand account of a traveler is therefore fitting.) Lead piece in the October 1816 issue and therefore one a reader might leaf through offhandedly, the anonymous review includes all the salient details used by the two poets, not least a description of the giant fallen statue of Rameses II—a description bound to fire the fancy of a distracted poet or two. Indeed, so much so that fancy soon replaced fact. The statue, which intact would have stood some seventy feet high, had been well known in the classical period, having been set at the back of the first court of the pharaoh's great funeral temple at Thebes, the Ramesseum, which lay across the Nile from Luxor. The statue was not standing but enthroned—not an orphan, not a lone figure abandoned amid empty sands.

Discussion of the statue and Shelley's sources is complicated by occasional confusion about the various statues in the area. In desert emptiness about half a mile south of the Ramesseum stand the twin statues of the earlier pharaoh Amenhotep III called the Colossi (sometimes simply Colossus) of Memnon. At the Ramesseum, apart from the colossal head and upper body of the great statue of Rameses, sit the legs and base of the shorter statue of the enthroned pharaoh whose head was taken to the British Museum. This survivor of what was once a pair flanking the entrance to the temple is called, misleadingly, the Younger Memnon. The other head sits on the sand at the temple.

There is evidence that Shelley may have seen illustrations of the Colossus of Memnon in Richard Pococke's *A Description of the East and Other Countries*, illustrations that also show the head and legs of the Younger Memnon. Pococke mistakenly believed a temple he saw at Luxor answered the description in Diodorus of the "sepulchre of Osymanduas."[37] Shelley may also have read the description of the Osymandyas statue by Dominique Vivant, Baron Denon, in a translation of *Voyage dans la basse et la haute Egypt* (1802), which contains a number of phrases that beckon toward the poem (my emphases below):

> At some paces from this gate are the remains of an enormous *colossus*; it has been wantonly *shattered.* . . . Is it the statue of . . . Osymandyas? . . . Osymandyas had . . . caused an inscription to be engraven *on the pedestal* of the statue, in which he defied the power of man to destroy this monument. . . . [The statue] has disappeared, the *hand* of time and the teeth of envy appear to have united zealously in its destruction, and *nothing of it remains* but a shapeless rock of granite.[38]

Since Smith and Shelley had many of the same fancies, and since both used the same spelling of Ozymandias,[39] either their conversation settled on detail after reading the review or they had read some source now forgotten. The translation of Diodorus quoted in the *Quarterly Review* began, "I am the king of kings, Osymandyas"—the inversion may be a clue that the poets did not use only the review but had seen, say, George Booth's translation of Diodorus. We know nothing about the form the competition or challenge took; but Shelley and Smith could not have been writing to the clock, because Shelley had drafted notes, as mentioned, now on the reverse of his fair copy of the poem. Rather, the poem may have taken a day or so, since Smith stayed only two days with Shelley after Christmas, and by early January Shelley's poem was in Leigh Hunt's hands. It's possible that Smith was still revising his own piece when Shelley's was published.

"Ozymandias" is not just about hubris; it's a tale of mortality. Poets long to be immortal, as immortal as gods—that is the point, the more so if the poet is an atheist. (Shelley was inspired by such objects even while despising those who had erected them.) If even the monuments of the great conquerors can vanish in a few millennia, however, what shall remain of those whose names are writ in water? As Keats put it, when speaking to the Grecian urn, "When old age shall this generation waste, / Thou shalt remain, in midst of other woe / Than ours."[40] That, at best, is the fate of poetry. E. M. W. Tillyard put the case more dryly: beholding the annihilation of the works of Ozymandias, he proposed, any conqueror would despair.[41] That was not the despair Ozymandias had in mind.

The very destruction or mutilation of artifacts makes them mutely eloquent (as we know from the recent brutal and senseless razing of monuments at Palmyra), especially when the past has been wrenched from its own country. The artifacts of empire were often orphans of war. Having conquered Egypt, Napoleon dispatched more than a hundred scholars and scientists to examine the wreckage of unnamed dynasties; when his fleet was defeated at the Battle of the Nile, his booty became the booty of England. This included the Rosetta Stone, which King George presented the British Museum in 1802. The Napoleonic army's work of scholarship, *Description de l'Egypte*, appeared in twenty volumes between 1809 and 1826.

The Parthenon marbles were transferred to the museum piecemeal, though the government showed no interest in the Earl of Elgin's rubble until after the rubble arrived. Would the Elgin Marbles, which Keats visited obsessively and Shelley at least on occasion (for some weeks in 1818, shortly after "Ozymandias" was published, he lived down the street from the museum),[42] have provoked half so many poems if the frieze had been left decaying upon the shattered temple atop the Acropolis? Not every poet is a Shelley, able to squeeze genius from the pages of a review—most poets want more access to the source of inspiration. Poetry is not, even so, an adequate excuse for pillage.

Perhaps, deep beneath the conscious play of mortality here, lies something unconscious: the idea that a king, in the body of the poem, has been reanimated from his amputated parts. Those limbs are the limbs of Osiris, surely; but they are also the limbs imagined by Shelley's young lover in *Frankenstein* more than a year before:

I had selected his features as beautiful. Beautiful!—Great God! His yellow skin scarcely covered the work of muscles and arteries beneath;

his hair was of a lustrous black, and flowing; his teeth of a pearly whiteness; but these luxuriances only formed a more horrid contrast with his watery eyes, that seemed almost of the same colour as the dun-white sockets in which they were set, his shrivelled complexion, and straight black lips. . . . Oh! No mortal could support the horror of that countenance. A mummy again endued with animation could not be so hideous as that wretch.[43]

A *mummy*! There is the center of the horror, the idea that even the ancient dead could return to life. Just as Byron may take credit for the vampires in our literature, Mary Shelley might be responsible for the reanimated mummies rife in Hollywood for most of a century.[44]

The deformed and mutilated head provides the link between Ozymandias and Frankenstein's monster, but the creature realizes as soon as he sees himself that he is a monster. Ozymandias's statue perhaps did not provide such enlightenment. We don't know how Frankenstein fashioned his brute—Mary Shelley is economical there, either through a delicacy at mentioning body-snatching (limbs not of Osiris but of the graveyard) or through a sense that the monster could have been created out of inanimate clay, for instance. That radical notion might have appealed to her atheist lover.

Shelley's work is a kind of reanimation, too—after millennia, the dead king speaks. The poem is neatly couched as two addresses: the traveler to the poet, and Ozymandias to anyone who passes. (It's hard to pin down the tone of the former—dumbstruck? overbearing? boastful?—but the arrogance of the latter is beyond mistake and not meant to be mistaken.) No wonder Shelley despised tyrants—they are the acknowledged legislators of the world. When Shelley said in "A Defence of Poetry" (1821) that "poets are the unacknowledged legislators of the world,"[45] it was at best a smiling untruth, just as false in Shelley's day as in ours. (Had Byron remained in England, he might eventually have possessed great influence in the House of Lords. No English poet so important came so close to legislation.) That doesn't mean poets are nothing; but to suggest they're more than they are is a mild act of hubris, if also of romance. Should there ever be a colossal monument to Shelley, that sentence, not a line of his poetry, will no doubt be inscribed upon the base.

The poem also overthrows convention's mild tyrannies about how poems come to be written. "Ozymandias" was written in competition, like an assignment in a poetry workshop; and its source lay at three removes from any view of the statue. (Magazines like the *Illustrated London News* and *Frank Leslie's Illustrated Newspaper*, with their wealth of wood engravings, had yet to be founded.) There was the ancient historian Hecataeus; there was Diodorus who paraphrased him; then the anonymous review, perhaps lying about Shelley's library, in which the details lay recorded; and at last Shelley and Smith. The poem, in other words, probably fell from a review that quoted a book that paraphrased another book. (Had the men seen the engravings in Pococke, they were of the wrong statue.) Poems written on commission, as Shakespeare's first sonnets may have been, are not by nature less felt, less authentic products of imagination than poems demanded by God. You might say that "Ozymandias" is a model of Romantic inspiration—what was the ruined statue but a folly, one you didn't have to pay masons to erect? Indeed, you didn't even need to see it.

Here Shelley has borrowed Byron's exoticism, his attraction to the tales of the Middle East in *The Giaour* and *The Bride of Abydos*. Shelley took his inspiration through reading, and it's good to be reminded that from Chaucer forward the secret history of poetry has been a history of reading. It's surprising how often post-Romantic poets look down their noses at poems derived from reading other poems—Chaucer and Shakespeare and Milton would not have condescended to poems that found their debts in old texts, and neither would Byron, Shelley, or Keats. Reading was part of their living world.

The centuries long ago took their toll of the ponderous hulk of Ozymandias, his bust lying cracked into puzzle pieces, his hands and feet disarticulated nearby. He lies facedown, as if he had slipped on a patch of desert ice. His excavated temples lie in beautiful ruins, but it isn't true that nothing beside remains. The mummy of Rameses II was discovered in 1881. A few decades ago, it was flown to France to kill the insects devouring him from within—that's the real curse of the pharaohs.[46] Like so much else, the mummy has found immortality under glass. You can see the king himself. He now lies safe in a museum.[47]

2. Frost's Horse, Wilbur's Ride

ROBERT FROST, "THE DRAFT HORSE"

American literature began with the horse. Our poetry had to wait for Whitman, but the stirrings of an American fiction—a fiction that did not slavishly imitate whatever the British were doing—can be found in the ride of the Headless Horseman. Like Frost a hundred years later, Washington Irving had to go to England to write his most original work, and he came bearing news of the backwaters. The British loved tales of empire, loved them long after the empire had collapsed, and the better when written by exotics. Irving was followed by Kipling, Frost, Walcott, Naipaul, and Rushdie.

Perhaps a national literature must begin in myth. "The Legend of Sleepy Hollow" gave nightmares to generations of children. Irving offered, not merely German folk tales transplanted to the New World, but a sense of the uncanny lurking on foreign ground (home yet not home with its *New* York, *New* Jersey, *New* London), the uncanny found in the more stiff-collared, psychological version of Nathaniel Hawthorne a couple of decades later.[1] Like James Fenimore Cooper, that other mythographer of the American east, Irving contributed more to American matter than to American style; his humor was so drily secondhand, so calcified and genteel, it had an almost anonymous character. A sentence will serve:

In this by-place of nature there abode, in a remote period of American history, that is to say, some thirty years since, a worthy wight of the name of Ichabod Crane; who sojourned, or, as he expressed it, "tarried," in Sleepy Hollow, for the purpose of instructing the children of the vicinity.[2]

If Irving's tales are almost unread now, they were not unread when Frost and Wilbur were boys.

We forget how much of the American myth was founded in nightmare rides. Revere's midnight gallop is part of our textbooks now—we can scarcely escape it—but, when Longfellow composed "Paul Revere's Ride" (1860), only a dozen Revolutionary veterans were still alive. (Tennyson wrote "The Charge of the Light Brigade" when bulletins from the Crimea were warm upon the table.) Until Longfellow, Revere had been just another obscure Boston silversmith. He owed his late fame less to his heroic dash than to the convenient rhymes upon his name. ("Prescott" and "Dawes" offered less attractive rhymes,[3] but William Prescott was the only rider to make it to Concord.) If there was Revere, whose fictive history we eagerly recall, there was also Israel Putnam, whose real history has been forgotten. That farmer-general, that latter-day Cincinnatus, raced eighty miles overnight to volunteer after the Battle of Lexington.[4] And what of Sybil Ludington of New York, called the female Paul Revere? (She rode twice as far as Revere—he might have been called the male Ludington.) Such headlong gallops did not stop with the Revolution. What of General Sheridan's frantic ride from Winchester, the subject of a poem much beloved in its day?[5]

The horse entered our poetry already lathered in exhaustion, and a century later found its place in our great pastoralist, Robert Frost.

THE DRAFT HORSE

With a lantern that wouldn't burn
In too frail a buggy we drove
Behind too heavy a horse
Through a pitch-dark limitless grove.

And a man came out of the trees
And took our horse by the head
And reaching back to his ribs
Deliberately stabbed him dead.

The ponderous beast went down
With a crack of a broken shaft.

And the night drew through the trees
In one long invidious draft.

The most unquestioning pair
That ever accepted fate
And the least disposed to ascribe
Any more than we had to to hate,

We assumed that the man himself
Or someone he had to obey
Wanted us to get down
And walk the rest of the way.[6]

"The Draft Horse" begins with the almost throwaway observations typical of Frost, but the balky lantern and frail buggy announce mishap and incipient disaster at the outset. Frost occasionally betrays the theme of a poem in the opening line (think of "Something there is that doesn't love a wall"), but he prefers to enter a poem by the side gate: "A lantern-light from deeper in the barn," "Out walking in the frozen swamp one gray day," "There were three in the meadow by the brook."[7] These aren't the stuff of pastoral so much as backward introductions to backwoods tales. (There were farmers long before pastoral poems; for all we know, with their long bets on the future, such men have always told stories sidelong, so as not to tempt fate.) Frost loved the quiet before drama—but he loved the quiet after drama, too. Very few of his poems, and perhaps none of his best, end on a dramatic note—his poetry was built for reflection over the ashes or the grave.

"The Draft Horse" doesn't take long to lay out this couple's plight:

With a lantern that wouldn't burn
In too frail a buggy we drove
Behind too heavy a horse
Through a pitch-dark limitless grove.

Part of this nightmare is that the grove is "limitless." Woods can be large, forests immense; but you can usually see from one side of a grove to the other—this half-real grove is half unreal. ("Grove" is without cognate in any Germanic tongue, its origins as mysterious as Frost's tale.)

Frost could not imagine the day when a reader wouldn't know a thing about buggies. The lantern is mounted outside. (The absence of a comma at the end of the first line might suggest otherwise.) A buggy is delicate by nature, not made for rough roads or the long haul, and too fragile here for how far the couple has to go (the buggy's load would have to be trifling)—besides, the horse is "too heavy." Why? Because, as the title has explained without explaining, it's a draft horse, thickly muscled, normally used for drawing a wagon or plowing. It's the wrong horse for the wrong carriage. If the couple do have a long way to go, the draft horse will be forever getting there. Draft horses, the Percheron or Belgian or Clydesdale, are famously docile—you have to be of mild temperament to pull plow or wagon all day.[8] They're plodders. A buggy wants a trotter with deep bottom.

Why is this woebegone couple using an ill-suited horse? The answer must be, because they have to—they no longer have anything better. Their trip is the embodiment of necessity—but, as so often, fate intervenes without warning:

> And a man came out of the trees
> And took our horse by the head
> And reaching back to his ribs
> Deliberately stabbed him dead.

The dark trees of "Stopping by Woods on a Snowy Evening" are as beautiful and hypnotic as the Sirens; but the grove is malevolent, haunted like Dante's wood of suicides. Frost piles up his matter-of-fact *ands*—what might seem like biblical anaphora reads like blackboard addition. (A more theatrical storyteller would have started the stanza with "Then.") Frost knows how dramatic the undramatic can be; the stranger simply steps from the grove and slaughters the horse. This is no accidental madman, but a man trained to the task. He's a good Stubbsian anatomist—he grabs the bridle to steady the beast for the fatal blow, knowing just where to strike between the ribs. The disturbing physical detail reads like an autopsy report. This Nemesis, this embodiment of random fate (or a preordained fate more awful for being planned), acts seemingly without motive. Perhaps he has an obscure grudge, perhaps he just hates horses—but Nemesis doesn't need motive. Frost comes fatally close, not to the fatalism he loved to toy with, but to the Greek notion of Anangke, or Necessity. This is a poem not about a depraved act of cruelty but about the consequences. The murderer disappears as soon as he stabs the horse—he's as much an instrument of the poem as an instrument of fate. (Poets are dismissive gods, too.) Seen in a sidelong way, he does no more than correct the mistake the couple have committed.

The melodrama is over almost before it has begun—the horse goes down. Frost is good at telling more than we realize. The sound of the splintered shaft (there would have been two, connected to the buggy by shaft clips) is more terrible, because more indirect, than anything he could say about the animal's death throes. There would have been a terrible tangle of harness, reins, buggy shafts, horse dying or dead, and blood. Nothing follows but a postscript: "And the night drew through the trees / In one long invidious draft." This afterthought is not the only case where Frost is clever with the trimeter—you can read the line most radically as an ionic followed by an anapest, with the load-bearing spondee like an announcement of doom ("And the | *Night drew* | through the *trees*"); but perhaps it sounds more sinuous, and sinister, as anapest-trochee-iamb ("And the *night* | *drew* through | the *trees*"), which requires a syntactic pause after *night*—the reversal of rhythm and slightly forced pause are eerie, with the emphasis on movement. It might be most telling, however, to scan this simply as anapest-iamb-iamb ("And the *night* | drew *through* | the *trees*"), which would put rhetorical stress on *through*—there would be little advantage to the meaning of rhythm here, if the line didn't sound so chilling that way. Effects are language plus meter, not meter alone. Stressed thus, the night slips through the wood like the murderer. If the night approaches only now, the grove must have been dark as a grave by evening, the draft horse finding the road only by feel and by the light of a lantern sputtering or defunct. The reference to *a* grove suggests the place is unfamiliar.

Americans did not invent the poetry of the gallop or canter. (The rhythm of prose is not quite the rocking horse of meter.) Browning's "I sprang to the stirrup, and Joris, and he" and Tennyson's "Half a league, half a league, / Half a league onward"[9] must plague any poet who writes of horseback—or, for that matter, *on* horseback. I don't believe that poetry has much mimetic faculty; but I'm willing to suspend my disbelief at the metrical choice here, in part because it makes no great difference and in part because the little difference rhythm makes is perhaps crucial to the routines of pause and release into which Frost's language has been cast—the movement, or in other words the rhythm, of understanding.

"The Draft Horse" requires only five sentences across these five stanzas—had Frost been liberal with semicolons, he might have managed it in three. The final sentence sidles toward moral knowledge of a bewildering kind:

> The most unquestioning pair
> That ever accepted fate
> And the least disposed to ascribe
> Any more than we had to to hate,
>
> We assumed that the man himself
> Or someone he had to obey
> Wanted us to get down
> And walk the rest of the way.

A buggy normally seats only two—the poem reveals nothing much about the couple; but, given Frost's compelled interest in husbands and wives, it's tempting to make the poem betray the exactions of marriage. Frost takes a whole stanza to describe the couple as a philosophic condition; yet the lines of the penultimate stanza are a dead end syntactically, lying in apposition to the sentence's real subject, "We." This puts the horse before the cart, if such a résumé is not to disrupt what follows. Think how much tension would be lost had the penultimate stanza begun, "We were the most unquestioning pair"—the ending would seem presumptive, instead of charged with the premonitions of syntax. Frost was always canny about syntax. (I admire the homeliness of a line that would otherwise be barbaric, "Any more than we had to to hate," which violates *The Elements of Style* in about four different ways, merely to hit the rhyme.)

The construction here is almost too sophisticated. (Country yarn-spinners don't need lumbering syntax to deceive their listeners.) The advantage of backing into the sentence is that when we finally reach subject and verb, they seem a revelation. The poem is based on false clues, of course. The title has all along been an act of misdirection, for the draft horse is only proximate to the argument (the poem would not have been wildly different had the couple been driving a good square trotter)—the title has let Frost undersell what follows.

The couple know who they are—they accept the virtues of their limitations. Never questioning fate, they ascribe nothing to hatred, or no more than they have to. (Indeed, if they are the "most unquestioning pair," they have almost made a vice of it—they're as docile and plodding as their beast.) This is Christian submission taken to a slightly deranged degree. They're not Manichaeans: they don't believe the universe a permanent struggle between good and evil. Yet they don't believe that evil does not exist.

Though it requires more strength than most Christians could muster, the couple refuse to act as if their lives were ruined by tragedy. This mysterious stranger, the instrument of fate or perhaps fate itself, must have *wanted* them to get down. (No other conclusion fits the naiveté of their philosophy.) If he had no motive, he must have his own Nemesis and his own employer. They have answered the God of Job with the forbearance of Christ.

This seems a sapheaded way of thinking; but, if the couple bewailed their fate in the dark grove, beyond any immediate aid (otherwise the husband would walk to a farmhouse and beg), they'd be better off dead. We know too well the preacher's graveside humbug—the Lord has taken your baby home; the death of the innocent is part of God's plan; the Almighty gives us no burden greater than we can bear. Such emollient lies are no comfort to the cynic, but this is not a poem about cynicism.

The poem would be an allegory, if we knew exactly of what. Even with their fragile buggy, and their muscle-bound horse, and their malfunctioning lantern, and the pitch-black grove without end, someone thinks this couple has it too easy. The action of their faith is to get down and walk. They must bear their burdens afoot, as Christ did to Calvary, and as imitation Christs do in penance. Half of Frost's brilliance is to leave the killing unexplained. It merely and terribly is, among the other unknowings of life. The couple don't speculate, because the universe's mysteries are inscrutable. The majesty of their philosophy, whatever it is, lies in their acceptance of whatever befalls them. Frost is mocking the couple—but he admires them, too. (Think how discomforting Frost is where someone *can't* accept fate, as in "Home Burial," or where the many shockingly can, as in "'Out, Out—.'") It's not an allegory—it's a parable.

"The Draft Horse" is ill at ease with a world reduced to science, but the poem implies that any response other than submission is fatal. (For the Old Testament Christian, God tries his faithful by humiliation.) We know we wouldn't act this way, and we're not sure we should—but we're not sure we shouldn't, either. Frost isn't interested in the horror of circumstance. His pathos lies in how people adapt—the daily grind is always, for the poet, the choice to live. There's a lot of death in Frost but a lot of survival, too—and it takes poems like "Home Burial" and "Snow" to force the confrontation. The couple are really too mild to be Stoics, just as they're not gloomy enough to be fatalists. (They also lack the rueful irony.) Their primitive faith is scarier than Christianity, invoking neither God nor Devil, just the unknowable agency that drives Frost's universe. (Frost was no believer, but he wasn't quite an unbeliever, either.) Modern examples of such behavior are rare; but I'm reminded of the Amish families in Nickel Mines, Pennsylvania, who a few years ago embraced the family of the man who had murdered five of their children in the village schoolhouse.[10] What irritates us about this couple is that they don't respond to the murder with righteous anger—it would be easy to see them as slightly stupid. The terror for a reader comes, not because they don't feel rage, but because they have mastered it. They submit to their fate and by doing so conquer fate. Such acts are difficult to bear. The couple is nearly as incomprehensible as the murderer.

In an undated blue buckram notebook,[11] Frost left a late draft of "The Draft Horse" that shows how subtly he wrestled with the occasion of verse. The original title of the poem was "Rather Pointed." "Too heavy a horse" was once "a great Percheron horse"—the revision's gain in implication is far greater than the loss of specificity. (This is a model of when telling is better than showing.) The effect would have been blunted, the couple's knowledge of the horse's shortcomings more opaque, had only

Rather Pointed

With a lantern that wouldn't burn
In too frail a buggy we drove
Behind a great Percheron horse
Through a pitch dark limitless grove

And a man came out of the trees
And took our horse by the head
And reaching back to his ribs
Deliberately stabbed him dead.

The cumberous beast went down
With the crack of a broken shaft.
The night sighed through the wooded grove
In a ~~one long terminal~~ draft.

The most unquestioning pair
That ever accepted fate,
And the ~~most~~ least disposed to ascribe
~~No~~ more than what had to to fate,

We assumed the man himself
Or someone he had to obey
Wanted us to get down
And walk the rest of the way.

Draft of Robert Frost, "The Draft Horse."
Source: Rauner Special Collections MS 02348, p. 6 recto,
Courtesy of Dartmouth College Library.

the breed been mentioned. In the third stanza, "ponderous" is merely "cumbersome"—a word so slightly wrong, perhaps it was just a place-holder until Frost thought of better. He fiddles with the next lines, having arrived at "The night sighed through the grove / In one long terminal draft." "Drew through the trees" is more insidious, ridding the wind of sentimental personification. (The night *draws*—from that ancient root that gives us "tractor"—just at the moment the horse can draw no longer.) "Invidious" is a judgment, "terminal" too knowing—and too meaningful, in an Empsonian way, for this couple straitened in what they can know.

Frost published "The Draft Horse" in his final book, *In the Clearing* (1962). I long thought it the best of his late work, a revenant among the case-hardened Yankee poems he wrote after fame got the better of him; but he told his biographer Lawrance Thompson that it had been written nearer 1920.[12] It might have been included in *New Hampshire* (1923) with the equally death-haunted (and horse-haunted) "Stopping by Woods on a Snowy Evening," the poem it genetically most resembles. "The Draft Horse" is one of the last uses of the American uncanny that began with Irving and Hawthorne. By the end of Frost's life it had been demoted to genre.

RICHARD WILBUR, "THE RIDE"

Frost knew by hard fact the behavior of the horse in "Stopping by Woods"—he kept horse and carriage (as well as sleigh, sulky, and democrat wagon) on his farm south of Derry.[13] The horses in "Stopping by Woods" and "The Draft Horse" have been closely observed, not imagined after some lesson in Dotheboys Hall. The culture of the horse lasted longer in America than in England, as a matter of poetic knowledge—but then American poets were more likely to have been plowed up on a farm. (In Seamus Heaney's childhood, his father's horses were stabled in part of the farmhouse, as was common when Ireland was still an agricultural country.) Horse-drawn streetcars vanished from Manhattan in 1917,[14] but until after World War II it was common to keep horses on the American farm. (They were driven off, of course, by the tractor.) Even in the suburbs now, the cult of the horse has not entirely been lost—indeed, the last public stable in Manhattan closed as recently as

2007.[15] For most British poets of the past century, however, riding a horse could be treated only nostalgically, as in anthology fluff like Alfred Noyes's "The Highwayman." I doubt English poetry has had a decent horseman since Byron.

The horse was probably domesticated upon the steppes, perhaps as early as six thousand years ago. The archeology takes us no further than the chariot graves a thousand years before Homer. Homer was no historian—he was ignorant of the tactics and weapons of Mycenaean warfare; indeed, his sense of how such battles were fought is confused and anachronistic. Though he retains a trace memory of the horse's importance in battle, he thinks chariots provided a taxi service for the likes of Achilles and Hector.[16]

The epithets of oral composition are often fossilized remains of a vanished world (just as idioms like *hue and cry*, *at loggerheads*, and *spick and span* retain linguistic fossils). Homer's running epithet for the Trojans was "breakers of horses," hence the irony—really the tactical joke—of gulling them with a wooden horse, which they mistook as an offering to civic pride by their vanquished enemy. Domestication has in fact left only the thinnest coat of civility on a beast essentially still wild. The horse quickly reverts to a feral state—apart from Przewalski's horse, on the Asian steppes (which has sixty-six chromosomes, not the sixty-four of the modern horse), there are no longer true wild horses, merely feral domestics.

THE RIDE

The horse beneath me seemed
To know what course to steer
Through the horror of snow I dreamed,
And so I had no fear,

Nor was I chilled to death
By the wind's white shudders, thanks
To the veils of his patient breath
And the mist of sweat from his flanks.

It seemed that all night through,
Within my hand no rein

And nothing in my view
But the pillar of his mane,

I rode with magic ease
At a quick, unstumbling trot
Through shattering vacancies
On into what was not,

Till the weave of the storm grew thin,
With a threading of cedar-smoke,
And the ice-blind pane of an inn
Shimmered, and I awoke.

How shall I now get back
To the inn-yard where he stands,
Burdened with every lack,
And waken the stable-hands

To give him, before I think
That there was no horse at all,
Some hay, some water to drink,
A blanket and a stall?[17]

"The Ride," published in 1982, throws us on horseback in medias res, without even the breathless preamble of "I sprang to the stirrup."[18] That is the course of dream—and perhaps only on re-reading the first lines does the reader notice the sly admission that this *is* a dream. The poem needs no cause but the ride itself (no reader really gives a damn about the news brought to Aix—and in any case Browning made the whole thing up), just as we don't know if Frost's doomed couple are abandoning a bankrupt farm or traveling home as best they can.

Wilbur's rider is cast into the midst of a blizzard, that terror for early settlers. A man could die within yards of his own door. The dream requires no reason for its terrors—if dreams permitted reflection, the real terror might be how the speaker got there in the first place. This is a more metaphysical point than it seems. The rider plunges forward, apparently all night. (This must be the night in the dream and the night of the dream—*apparently*, because dream imagination may be almost instantaneous, then retrospectively filled out and given body.)

In small ways, Wilbur allows the dream its absurdities—the ability to ride without holding rein, the "magic ease"—but its illusion is rooted in a sharpened experience of the character and provision of riding. A rider hugging the horse's neck would receive a fair amount of heat from the beast, and there are convincing records of long-distance nightlong rides like Israel Putnam's. Such a ride can't be taken at a gallop. No horse can gallop for ten hours; for long rides, an easy lope or Wilbur's "quick, unstumbling trot" is necessary. (Thoroughbred races give a misleading impression of stamina—blood horses can go flat out for a mile or so, but at the end they're knackered.)

"The Draft Horse" is set during a blackout, in a tar-black grove with no lantern to see by; Wilbur's dream vision lies in a whiteout, the nothing's nothing of blizzard. (The seeing imagine that the blind are plunged into unearthly darkness, but some live in the swirling of an inner snowstorm.) Being lost may be, as I suggest, a metaphysical condition—one of the poem's quiet virtues is that this does not exhaust the subject. The first five stanzas of "The Ride" live on trust—the rider abandons himself to the horse. Trust, however, is the medium of betrayal. The "pillar of his mane" must mean, by metonymy, the neck of the beast; if you cling to a pillar, you grasp a symbol of strength. No one thought that the blind Samson (blindness often being mistaken for weakness) could bring down the pillars of the temple.

This reading of "pillar" is no more than a likelihood, because it's a word that has so much metaphorical substance—there is Jesus's pillar of flagellation; the Scottish pillar of repentance (the whipping post); the pillars on which the earth rests; the Pillars of Hercules; the upright post in a harp; the phrase "from pillar to post" (which comes from tennis); various uses in anatomy, metallurgy, conchology, typography, mining, horology, and dressage; and of course the compounds of pillar box, pillarbrick, pillar dollar, pillar drill, pillar hermit (like St. Simeon Stylites), and much else, none of them apparently relevant to the *pillar of his mane*.

The blizzard dissipates. Just as an inn appears, the dreamer wakes. The rider's first reaction on escaping the dream is not relief but the terror of having left something unfinished—a sophisticated version of thinking in Ohio that you left the stove on back in Massachusetts. If sleep offers the absolution of our cares, sometimes waking relieves us of the burden of sleep, like the dream of murder (though that is not necessarily unpleasant). "The Ride" leaves us in a state of sin, in other words—and the worse for being imaginary, for who can ever be released from an imagined state of sin? Even the dreamer admits that in an instant he will realize there was no horse. Yet for that instant, a terrible obligation descends—and the guilt is not, as so often in dreams, over the adultery indulged or the murder committed, but over something never done at all. Damnation is the guilt of having left something forever undone, something that can never be atoned for.

In the dawn of that earlier Wilbur poem, "Love Calls Us to the Things of This World," the sleeper is roused to a half-waking state where things are not what they seem. The simplicity of "The Ride," in a poet once so deliriously baroque, pares away the literary accretion of consciousness. Dreams often fail to provide the gratifications foreseen. No wonder, having woken, we so often want to return. The only relief will come in the realization that the horse never existed. And perhaps not even then.

Wilbur has been given too much credit for his essential good nature, as Frost has suffered for his pretense of wisdom. Here, however, the later poet offers terror without catharsis. "The Ride" denies those satisfactions a rhymed poem usually promises in its perfected form. The form does not bring analysis to extinction—the reader is refused release, the matter left undone, even when the manner is at rest. This is the proximate condition of life when it longs for the absolution of death.

Wilbur's dream was part of a past itself already unreachable—at least, the sort of inn where you could get hay and a stall hasn't been much available in our country since shortly after the Model T rolled out. (It would be too much to imagine that Wilbur is alluding to the inn where Christ was born—the magi could not have ridden horses.) That makes the predicament of the dream horse more pathetic. The poem ends on a question to which there is no answer—but there are some debts we can never repay. There is always darkness at the edge of Wilbur's brightness; behind that good cheer lies the shadow of mortality. In "The Ride," this is not simply joined to the matter but embraced in some damp wedding of the soul.

Where Wilbur's rider plunges "on into what was not," the literal emptiness of the dream might be thought the figurative emptiness of the imagination (for the dreamer there is no there there). The plummet into a world of nothing is, for a poet, always preliminary. The real blizzard, in no way trivially, is the stark emptiness of the page; but this poem is an *ars poetica* in the weakest sense, the sense of Stevens's "The Snow Man," where the speaker, like a poet, is *nothing himself* and where at last, in the absoluteness of perception, he beholds "Nothing that is not there and the nothing that is." There is no better description of the burden, and the gift, of modernism's impersonality.

CODA

We have left undone those things which we ought to have done;
and we have done those things which we ought not to have done.

"The Ride" is an homage to "The Draft Horse," borrowing the meter (Frost the more liberal with anapestic substitution) and reworking the quatrain (Frost's is *abcb*, Wilbur's *abab*). Both are indebted to our long identification with the animal that was necessary to our farming, our mails, our military, our modes of travel, and the romances spun around the struggle for the land itself. The horse was once the most valuable thing a common man could own; it was his guarantee of independence. (A good horse was more expensive than a good car today.) Wilbur has taken a poem of philosophic acceptance and made it one of psychological torment—not what the world does, but what we do to ourselves; not what the world asks, but what we ask of ourselves. The Sermon on the Mount might be Frost's text; the Book of Common Prayer, Wilbur's. There's an old quarrel between resignation and guilt—acceptance over what is versus guilt over what was. (There is a theological argument over which is worse, the sin of commission or omission—in narrow legal terms, omission can also be punished severely. One term for it is guilty knowledge.)

In folk etymology, the nightmare has something to do with a horse; but the *mare* is instead the Anglo-Saxon's malign, suffocating spirit that squats upon your chest. (Wilbur's night mare turns out to be a nightmare, of a sort.) Tales of running or being chased are no doubt lodged deep in the reptilian brain—indeed, the dominant motif of horror is being hunted by an unkillable foe. The *Terminator* movies, like "The Legend of Sleepy Hollow," deftly reinvent "Sir Gawain and the Green Knight"— and earlier, in the chases of Burns's "Tam O' Shanter" and Bürger's "*Der Wilde Jäger*," the ordinary horror has been made the horror of art. Perhaps the dream of riding is the conceit of a brain rationalizing what used to be known as Wittmaack-Ekbom's Syndrome, now comically called Restless Legs Syndrome, a condition first recorded by Thomas Willis, one of Charles I's physicians. (Willis coined the term "neurology," and a portion of the brain is still called the "Circle of Willis.") When a sleeping dog twitches its limbs, we assume it is dreaming of hunting; but perhaps the prey is merely the invention of a canine brain trying to keep the dog asleep, as the human dreamer turns the annoying alarm clock into a car alarm or ringing telephone. But what is being chased by a ghost, or an apparition, or even a living enemy, to that of being chased by another poem?

A poem sometimes lies in the shadow of the poem that provoked it. A great sonnet darkens both Frost and Wilbur, Milton's about duty.

> When I consider how my light is spent
>   Ere half my days, in this dark world and wide,
>   And that one talent which is death to hide
>   Lodged with me useless, though my soul more bent
> To serve therewith my Maker, and present
>   My true account, lest he returning chide,
>   "Doth God exact day-labour, light denied?"
>   I fondly ask. But Patience, to prevent
> That murmur, soon replies: "God doth not need
>   Either man's work or his own gifts: who best
>   Bear his mild yoke, they serve him best. His state
> Is kingly; thousands at his bidding speed
>   And post o'er land and ocean without rest:
>   They also serve who only stand and wait."[19]

"When I consider how my light is spent" marks blindness as a physical crippling that makes a moral failing inevitable and asks a question not the least rhetorical—how can a man serve his God if he cannot do his job? "Patience" is the personification of an old virtue as much pagan as Christian—it retains the dark undercurrent of the original almost sacred idea embodied in Frost's couple: the "calm, uncomplaining endurance of pain, affliction, inconvenience" (*OED*).

Milton's poem is transparently about writing poetry. Thousands of couriers already bear the word of the Lord (they are his mail service); but others must stand by, awaiting His call, no doubt bored and anxious—patience is the hardest of virtues, far harder to practice than faith, hope, or charity, whose rewards are more immediate. For a poet worried about the cost of blindness to his art, worried that his art may be extinct, Milton provides his own answer in writing the sonnet—that call is the vocation of poetry. Being called to an action is no small part of the bewildering faith of Frost's couple and the duty implicitly felt by Wilbur. (Guilt can be triggered by illusion—that is the pity and terror of art.) Poets are haunted by poets because beneath every poem lies another poem avoided, cannibalized, stolen, or betrothed. Milton's patience tells him that numberless messengers already carry the Lord's dispatches. But how did those "thousands at his bidding speed"? They sped by horse.

3. Lowell's Skunk, Heaney's Skunk

Robert Lowell, "Skunk Hour"

Nautilus Island is a rich man's island in Penobscot Bay, standing at the head of Castine Harbor. Still privately owned, its forty acres could fit comfortably into Boston Common. Until recently you could rent the island's main house or Cape Cod cottage by the week—or both, and for about as much as a clerk in a bait shop makes in a year.[1] This Maine island is rich in its histories—Indian shell-middens mark its shores, within sight of the ruins of a British gun emplacement captured during the Penobscot Expedition, which led to the most disastrous American naval defeat before Pearl Harbor. (The British had christened the island after HMS *Nautilus*, a sixteen-gun sloop.) History may trouble a poem like "Skunk Hour" even when the poet chooses not to acknowledge its reach.

The main house sits atop a bluff across the water from Castine, whose cottages rise in orderly rows up the hills from the bay. Starting in 1955, Lowell spent many summers there in his cousin Harriet Winslow's house on the village green.[2]

Skunk Hour

(For Elizabeth Bishop)

Nautilus Island's hermit
heiress still lives through winter in her Spartan cottage;
her sheep still graze above the sea.
Her son's a bishop. Her farmer

is first selectman in our village;
she's in her dotage.

Thirsting for
the hierarchic privacy
of Queen Victoria's century,
she buys up all
the eyesores facing her shore,
and lets them fall.

The season's ill—
we've lost our summer millionaire,
who seemed to leap from an L. L. Bean
catalogue. His nine-knot yawl
was auctioned off to lobstermen.
A red fox stain covers Blue Hill.

And now our fairy
decorator brightens his shop for fall;
his fishnet's filled with orange cork,
orange, his cobbler's bench and awl;
there is no money in his work,
he'd rather marry.

One dark night,
my Tudor Ford climbed the hill's skull;
I watched for love-cars. Lights turned down,
they lay together, hull to hull,
where the graveyard shelves on the town. . . .
My mind's not right.

A car radio bleats,
"Love, O careless Love. . . ." I hear
my ill-spirit sob in each blood cell,
as if my hand were at its throat. . . .
I myself am hell;
nobody's here—

only skunks, that search
in the moonlight for a bite to eat.
They march on their soles up Main Street:
white stripes, moonstruck eyes' red fire
under the chalk-dry and spar spire
of the Trinitarian Church.

I stand on top
of our back steps and breathe the rich air—
a mother skunk with her column of kittens swills the garbage pail.
She jabs her wedge-head in a cup
of sour cream, drops her ostrich tail,
and will not scare.[3]

Any poet may be lucky, but a good poet knows how to take advantage of accident. The *Nautilus* was also Captain Nemo's vessel; and something of Verne's character, of a man set apart from his fellows, survives in this hermit with aesthetic designs. The portrait begins in decay, the long decay of traditions never revitalized, the short decay of the nouveau riche and the tradesmen who prey on them. The poem might itself be a study in faltering convention, with its slapdash, irregular rhyme and straggling unmetrical line—they were certainly a smack at tradition when the poem was published in *Partisan Review* in 1958 and collected in *Life Studies* the following year. Unmetered, but not without an ear for meter—the initial nouns and adjectives drum their first syllables, like a Vachel Lindsay tattoo (even the exception, "first selectman," drums as a phrase). A few months before drafting the poem the year before, Lowell had started to disrupt the niceties of his strict formal style during a West Coast reading tour.[4]

"Skunk Hour" begins with this superannuated heiress, hidebound, cocksure, senile—Lowell often played the card of his Puritan ancestors, and he played it hard. He recognized that the clannish descendants of the Pilgrim fathers were often inbred and impotent. ("Sterility howls through the scenery," he said in "On 'Skunk Hour.'")[5] Lacking new blood, they were living on principal. There's a Tory taint to this ghost of Nautilus Island—the privacy she requires is that of "Queen Victoria's century," as if she were the Revolution's last Tory loyalist. (For an American to refer to the nineteenth century thus is as much a faux pas as for him to bow to a king.) Victims of primogeniture, the younger sons of British gentry had been packed off to the church, the army, or Parliament—her son has taken the vows and risen to the robes, but it's her farmer who has stepped into politics. His British equal, if he didn't own a house, would not even have had the right to vote before 1918.

The poem quietly remembers the old antagonisms of the Revolutionary War, which was our first Civil War. About a fifth of the colonials stood with the king, and as many as half didn't much care for one side or the other.[6] The property of Tories was often seized without compensation. (The American Indian was not the only American to lose his land without being paid.) The heiress lives on once disputed ground, proprietor of her own St. Helena, or simply an American whose time has passed her by, like the original owners of the ghostly Manhattan mansions now home to Ralph Lauren and Cartier.[7]

Yet things endure—she *still* lives, the sheep *still* graze. (So close a repetition passes into the small dramas of rhetoric—of surprise, or wonder, or disgust.) The heiress is rich enough to buy up ugly cottages spoiling her view and stare them into ruin, as if they were follies at the end of some duchess's garden. (Lowell does not say whether these are humble saltboxes or some postwar Down East ugliness.) The real hermit heiress of Nautilus Island was the widow of the geologist John Howard Wilson, whose collections form the core of the Castine museum. Georgia Johnson Wilson died in 1965 at the age of eighty-three.

It takes a particular aesthetic conscience to think a ruin more poetic than clapboard or shingle vernacular architecture—but the heiress is half a Romantic, for any Romantic is a dictator of taste, and she has the money to indulge her outrage over such lèse majesté. "Hierarchic privacy" is a nicely judged phrase—anyone who has walked through a saltbox cottage will know that privacy in such quarters is a vacant wish. The antique ways are gradually falling into desuetude; and this old dotard, in her dotage, lives in Spartan parsimony—a New England hardiness taken to foolhardy extremes, or simple penny-pinching. (She's living in her cottage, then, not the main house—down-at-heels English lords have been known to do the same.) Does she show the sturdy character of the old Johnny Cake, the sharp practice of the Yankee peddler, or is she simply a nut who's going to freeze to death one December?

The true New Englander stays in his godforsaken port past Labor Day, when summer visitors flee to the cities. (Not twenty years after *Life Studies*, down the coast in Provincetown, most of the shops still shuttered themselves for winter, and many of the residents went on welfare.) The privilege of old money, however, sits ill with the town's economic collapse. The "summer millionaire" in his L. L. Bean gear has vanished, his yawl auctioned off to the local lobstermen, his wealth as fleeting as the Maine summer. He's gone bankrupt, or perhaps just lost interest in playing the Penobscot yachtsman—"We lost" makes his absence seem the town's fault. Lowell's use of colloquial phrase was always acute.

A yawl is a two-masted vessel, with a mizzenmast aft of the main—nine knots is extremely fast for such a boat. Perhaps Lowell knew that originally this was a fishing-boat rig, so there's some justice to its defeated afterlife, sweeping busily, bossily, about the harbor to check the traps. New England lobstermen are extremely territorial—if you come from a neighboring town, you can lay lobster pots only at the risk of life and property. The locals have had their poetic vengeance upon the rich, but it's thin compensation. The bay's lobsters and clams, as well as the fish in the Georges Banks (fished out a few decades later), may sustain a subsistence economy; but already half a century ago such precarious towns could not thrive without summer visitors.

These early stanzas mark the derangements of order now threatening the community. Even nature is at odds with itself, some sort of infective stain covering Blue Hill. (The landmark, like the village named for it, lies on the other side of the peninsula from Castine.) Lowell later admitted that this was only the "rusty reddish color of autumn,"[8] but his language gives it a pathological cast.

The last of the three exemplary portraits that open the poem, unremarkable at the time, is now the most controversial. You can say a lot of bad things about Lowell's phrase "fairy decorator" before you come to any good ones. The decorator was a type, as was the homosexual hairdresser. Lowell was not alone then in thinking homosexuality a perversion of instinct—American psychiatry agreed with him. Such language would be vile now, as it was vile then; but the critic must examine the reach and intention of 1957. The casual aspersions on the decorator's manhood come from a speaker himself unmanned, but then the vile is often an assertion of virility. There is something apart from an expression of beleaguered masculinity, whether Lowell heard it or not: the decorator is the merchant Puck of this town, with his powers of metamorphosis. What is the speaker's hope but to be transformed? Dividing the phrase "fairy / decorator" releases the folklore locked within—following so closely the woodland of Blue Hill, the phrase quietly suggests that even the local supernatural figures have fallen on hard times. The fairies have had to move out of the woods and set up shop.

The use of slang always carries a risk. During the Revolution, the British sang, "Yankee Doodle came to town / Upon a little pony, / He stuck a feather in his hat / And called it macaroni."[9] We no longer hear the slander in "Yankee Doodle"—"Yankee," though of uncertain origin, was derogatory, and a doodle was a fool. "Macaroni" now requires a footnote (he was a London dandy—a hayseed with a feather in his hat is no macaroni), while the casual slurs of Eliot's "squatting Jew," or Pound's "kike," or Marianne Moore's "coon," or Wallace Stevens's "nigger," or William Carlos Williams's "wop" are now taboo. Yet all were used in poems or letters as if perfectly natural. We can convict the poet only if we also convict the time, because the poet is rarely better than his time. Only his poems may be, by grace or imagination.

The decorator trades in the cobbler's bench and fisherman's net, the cast-off kit of workmen—the honesties of labor have been perverted into the dishonesties of kitsch. It's another sign of decay. (Many restaurants and fish markets required a nautical theme, and thousands of middle-class homes once used a cobbler's bench as a coffee table.) To decorate a room with such things makes them battle trophies—the modern world, having triumphed over hand labor, now sentimentalizes it. Yet the decorator's shop is failing, the local businesses and middle-class housewives either sated by such junk or deserting the rundown port. That the decorator would prefer marriage is a further comic reversal, a sour judgment on interior decoration or marriage, it's hard to say which—though perhaps, like many in that day, Lowell believed the man was homosexual by choice.

The poem has a long opening—it takes its time, lingering over the setting until the reader might think that setting is all. At its midpoint, the poem shifts from exterior to interior, from ill landscape to the ill landscape within, and particularly from *our village, our summer million-aire, our fairy decorator* to *my Tudor Ford, my ill-spirit, my mind's not right*. Lowell claimed that the poem "was written backward, first the last two stanzas, I think, and then the next-to-last two,"[10] which suggests, not the crooked path of imagination (many a tale is best told backward, and many a tail flourished in retreat), but a fruitful way of fixing the barren ground of private life in local landscape and local economy. The stanzas on the private life alone, he must have realized, would lack contrast and setting.

One dark night,
my Tudor Ford climbed the hill's skull,
I watched for love-cars. Lights turned down,
they lay together, hull to hull,
where the graveyard shelves on the town. . . .
My mind's not right.

The bleak night, the lone pilgrim climbing the hill—we are at the opening of the *Inferno*, transposed to the day of the internal combustion engine, that devil's device. (Blake's "dark satanic mills," steam powered or water driven, were never far off in New England.) The Tudor Ford was a jaunty lightweight sedan introduced in the twenties, but by the fifties it had become a stolid and ugly heap. The lovelorn speaker probably drives this bulky later version. Sullen and low-browed, it's a car for private brooding, for lurking in the shadows, a car that might develop an unhealthy interest in love-cars. The model had two doors—there's a levity to the pun, a levity masking a seriousness, since a royal dynasty has been reduced to selling automobiles, another sign of that fallen world, or perhaps merely a more democratic one, because a Yankee independence of spirit infuses the poem, even if that spirit must live on scraps. Perhaps such uses of modern trade are no worse than the royal warrants dynasties since the Plantagenets have granted their favorite shopkeepers. (Current holders include Bacardi for vermouth, Kellogg's for cereal, Kimberley-Clark for toilet paper, Xerox for photocopiers—and Ford for cars.) Ford also offered a Fordor—a groaner of a pun even more excruciating, if possible.

The descent the poem will shortly make into the speaker's hell is for a moment suspended. He watches his cars the way Dante contemplated his sinners. (We have perhaps happened upon the second circle, where the poet watched the whirlwind that bore the lovers Paolo and Francesca.) The voyeurism is both the wounded soul's recognition of unhappiness and an attempt to reach the normal life availing elsewhere. The allusions are more than usually impacted here—the "hill's skull" invokes the horror of Golgotha, while hinting that we are delving into a man's skull, that is, his psychology. (The later incarnation, some might say, of that serious Victorian science, phrenology.) On this ground of death, the "graveyard shelves on the town"—as if the crucified thieves of Golgotha have been buried beneath slate slabs or granite crosses.

Those love-cars lie in happy, fructifying, carnal opposition to the corpses below. The speaker has been drawn to the local lover's lane, a retreat that in small towns of small cottages is nearly a necessity. Even at the point of admitting madness, he drolly suggests (or the language allows) that the cars themselves are mating, "lights turned down" romantically—they "lay together" in the old phrase, "hull to hull" in Lowell's new one. Couples don't go to such places if they're married, at least to each other—besides, in such a town everyone knows your car. Here the pervert is watching the illicit. (Peeping Tom, no criminal in common law, was usually prosecuted merely for disorderly conduct.) Sex in American cars deserves a longer disquisition—such things were more comfortable when the back seat of Detroit's sedans was about the size of a hotel bed.

Lowell's secrets were not always his own—he took from his life what he required and faked the rest. He admitted that the lead soldiers from Dijon in his memoir "91 Revere Street" were a counterfeit Flaubertian detail, so far as Dijon was concerned. (The particulars *look* stolid and exact: "hand-painted solid lead soldiers made to order in Dijon, France.")[11] Lowell found the germ of his lover's lane in Logan Pearsall Smith's autobiography, *Unforgotten Years*. When Whitman lodged for a month at the Smith family home in Germantown, northwest of Philadelphia, Smith's father used to take the poet on afternoon excursions through Fairmount Park, where they would "drive as close as they could behind buggies in which pairs of lovers were seated, and observe the degree of slope

towards each other, or 'buggy-angle,' as they called it, of these couples."
Seeing the lovers embrace made the men cheerful. (Whitman, in Smith's
rhetorical gassiness, "ever honored that joy-giving power of nature sym-
bolized under the name of Venus.")[12] Not prurient or salacious voyeurism, then, but the warmth of watching a private happiness.

The poem keeps close its use of the source, but the desperation for
healing and renewal does not entirely erase the degradation of the act. If
there are losses the poem cannot admit, that partially accounts for its
power. All Lowell's adulthood, he suffered violent attacks of manic
depression—his biography taints these lines. Here, as so rarely in life, he
seems alert to the onset of the symptoms (present-tense poems are always
retrospective, one way or another). If there's a healthy voyeurism here,
tinged with innocence, there's an unhealthy one tinged with guilt, or
shame, or perhaps envy.

The reader wants to pass through the veils of language to the naked
life, to Lowell's naked life—that is the intimacy poetry promises, even if
the life of the poet is a fiction. Poetry offers the experience of private revelation, of secrets whispered and longings blurted out (I am avoiding
the word *confession*). To go no further back than the Elizabethans, think
of Wyatt. Think of Donne. Critics often feel obliged to treat poems as
dispassionate fictional acts, as the New Critics preferred, even if on occasion biography drags us closer to the meaning. We do not have to think
the poet on oath or take the revelations of poetry on trust. If to scour
the art for clues to the life compounds one fiction with another (poetry
is autobiography's fiction), refusal to bring the life to bear can be willful
blindness.

"My mind's not right"—the phrase lies in the shock of saying, as well
as in what it fails to say. Lowell no doubt means only *not well* or *half mad*;
but, if a mind is not right, it's wrong. Wrongness of mind is the condition of evil. Dramatically, this recognition scene limits the damage of the
speaker's voyeurism, assuaging the reader's unease. Yet there are no cars
on this bleak night.

A car-radio bleats,
"Love, O careless Love. . . ." I hear
my ill-spirit sob in each blood cell,

as if my hand were at its throat. . . .
I myself am hell;
nobody's here—

A car radio—but it must be the speaker's car if nobody else lurks there (unless he's suffering auditory hallucinations, a symptom of psychosis). "Careless Love" is an old blues standard (the line usually rendered as "Love, O Love, O careless Love"—the falling rhythm of the poem's opening). Bessie Smith sang a hypnotic version in 1925; but Lowell was probably thinking of the B-side recorded by Fats Domino in 1951, likely still played on AM radio. (FM radios appeared in cars in 1952, but they were very rare until the 1960s.) The echo of "car" in "careless Love" might be whimsical if it weren't pathetic and sad. "Bleats," the echo of those island sheep, could be here merely for the rhyme, among the most off-kilter in the poem; but it suggests pathos heard without sympathy, as if the speaker were dismissive of such desires, even his own—dismissive, or scathingly critical. "Bleat" and "throat" lie near each other only when the hand at the throat bears the sacrificial knife.

The ill-spirit is a bullying reminder of infection and contagion, yet the poem is rich enough in its references for other meanings to sidle in. A man's nature was once supposed to be dominated and influenced by two spirits, a good genius and a bad. (The *OED* reminds us that Christians called them angels, as in Lincoln's phrase, the "better angels of our nature.") An "ill-spirit" is not the same as an ill spirit. Lowell's hyphen dampens the primary meaning, a spirit itself unwell, sick down to the body's very cells—it's a terrifying diagnosis of the early stages of an attack. The fever of illness has become moral pathology. The "ill-spirit" might therefore be taken, though this pushes the meaning a little hard, as a bad genius now inhabiting the whole body. (If we let biography intrude at all, we should not forget that Lowell was more than once accused of choking his lovers—"my hand . . . at its throat.")[13] The poet who rhymes "blood cell" with "hell" must allow that cell some hint of imprisonment, a pun often passing off lightly the stain of seriousness.

What else is that guilt composed of? When Lowell's mania came on, there was usually a girl involved. Careless love, the love-cars—perhaps the speaker is thinking of adultery. We are on thin ground here, because the only mention of a wife lies in "our" back steps, and therefore perhaps the other "our"s as well (a wife was more evident in earlier drafts)[14]—it requires a leap of faith into the faithless. Yet without the "love attack," as it once was called, the symptoms seem incomplete.

The first half must now be reinterpreted by what we learn of the speaker's motives and state of mind. With "My mind's not right," Lowell becomes—as so rarely in poetry, that medium of confession and denial—an unreliable narrator. ("My Last Duchess" is perhaps the most famous example.) Everything the speaker has said about the town's infections and decay must be reexamined—as with the Devil, nothing can be taken on trust, not even that the speaker's revelation contains an apology for a view morbid or skewed.

"I myself am hell" was immediately recognized as Lowell's nod to Milton's Satan: "Which way I fly is hell; my self am hell."[15] In that deepest hell of self, one may be imprisoned without bars, in a land so vast there are no walls: the prison cell, like the monk's cell, is insufficiently large; but there are worlds whose prison is insufficiently small. Milton's idea was not Milton's alone. In *Religio Medici* (1643), Thomas Browne wrote, "The Heart of Man is the place the Devils Dwell in; I feel sometimes a Hell within my self"; Marlowe's Faustus earlier lamented, "But where we are is hell, / And where hell is there must we ever be."[16] Worse, even in the lowest hell, says Milton's Satan, there is always hell even lower, "To which the Hell I suffer seems a Heaven."[17] Milton's context, however, should not be forgotten. The fallen angel speaks in the dark of his greatest despair (akin to the depressive gloom of Lowell's speaker), just before he spies Eden, the Eden that gives him purpose:

All hope excluded thus, behold in stead
Of us outcast, exiled, his new delight,
Mankind created, and for him this world.
So farewell hope, and with hope farewell fear,
Farewell remorse: all good to me is lost;
Evil be thou my good.[18]

We would take the allusion too far to think that in "Skunk Hour" the speaker's longing will become Man's fall, but the love-cars are a hope withdrawn. "My mind's not right" is what Satan cannot say; it is Satan without hubris—that is what terrifies about Lowell. He has fallen even lower than Satan, the mark of his humanity also the zero point of absolute negation. The pathos of the town's fall is that for centuries it thrived—once it did not need tourists. If all good to the speaker has been lost, where in this Paradise Lost along the Maine coast can some evil be a good?

"Nobody's here" is not, not just, the recognition that the graveyard is empty of cars this bleak night, but that the speaker himself is no one and nothing. We have come at last to the dark night of the soul, the night of St. John of the Cross, as Lowell assumed the reader would know. (Did he also hope the reader would remember that, when St. John wrote, he lay in prison, having offended his own order, the Carmelites?) We have arrived at the "skunk hour," the hour of moral scavenging, of the dark scrabble for survival. Here at last the poem fills with life, if only blind animal life, for the lines on the cemetery do not end with a period:

nobody's here—

only skunks, that search
in the moonlight for a bite to eat.
They march on their soles up Main Street:
white stripes, moonstruck eyes' red fire
under the chalk-dry and spar spire
of the Trinitarian Church.

The march of the skunks would usually take place in high summer, and Lowell has made a hellish burlesque of the town's nineteenth-century traditions. Summer, the high-school band marching up Main under the white stripes—the red and white stripes—of the American flag: the skunks are making bleak mockery of the Fourth of July parade (in low light, red and white *read* as black and white). The connections are perhaps subconscious, though Lowell was a student of American holiday and ceremony, as any poet would be who had written "Thanksgiving's Over," "Christmas in Black Rock," "Memorial Day"; yet the skunks celebrate that Yankee independence Lowell seeks to recover. (Lowell provided his own sharply political observation of the Castine parade in "Fourth of July in Maine," addressed in heroic couplets to Harriet Winslow.) Independence Day marks that founding rupture from British manners, British royalty, when a man's destiny became democratically his own. It would be fanciful to hear *star* in that spar spire, not just in the unused echo of rhyme, but in the church that began with magicians following a star—the comet of Bethlehem, as Origen had it.

"Nobody's here"—the line would fit slyly into book 9 of the *Odyssey*, where Polyphemus's vengeance is frustrated by the cleverest pun in Homer. (If we reach for the virtue of accident, the name of the captain of the *Nautilus* meant Nobody, too.) The syntax slips here—Lowell was no master of punctuation, and his publishers seemed often in fear of him, elsewhere in his poems allowing misspellings like *Chevie* or *placques* to pass without correction.[19] (As a young man, Lowell had written his former teacher Richard Eberhart, "Mis-spelling seldom obscures meaning.")[20] The comma after "skunks" should not lie before a restrictive relative; otherwise we're likely to read "that" as not pronoun but adjective, which would make the syntax oddly elliptical: the only inhabitants of the cemetery are not "skunks that search in the moonlight" but only (1) skunks and (2) a particular "search / in the moonlight." The comma makes a difference, the difference of confusion. Dropping it would have been clearer—yet there's a more cunning ambiguity. If nobody's at the cemetery, only skunks, then this speaker has already made common cause. What is a voyeur but a moral skunk? The judgment would be harsher had Lowell not written in a letter to Elizabeth Bishop, "I'm a skunk in the poem."[21]

Except during breeding season, the skunk is solitary and nocturnal (more accurately, crepuscular), as well as omnivorous. Insects, rodents, fruit, grubs, even bees—skunks have learned to take their menu broadly. No doubt that was the menu in Paradise, where everything must have been delicious, not just the apples. The beast is an old creature in the mythologies of this historical ground—the name derives from an Algonquin word meaning, in the local Abenaki dialect, the urinating fox.[22]

Lowell lightens the scavenging for survival with the cheerfully colloquial "bite to eat," as if the skunks, foraging in that lonely graveyard, their eyes red as a devil's, might have walked into a diner and ordered the blue-plate special. The poem has collapsed local geography into rough

Aristotelian unity: the sharply angled Trinitarian Church sits sharply upon Main Street, almost half a mile away from the graveyard; Lowell's summer house lies between them to one side of the green. The mast-like spire, stiffly visible from Nautilus Island, rises as if from a ship in drydock or washed up ashore. (The ship's-keel roofs of medieval churches suggest how closely allied to shipbuilding were the aspirations of theology—and the beginning of Christ's mission.) Lowell doesn't press the point. He merely reveals it (adjectives expose even as they restrict), just as the dry chalk might serve for the desiccation of religion. Yet the church quietly embodies that Yankee spirit. It's a Congregational church, whose congregation alone determines the religious practice and doctrine. (Harvard and Yale were founded as Congregational institutions.)

Lowell changed his religious principles so often that it's difficult to know whether the dry spire represents a Catholic's view of Protestants, an Episcopalian's view of Protestant American sects, or a doubter's view of the false promise of the whole Christian enterprise. In the fall of 1955, before the poem was written, Lowell left the Catholic Church (a convert, he had an on-again, off-again dalliance with the faith) to rejoin the Episcopalians;[23] but the poem seems skeptical of the grace offered and the salvation vouchsafed.

The skunks make three appearances: scrounging at the cemetery; marching up Main Street, away from the harbor; and swilling from the garbage pail near the speaker's back steps—they're not the same skunks, but probably three different groups forced into what seems one appearance. Their dinnerware must be a small pail for kitchen waste, not the taller trash-can a skunk would find difficult to tip over. Why has the speaker gone out to the steps? We don't need a reason, because the poem doesn't require it; if we wanted one, it would be to empty the day's garbage or because he heard the skunk disturb the metal lid of the pail—or perhaps in despair, merely to escape the house for a moment. When the mother skunk *will not scare*, it must be the speaker who can't shoo her. The physical geography doesn't matter—when a poem makes a dream landscape, it's not a fault of but a device of imagination.

Here the poem turns toward the simplicities of the animal world, the human one having proven so tainted with compromising economies. Nature may be red in tooth and claw (a practical Marxist lives off the waste of capitalism—the skunk is successful in a way the decorator is not), but nature reduces complex psychologies to instinct. The mother skunk's fearlessness has been bred into a long Darwinian order—her primal drive is to feed her kits.

> I stand on top
> of our back steps and breathe the rich air—
> a mother skunk with her column of kittens swills the garbage pail.
> She jabs her wedge-head in a cup
> of sour cream, drops her ostrich tail,
> and will not scare.

The skunk is a fierce, well-armed matriarch, like Lowell's mother. That's a very different kind of love from what the speaker seeks—yet the moral taken is of facing up to fear, not being scared or scared off. Where Lowell's family drama forces its way into his early poems, the organization almost always requires a rejection of the father—Lowell famously knocked his father down, Oedipal fashion, over the poet's college romance.[24] His mother is the more Protean figure, both the castrating Medea of "91 Revere Street" and the domineering yet almost admirable monster of "Sailing Home from Rapallo." Lowell's daughter Harriet was six months old when he began "Skunk Hour," and a parent's obligations may lie in the background. She was named for the Winslow cousin who eventually willed Lowell's wife the Castine house.[25] Here, on "our" back steps, presumably with the baby Harriet asleep or almost asleep indoors, the young father, the man seeking love-cars, has quietly been recalled to the burdens of home. A man must face his responsibilities.

Why did he need to be recalled? In early August 1957 at Castine, Lowell began to spiral out of control. He later apologized for his "frenzied behavior" and his "slip into the monstrous."[26] He had been particularly drawn to the company of one summer visitor, an old friend, a poet to whom he had almost proposed, which he called "*the* might have been."[27] The poet was Elizabeth Bishop, to whom he dedicated "Skunk Hour."[28] Even more than "Water," it is his great love poem to her. If she is the absent love, the careless love missing from his symptoms, it explains what he wrote after she fled from Castine: "My disease, alas, gives one (during its seizures) a headless heart."[29] The dark night of the soul is love, not faith. Lowell must have believed, against all evidence (recall his portrait of the fairy decorator), that she could choose not to be homosexual—but then lovers believe so many silly things.

Bishop's "The Armadillo" was published in the *New Yorker* on June 22, 1957, weeks before her visit. (He'd seen the poem with others she'd recently sent and called it "one of your three or four very best.")[30] He wrote her in September that he'd started half-a-dozen poems, one "called 'Skunk Hour,' not in your style yet indebted a little to your 'Armadillo.'"[31] In a letter the next spring, he confessed that he'd compared the two poems in class "and ended up feeling a petty plagiarist."[32] Her dedication of the poem to him came only when she published *Questions of Travel* in 1965 ("since you have liked it," she wrote).[33] He'd taken to carrying her poem in his wallet.[34]

Lowell struggled to bring "Skunk Hour" to term. He attempted to crowd the material into stanzas of various sizes, titling some drafts "For Elizabeth Bishop." In one untitled draft that survives among his papers at Harvard, two seven-line stanzas form what might be called an accidental sonnet. The pentameter galumphs along unconvincingly, but in this draft two people—obviously Lowell and Bishop—take a moonlit drive up a hill's "bald skull above the bay / To watch the moon whose mind is not quite right." The poem ends with the moon "above the chalk-white and pure spire of a Maine church."[35] Such false starts reveal how cunningly, compellingly, Lowell shuffled his images—yet he still reverted to staid pentameter months after the March trip to the West Coast in which he learned "to add extra syllables to a line to make it clearer and more colloquial."[36] In another precursor to "Skunk Hour," titled "Inspiration" and far closer to the later poem, the poet is the one who finds "there is no money in this work, / You have to love it."[37]

Could the frightening, unfrightened matriarch not be an animal incarnation of his wife, now restored to dominance? That would give a new reading to "will not scare," because it was Elizabeth Hardwick who bore the burden of Lowell's bouts of mania, Lizzie who managed his illness and braved the amours that accompanied it. That does not preclude the skunk from being the manifestation of both mother and wife, something that would have scared either—or merely the animal other, that familiar of a world whose arguments are simple.

The air is rich, even if the town is not—rich with the stink of skunk and garbage. (We talk of someone making a stink.) The skunk's perfume is acrid, foul, so there is some irony when the rotten speaker revels in the rotten odor of it. (Encountering a skunk on his voyage on the *Beagle*, Darwin wrote, "Whatever is once polluted by it is forever useless.")[38] Whether in decaying garbage or on the skunk's ripe scent, life itself rises from the mulch of rot, which is another way evil can be made good.

Through Lowell's enjambment, the speaker stands *on top*, like a conqueror—but only "on top / of our back steps." (The poem is full of short rises and dying falls—the heiress . . . in her dotage, the millionaire . . . whose yacht is sold. Even the "hermit / heiress" contains its small drama of opposition.) The poem has passed from the disease of the world to the disease within, from the impoverished economy to salvation and renewal—and without an hour wasted in psychiatry. In later terms, the poem might be called self-medicating.

In coastal towns, skunks like to breed under the beach houses raised on wooden pilings. Skunks mate in March and give birth in May. The kits leave the mother by the end of July. Lowell's hellish parade should be held at midsummer, not when the leaves are turning. If it's not poetic license, it's another way in which the time is not right. (Henry Erhard, animal-control officer of Castine, has confirmed that fall is too late to see such things there.)[39] The bestial world knows how to survive on garbage—salvation lies in the scrabble of animal existence, not the civilized tally of losses that mark the first four stanzas, like a town corporation's annual report of profit and loss. If there's a death instinct, the skunk represents the life instinct—protective, feral, cunning, indomitable, incapable of bleating in self-pity, "Love, O careless Love."

Lowell told Bishop that "Skunk Hour" was an homage to "The Armadillo"; but the drive toward raw survival is closer to another poem in *Questions of Travel* (1965), "The Burglar of Babylon," where slums overrun the lush hills of Rio. Bishop's "fearful stain" seems to lurk behind the "red-fox stain that covers Blue Hill"; her "hill of the Skeleton," the "hill's skull"; her slums overrunning the hills, the Maine port's rundown cottages. Alas, she did not write the poem until 1963.[40] Lowell saw it in the *New Yorker* the following year. It's not impossible that "Skunk Hour" lies unconsciously behind *her* stray details—the themes fretted both poets.

"Skunk Hour" spirals inward like the nautilus shell, from the demented heiress's willed Spartan life to the bare subsistence of the scavenger—without the moral implicit in the close, the poem would be a portrait of one barrenness after another. Yet something would be lost if Lowell's chalk-dry humor were not recognized. Ian Hamilton, his biographer, is acute in calling the opening stanzas "lightish social comedy."[41] Lowell probably meant the "fairy decorator" to be teasing, not repulsive, even if the character is excruciating now—like every Hollywood scene with an eye-rolling black maid or cook. It presses the accidental symbol too sharply to note that the nautilus's back-curving corridor maps Dante's spiraling descent through the *malebolge*. Still, the heiress must be living on investments, the millionaire is not what he seems (he should wear not L. L. Bean togs but the lead cloak of the hypocrite)—Lowell's thieves' row of characters might be found in the seventh circle (usury and sodomy) and the eighth (fraud). There's no specific place for voyeurs in the *Inferno*, but they might be cast in the eighth circle among the sowers of discord, their wounds torn open even as they heal. Milton's lines in the first book of *Paradise Lost* might trouble the speaker here: "The mind is its own place, and in itself / Can make a heaven of hell, a hell of heaven."[42] And the skunk? The skunk is Lowell's Virgil, leading him out of that dark night—to the luxury of Purgatory, if no higher.

SEAMUS HEANEY, "THE SKUNK"

Seamus Heaney used to tell of the day Lowell was driven through Ireland in Michael Longley's rattletrap car. After a long ride, the American turned to the driver and said, "Michael's car is a bundle of *wounds*." With Heaney's accent, that became "wooooonds." If *Life Studies* (1959) is a collection of wounds, *Field Work* (1979) two decades later is a collection of healings. "The Skunk" is not a direct answer to Lowell, because only a parody is a cross-examination; but Heaney's poem lives in the shadow of "Skunk Hour." The ways in which it deviates are the ways in which the later poem exists in quiet and helpless counterargument.

"The Skunk" begins with one of those small patents we call style. Heaney sounds his descriptions the way hard taps secure a nail, loving his adjectives by threes and even fours. He sidles toward description as if each modification were a hypothesis:

THE SKUNK

Up, black, striped and damasked like the chasuble
At a funeral mass, the skunk's tail
Paraded the skunk. Night after night
I expected her like a visitor.

The refrigerator whinnied into silence.
My desk light softened beyond the verandah.
Small oranges loomed in the orange tree.
I began to be tense as a voyeur.

After eleven years I was composing
Love-letters again, broaching the word "wife"
Like a stored cask, as if its slender vowel
Had mutated into the night earth and air

Of California. The beautiful, useless
Tang of eucalyptus spelt your absence.
The aftermath of a mouthful of wine
Was like inhaling you off a cold pillow.

And there she was, the intent and glamorous,
Ordinary, mysterious skunk,
Mythologized, demythologized,
Snuffing the boards five feet beyond me.

It all came back to me last night, stirred
By the sootfall of your things at bedtime,
Your head-down, tail-up hunt in a bottom drawer
For the black plunge-line nightdress.[43]

The long description in the opening lines by a distance precedes the
thing described—the adjectives parade the skunk. The syntax is unusu-
ally disengaged; one could start a pub brawl over where the modifiers
shift to the vestment—*up* is the tail, but the transformation could occur
on any adjective following. There is an additive quality to adjectives, at

least until there's a subtractive one, since more do not necessarily cinch a description more tightly—at a certain point the noun begins to slip away. (A mathematics of poetry has not yet been developed, but such frenzied compiling might be like a parabola approaching a directrix—it comes near, then flees.)

The poem starts arrière-guard, with the tail—it's a poem about tails, and a tale about a tail. Black with a long high-tau cross in front (the capital Greek tau ["T"]), the crosspiece so close to the chin only the long vertical stripe may be noticed, a funeral chasuble may be richly figured, which the figure of "damasked" requires. The metaphor confers on the skunk a certain Crusader antiquity (the original damasks were woven in Damascus) as well as richness: in *Epicoene*, Ben Jonson mentions a damask tablecloth that cost eighteen pounds.[44] At about that date, by one source, ten thousand bricks cost just under seven shillings. You could have bought more than half-a-million bricks with eighteen pounds, enough for a wall two miles long and six feet high.[45]

What has died here? What are the obsequies for? The life of the poem begins with this funeral; but the skunk has come before, *night after night*, like a recurrent dream. Expectation always lives at the heart of arousal. One of the poem's acts of graciousness and confidence is the way it winds toward its subject with a certain leisure (like a nautilus shell, perhaps)— Lowell's poem is looking for a way out, Heaney's a way in, because his is constructed like a mystery. In a quiet way, the poem's blacks and whites are indebted to film noir. He sets the scene: the desk light cast dimly upon the verandah (in California, we shortly learn); the refrigerator shuddering into silence, the oranges ripening or ripened on the tree—but the refrigerator *whinnies* like an animal, the oranges *loom*. (Is it intensification or merely slack repetition to be told that the oranges hang on an orange tree?) With a certain abruptness, however, the speaker announces, "I began to be tense as a voyeur." The diagnosis may be as much a mystery to him as it is to the reader—it comes as an unexpected shock. It's like Heaney to make something so sinless appear a sin—perhaps, in the words of a famous American peanut-farmer, it's only a sin *in the heart*.[46]

Both poems revel in their orders, Lowell's built into sestets and Heaney's dragged into quatrains. (The poems have a catch-as-catch-can feeling without being formless—that's part of their charm.) The rhyme scheme of "Skunk Hour" is ragged, irregular, lines written in the ghost of meter. "The Skunk" travels through a more cocksure free-verse, with occasional rhymes by chance or fancy (*visitor* / *voyeur* / *air* end the first three stanzas, but *useless* is a long dozen lines from *nightdress*). The stray acknowledgments to "Skunk Hour"—the funeral mass that echoes the cemetery scene, the paraded tail that remembers the march up Main, the skunk itself—have prepared the comic incarnation of Lowell's voyeur. Yet where the American's admission, midway through the poem, clarifies the actor and act, in Heaney we are a distance from understanding. Lowell has things he can't say, Heaney things he won't, not yet—the latter is a contrivance, but literary contrivance must be repaid in dramatic effect.

The next stanza begins with an apparent irrelevance:

After eleven years I was composing
Love-letters again, broaching the word "wife"
Like a stored cask, as if its slender vowel
Had mutated into the night earth and air

Of California.

These are plain facts, not so plainly. Here the complicated construction of time in the poem is made half clear. The husband is away in California, away long enough to find himself projecting his longing onto passing scavengers. He's writing his wife love letters—if the poem is lodged in biography, Heaney went to Berkeley as a visiting professor in 1976, this time without his family, unlike his visit a few years before. Eleven years. Heaney married Marie Devlin in 1965,[47] so those letters take him back to the last days of courtship.

Airmail letters, at thirty-one cents an ounce, would have taken a week to arrive in Ireland.[48] In those days, overseas phone calls cost a minimum of $9.60 per three-minute block[49] and were therefore usually avoided (that would be approximately $40 now); but writing letters from such a distance creates a curious disconnection, answers often crossing new questions in the mails. The last days of courtship are very different from the middle days of marriage, the former marked by what wedlock sometimes lacks—anticipation. The poet has been thrown back on feelings buried in the gratifications of marriage, gratifications perhaps grown slightly common. The letters make him feel again like that young suitor, the guilt all the stronger if he finds himself looking forward to those nightly visits. It's emotional adultery, when he might instead be longing for his absent wife.

A poem can survive mysteries never quite explained, and in these lines perhaps some of the mystery is a mystery still. The lovelorn speaker broaches the cask of the word "wife" as if it had long been in storage—its vintage has been aging peacefully (wines mature in oak before they're bottled). The olfactory ripeness of the poem will shortly appear, but at this moment we should not ignore the carnal desires implied. *Broaching* a subject is a softened figure of the original meaning of piercing or stabbing (to broach a topic now is merely to introduce it). Heaney likely uses *broach* because you can broach both a cask and an idea (Pepys *broached* a "vessel of ale," *OED*). European dictionaries of the day—French, Spanish, even Swedish—each had a term for "to broach a virgin," and "tap a virgin" was the English equivalent.[50] Only the ghost of violation and release remains, but it's hard to ignore the sexual slang hovering behind—*bung-hole* has long been a synonym for anus.[51]

That much is clear, but to broach the "word 'wife' / . . . as if its slender vowel / Had mutated into the night and air // of California" somewhat defeats me. The "slender vowel" must be "i" or "I." The word "wife" is a cask breached or broached; its scent floats upon the California air, the way a woman's scent, or her perfume, rises off a pillow when she's gone. She is perhaps the "I" upon the air. That may be all—but there may be something further, some sense where the letter "i" comes into play, and where the "spelling" of absence in the next lines is more than wordplay ("love-letters" could be another pun):

> The beautiful, useless
> Tang of eucalyptus spelt your absence.
> The aftermath of a mouthful of wine
> Was like inhaling you off a cold pillow.

Wife is perhaps not a word he used in the intimacy of home—writing it from a distance would have a special frisson—and therefore spectral presence. (Something spelled is also spelled out.) He might mean, "The self I am only when thinking of you as my wife suddenly appeared in California" or "I began to feel detached and disembodied, thinking of you so far away." "I had a whole house to myself for the term," Heaney later recalled. "[The owners had] told me to look out for this skunk and her family and, if they appeared, to keep very still. . . . To this day I associate that visitation with the erotic."[52]

Sensuality, for Heaney, is sometimes introduced as scent or taste. Is there no sexual hint in "Oysters": "My tongue was a filling estuary . . . / As I tasted the salty Pleiades. . . . / I saw the frond-lipped, bring-stung / Glut of privilege"? Heaney may be the most olfactory poet since Shakespeare, whose works contain some thirty references to "perfume" and almost ninety to "smell" and its close relations (though not quite twenty to "stink"). The alien scent of eucalyptus reminds the speaker of all the losses around him, spelling in a different way, like Circe. Replacements invoke absence, and fail to replace.

The eucalyptus is itself a foreign invader, introduced to California by Australian Forty-Niners, no doubt as a reminder of home, unless the seeds were caught in their trouser cuffs. Berkeley, like Lowell's Castine, rises on hills above a bay, San Francisco Bay. During the Gold Rush, San Francisco expanded with breathless speed—arriving ships lost their entire crews and even their captains to the mines. Scores of abandoned vessels lay at anchor. Some became hotels or warehouses; others were sunk as foundations for new buildings, land was so valuable. The city gradually crawled out into the bay. What became San Francisco's Barbary Coast was originally called Sydneytown, and the inhabitants—many of them freed prisoners or ticket-of-leave men, criminal, violent, and rowdy—were called Sydney Ducks. The orange, too, is foreign to the Americas, introduced to the Caribbean by Columbus and to Florida by Ponce de León. The speaker may be unaware of their history, but these old immigrants surround his temporary immigration.

Perfumes are often ghosts, emanations of lost time. Scents lie deep in neurological memory, as if we were still primitive mammals, depending on our noses to detect ripeness—or rot, for that matter. (The physicist Richard Feynman once showed, as a party trick, that the human nose is powerful still—he could detect a man's scent almost as keenly as a bloodhound.)[53] Lowell rarely mentions smell—the rich air of Castine and its skunks is unnatural in his work. He's more often a poet of needling visual imagination.

In California, the richness ripens into absence—if Heaney were back in Ireland, he would not be smelling eucalyptus. The lingering odor of a mouthful of wine, presumably drunk alone, becomes part of this longing in the nose—the act of smelling the beloved is now remembered, smelling the trace of her perfume on the cold pillow. Those scents can drive a lover almost mad. The moment ought to be preserved, for all it says about marital intimacy—the traces we leave for our lovers, the presences those absences are.

Such desires grow stronger the longer they are endured. At this moment of intense yearning the poet, in a coup de théâtre, dispatches to the stage that most unromantic animal, the skunk. The scent of the lover draws us forward; the skunk's stink drives us away. If there's a tour de force there can be a tour de farce—the farce embedded here underlies Warner Brothers' cartoon skunk, the suave and perpetually lovelorn Pepé Le Pew, his voice imitating Charles Boyer, the great screen-lover. Desire can rise up even in the face of the unromantic, but desire passed off as comedy.

> And there she was, the intent and glamorous,
> Ordinary, mysterious skunk,
> Mythologized, demythologized,
> Snuffing the boards five feet beyond me.
>
> It all came back to me last night, stirred
> By the sootfall of your things at bedtime,
> Your head-down, tail-up hunt in a bottom drawer
> For the black plunge-line nightdress.

And there she was—the peripeteia fulfills the expectation announced in the first stanza. *Here* she is—not the lover but the skunk. Perhaps only on second reading is it plain how much the armature of the poem depends not on arrival but expectation. The skunk is greeted by an extraordinary gout of adjectives, six in all, in pairs of rising opposition (*intent* is only thinly at odds with *glamorous*, but *mythologized* a U-turn from *demythologized*)—the sort of attention that in a sonnet would be visited upon the lover alone. It's as if a cask of adjectives had been broached. (Perhaps it's merely wishful to think that Lowell's skunk mythology is demythologized here.) The mechanism of desire should remind us of Shakespeare's devious sonnet of backhanded compliment, "My mistress' eyes are nothing like the sun."

"The Skunk" is an homage to Mrs. Heaney's bottom—it's hard to deny. The intensity of desire; the irrational, whimsical projection onto the skunk; the comic perversion of being a voyeur of skunks: the already twisted elements of this love affair with Nature have been married in this final droll epiphany. The poem, the last stanza wryly reveals, has all been a flashback, those California dreams (what happens in Berkeley stays in Berkeley, apparently) forgotten after the poet returned home. Forgotten, or repressed. The tail begot a tale; but told the other way, headfirst, it would have lost half the mystery of longing—what is now climactic would have been anticlimactic. The poem knows it must hold the moment of recognition in reserve.

There she is. His wife has shed her clothes before bed; but, instead of standing naked before him, she grubs in the bureau drawer for a sexy nightdress, so she can re-robe and re-disrobe. (The moment is tender in its domestic comedy, its play of knowledge and anticipation.) No—*the* sexy nightdress, so both already know its effect on him. *Sootfall* deserves a minor disquisition in the gallery of Heaney's coinages. Her clothes are perhaps black as soot; but soot must follow a blaze, like desire—and where there is soot, as in a chimney, another fire may come. Ass tipped in the air, nose to the ground like that California skunk, head wedged like Lowell's skunk—*bottom* drawer is an accidental pun that almost tips the ending into farce. Nevertheless, you must have a strong marriage to describe your wife as a skunk.

Yet the sexiness of Mrs. Heaney's bottom would be lost if at that moment we thought of the skunk's anal scent-glands, or of what happens after the skunk adopts the tail-up posture. A good poem knows what to leave out, and a good poet how to distract the reader. (Similarly, if Mrs. Heaney is going to don the black nightdress, the skunk's chasuble, the priest's vow of chastity might have come modestly into play. There must be a quiet thrill in seducing a priest, especially a female priest.) We should not ignore that, among primates, the tipped-up bottom is an act of "presenting," in a meaning not available in the *OED* (the technical term is "lordosis"). The female offers herself, ready to be mounted.

What has died? Certain longings, certain illusions. In the restoration of domestic harmony, there's loss of the freewheeling fantasy of distance, loss of the pang of mock adultery. Seeing your wife naked once more, there must be a guilty shiver in suddenly recalling the tail-up prowl of the skunk, as one might a casual adultery conducted thousands of miles away—it's as if, having left your mistress, you go home to find your wife dressed as your mistress. In the Freudian comedy, the displacement has been displaced.

Where the skunk received the longing due the wife, the wife has been magnificently transformed into a skunk—indeed, full of animal desire, she's about to dress as a beast (as Queen Pasiphaë concealed herself in the wooden cow), the nightdress plunging between the breasts and perhaps as far as the belly, revealing her white skin like the skunk's white stripe. Her lingerie has become a chasuble. It's almost a lost scene in Shakespeare, or a lost passage from Ovid—the wife dressing as the skunk to attract her husband, who has a thing for skunks. The poem invokes ceremony without being ceremonious.

The comedy wheels in various directions—perhaps no poem more tender has ever been devoted to a wife's bare ass. You might say that some four centuries after Titian[54] and Cranach discovered women's bottoms,[55] Heaney has at last taken the rear into poetry. Marital harmony restored, the poet again in possession of the memory of loss that ought to make this homecoming the more affecting, the poem, like movies of a certain day, demurely takes its leave before the real action begins. What is more potent than a love potion—Eucalyptus #5, perhaps—that leads to a moment of comic bestiality? All along the poet has been not Circe but Puck—for Puck gave Bottom the head of an ass. If that's a joke too far, then life has restored to the wife the spirit of an animal.

CODA

"Skunk Hour" was written during the last years of the Eisenhower administration, and something contrary to the smugness of those rootless years infuses the tone. We never escape the land of pastoral, the Lowell pastoral of collapse and moral decay, the fraught surroundings that act as a descent into hell, for the outer world is always a manifestation of spirit—it's not for Lowell to offer comic relief or the oppositions of comedy. Aren't such collapses also kin to those ruins the Romantics found such an apt source of contemplation, these memento mori the reminder that, however grand the palace, or abbey, or monument to victory, after some centuries it will be no more than a ruin, and a monument to ruin?

Among mammals the skunk is among the most reviled, the most associated with comic misapprehension—not for lowly mores (as a parent, the mother skunk is fiercely loyal), but for the Darwinian accident of its smell. In both "Skunk Hour" and "The Skunk," this unhappy state suggests the disorder of the world, which the poems set to rights—sanity and marital love are the steady states toward which the unexpected symbol drives. Heaney's skunk does not overturn Lowell's world so much as genially rewrite it. The Main Street parade of skunks becomes the tail that parades; the night voyeur of love-cars the skunk's nightly voyeur (both men take a slightly unnatural—and slightly pathetic—interest in skunks); the scavenging skunk with her head stuck in a sour-cream cup the wife with her head in the bureau drawer; the promise of sex in the love-cars the promise with which "The Skunk" abandons us, voyeurs ourselves. At the heart of both poems stand marriage and a wife.

Both poems are about love, but more accurately they're about longing—*love* is a word Lowell mentions only in quotation. The steady sanities to which he would like to return, the disordered world that ought to be set aright, lie partly in his own unstable mind; while the desire Heaney feels for his wife cannot be registered except at distance— cunningly, he recalls the loneliness a world away when his sexy wife kneels there in the room, bottom up. Is that a deeper solitude, or a more sublime satisfaction, feeling the retrospective tinge of loneliness and the retroactive gratification of loss? Or, as Empson might have had it, both at once, loss and fulfillment, emptiness and surfeit—eating your cake then having it, too. Yet in Heaney's poem the word *love* is never mentioned— it merely suffuses the air like a whiff of perfume.

If "Skunk Hour" worries its way toward the restoration of marriage, in Heaney's the marital bonds are unified and sustained by the act of memory, by the complicated backdrops of pasts to which the present must come. "The Skunk" could not have been written entirely innocent of Lowell's skunk; yet such knowledge is not, in a poem, necessarily guilty. One can take the hint, as the phrase goes, knowing in an instant that one's handling, one's regard, one's perception will be different—the later poem becomes an intricate act of homage and forgetfulness (indeed, the homage to and forgetfulness of the wife in "The Skunk" are almost imitative acts). Heaney is indebted without remaining in debt. The night hours of the poets' sanities, their last resolves, are different, however— one welcomes himself back to the marital bed, the other finds only a temporary stay against madness. In December 1957,[56] Lowell had a complete breakdown and was hospitalized. We are reassured in the later poem to the degree we are left ill at ease in the earlier.

It would be easy to say that "The Skunk" uses the slippery, unreliable passage of time the way "Skunk Hour" exploits the collapsed unities of space. (Lowell's poems are often drawn to spatial circumstance—he had a painter's eye, an intimating control of foreground and background.) For the poet, figure and ground are often circumstance and philosophy, or act and meditation—meditation is the poet's equivalent of clouds and river in the misty distance. Peculiarly among his contemporaries, Heaney is a poet always aware of the clock—he has a complicating sensitivity to verb tense, and his poems are not always told front to back. The past and present in his poems are always contending—the past is the shadow on the future, the present the projection of the past.

The indomitable life and fulfilled being that drive both poems derive from the mother skunk, the possessive instincts of maternal love fending off the capitulation to death. Lowell's Catholicism (or, later, ex-Catholicism) seems to have responded more viscerally to the self-sacrifice of the Madonna and Magdalen than to the self-abnegation of the Christ—perhaps Lowell felt he already possessed too much grandiose sacrifice in his character, or perhaps he didn't like to share top billing. In his mania, he often suffered delusions of grandeur. What better delusion than to adopt as your own the words of Satan, or Milton? (In one bout of madness, Lowell believed he *was* Milton.)[57]

"Skunk Hour" is about invaders, too—in the disorders to the natural order, in the visits of the millionaire (doubly disordered, rather than a reversion to order, when he goes bankrupt or vanishes), in the fairy decorator (again, doubly perverse—he'd rather marry), in Lowell's haunting of the lover's lane, and at last in the nocturnal march of the skunks. Heaney is the alien in California, Lowell the New Englander not quite belonging to the town—he was a fallen Brahmin, no Down Easter.

If the poems are about displacement, we should recognize that these are modern pastorals and that what has been shoved aside is not the speakers, or not the speakers alone, but the natural world. Nature has been overrun, but part of Nature—seagull, coyote, raccoon, bear, fox—thrives on the castoffs of man. These visitations by the skunk are reminders of a natural order lost. Lost, but in some way found again, as Adam and Eve lost a paradise but found a world. You might think Lowell's was an ecological poem avant la lettre; but both poems are just as much actions of moral philosophy, trespassing into the comic wryness of Aesop's fables. Man invades nature; but, as so often in love, the bestial invades man. How Romantic. How romantic.

4. Longfellow's Hiawatha, Carroll's Hiawatha

The Name and Nature of Parody

HENRY WADSWORTH LONGFELLOW, THE SONG OF HIAWATHA / LEWIS CARROLL, "HIAWATHA'S PHOTOGRAPHING"

Henry Wadsworth Longfellow was the great literary man of his day. Modest, widely if not wisely adored (the poets loved by one generation are most at risk when the next scorns its elders), he was visited by the small and great (from neighborhood children to the emperor of Brazil), burdened with honors (receiving a chair carved from the remains of the famous spreading chestnut-tree), and made an object of public sympathy when his second wife died in an accidental fire. Longfellow was so well known that his birthday was marked in public schools, and after his death his face pasted on a brand of cigars. Admirers built replicas of his Cambridge house in Detroit, Minneapolis, Great Barrington, and Evanston—late into the 1920s, Sears, Roebuck still sold plans for a version of the house. Though it had been Washington's headquarters during the siege of Boston, Craigie House was ever after remembered as the home of Longfellow.

Yet the chill of the future was felt as early as 1856, when a London reviewer asked of Whitman, "Is this man with the 'barbaric yawp' to push Longfellow into the shade, and he meanwhile to stand and 'make mouths' at the sun? The chance of this might be formidable were it not ridiculous."[1] The fatal question had been posed. By 1868, a reviewer for *Chambers's Journal of Popular Literature, Science, and Art* could tout Whitman as the "first characteristic poetical writer that the United States have produced. Longfellow is but Tennyson and water."[2]

When we think of Longfellow now, he seems little better than a city-bred Whittier, a Norman Rockwell avant la lettre, always ready to take some homebound scene, lay on a few schmaltzy touches, and varnish it up. Where Frost is weak, he sounds most like Longfellow (the ending of "'Out, Out—'" does not quite salvage the poem from Longfellowish melodrama).[3] It's fortunate that Frost only occasionally falls victim to the tear-stained side of Yankee wisdom, and unfortunate that he's often represented in anthologies by just those poems where he succumbs.

Longfellow was the poet of the age, so long as it was the age. Yet no man can be all good who writes little but sentimental tosh:

> I hear in the chamber above me
>> The patter of little feet,
> The sound of a door that is opened,
>> And voices soft and sweet.
>
> From my study I see in the lamplight,
>> Descending the broad hall stair,
> Grave Alice, and laughing Allegra,
>> And Edith with golden hair.[4]

Longfellow excelled at slick-tongued bathos that embodied the sentimental impulses of popular journalism—but his audience was surprisingly broad. Presented to Queen Victoria in 1869, he made a self-deprecating remark about his fame. Her majesty replied, "Oh, I assure you, Mr. Longfellow, you are very well known. All my servants read you."[5]

However revered he was below stairs at Windsor Castle, there were readers of more captious temper. The characteristics that once made Longfellow cherished make him look fatuous now, but they already looked fatuous to those who parodied him with malicious glee. (It's a mistake to condemn a time for its best sellers or think it redeemed by its iconoclasts—yet both reveal something of the age.)

Take Longfellow's solemn bucket of maple sap, "A Psalm of Life":

> Tell me not, in mournful numbers,
>> Life is but an empty dream!—
> For the soul is dead that slumbers,
>> And things are not what they seem.
>
> Life is real! Life is earnest!
>> And the grave is not its goal;

Dust thou art, to dust returnest,
> Was not spoken of the soul.[6]

Longfellow had many parodists, good, bad, and indifferent; but only a malevolent genius could have turned this into a poem about life insurance:

Tell me not in mournful numbers,
> Life Assurance is a dream,
And that while the public slumbers,
> Figures are not what they seem![7]

When parody applies the outer shell to a subject wholly unsuitable to the gravitas of the model, it turns topsy-turvy every verity the original holds sacred. Longfellow's booming pieties about the living who think only of the afterlife are honorable enough. He wanted people to live in this world, while they lived. Life insurance is the bet the living make against death, the bet the bettor can't live to see paid off—the parody suggests that once the insured is dead he'll be cheated. (Religion has often been thought to be a similar gamble—hence Pascal's wager.) One may agree with the poet's sentiments but not with his sentiment.

In Longfellow, far too many ideas come with an improving lecture attached—though you may applaud the idea, it's hard to stand the lecture. The rhetorical bullying, righteous as a holiday Christian's, is almost worse than the theological bullying it abhors. It took another parodist to sense that such breast- and brow-beating were little better than advertising:

Tell me not in doleful murmurs
> Ink is but a mouldy stream!
And the pen it rusts, and murders
> Writing paper by the ream!

Thatcher's Ink is Ink in earnest!
> And to rust is not its goal;
Mud thou art, to mould returnest,
> Was not spoken as its dole.[8]

Turning Adamic dust to mud is an exquisite touch. Here, here too, the reversals work more deeply because the subjects have unlikely alliances. Ink seems to promise a life in words everlasting—as do poems, for that matter. Much though Longfellow ballyhooed the engaged life, he was writing at one remove from life. That might be too subtle a reading of the parody, but even parody may be wiser than it knows. The poet who could thunder, "Art is long, and Time is fleeting, / And our hearts, though stout and brave, / Still, like muffled drums, are beating / Funeral marches to the grave,"[9] is stripped and shown up as a handwringing ninny by the parodist who answers, in antiphonal chorus, "Blots begone! Vile ink be fleeting! / Penman, be no more a slave! / Let all other inks go beating / Funeral marches to their grave!"[10]

It's not clear if Thatcher's Ink could be found at the local stationer's (one T. Thatcher was the author of the parody). A. E. Housman, however, while still a student at Oxford, pursued an attack similarly commercial against this most commerce-minded of poets, interpolating lines into Longfellow's "Excelsior"—the odd lines are Longfellow, almost exactly, and the even, Housman:

> The shades of night were falling fast,
> And the rain was falling faster,
> When through an Alpine village passed
> An Alpine village pastor:
> A youth who bore mid snow and ice
> A bird that wouldn't chirrup,
> And a banner with the strange device—
> "Mrs. Winslow's soothing syrup."[11]

The knockabout comedy continues for another two stanzas, as devastating to Longfellow's Horatio Alger–ish moral boosterism as Lewis Carroll's "The White Knight's Song" was to Wordsworth's. Housman may not have known that the active ingredient in Mrs. Winslow's syrup was morphine—the syrup was implicated in the deaths of numerous babies.[12]

The art of parody lies, not just in imitating the meter and rhyme scheme (slipping into the form as if it were a set of old clothes), but in reframing the subject to make it ludicrous, meanwhile adopting the form with such style that the original seems almost the imitation. Parody finds a fracture in behavior—its caricatures exploit what is usually an innocent violation of good manners (bragging, pomposity, Wordsworth-itis). Often parody is the vengeance of experience upon innocence, the knowing upon the unknowing, the literati upon the middlebrow—at least, when it is not the reverse. Parody is one of the democratic arts—it pulls down the man on the pedestal and raises the man from the gutter, unless it parodies him, too. Longfellow, whatever his highbrow appetites, exemplified the solid middle-class values of the village banker—hard work, responsibility, yearning for hearth and home, and a good old-fashioned physic of American mawkishness.

Even Longfellow's most beloved poems were not immune. Indeed, what made them beloved made them readier targets, not least because a certain homely fatheadedness is always a painted bull's-eye for the cynic. Many schoolchildren of a certain age still recall with horror having to memorize "The Village Blacksmith":

> Under a spreading chestnut-tree
>   The village smithy stands;
> The smith, a mighty man is he,
>   With large and sinewy hands;
> And the muscles of his brawny arms
>   Are strong as iron bands.
>
> His hair is crisp, and black, and long,
>   His face is like the tan;
> His brow is wet with honest sweat,
>   He earns whate'er he can,
> And looks the whole world in the face,
>   For he owes not any man.[13]

This ode to four-square Yankee independence is so drenched in the sweat of nostalgia, it's hard to understand why the poet wasn't laughed off the shelves. In his review of *Ballads and Other Poems* (1841), Poe praised the poem as "*nearly true*," having remarked that Longfellow's verse would "find stern defenders . . . so long as the world is full to overflowing with cant and conventicles."[14]

Poe had some years before accused Longfellow of plagiarism (this was like the hammer calling the anvil black), though the New England poet was guilty of little worse than pilfering ideas, after the manner of the day.[15] Still, the curious thing about Longfellow is that, even if you've never read the poems, when you come to them you're sure you've read them before. He had a gift for swallowing literature whole and producing something insufferably commonplace—Homer and Dante and Milton went in, and out came sausage. There's hardly a cliché that Longfellow could refuse when offered, and hardly one he wouldn't otherwise drag in by brute force. It's not surprising that such a poem would be answered, some decades later, by "The Village Schoolboy":

> Under the garden apple-tree
>   The village schoolboy stands;
> The boy, a nasty boy is he,
>   With muddy, filthy hands;
> And the mussel-shells he's playing with
>   Are pick'd from dirty sands.
>
> His hair is short, and red, and straight,
>   His face is like the tar;
> He cries and bawls when mother calls,
>   You hear him near and far,
> And when he gets a chance he steals
>   The sugar from the jar.[16]

You wonder if by "dirty" the parodist meant "fouled with sewage"—not an impossible thought even late in the century. That would make the boy's hand in the sugar jar more piquant.

When you think of Whitman's poems, you think of what they include; when you think of Longfellow's, you think of what they leave out—here are the things about a village that Longfellow left out. (Parody is always a form of criticism, often with a cheerful show of moral turpitude attached.) With his plummy sentiments and naive portraits of village contentment, Longfellow makes Edgar Lee Masters look like a barn-burner. It's tempting to see the mayhem with which "The Village

Schoolboy" ends, not as the echo of the ringing blows of the blacksmith, but as the projection of the reader's temptation to go after the poet with brickbat and cudgel: "His father smacks him in the face, / He pulls him by the nose, / The village schoolboy only cries, / And crying—off he goes."[17]

Longfellow was part of the great age of American reinvention, when poets born a few decades after the Revolution—and still paying their debts to whatever was being written in London (it was not until Whitman that things began to change)—created a faux America of honest mechanics and kindly shopholders, homespun virtues and genteel manners, an America that would not scare away a dollar of foreign trade. Unfortunately this pretty picture was marred by the travel memoirs published whenever an Englishman happened to visit the place, most notoriously Dickens's *American Notes for General Circulation* (1842), whose very title raised suspicion about American currency, and Mrs. Trollope's *Domestic Manners of the Americans* (1832). Frances Trollope, the novelist's mother, had opened a department store in Cincinnati—when it proved an abject failure, she was witty in her vengeance. The remaking of America included rewriting the past in romantic and heroic terms. "Paul Revere's Ride" (1860), a late example but one of the most famous poems of the day, was Longfellow's excuse for nonsense history, hardly forgivable even as a call to arms on the eve of a more disastrous war. The painting *Washington Crossing the Delaware* (1850) was among the contributions by other arts to this indulgence in romantic drama over history—Emanuel Leutze's portrayal might have been accurate if not for the flag, the boat, the ice, the weather, and the time of day.[18]

Heroic poems were America's earliest theme park—though, if Longfellow is bad, there are poets far worse, poets who did nothing but produce pulp sentiment. Alas, even his set pieces, like "The Jewish Cemetery at Newport," are disfigured by deadening adjectives, bloated rhetoric (the "groaning earth in travail and in pain"), a sweet tooth for histrionic metaphor ("they keep / The long, mysterious Exodus of Death"), and the occasional accidental comedy (the dead lie "Silent beside the never-silent waves, / At rest in all this moving up and down!").[19] Longfellow's heart is often in the right place (not always just pinned to his sleeve), but his airy rectitude is difficult to take. He lets any breath of fancy overwhelm the facts—the Jews whose graves so puzzled him were merely Sephardic Jews, remnants in Newport of the diaspora from Spain and Portugal. Their presence was no stranger than that of the Portuguese fishermen who lived in many coastal New England villages.

Most members of the American Renaissance were more steely-eyed (Hawthorne, Emerson, Thoreau—and Melville everywhere except in his poems). Parody provided rude contrast to Longfellow's samplers and needlepoint—the parodist was not afraid to write of the village blacksmith as he likely was:

> Under the spreading chestnut tree
> The village blacksmith stands,
> The smith an awful cad is he
> With very dirty hands.
> For keepers and the rural police
> He doesn't care a hang.
> He swears, and fights, and whops his wife,
> Gets drunk whene'er he can;
> In point of fact, our village smith's
> A very awful man.[20]

This anonymous piece dates to 1873, yet it sounds like a lost work by W. S. Gilbert. Indeed, there's a curious echo in King Gama's song, "If You Give Me Your Attention," from *Princess Ida* (1884): "I love my fellow creatures—I do all the good I can— / Yet everybody says I'm such a disagreeable man!"[21] The growls of the parody (Longfellow could incite other poets almost to violence) would sound light and jaunty set to Sullivan's music—Gilbert's fourteeners are just Longfellow's ballad measure without the line break. The sentimentality of the original would have turned burlesque in such a melody, for Longfellow's most damaging parodist was himself.

The British were not above using Longfellow to sneer at their own targets, like the village coquette: "Under a spreading Gainsborough hat / The village beauty stands, / A maiden very fair to see, / With tiny feet and hands, / As stately, too, as if she owned / The squire's house and lands."[22] After the sprightly opening, however, the poem seems to forget why it was written. (Parodies are hard to sustain—many falter long before the end, and most are good only in fits and starts.) The original provides a formal scaffolding, so only a mild dash of cleverness, added to a large dose of maliciousness, is required to get parody up and running—if it follows the original rhyme-scheme too slavishly, however, the parodist may soon be backed into a corner. Very few parodies offer the integration of the original—the aesthetic logic, the progress of argument or narrative, the justice of an ending. When you look at twenty or thirty parodies of the same poem, how tedious most of them are! A good parody requires not much less talent than the original, and a great one perhaps a visitation of the demonic.

When Longfellow was forty-one, his infant daughter Frances died. Weeks later, he wrote "Resignation." An infant's death is heartbreaking—the death of a child was often a nineteenth-century excuse for weepy moralizing. Better artists used such deaths with a violence that drove past sentiment, though almost inevitably there were tears, too. Think of the dead children in *Jude the Obscure*, murdered by the half-brother who afterward hanged himself, leaving the terrible note: "Done because we are too menny."[23] There's an apocryphal tale that crowds on the Manhattan docks waited for the crucial installment of *The Old Curiosity Shop*, shouting to an incoming ship, "Is Little Nell dead?"[24] Still, the ferocious critic Francis Jeffrey was found sobbing over the fatal chapter, and the Irish MP Daniel O'Connell was so upset when he came to her death that he threw the novel out a train window.[25] (On the other hand, Oscar Wilde characteristically remarked, "One must have a heart of stone to read the death of Little Nell without laughing.")[26]

Then there's Longfellow:

There is no flock, however watched and tended,
    But one dead lamb is there!
There is no fireside, howsoe'er defended,
    But has one vacant chair!

The air is full of farewells to the dying,
    And mournings for the dead;
The heart of Rachel, for her children crying
    Will not be comforted![27]

The dead lamb is bad enough, but the busy clutch of exclamation points is worse, as is the poet's reassurance in the following stanza that "oftentimes celestial benedictions / Assume this dark disguise."[28] *Celestial benedictions!* This is Longfellow at his most maudlin, taking the conventions of grief ("God works in mysterious ways," "God will provide," "She is going to a better place") and wringing them for all the barley water he can. Like Satan's discovery that for every hell there's a hell still lower, you can never measure Longfellow's sentiment, because there is always an abyss of it lower still.

Yet Longfellow did know terrible grief before and after the death of his daughter. His first wife died after a miscarriage while the couple were touring Europe; his second, the beloved Fanny, burned to death after passing her sleeve against a lit candle or stepping carelessly on a parlor match and igniting it. Longfellow suffered severe burns to his face while trying to put out the flames that engulfed her. To cover his scars, he grew the long beard. The depths of his anguish are unquestioned; but authenticity of feeling never guarantees the art, and Longfellow's sorrow for his dead daughter did not prevent parody.

The long-forgotten poet Elizabeth Akers Allen wrote a reply to "Resignation" under the same title, a reply fairly sparkling with proto-feminist irritation:

> There is no sister-band, however tended,
> > But one young bride is there;—
> There is no fire-side, howsoe'er defended,
> > But has one vacant chair.
>
> Our home is full of mingled smiles and sighing,
> > Our fairest one has fled!
> And baby Ned, for his lost sister crying,
> > Will not be comforted![29]

She follows the original almost exactly, straying from the rhyme scheme only twice, often reusing Longfellow's line, and on occasion nearly Longfellow's stanza. Few nineteenth-century poets approach marriage with such a cocked eye—there were evil husbands enough in the literature of the day (the duke in "My Last Duchess" was the worst of a long line), but rarely such a sidelong glance at the institution. (Clough in *Amours de Voyage* is good on the travails of courtship, but Meredith's excoriating "sonnets" in *Modern Love* are almost unreadable.)

Allen transforms Longfellow's "What seem to us but sad, funereal tapers / May be heaven's distant lamps"[30] into "We read her marriage notice in the papers, / And trim hope's brightest lamps."[31] Longfellow pictures the child in heaven:

> In that great cloister's stillness and seclusion,
> > By guardian angels led,
> Safe from temptation, safe from sin's pollution,
> > She lives, whom we call dead,
>
> Day after day we think what she is doing
> > In those bright realms of air;
> Year after year, her tender steps pursuing,
> > Behold her grown more fair.[32]

Allen offers instead the young wife in her new household, an obituary of ruined hopes:

> In that great cloister's stillness and seclusion,
> > By his old mother led,
> Safe from "young company" and mirth's intrusion,
> > She lives,—the same as dead.
>
> Day after day we think what she is doing
> > In those old dismal rooms,
> Year after year, her toilsome way pursuing
> > With stew-pans, mops and brooms.[33]

Marriage, these devastating stanzas imply, is a fate awful as death. "Her Father's mansion" becomes "her husband's mansion," and "Christ himself doth rule," tellingly, "own a husband's rule."[34] The transformation is as neat as the stiletto Allen inserts into the bloated corpus of nineteenth-century sentiment.

Parody is always double edged and Janus faced—it must look sharply to its victim while looking out for itself, for a bad parody is worse than no parody at all. There is parody as comic burlesque and parody cunning in its criticism, parody purgative and parody merely parasitic (or perhaps epiphytic). Parody is the catcall or Bronx cheer to all things that take their seriousness too seriously—it supplies what has been left out or suppressed, offering mockery where there should have been self-mockery. Even Homer was parodied—and, if the catalogue of ships in book 2 of the *Iliad* were not the oldest section of the poem, it would be the earliest and most brilliant parody.

American literature at last came into its own in the decades of the 1840s and 1850s. Three generations after the Revolution, our poetry and fiction were still largely English colonies. Emerson had called for an American poetry in his essay "The Poet" (1844):

> We have yet had no genius in America, with tyrannous eye, which knew the value of our incomparable materials, and saw, in the barbarism and materialism of the times, another carnival of the same gods whose picture he so much admires in Homer; then in the middle age; then in Calvinism. Banks and tariffs, the newspaper and caucus, methodism and unitarianism, are flat and dull to dull people, but rest on the same foundations of wonder as the town of Troy, and the temple of Delphos, and are as swiftly passing away.[35]

He was not long in receiving a reply. Perhaps *Leaves of Grass* was not quite the poetry Emerson imagined (if someone could have imagined it, it would have been written all the sooner); but Whitman embodied the breathless outrageousness of American life, using English as Americans did, without the pretense of London literary language.

Emerson's call was not answered by Whitman alone. Longfellow had the learning and leanings of a classicist. Fluent at fourteen in Latin and Greek, he graduated four years later from Bowdoin. (At seven his headmaster had said that he stood in Latin "above several boys twice as old as he.")[36] During a three-year tour of Europe, he studied French, Spanish, and Italian, making a start on German and possibly Portuguese. After lecturing a few years at his alma mater, he spent another year and more in Europe, an offer from Harvard in hand, studying Swedish, Dutch, Danish, and Old Icelandic.[37] By his late twenties, he was professor of modern languages at Harvard. The boy who translated Horace later became the first American translator of the *Divine Comedy*—it's not surprising that he would look to his learning (and backward rather than forward) for a model that could shape American experience.

Among all the works of Western literature, Longfellow chose the *Kalevala*, the collection of heroic lays that became the national epic of Finland. (He adopted the standard Finnish meter of trochaic tetrameter probably in part for its strangeness to the American ear, though in all likelihood he knew the poem only in German translation.)[38] The author, Elias Lönnrot, was one of the great collectors of folk songs, the equal of Bishop Percy or Francis James Child,[39] but a collector with larger ambitions. Having mustered his raw material on numerous field trips, he composed the epic by fusing and editing the old lays, probably adding some new lines of his own.

Longfellow's desire for an American saga, with a warrior who could stand among the ancient heroes, was grounded in contemporary study of early epic. The Icelandic Eddas were collections of individual lays— and by the eighteenth century some critics believed the *Iliad* and the *Odyssey* compiled from such preexisting songs. A gathering of passions informed the creation of *The Song of Hiawatha*, which the poet referred to as his "Indian Edda":[40] curiosity about American Indian folklore, not yet considered part of an American literature; sympathy for the race that had originally occupied the continent, mingled with a good deal of maundering; and knowledge that the Finnish tale was a modern construction. (The first version had been published in 1835, the year Longfellow traveled through northern Europe.)

This sense that America needed a literature of its own had been a long while simmering. In his commencement address at Bowdoin in 1825, Longfellow declared, "Thus shall our native hills become renowned in song, like those of Greece and Italy. Every rock shall become a chronicle of storied allusions; and the tomb of the Indian prophet be as hallowed as the sepulchres of ancient kings."[41] This from a boy of eighteen. Still in his twenties, he wrote in "Defence of Poetry," "Let us have no more sky-larks and nightingales. . . . A painter might as well introduce an elephant or a rhinoceros into a New England landscape." He claimed, "It is not necessary that the war-whoop should ring in every line, and every page be rife with scalps, tomahawks and wampum. Shade of Tecumseh forbid!"[42] Yet a quarter of a century later, he succumbed.

Hiawatha arrived at an opportune moment for the poet. When we think of the modernists, we think how different they were from generations of poets, like the Romantics, able to devote their time to poetry. Eliot was a banker and an editor, Williams a pediatrician, Stevens an insurance executive, Frost a teacher and failed farmer, and Moore for a time editor of the *Dial*. (Only Pound supported himself entirely by his pen—yet even he had once been a college instructor of French and Spanish.) Such poets knew what it was like to earn money for something other than poetry. Their poems sometimes record the remnant memory of labor, and they each wrestled with finding hours for art after a day exhausted by work. To say that the honesties of labor wormed into the poetry might be an exaggeration—but, if the honesties can sometimes be found there, so can the dishonesties.

The modernists were not the first generation of American poets forced to earn a wage. Philip Freneau had been a ship captain and, farther back, Edward Taylor a preacher—such men would never have thought poetry an adequate (or perhaps even honorable) way to make a living. In pre-Revolutionary America, poetry could not have paid enough to support a man; after the Revolution, things were little better. Few writers of the American Renaissance made a living by the pen—what income they enjoyed came largely from American sales, for international copyright was in its infancy. Melville had been a sailor and became a customs inspector; Holmes was a doctor and Harvard professor; Whitman and Whittier, newspaper editors; Thoreau, a maker of pencils. Emerson—a pastor, then a lecturer; Hawthorne—weigher and gauger in the Boston Custom House, surveyor, then United States consul at Liverpool; Bryant—a lawyer and hog reeve of Great Barrington, but for most of his life a newspaper editor. Longfellow remained a college professor into his late forties.

Copyright law for American authors published in Britain started to change in the 1840s, but British authors went unprotected in America until the end of the century. Writers as important as Dickens, who received no American royalties for his early novels, might gain an official

American publisher who still had to compete against a slew of pirates. Longfellow himself lost a fortune in British sales, but the great success of his epic in America meant that he never had to teach a class again.

The Song of Hiawatha was published in November 1855, a few months after *Leaves of Grass*. The poem was a very different response to Emerson's call. Though the sage of Concord admired Longfellow's poetry, his reaction was remarkably cool: "Sanborn brought me your good gift of Hiawatha. . . . I have always one foremost satisfaction in reading your books that I am safe—I am in variously skilful hands but first of all they are safe hands."[43] That is hardly the rousing endorsement offered Whitman: "I greet you at the beginning of a great career," an arch piece of flattery the poet printed on the spine of the second edition of *Leaves*.[44]

Emerson was robustly ignorant about Indians, writing Longfellow, "The dangers of the Indians are, that they are really savage, have poor small sterile heads,—no thoughts, & you must deal very roundly with them, & find them in brains; and I blamed your tenderness now & then, as I read, in accepting a legend or a song, when they had so little to give."[45] "Savage" is too broad a brush, but he was not wrong about the raw violence that terrified settlers—Longfellow produced the Disney version of Indian life. If Emerson was cool, others were cooler—the reviewer for the *Boston Daily Traveller* wrote that "rendered into prose, *Hiawatha* would be a mass of the most childish nonsense that ever dropped from human pen."[46]

Hiawatha, like *Leaves of Grass*, cast itself in a strange rhythm and found its ambition in native soil. Yet where Whitman used a medium that both was and was not American speech, Longfellow forced his mythic pastiche into the tub-thumping or tom-tomming Finnish meter (Longfellow was Vachel Lindsay before his time):

> By the shores of Gitche Gumee,
> By the shining Big-Sea-Water,
> Stood the wigwam of Nokomis,
> Daughter of the Moon, Nokomis.
> Dark behind it rose the forest,
> Rose the black and gloomy pine-trees,
> Rose the firs with cones upon them;

Bright before it beat the water,
Beat the clear and sunny water,
Beat the shining Big-Sea-Water.[47]

The ink was hardly dry before the parodies came rollicking forth. *Hiawatha* was, not just absurdly popular (the book almost sold out the day of publication, November 10), but widely imitated—a fashion for trochaic tetrameter was born on the instant. Two weeks later, in its weekly "Gossip" column, the *New York Daily Times* reported, "The madness of the hour takes the metrical shape of trochees, everybody writes trochaics, talks trochaics, and think[s] in trochees. People talk trochees in the street; merchants ask the price of raw material in that strain, and even ladies retail the scandal of the day in trochaic measure." Examples were appended. Longfellow was called a "sort of Columbus in metres."[48]

The morn of Christmas Eve, the *Times* reviewed a play opening that night at Wallack's Theatre, one prefaced by what must have been the poem's first published parody of real length:

Ask you—How about these verses,
Whence this song of Pocahontas,
With its flavor of Tobacco,
And the Stincweed—the Mundungus,
With its pipe of Old Virginny,
With the echo of the Breakdown,
With its smack of Bourbon whiskey,
With the twangle of the Banjo;
Of the Banjo—the Goatskinnet,
And the Fiddle—the Catgutto,
With the noisy Marrowbonum.[49]

This went on for some hundred lines. The playwright was John Brougham; the play, *Po-ca-hon-tas; or, The Gentle Savage*. Brougham's lines are much closer to American demotic than Longfellow's charmless sublime, which is like a preparatory oil sketch for some wall-filling mural of the northern woods. With the catgut fiddle and goatskin banjo (you can find *twangle* in Walter Scott: the "Spaniard did nothing but stalk about and twangle his guitar"),[50] the clatter of the marrow bones, the whiskey and the rollick of the breakdown, the poem catches the nervy boisterousness of American life—recall Whitman's "I loiter enjoying his repartee and his shuffle and breakdown."[51] The breakdown was a riotous improvisation of leaps and kicks. In a version shot by Edison on kinetoscope in 1894, the dancer leans, falls over on his back, and somersaults upright—it's the ancestor of breakdancing. Brougham saw something American in the meter's rough cascade. Perhaps Longfellow thought that his catchy trochaics provided, not just an American idiom, but an American rhythm.

The opening night of *Po-ca-hon-tas* came days before Longfellow's epic was itself reviewed in the *Times*. The review was not kind:

> We doubt very much if Mr. Longfellow has done the world of poesy any service by producing it. . . . In "Hiawatha," grotesque, absurd and savage as the groundwork is, Mr. Longfellow has woven over it a profuse wreath of his own poetic elegancies. It resembles a Hindoo monster, which, having lain neglected in the temple, has been sought by the ivy or the woodbine, that, clambering over its hideous features, have masked the deformity with exquisite foliage. . . . It is only when you have thrust the adventitious growth aside that you start to find yourself face to face with the ugly, clumsy monster. . . . "Hiawatha" is an experiment and—a failure.[52]

The high-toned mythmaking of *Hiawatha* presents a version of the Indian suitable for the ears of schoolchildren (ritual mutilations and the near slavery of Indian women, for example, go unmentioned). The Indian tales Longfellow adapted, heavily reworked and rewritten, came already filtered through the scarcely reliable versions of Henry Rowe Schoolcraft.[53] They are little better than James Fenimore Cooper's fancies about the Mohicans, which Twain treated with admirable contempt. Though in 1855 those willing to speak well of the Indian were a minority, Whitman's detached portrayal of a wilderness marriage ("I saw the marriage of the trapper in the open air in the far-west. . . . the bride was a red girl")[54] was far more unsettling than Longfellow's whimsies. Such unions were common in the west, where they attracted little comment even late in the century—the Indian wife, always useful as a translator, was called a "sleeping dictionary," and the children were often considered great beauties.

Hawthorne, Longfellow's friend and classmate at Bowdoin, thought *Hiawatha* the "annexation of a new dominion to our poetical territories"[55] (he was probably recalling the annexation of Texas a decade before), yet he enclosed in a letter to his publisher some verses he'd been sent:

> Hiawatha! Hiawatha!
> Sweet Trochaic milk and water!
> Milk and water Mississipi [*sic*]
> Flowing o'er a bed of sugar!
> Through three hundred Ticknor pages,
> With a murmur and a ripple,
> Flowing, flowing, ever flowing—
> Dam the river!—damn the poet![56]

Hawthorne was delighted when one of his friends, Henry Bright, satirized him in the measure:

> Should you ask me, "Who is Hawthorne?
> Who this Hawthorne that you mention?"
> I should answer, I should tell you,
> "He's a Yankee, who has written
> Many books you must have heard of;
> For he wrote 'The Scarlet Letter'
> And 'The House of Seven Gables,'
> Wrote, too, 'Rappacini's Daughter,'
> And a lot of other stories;—
> Some are long, and some are shorter;
> Some are good, and some are better.
> And this Hawthorne is a Consul,
> Sitting in a dismal office,—
> Dark and dirty, dingy office,

Full of mates, and full of captains,
Full of sailors and of niggers,—
And he lords it over Yankees."[57]

Parodies of epics cannot follow the model line by line—they must steal whatever they will of the manner and remain loyal to the form while finding a subject intolerant of the original. Long parodies are therefore the more suited to comic invention. The parodists realized something Longfellow could not: that the measure was far better adapted to burlesque than to weepy tragedy and that the variations and repetitions that make *Hiawatha* so wearisome were already comic by misadventure if not intent. Some poems are self-parodic before they're ever parodied.

The year after publication, *Hiawatha* was subjected to a book-length parody, *The Song of Milgenwater*, "translated from the original Feejee" by Marc Antony Henderson, "Professor of the Feejee Language and Literature in the Brandywine Female Academy."[58] (Feejee or Feegee was the contemporary spelling of Fiji.) This was the first edition—in the second, issued the same year, the hero was rechristened Milkenwatha. Lest the reader not get the joke, the new publisher was "Tickell & Grinne." Longfellow's poem remained popular enough that third and fourth editions of *The Song of Milkanwatha* were issued some thirty years later.

Henderson, the pseudonym of Reverend George A. Strong, had a viper's sense of Longfellow's weaknesses. His answer to the inane passage on "Hiawatha's Wooing" (which opens, "'As unto the bow the cord is, / So unto the man is woman, / Though she bends him, she obeys him, / Though she draws him, yet she follows'")[59] achieved by wit what Elizabeth Akers Allen did by wry substitution.

Just as, to a big umbrella,
Is the handle, when it's raining,
So a wife is, to her husband;
Though the handle do support it,
'T is the top keeps all the rain off;
Though the top gets all the wetting,
'T is the handle bears the burden;

So the top is good for nothing,
If there isn't any handle,
And the case holds, vice versa.[60]

To this passage, he added a sly note: "Umbrellas are known to have been in common use in these islands, from the earliest times. They are, invariably, constructed of sheet tin."[61] So much for the usefulness of women—or men.

In Longfellow's version, Hiawatha's wife, Minnehaha, dies during a famine. Henderson does not permit such tragedy—at the climax of the tale, Milkanwatha's Pogee contracts a fever the savage doctors prove unable to cure. Seemingly dead, she is wrapped in a blanket and dropped unceremoniously into the river. Milkanwatha leaves his people to follow her body but finds her miraculously restored:

> For the water's sudden coldness,
> From her silent stupor waked her,
> From the swooning of the Fever,
> Which, in vain the wise old doctors,
> Which the Ague, vainly shaking,
> Tried to make her wake up out of,
> In the wigwam of Marcosset;
> And our hero, rushing to her,
> Clasped her in his arms, exclaiming,
> "Lo! I see, my duck, my darling,
> See the moral of this matter,
> See the lesson that it teaches;
> What the Allopathic Practice
> Was unable to accomplish,
> Lo! How quickly was effected
> By the Plunge-bath, and the Blanket,
> By the use of *Hydropathy*."[62]

Milkanwatha vows to return to his village, bearing this remarkable medical advance. Longfellow, as it happens, was himself a fervent believer in hydropathy—"It is useless for me to reiterate, like an idiot or a parrot," he wrote a friend, "my one idea 'Water Cure.'"[63] (Allopathy was the term used by homeopaths for modern medicine, presumably unavailing in this case. Henderson's portrayal of the tribal doctors examining Pogee's tongue and then uselessly wailing and lamenting is a neat and nasty turn.)

The parodist had an acute ear for Longfellow's absurdities—he matches the poet's dewy-eyed embrace of Indian names:

> Here he saw the Melee-wee-git,
> Lightning-bug, the Melee-wee-git,
> Saw the Feesh-go-bang, musquito,
> Saw Snappo, the pinching-beetle,
> Saw the dragon-fly, Snap-peter,
> And the flea, Sticka-sting-wa-in.[64]

The names sound like island Pidgin—but perhaps some of the jokes are now lost. Sticka-sting-wa-in is approximately "Stick-a-sting-in" (in the third edition, the line was altered to "And the flea, too, Sticka-ta-wa-in").[65] Is Melee-wee-git "Mealy Widget"? No, because "widget" dates to almost a century after. A "get" was a child or offspring (i.e., something gotten or begotten), so a "wee get" would have been a runt or small child, "melee" perhaps combining the sense of *mealy* and *melee*. "Brek-e-kex-co-ax, the bull-frog," which figures elsewhere, is of course an allusion to Aristophanes.[66] Parodists and their audiences were learnèd in those days.

Longfellow's soothing adaptations of Schoolcraft's Indian myths find their match in the tale of Bee-del, the fat brave (from "beadle," no doubt—like Mr. Bumble, made the butt in *Oliver Twist* two decades before). It also gives Henderson an opportunity to mock Longfellow's slightly ridiculous and longwinded manner:

> But he waddled from the corner,
> From the wigwam slowly waddled,
> Went and stood upon the hill-side,
> Slowly sat down, slowly laid down,
> Doubled up and started rolling;

> Rolled right onward, forward, downward,
> Down the green and sloping hill-side,
> Down the hill-side kept a-rolling;
> And his mother stood and watched him,
> Wond'ring when he 'd stop a-rolling.
>   Nothing more was heard of Bee-del,
> For six months and something over;
> But, one morning, while a-baking,
> Bee-del's mother heard a rumbling,
> Like a big stone, tumbling downward
> From the hill-top, up above her;
> Went and looked, and there came Bee-del,
> Came the fat man, rolling, rumbling,
> Came a-rolling toward the wigwam,
> Came and rolled in through the back-door,
> Rolled right up into the corner,
> And remained rolled up, in silence.[67]

Bee-del, it turns out, has rolled all the way around the globe.

The most notorious savaging of Longfellow's style, however, derived from the passage on Hiawatha's mittens:

> He had mittens, Minjekahwun,
> Magic mittens made of deer-skin;
> When upon his hands he wore them,
> He could smite the rocks asunder,
> He could grind them into powder.[68]

Henderson could not resist the temptation offered:

> From the squirrel-skin, Marcosset
> Made some mittens for our hero,
> Mittens with the fur-side, inside,
> With the fur-side next his fingers
> So 's to keep the hand warm inside;
> That was why she put the fur-side—
> Why she put the fur-side, inside.[69]

This has in turn been endlessly elaborated by other parodists. Herbert Ponting, the photographer for Robert Falcon Scott's disastrous South Pole expedition, wrote a wearyingly long contribution titled "The Sleeping-Bag,"[70] which might now seem funnier but for his association with tragedy.

It's hard to imagine a book-length parody of an epic these days, but then we have so few epics. Indeed, there was one parody even longer than *Milkanwatha*—namely, *Plu-ri-bus-tah: A Song That's-By-No-Author*, by Q. K. Philander Doesticks, also published in 1856.[71] No book of American poetry before or after *Hiawatha* so quickly attracted humorists trying to cash in on a sudden craze, though no doubt *Leaves of Grass* would have been more widely parodied had Whitman sold as many as copies as Longfellow.

If the original has a form telling enough, the parody no longer need refer to the source at all—the form alone is enough to call it to mind, no matter how distant the subject from Indian maidens or mittens. In an anonymous poem from the New York *Evening Mirror* (taken here from its reprinting in the *Perth Gazette*), a girl named Pinky Winky badgers her father to tell her the best breakfast food. As she rejects each in turn, his replies grow increasingly indignant and her despair ever greater. One of his suggestions is "sausage":

At this answer, Pinky Winky
Turned her little saucy nose up,
Saying pertly, smartly, tartly:
Sausage, sausage, always sausage—
I am tired to death of sausage—
Sausages are fat and greasy
Sometimes made 'tis said of puppies;
Puppies juvenile and tender,
Which come to their end untimely.
No, my venerable Father,
If you love your Pinky Winky,
Don't by any means have sausage![72]

One of the Forty-Niners (many of them Australians) thought this the finest parody of *Hiawatha* he had read.[73]

Parody is often passive-aggressive when not simply aggressive—it conceals an attack beneath a mask of humor. (Chaucer's phrase was the "smiler with the knife.")[74] Once the parodies have severed themselves from the subject, something is lost—or everything is lost, except the absurdity of the form itself. It takes no great poetic gift to ramble on in Longfellow's form—an unpublished parody might have been called "An Ode to Mud":

> Gracious town is Kennebunkport,
> With its houses white and clapboard,
> Roofs of gray and closely shingled,
> Picket fences need much tending,
> Rotten fences to be mended
> By the moleskin-trousered workman,
> Whitewashed by the low-browed painter,
> By the paint-bedaubèd painter.
> Streets of mud are heavy going
> In the town of Kennebunkport,
> Rains come falling in all seasons,
> Mud that blooms in walks and alleys,
> Mud that sticks to boots and dresses,
> Mud upon the stoop and doorstone,
> Mud upon the stairway railing,
> Mud on coverlet and quilt-top,
> Mud in closet, mud on curtain,
> Mud on Bridie's nose and apron,
> Mud that marches to the parlor,
> Mud within the sacred parlor,
> Worked into the Turkey carpet
> Like a sacramental object—
> Sacrilegious, mud on carpets;
> Blasphemous, the mud returning;
> Resurrected, six months running.[75]

Still, something lost may be resurrected if the parodist has genius, and perhaps the only comic genius who treated *Hiawatha* was Lewis Carroll.

The title of his parody was "Hiawatha's Photographing," first published in the magazine *The Train* in 1857. It opens:

> From his shoulder Hiawatha
> Took the camera of rosewood—
> Made of sliding, folding rosewood—
> Neatly put it all together.
> In its case it lay compactly,
> Folded into nearly nothing;
> But he opened out the hinges,
> Pushed and pulled the joints and hinges,
> Till it looked all squares and oblongs,
> Like a complicated figure
> In the second book of Euclid.
>
> This he perched upon a tripod,
> And the family, in order,
> Sat before him for their pictures—
> Mystic, awful, was the process.
>
> First, a piece of glass he coated
> With collodion, and plunged it
> In a bath of lunar caustic
> Carefully dissolved in water—
> There he left it certain minutes.
>
> Secondly, my Hiawatha
> Made with cunning hand a mixture
> Of the acid pyrro-gallic,
> And of glacial-acetic,
> And of alcohol and water—
> This developed all the picture.
>
> Finally, he fixed each picture
> With a saturate solution
> Which was made of hyposulphite
> Which, again, was made of soda.
> (Very difficult the name is
> For a metre like the present,
> But periphrasis has done it.)[76]

The parenthetical metacommentary is reminiscent of a parody in *Punch* the year before: "Henry Wadsworth, whose *adnomen* / (Coming awkward, for the accents, / Into this his latest rhythm)."[77] Photography was an art in which even amateurs could excel—Oliver Wendell Holmes was an enthusiast who invented the handheld stereoscope. Carroll was himself a photographer of extraordinary gifts, so perhaps some of his frustration with sitters leaked into his hilarious polemic.

Hiawatha provoked a poetic ingenuity unavailable in most parodies of Longfellow. Carroll had too much good sense to overdo the original's tedious repetitions. In his poem, Hiawatha tries to take portraits of the members of a large English family, but each photo fails miserably. The sitters individually reveal themselves to the artist, despite the failure of the art. The mother, for example:

> She came dressed beyond description,
> Dressed in jewels and in satin,
> Far too gorgeous for an empress.
> Gracefully she sat down sideways,
> With a simper scarcely human,
> Holding in her hand a nosegay
> Rather larger than a cabbage.
> All the while that she was taking,
> Still the lady chattered, chattered,
> Like a monkey in the forest.[78]

The subject has turned from Longfellow to Victorian pretensions (the portrait of the eldest son makes quiet fun of Ruskin), the very pretensions so crucial, across the Atlantic, to the high-collared manners embodied in Longfellow's verse. His attitudes were so stalwart, so T-squared, so tightly waistcoated, he exemplified middle-class sententiousness—Longfellow wrote poetry of the parlor, by the parlor, and for the parlor. Carroll's cruelties are not only to the style—they also attack this poet's unhappy lack of cynicism. Carroll was ideally placed as a captious observer of the mores of the day—he indulged here in social observation that rarely reached the pages of the Alice books (it permeated *Sylvie and Bruno*, of course, which was distinctly unpopular).[79]

The case could be made that Carroll was parodying only the medium of Longfellow's verse—he may not have cared a fig for Indians. The civilized Hiawatha, however, was an implicit criticism of the ambitions of America itself, those less agreeable manifestations of Manifest Destiny. What was the purpose of empire but civilizing the savage, of someday making all the savage Hiawathas into portrait photographers? Besides, who are the real barbarians in Carroll's poem? Here the parodist has become a satirist.

Carroll takes up the case of the eldest daughter, who

Only begged she might be taken
With her look of "passive beauty."
Her idea of passive beauty
Was a squinting of the left-eye,
Was a drooping of the right-eye,
Was a smile that went up sideways
To the corner of the nostrils.[80]

"Passive beauty" was an ideal of the day and goes back at least as far as Wordsworth's "And to enliven in the mind's regard / Thy passive beauty,"[81] spoken of his baby daughter. Eventually the poor photographer gives up trying his portraits severally:

Finally, my Hiawatha
Tumbled all the tribe together
("Grouped" is not the right expression),
And, as happy chance would have it,
Did at last obtain a picture
Where the faces all succeeded:
Each came out a perfect likeness.
Then they joined and all abused it—
Unrestrainedly abused it—
As "the worst and ugliest picture
That could possibly be taken.
Giving one such strange expressions!
Sulkiness, conceit, and meanness!

Really any one would take us
(Any one that did not know us)
For the most unpleasant people!"
(Hiawatha seemed to think so—
Seemed to think it not unlikely.)
All together rang their voices—
Angry, loud, discordant voices—
As of dogs that howl in concert,
As of cats that wail in chorus.[82]

Perhaps the howling dogs and wailing cats are the adequate symbols of Longfellow's verse. As a poet, he was always a little more interested in sound than sense, if we can include the sentimentalities that lie beneath sense. The sonorities that reached a dead end with Swinburne and are irritating even in Poe and Tennyson lodged all too early in Longfellow (Carroll in another mood might have called them *snorities*). The Fireside Poets (Longfellow, Bryant, Holmes, Lowell, Whittier) were all afflicted by a taste for beauty oversugared and full of niceties of self-regard, which to the more jaundiced reader look like niceties of humiliation. Generations of grade-school students were browbeaten to get such verse by heart—how much livelier the school day might have been had they been required to memorize Carroll or Henderson instead.

Longfellow no doubt had a sense of humor, but not about his poetry. Of the many parodies he suffered, he wrote in 1870 that the "better they are done, the worse they are in their effects; for one cannot get rid of them, but ever after sees them making faces behind the original."[83] There are parodies after which the original survives, more or less unscathed (the author perhaps even flattered by the attention), and parodies after which the original can never be read in quite the same way. A poet well parodied seems to get no worse than he deserves—the parodist is only a critic not afraid to make faces. To those who do not like a poet's verse (and even to some who do), parody provides a cathartic release. Parody is the daimon that rescues poetry from its better nature, for in poetry the better angel is always Lucifer in disguise.

Longfellow's verse suffered from his ambitions. It was not the worst thing to have conceived an American epic so early in the history of the republic, nor was it preposterous to attempt to reduce the scattered tales of the American Indian to the kind of artificial narrative that shaped the *Kalevala*. (The myths prove more interesting as anthropology than as literature.) A poet a little circumspect might have seen that the idea was fatally crippled by the sentimental views Longfellow adopted for nearly everything that came under his pen, but they were the views of the age. The poet of Craigie House was always ripe for parody—had he not existed, the parodists would have had to invent him.

5. Keats's Chapman's Homer, Justice's Henry James

JOHN KEATS, "ON FIRST LOOKING INTO CHAPMAN'S HOMER"

At the dawn hour one morning in October 1816, a young man set out toward the Thames from Little Warner Street in Clerkenwell. He likely passed down St. John's Street, turning beyond Smithfield Market through Newgate Street and Cheapside before coming to the long slope of Grace Church Street. The city's silence would have been broken only by the early journeys of the laboring poor and traders heading to the markets.

The beaky-nosed youth ran what he called the "Gauntlet over London Bridge" and headed into the Borough, a "beastly place in dirt, turnings and windings," as he had described it to a friend days before.[1] Less than a decade later, Dickens lived a little further south off Borough High Street, an area he recalled in *The Pickwick Papers*:

> If a man wished to abstract himself from the world; to remove himself from within the reach of temptation; to place himself beyond the possibility of any inducement to look out of the window, we should recommend him by all means to go to Lant Street. . . . The majority of the inhabitants either direct their energies to the letting of furnished apartments, or devote themselves to the healthful and invigorating pursuit of mangling. . . . The population is migratory, usually disappearing on the verge of quarter-day, and generally by night. His Majesty's revenues are seldom collected in this happy valley, the rents are dubious, and the water communication is very frequently cut off.[2]

His portrait of the rooms of the impoverished medical student Bob Sawyer is probably a fair description of the local lodgings in Keats's day.[3]

Over the bridge, the young man crooked left into Tooley Street and shortly right into Dean Street, where his lodgings lay almost across from a Baptist chapel.[4] He had chosen to stay near Guy's Hospital, where he was licensed as apothecary and surgeon. A week or two later (on the twenty-ninth or thirty-first, the date still disputed),[5] he would turn twenty-one and be able to practice. That year, 1816, had been the famous Year Without a Summer—through most of October, dawns were cloudy or rainy, and after the middle of the month mornings had usually fallen into the forties.[6] Perhaps the young man lit a fire before he sat down to write.

This not quite boy—brown-haired and hazel-eyed like his late father, and according to Leigh Hunt "under the middle height"[7]—had been visiting that friend, Charles Cowden Clarke, once his tutor in Enfield, a village just north of London where Clarke's father ran an academy. When Clarke came down to breakfast later that morning,[8] he found on the table the poem the young man had written after crossing the Thames at dawn. The former student was John Keats. The later, slightly revised version of the poem read:

On First Looking Into Chapman's Homer

Much have I travell'd in the realms of gold,
    And many goodly states and kingdoms seen;
    Round many western islands have I been
Which bards in fealty to Apollo hold.
Oft of one wide expanse had I been told
    That deep-brow'd Homer ruled as his demesne;
    Yet did I never breathe its pure serene
Till I heard Chapman speak out loud and bold:
Then felt I like some watcher of the skies
    When a new planet swims into his ken;
    Or like stout Cortez when with eagle eyes
He star'd at the Pacific—and all his men
Look'd at each other with a wild surmise—
    Silent, upon a peak in Darien.[9]

The earliest surviving copy is fairly clean, with straggling lines at the long edge linking the rhymes. The handwriting shows no sign of hurry, betraying only one second thought ("low-browed" Homer, which makes him sound broody and threatening, has been improved to "deep-browed"). This is probably the very sheet that landed on Clarke's breakfast table before ten a.m.,[10] enclosed in a now vanished letter (or at least an address leaf).[11] Like Wordsworth, Keats sometimes composed his lines before writing them down—this may be his original draft.[12] Most critics see the marginal scrawls as Keats's blueprint of a Petrarchan sonnet, set down as he began; but they seem more an afterthought, scratched against the right edge by a hand much less deliberate than the bold one that composed the poem. Keats may have been checking the rhyme scheme before dispatching the poem—or perhaps it was Clarke, after receiving it.

Why was Keats out walking that cool dawn? All night the two young men had worked through a translation of Homer by the Elizabethan playwright George Chapman. Clarke had borrowed a rare copy of the c. 1614 folio, one that belonged to Thomas Alsager, a theater critic who became the "reporter of the state of the money-market" for the *Times*.[13] The two poets were fortunate to have the chance to pore over it—there was no modern edition of Chapman for another generation.[14]

When Clarke came to remember that evening, he said that Keats had left at "day-spring" (it's too much to hope that this echoed Cowper's translation of the *Iliad*—"the day-spring's daughter rosy palm'd").[15] Keats might have prolonged the hour because in the dark he didn't care to walk back into the Borough, a haunt of thieves; but the young men were night owls—of their long evenings, Clarke charmingly quoted Thomas Browne, more or less accurately: "We were acting our antipodes—the huntsmen were up in America, and they already were past their first sleep in Persia."[16] The exact time scarcely matters. A man's watch was an approximate thing before railroads, if a man carried a watch at all. Still, "day-spring" would be near six a.m. in London at mid-October, the sun rising about half an hour after.

Clarke does not reveal how the letter arrived—he says only that Keats "contrived that I should receive the poem from a distance of, may be, two miles."[17] Someone else must have been home to lay it on the

John Keats, manuscript of "On First Looking Into Chapman's Homer."
Source: MS. Keats 2.4, Houghton Library, Harvard University.

table—Clarke says he was alone in the house, which belonged to his brother-in-law, so perhaps a domestic.[18] (Domestics, being invisible, did not count.) How might a man send a letter across London in 1816? The short stretch of Dean ran into Tooley Street, which in 1807 was described in Edward Pugh's *London* as "long, but in some parts narrow, and . . . in general exceedingly dirty, owing to the great number of carts continually passing with goods from the different wharfs on the south side of the river Thames."[19] At the end of the month, on what may have been his birthday, the poet posted a letter to Clarke from the receiving house along Tooley.[20] Keats need have done no more than drop the letter into a box there. London's Twopenny Post was a modern convenience—letters could be paid for on delivery.[21]

The walk from Clerkenwell, a good two miles, would have taken Keats the better part of an hour, especially if he spent time musing over the passages from Homer that had so entranced him. Two sonnets Keats wrote about the same time, "Keen, fitful gusts are whispering here and there" and "On Leaving Some Friends at an Early Hour," record, at least in part, his walks home from Hampstead.[22] Like Wordsworth, Keats may have composed while he walked.

Even had lines formed as the poet found his way back to the Borough that dawn, it's unlikely that he could have arrived home, perhaps lit a fire, written what may be the sole draft, read it over, then posted it to his friend, all before the eight a.m. pickup for London's second delivery. That would have placed the poem in Clarke's hands between ten and eleven later that morning.[23] It's useless to chop minutes two centuries after.

Keats was known to write in white heat and almost without correction.[24] (The evidence of his drafts recalls what the editors of the First Folio wrote of Shakespeare—"We have scarce received from him a blot in his papers.")[25] The morning may have been cold—Keats might have hurried home, or left slightly earlier than dayspring. Still, considering all the small impedimenta (warming his fingers; sharpening a quill, common use of steel nibs being a few years in the future; addressing a sheet; folding up the poem; sealing it with wax, which required a candle flame; taking the walk down Tooley) and at least some time thinking over his words, the timing is difficult.

How could Clarke have received the letter, if not by post? Keats had no servant. Having not yet been to bed, he would likely have been too exhausted to deliver the poem himself and steal back to Southwark. His biographer Robert Gittings claims it was carried by an "early-morning postal messenger."[26] (Others vaguely say "messenger" or "courier" or "postboy.") The Twopenny Post had six daily deliveries—a letter posted by ten that morning would have reached Clarke with the third delivery, between noon and one or one-thirty p.m.[27] Why then go to the expense of hiring a man, perhaps a servant at a nearby inn? (There were large coaching-inns in Borough High Street.)[28] Because on one day of the week there were no deliveries. If Keats wrote "On First Looking Into Chapman's Homer" early on the morning of the Sabbath, that would explain his failure to use the Twopenny Post. The date of the poem, written sometime after the ninth,[29] would then probably be the morning of October 13 or 20, or even as late as October 27.[30] Keats and Clarke had dined at Leigh Hunt's on Hunt's birthday, October 19, the occasion on which Hunt and Keats first met; and the loan of Chapman may have come through Hunt, a good friend of Alsager's.[31] It is all no more than a possibility.[32]

Had Keats hired a man, he must have felt the occasion important—the gesture certainly showed Romantic intensity. (It would have taken more time, and more care, than walking to the receiving house.) After the night-long session with the old folio, the sonnet was a mark of gratitude—and perhaps he was eager to share his own astonishment at a poem that had arrived like a bolt of lighting. His previous verse had been earnest, and terrible.

Though Keats had studied Latin and French at Enfield, he had left, probably at fifteen, with no Greek.[33] (Charles Armitage Brown claims that a few years later, about 1818 or 1819, the time of *Hyperion* and *Lamia*, Keats was "deeply absorbed in the study of Greek and Italian"—this might have been part of a yearning to read Homer plain.)[34] Like Clarke, he knew Homer through the teeter-totter of Pope's couplets, whose formal antitheses decked out the bard in the raiments of some courtier to George I. Like many poets of the day, Keats despised the Augustans, mocking them rather amusingly in "Sleep and Poetry" ("with a puling infant's force / They swayed about upon a rocking horse / And thought

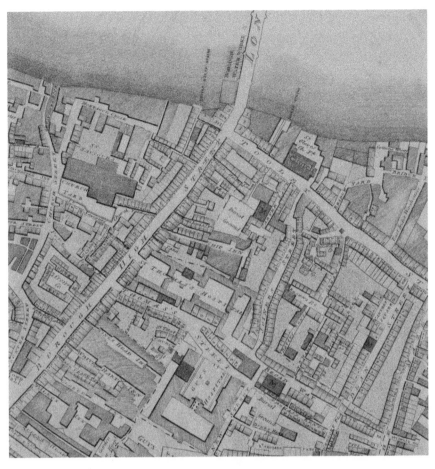

Map of Southwark in 1813. Dean Street runs north near the far right of the map.
Source: Richard Horwood's Plan of the Cities of London, Westminster and Southwark.
Published by William Faden, 1813.
Courtesy London Metropolitan Archives, City of London.

it Pegasus").[35] He would have agreed with the classicist Richard Bentley, who condescendingly remarked, "It is a pretty poem, Mr. Pope; but you must not call it Homer."[36]

The young men had spent the evening ravaging through the folio, looking up what Clarke called the "'famousest' passages, as we had scrappily known them in Pope's version."[37] Decades later, when he wrote down his recollections of Keats, Clarke recaptured their excitement. He remembered four passages in particular, the quotations filled with Chapman's brusque attractions. From the third book of the *Iliad*, Clarke showed Keats the portrait of Odysseus, where the Trojan Antenor said that, when the Greek rose to speak, his words "flew about our eares, like drifts of winters snow."[38] Compare Pope's long-winded, almost comical,

> But, when he speaks, what Elocution flows!
> Soft as the Fleeces of descending Snows
> The copious Accents fall, with easy Art;
> Melting they fall, and sink into the Heart![39]

The "easy Art" and melting snowflakes are pure Pope, and purely Pope—Chapman captures the terrible force of Homer's blizzard. This was part of a longer passage Keats and Clarke examined, "that perfect scene of the conversation on Troy wall of the old Senators with Helen."[40] As he doesn't quote more than the portrait, we have to guess where else in the passage Keats's interest fixed. Perhaps, with his fondness for grasshoppers, he responded to Chapman's description, early in the scene, of the nattering old warriors:

> And, as in well-growne woods, on trees, cold spinie Grashoppers
> Sit chirping, and send voices out, that scarce can pierce our eares,[41]

a comparison Pope renders more clumsily. His elderly Trojans

> In Summer-Days like Grashoppers rejoice,
> A bloodless Race, that send a feeble Voice.[42]

As Homer has them lighting on trees, the insects are probably cicadas. This famous image drew a long note from Pope defending it ("one of the justest and most natural Images in the World"),[43] but Chapman's version is more fully blooded in bloodlessness. Still, he cannot entirely be trusted. When Helen names the Greeks in distant view, Chapman makes Agamemnon a head taller than other great Achaean warriors, while Homer leaves him a head shorter.[44]

Having possessed the folio for some time, Clarke may already have scouted extracts for his young friend, who loved poetic language thickened with imagery. Clarke recalled that at about sixteen the poet had carried off a volume of *The Faerie Queene* and gone through it "as a young horse would through a spring meadow—ramping!"

> He especially singled out epithets, for that felicity and power in which Spenser is so eminent. He *hoisted* himself up, and looked burly and dominant, as he said, "what an image that is—'*sea-shouldering whales!*'"[45]

That quality is missing from Pope's emollient verse.

The Augustan doesn't always have the worst of it. Though Clarke mentions[46] the moment in *Iliad* 5 when Athena lit Diomedes's shield and helmet with living fire, Chapman's bouncy rendering,

> Like rich *Autumnus* golden lampe, whose brightnesse men admire,
> Past all the other host of starres, when with his chearefull face,
> Fresh washt in loftie Ocean waues, he doth the skies enchase,[47]

is inferior to Pope's

> Th' unweary'd Blaze incessant Streams supplies,
> Like the red Star that fires th' Autumnal Skies,
> When fresh he rears his radiant Orb to Sight,
> And bath'd in Ocean, shoots a keener Light.[48]

Enchase means to set with a gem, here the red star hung in the skies. The glamour of Chapman's translation may have come partly from its physical presence—the large volume, published almost exactly two centuries before, had been printed in rich Jacobean orthography: "Fresh washt in loftie Ocean waues." The initial and medial *s*'s were long *s*'s (in a double *s*, only the first letter), another way Chapman's language had the patina of antiquity. (Editions of Pope retained the long *s* into Keats's day, but the typography was more orderly and legible than in Chapman's folio. By the time Keats wrote his sonnet, the old letter-form was passing out of use.)[49] The slower you read Chapman, the less irritating his fourteeners, the more magnificent and generous his language. If Chapman's translation is more vigorous, more filthy with particulars, Pope has his polished grandeur and formal elegance.

The two night-readers also studied Neptune's thundering progress toward the Greek ships in book 13—Chapman there is good ("Three steps he onely tooke, / Before he far-off *Ægas* reacht; but with the fourth, it shooke / With his drad entrie"),[50] yet Pope is better:

> Fierce as he past, the lofty Mountains nod,
> The Forests shake! Earth trembled as he trod,
> And felt the Footsteps of th' immortal God.[51]

In the final passage, the wreck of Odysseus from book 5 of the *Odyssey*, Clarke recalled the specific line where Keats gave him the "reward of one of his delighted stares."[52]

> Then forth he came, his both knees faltring; both
> His strong hands hanging downe; and all with froth
> His cheeks and nosthrils flowing. Voice and breath
> Spent to all vse; and downe he sunke to Death.
> *The sea had soakt his heart through*: all his vaines,
> His toiles had rackt, t'a labouring womans paines.
> Dead wearie was he.[53]

The italics are Clarke's.

Though Chapman translated the *Iliad* into fourteeners, his *Odyssey* is pitched into pentameter couplets violently enjambed, unlike Pope's. The Augustan's translation is not awful, but Clarke rightly casts scorn on the couplet that corresponds to the line: "From mouth and nose the briny torrent ran; / And lost in lassitude lay all the man."[54] He grubbed the Pope up for Keats on a later occasion, he remembered, so that momentous first evening they didn't have the Augustan before them. Clarke could scarcely conceal his delight at the memory, for he italicized Pope's pallid second line and marked it with three exclamation points. "Chapman supplied us with many an after-treat,"[55] he wrote, so he must have kept the old folio for some time. Pope's *Odyssey* is not all Pope— half the books were translated by hirelings and touched up by the master.

Much in "Chapman's Homer" is clear on first reading, and much hovers at the edge of clarity. The first stanza is the reminiscence of a poet-traveler, an occupation unknown until Alphonse de Lamartine named it in 1835.[56] The world Keats invented is at once physical and metaphorical (call it a world existing in the physics of metaphor), fancifully packed with realms, states, kingdoms, each carved out by a poet, or granted by Apollo—on this imagined globe, the greatest poets rule the largest emperies. Keats, who had ambitions, and might have longed for a small city or two, reads the map of imagination onto the map of the world. Homer and Shakespeare must have been his Alexanders, and Dante and Ariosto and Tasso monarchs of vast lands—the undertone of conquest should not be ignored. (For Keats's ranking of his predecessors, see "Ode to Apollo" and his letter to Benjamin Haydon of March 25, 1818: "When I die I'll have my Shakespeare placed on my heart, with Homer in my right hand.")[57] The bards hold their lands in fealty, and for the conquistadors fealty was a license to conquer.

The young poet has journeyed through the realms of gold (every great poet is a Golden Age—and Keats had already begun a sonnet with "How many bards gild the lapses of time!"),[58] picking up knowledge like a gypsy scholar, but not to one land closed by his ignorance of ancient Greek— that wide expanse ruled by Homer. Homer's epics had been lost to Western Europe for a thousand years—even Petrarch failed to find someone who could translate them or teach him Homeric Greek. Not until decades later was Homer reclaimed for the Western tradition. Why not travel to a land you wanted to see? Because, if you didn't know the language, you would need a translator. At Enfield, Keats had studied his Latin and French, studied them hard, beginning a translation of the *Aeneid* he finished while apprentice to the surgeon-apothecary Thomas Hammond.[59] Though aware of his otherwise inadequate education, Keats was a striver.

He had, perhaps, the fantasy that the greatest poet of the ancient world held the key to poetry itself; apparently he didn't know the medieval and Renaissance Latin translations, which often showed great fidelity to the originals.[60] Pope's version, from which Keats occasionally drew allusions in his letters,[61] was useless to someone who wanted to understand why Homer was accorded his place *primus super pares*. Keats was not, however, without a touch of arrogance. The following spring he wrote that lines from Pope's translation, read out by his brother Tom, "seem like Mice to mine."[62]

Some critics have located Keats's islands in the Mediterranean. Though the sea of Odysseus has a few western islands, it lacks realms of gold. Keats must have been thinking of the Spanish Main, from which for some three centuries treasure ships had sailed back to Europe. In the indentures of this imagery, the geographical becomes metagraphical. A few years later, in "A Defence of Poetry," Shelley wrote that "poets are the unacknowledged legislators of the world."[63] Keats made them kings.

LOW-BROWED

In the copy of the poem probably sent to Clarke, Keats called Homer "low-browed," then scratched it out. He could not have meant the bard a Neanderthal (Neanderthals were not described for another half-century), but a low forehead had long been a defining feature of the ape (*The Tempest*: "We shall . . . all be turn'd to Barnacles, or to Apes / With foreheads villanous low").[64] "Having a low forehead," Ash's *New and Complete Dictionary of the English Language* (1775) defines the compound;[65] but in 1816 "low-browed" was rarely if ever used of people. It was an architectural term applied to doors, caverns, windows, roofs, cottages, anything that might have a low entrance (the way a man might lower his brows over his eyes)—hence, as the *OED* has it, "dark, gloomy." It was also applied to rocks of a beetlish appearance, no doubt due to the "low-brow'd rocks" in *L'Allegro* (Pope later borrowed the term).[66] "Beetle-browed" goes back at least as far as Langland, often with the sense of "reproachful," and later "sullen" or "surly."[67] The *OED* does not record any "low-browed" people before 1855, though the dictionary's dating must always be treated skeptically—an 1829 issue of *Blackwood's Edinburgh Magazine* describes a man as "smug-faced, smooth-haired, low-browed, pug-nosed, cock-chin'd," while the *Spectator* in 1841 refers to a "faction of low-browed, sketching clubbists," the term referring to the artists' brutishness rather than their fierce concentration.[68] Keats could have found the idea in Chapman, had he and Clarke paged through *Iliad* 17: "And lets his rough browes downe so low, they couer all his eyes. / So *Aiax* lookt"—but why would Homer look so?[69] Keats must have felt "low-browed" mistaken or ambiguous—it may have been only a brief place-marker for some better epithet, or more likely an error in judgment immediately corrected. "Deep-browed" was his own coinage.

What might he have *meant* by "low-browed," though? Given its use in architecture, perhaps he thought that Homer, like a low doorway or a low room, was difficult to enter (for Keats, before he heard Chapman, virtually impossible). "*Deep*-browed" would then be simply a variation— a man whose brows so hooded his eyes that, in a surprisingly old sense, he was *hard to read*. So the man, so the work.

PURE SERENE

The final lines of the octet lie waiting to complete the complex thought Keats has slowly developed. They are perhaps the first sign in his poetry of a power to surprise beyond the mere register of the words. "Pure serene" is Romantic guff, perhaps a nod to Coleridge's "Hymn Before Sun-Rise" or Henry Cary's translation of Dante, which Keats owned and where the phrase occurs twice.[70] Through the previous century, the phrase appeared often enough in scientific and medical papers or travel journals as an adjectival phrase describing the atmosphere ("the sudden mixture of the pure serene air above the clouds").[71] Keats might have met it elsewhere in his vagabond reading. At this period, the noun "serene" meant "fine quiet weather," "serenity," and most pertinently an "unruffled expanse of clear sky or calm sea," as in Byron ("Kissing, not ruffling, the blue deep's serene") and Cowper ("The bark that plows the deep serene"), to use the *OED*'s examples. In these stray meanings Keats has prepared, perhaps unknowingly, the startling images that close the poem.

The effect (where effect is not logic) is that the paradisal freshness, the simplifying quiet, of line 7 is disrupted by the mortal thunder of Chapman. Effect has preceded cause—Keats's logic, logic rather than effect, is that the violent storm leaves a freshness after, like the ozone released by the lightning bolt. A man in the miasmic warren of Dean Street might well pine for the pure serene. (Only a few months before, he had begun a sonnet, "To one who has been long in city pent, / 'Tis very sweet to look into the fair / And open face of heaven.")[72] There follow, as if Keats had been reading the *OED*, the clear night skies of Herschel and the calm sea of Cortez. Certain ideas roil about a poet's imagination. At Margate that August, Keats had ended a sonnet with "wonders of the sky and sea."[73]

"Chapman's Homer" requires only two sentences, one cobbled from statements cast from present-perfect reminiscence ("Much have I travell'd . . . ," "Round . . . islands have I been"), the other an admission in past-perfect foreknowledge ("of one wide expanse had I been told"), rising through simple past toward a recognition ("did I never breathe its pure serene") qualified by the independent clause that ends the octet ("Till I heard"). The volta is sandwiched between two measures of time ("Till . . . : / Then . . ."), marked by a subordinate conjunction and an adverb, one rising toward the climax, the other falling away. The consequence of revelation ("Then felt I") leads to the two similes that form the sestet. This progress of revelation—condition, development, climax, consequence, figurative comparison—brings us exactly to the moment the night before. Tense is crucial: how much more offhanded and detached the poem would have seemed had he begun, "Much had I travell'd." Keats's tendency toward Romantic mooniness is here denied in his control of tenses.

The poet perhaps had something like his rhymes in mind from the start. The plain "seen" and "been" become the more fanciful "demesne" and "serene." It seems improbable that he'd written the first pair and then had a stroke of luck—yet "serene" was a much later second thought. In the copy dispatched to Clarke, the line read, "Yet could I never judge what men could mean," the sort of bland, rhyme-filling line a poet in a hurry might set down until he could think of better, if he could think of better. (Clarke later recalled that the draft read, "Yet could I never tell . . ." His memory may have faltered there.)[74]

Keats told Clarke that the original line "was bald, and too simply wondering"[75]—bald, presumably, of metaphor or real thought. The replacement keeps the lineaments, "Yet —— I never ——," though the more natural wording might have been "Yet never did I . . . ," which gives more vigor to "never." (The line has often been misquoted this way, even by Helen Vendler.)[76] The original line suffered from other problems—the repetition of "could" is enough to suggest that Keats hadn't completely escaped his student verse, and "men" risks confusion with the very different body of "men" five lines later. Besides, though "what men could mean" underlines the poet's ignorance of Homer, the line repeats the gist of "had I been told." It's not a ruinous recurrence, but "serene" anticipates the staring of Cortez and the silence with which the poem ends.

The original line survived into the publication of the sonnet in Leigh Hunt's *Examiner* a few weeks later, on December 1.[77] Hunt, in his brief article on the poet, mentioned "one incorrect rhyme, . . . easily altered"[78]—he meant the exact rhyme of "demesne" and "mean." Keats's motive may therefore have been merely technical, and a way to please Hunt, his new acquaintance. The poet's rhymes were often abused—he was called a "very facetious rhymer" by one critic; another remarked that, having written a "line at random," the poet "follows not the thought excited by this line, but that suggested by the *rhyme*."[79] Here Keats is perhaps glimpsed in the act of composition—having written "ken" and "men," he's unlikely simply to have happened upon "Darien." Once the word occurred to him, however, triggered by his inaccurate memory of Balboa or by some rhyming thought of "men in Darien," he could easily have worked backward, "men" proving easy to manipulate and "ken" being just makeweight. The earlier use of "men," however, would have to go.

Keats might have been pardonably proud of "pure serene." The sonnet would have been extraordinary without that line, but something would have been lost, even were the fine knitting of the images of sky and sea mere accident, not calculation. The use of the noun for clear sky or calm weather (extending to metaphorical readings of mood and feeling) is itself of interest, since it gradually replaced and then wrote out of existence the earlier noun *serene*—a fine mist or rain, thought to be unhealthy, falling after sunset in equatorial countries.

TILL I HEARD CHAPMAN SPEAK OUT LOUD AND BOLD

In each stanza, the second appearance of a rhyme explains or elaborates the first. The "realms of gold" are those that "bards in fealty . . . hold." The passive receipt of knowledge, like a schoolboy's ("Oft . . . had I been told"), becomes a second listening—to Chapman speaking "loud and bold."

The force and passion of Chapman's oratory are reminiscent of the passage Clarke had shown Keats:

> He stood a little still, and fixt upon the earth his eyes;
> His scepter moving neither way, but held it formally,
> Like one that vainely doth affect. Of wrathfull qualitie,
> And franticke (rashly iudging him) you would have said he was,
> But when out of his ample breast, he gave his great voyce passe,
> And words that flew about our eares, like drifts of winters snow;
> None thenceforth might contend with him.[80]

"Vainely doth affect" meant "vainly tries [to speak]." Odysseus, though seemingly shy, spoke with such vehemence, when he did speak, that his words were a blizzard against which no man could stand. Pope, in his gentler version, misunderstood the point.

How did the long-dead *Chapman* speak, however? By being read aloud. Keats and Clarke were used to reading to each other (the habit dated back to Enfield).[81] It's unlikely that this night was different—how can a poet hear the sonorities of a passage, its very speech becoming speech, without reading it aloud? Keats's friend George Felton Mathew recalled that, when reading aloud, the poet never had "tears in his eyes" or a "broken voice."[82] We have a stronger clue in Benjamin Haydon's recollection of the young poet reciting the "Ode to Pan" from *Endymion*: "I begged Keats to repeat it—which he did in his usual half chant, (most touching) walking up & down the room." (Haydon called the lines "exquisite"—Wordsworth, who had just been introduced to the young poet, did not agree.)[83] Keats may have been a gentle but not sentimental reader. Perhaps Clarke gave Chapman the thunder of Odysseus. This was not just Keats's first reading of Homer, Chapman's pure Homer, but his first listening.

Clarke's further testimony about the evening can be found in the notes from which he later wrote up his recollections: "How distinctly is that earnest stare, and protrusion of the upper lip now present with me, as we came upon some piece of rough-hewn doric elevation in the fine old poet. He sometimes shouted."[84] This was probably Keats's reaction, not his style of reading; but recall how Odysseus stared at the ground before he spoke. (The slippery pronoun is delightful—it's not at first clear whether the shouts are Chapman's or Keats's.) This all-night frolic, punctuated by whoops and yelps, probably confirms that the house was empty apart from a servant or two, whose feelings would not have been consulted. With its silent or dumbfounded stares, its stentorian voice ("loud and bold"), the sonnet perhaps retains a ghostly recollection of that evening over the ancient folio, Keats excited almost past bearing. His old tutor would have seen this at once, reading "Chapman's Homer" at his table. Had Clarke been the loud and bold reader, he would have been delighted by the tacit acknowledgment. None of this is necessary to the meaning; but it might explain the spur to Keats's imagination, or at least his hurry to get the poem to Clerkenwell. In a poem so intensely about looking ("kingdoms seen," "watcher of the skies," "into his ken," "eagle eyes," "star'd," "look'd"), "told" is the echo of rumor or lecture; but the almost jubilant "loud and bold" is the sole recognition of the voice of oral poetry.

"Speak out" had so many meanings in Keats's day, it would be difficult to specify which was primary—they range from the redundant ("To talk in a loud voice, or so as to be heard distinctly") to meanings not mutually exclusive ("To talk freely or unreservedly," "To break into speech," "To utter; to make known in words; to declare openly or clearly"). No doubt such meanings form a crowded complex, none entirely exhausting the poet's sensitivity to language. The *OED*'s most interesting possibility, however, is a rare poetic usage, unfortunately always recorded as transitive: "To create by speaking." The first citation is from Abraham Cowley, "They sung how God spoke out the worlds vast ball." Cowley invented the irregular ode Keats later took up, though the young poet was probably borrowing from Wordsworth and Coleridge. What unnamed world could Chapman have created for Keats? Homer's, of course. (And, by insinuating irony, what is the next link in this chain of association but the "worlds vast ball" discovered by Herschel?)

The following spring, May 1817, it must have hurt Keats mortally to read in the *European Magazine* his old friend Mathew's review of *Poems*, the young poet's first book. Keats should not be said, the critic argued, to eclipse better poets simply because he was "pouring forth his splendors in the Orient." Having groused about the "slovenly independence of his versification," the critic came to the sonnet. Though "absurd in its application," it was a "fair specimen" of the good sonnets in the book. Even so:

> "Till I heard Chapman speak out loud and bold" however is a bad line—not only as it breaks the metaphor—but as it blows out the whole sonnet into an unseemly hyperbole.[85]

Mathew objected to just what later readers would admire—the injection of personality. The critic's strictures are not so much undeserved as misapplied. After lines of wan, conventional writing, with the whiff of antique gods and medieval fiefdoms hanging about them, Keats had broken into a modern register. The sonnet has often been the form through which the modern muscles in—modern diction and modern airs mark the sonnets of Milton, Wordsworth, and Auden. Keats has fallen far from Apollonian inspiration, fallen for a mere translation (anyone with half an education could have read ancient Greek), yet his tone is triumphant. It's as if Odysseus had spoken to him—as, in a way, he had. Mathew's final judgment of Keats, however, was that

> the mere luxuries of imagination, more especially in the possession of the proud egotist of diseased feelings and perverted principles, may become the ruin of a people—inculcate the falsest and most dangerous ideas of the condition of humanity—and refine us into the degeneracy of butterflies that perish in the deceitful glories of a destructive taper.[86]

That tells us as much about the critic as it does about the importance of poetry in 1817. (By "butterflies" he probably meant "moths.")

Many phrases from "Chapman's Homer" had been used by earlier writers: "goodly states" and "wide expanse"; "his demesne" and "pure serene"; "loud and bold" and "with eagle eyes"; "wild surmise" and even, in a poem by one N. Sloan in the *European Magazine* of May 1808, "realms of gold," all but the last pair frequently enough that Keats might have known them.[87] A poem is often composed in part of familiar phrases—Homer, as Milman Parry showed nearly a century ago, is brilliantly patched with timeworn epithets and stock formulae. The poet's task is the invention of the new on ground long trodden, just as the watcher must scan a sky long watched.

SOME WATCHER OF THE SKIES

The poem closes with two images among the most memorable in English poetry, images through which Keats renders in emotion his discovery of Homer, and does so by indirection. (Eliot would have had to look no further than Keats for such a pure example of the objective correlative.) The speaker of the poem is only figuratively a traveler; in the last lines, the metaphors are therefore meta-metaphors. Through the old folio, Keats could hear the bard of two-and-a-half millennia before. Pope had blocked the view of Homer; Chapman gave a glimpse, sometimes better than a glimpse, of what had been missed. A later critic, George Gilfillan, called Chapman's the "only translation which gives the savageism, if not the sublimity of Homer—his wild beasts muzzling and maddening in their fleshy fury, and his heroes 'red-wat-shod.'"[88] (Just two months before that October evening, Leigh Hunt had called Chapman's Homer a "fine rough old wine"—recall that probably through Hunt the borrowed volume came.)[89] Though the images might seem to aggrandize the moment a poor young man, one who had never written a good poem, finds a voice of magnificent power (it's only a poem about reading, after all), they represent the importance of Homer to *him*.

The similes allow Keats to specify and magnify a feeling otherwise difficult to measure, capable of measure only by comparison to two transforming discoveries remembered from his reading in astronomy and history (this is also a poem about metamorphosis through reading). Both events changed the boundaries of the known.

A NEW PLANET SWIMS INTO HIS KEN

The Babylonians knew six planets in the solar system, from Mercury out to Saturn, all visible to the naked eye. Critics usually say that the "new planet" is a reference to William Herschel's observation of Uranus in 1781, the first planet discovered since antiquity. Keats had almost certainly read of the discovery in John Bonnycastle's *Introduction to Astronomy* (fifth edition, 1807), which lay on his shelves—he had won it as a school prize at Enfield.[90] More recent discoveries have been forgotten, however. When Keats was a boy, newer planets had been found, namely Ceres (1801), Pallas (1802), Juno (1804), and Vesta (1807), now called asteroids.

Bonnycastle mentioned two of these planets in the edition Keats owned (in the seventh edition of 1816, all four were present in detail).[91] Indeed, the title of the chapter in which the poet read of these unknown worlds was "Of the New Planets, and Other Discoveries." To Keats, it must have seemed that the sky was full of undiscovered bodies and that any watcher of the skies, if only he scanned the heavens long enough, might discover a planet. (In Keats's day, a watcher who hoped to see something new would need a telescope.) This may explain why Herschel is unnamed—after all, Keats could have written, "like some Herschel of the skies." The "new planets" in Bonnycastle were pointed out half a century ago, but they have rarely been mentioned since.[92]

Keats's biographer Nicholas Roe argues that an equal or greater influence on Keats's attention to the skies was the "living orrery" established by the founder of the Enfield school, John Ryland. According to *Rylandiana*, boys were handed cards and made to act out the motion of the planets around the sun, "giving each boy a direction to move from east to west; Mercury to move swiftest, and the others in proportion to their distances, and each boy repeating in his turn the contents of his card, concerning his distance, magnitude, period, and hourly motion."[93] However schoolboyish the method, it would have fixed in Keats's mind the great mechanical system of the planets.

When a "new planet swims" into the vision of the astronomer, it must have a medium through which to swim. Keats is probably thinking of the aether. Astronomers would believe until Einstein that the stars and planets moved through the heavens suspended in this substance—Keats would have read in "An Explanation of the Principal Terms" in his copy of Bonnycastle that "ether" was a "fine subtile fluid."[94] Indeed, the poet had recently ended a sonnet with what seems an eerie premonition of the line in "Chapman's Homer": "E'en like the passage of an angel's tear / That falls through the clear ether silently."[95] That a planet moves at all, relative to the stars, made the Greeks name it "wanderer." Only by accidental grace does "aether" in Greek mean something very close to "pure serene."

Why this particular act of discovery? All night Keats had been soaked through with Chapman's imagery. We cannot know the way his imagination worked—he may have happened on his images by devious course. Yet one of the passages Clarke recollected, as noted earlier, described the flaming light from the shield and helmet of Diomedes: "Like rich *Autumnus* golden lampe, . . . / Fresh washt in loftie Ocean waues, he doth the skies enchase."[96] (The light of bright stars close to the horizon passes through a thicker layer of air, shimmering as if immersed—or as if emerging from the waves.) What is the golden lamp of Autumnus? Sirius, the Dog Star, the brightest star in the night sky, which appears over the southern horizon in autumn. Had the passage made Keats think of the heavens, his imagination might have passed easily to the planets, sometimes called stars, as Venus is still the morning or evening star. Keats wrote to Fanny Brawne, "I will imagine you Venus tonight and pray, pray, pray to your star like a Hethen."[97]

OR LIKE STOUT CORTEZ

Keats had traveled in the realms of gold because he was too poor to travel anywhere else. Indeed, he may then never have been farther than Margate, where a few weeks before he had stood upon a cliff and seen the wide expanse of the North Sea.[98] Keats had every intention of becoming a real traveler, but his travels too often were visions unfulfilled—he was to propose trips to the Continent, or just to Lisbon or Scotland. Later, he wanted to sail to America to see his brother George. He had his few journeys, but dreamed of more. Less than two years before he died at Rome, he was thinking of a voyage to South America, or of joining an Indiaman as a surgeon.[99]

As a schoolboy, Keats had devoured travel books, histories, and mythology.[100] He had read William Robertson's *History of America* (1777) at Enfield and later owned a copy.[101] Robertson was a famous historian in his day, the rival of Gibbon and Hume. It is usually thought that Keats was recalling, with some confusion, the historian's description of Balboa's discovery:

> Balboa commanded his men to halt, and advanced alone to the summit, that he might be the first who should enjoy a spectacle which he had so long desired. As soon as he beheld the South Sea stretching in endless prospect below him, he fell on his knees, and lifting up his hands to Heaven, returned thanks to God. . . . His followers, observing his transports of joy, rushed forward to join in his wonder, exultation and gratitude.[102]

Perhaps, as Richard Garnett pointed out more than a century ago,[103] Keats was influenced by other sources, like the remarks by William Gilbert that Wordsworth fondly quoted in a note to *The Excursion* (1814):

> A Man is supposed to improve by going out into the *World*, by visiting *London*. Artificial man does; he extends with his sphere; but alas! that sphere is microscopic: it is formed of minutiae, and he surrenders his genuine vision to the artist, in order to embrace it in his ken. His bodily senses grow acute . . . ; while his mental become proportionally obtuse. The reverse is the Man of Mind: He who is placed in the sphere of Nature and of God, might be a mock at Tattersall's and Brookes's [*sic*], and a sneer at St. James's; he would certainly be swallowed alive by the first *Pizarro* that crossed him:—But when he walks along the River of Amazons; when he rests his eye on the unrivalled Andes; . . . Or contemplates, from a sudden Promontory, the distant, vast Pacific—and feels himself a Freeman in this vast Theatre . . . —His exaltation is not less than Imperial.[104]

In his ken! "Ken" may not have been a makeweight after all. (Wordsworth thought the Gilbert "one of the finest passages of modern English prose.")[105] In this paean to the benefits of the grand tour, a tour that included the Romantic sublime of the Andes and the Pacific, Keats might have found justification for the vision of the artist. His travel may have been largely in books (indeed, the poem is a homage to his books); but he was free to be a man of mind, and his reading could take him much farther than London. He was not the man for Tattersall's, the famous horse auctioneer with a sideline in betting, or Brooks's, the gentleman's club notable for gaming (St. James's Street was full of coffeehouses and clubs). The coincidence of "in his ken" with the view of the Pacific suggests that Keats took this passage deeply to heart. He of course had read *The Excursion*. Just over a year after "Chapman's Homer," the poet wrote his friend Haydon "that there are three things to rejoice at in this Age—The Excursion[,] Your Pictures, and Hazlitt's depth of Taste."[106]

Critics have sometimes suggested that Keats's error was influenced or encouraged by the passage in Robertson where Cortez looks from the heights upon the "vast plain of Mexico."[107] Given the devious methods of imagination, the notion can't be entirely disregarded; but the scene bears little relation in detail to Balboa's discovery of the Pacific, while the mood is less dramatic than the description of his "transports of joy" and the "wonder, exultation and gratitude" that gripped him and his men.[108]

Why would Keats have remembered *this* discovery, however falsely? Balboa did not march his men across the isthmus in search of a new sea. As Robertson's history reminds us,

> A young cazique . . . tumbled the gold out of the balance with indignation; and, turning to the Spaniards, "Why do you quarrel (says he) about such a trifle? If you are so passionately fond of gold . . . , I will conduct you to a region where the metal . . . is so common that the meanest utensils are formed of it." . . . Balboa and his companions inquired eagerly where this happy country lay, and how they might arrive at it. He informed them that at the distance of six suns, that is of six days journey towards the south, they should discover another ocean, near to which this wealthy kingdom was situated.[109]

Balboa sought realms of gold. He found something greater, the ocean that would bind the fragments of the known world. On the far side lay China—half-a-dozen years later, Magellan's ships set sail on the voyage that circumnavigated the globe. Keats too found something, perhaps. The discoveries of Herschel and Balboa each owed a debt to chance (that young cazique!), like Clarke's timely acquisition of the borrowed folio.

The scholarly consensus is that the young poet, rushing to judgment that October morning, muddled his schoolboy reading. Clarke remarked that Keats possessed a "tolerably retentive memory" as a student,[110] but the conquistadors had a tangled history. What became the most famous example of a poet getting the facts wrong was so trivial at the time that apparently no one noticed. It is usually said that the mistake went unrecognized until 1861, when Tennyson mentioned it to Francis Turner Palgrave, then compiling his *Golden Treasury*.[111] However, in an 1845 review of the new edition of Leigh Hunt's *Imagination and Fancy*, the anonymous critic notes the error and amusingly proposes that the line be changed posthumously.[112] The mistake was not made to satisfy the meter, since "Balboa" has the same metrical profile as "stout Cortez," which—the meter tells us—must have been pronounced COR-tez. ("Stout" did not then usually mean thickset or overweight, retaining the older meanings of proud, valiant, determined.)

The title Keats used in the copy he sent Clarke was "On the first looking into Chapman's Homer"—*the* first looking. This might have been a slip—yet it suggests that, for Keats, his first real encounter with Homer, even through the medium of Chapman, ranked with discovering a new planet or a new sea. One can cut too fine in parsing a meaning. The second man to discover the Pacific will not be found in history books, though the vision may have been no less astonishing.[113]

Coasting among his islands and visiting new realms, Keats seems less a conquistador than an Odysseus—but we can ask too much of metaphor. It's amusing but irrelevant that Herschel did not know exactly what he'd seen. He thought at first the blur in the glass was a new comet, a rare enough achievement (less than a dozen had been found that century). Even in the scientific paper announcing the news, he was too diplomatic to do more than strongly imply that it was a planet. Keats's deep-felt wonder on looking into Homer, his setting the moment at one with the great discoveries of science and exploration, only confirm Clarke's portrait of his boyish passions—the young Keats who was moved to tears reading aloud from *Cymbeline* and given to "ecstatic" exclamations about Spenser.[114]

EAGLE EYES

Poems often need a bit of padding, and in a labyrinthine form like the sonnet an obvious rhyme can be a gift. Still, Cortez's "eagle eyes" are curious. The ocean was lying directly before him—he could have been blind and not missed it. The common phrase normally referred to keen sight, as in the *OED*'s citation from Thomas Dekker, "Women haue eagles eyes, / To prie euen to the heart." (Keats's "eagle" was deliberate, because in the earliest version he had written "wond'ring eyes," another bit of juvenile stuffing.) Perhaps the sense in Keats is closer to "predatory" (Dekker may partly embrace this shading), as if new realms of conquest had suddenly been opened. Leigh Hunt remarked that Titian had captured these eagle eyes in the conquistador's portrait (he does not claim that Keats had seen it), yet no such painting is known.[115] Beyond that sea lay other lands, even continents, all yet unconquered. Keats's Cortez was not thinking of the sea—what he saw was possibility.

For whom does a conquistador conquer? For his king. (Robertson: "Balboa advancing up to the middle in the waves with his buckler and sword, took possession of that ocean in the name of the king his master.")[116] Balboa carried back riches in gold and pearls from his march across the isthmus—booty from local tribes, freely or not so freely given, force of arms ever the handmaiden of extortion.[117]

The watcher of the skies is neatly parallel—the discoverer of a planet is allowed to name it, figuratively setting a flag upon it. Herschel christened the new planet Georgium Sidus, the Star of George, for the king of England, the German king of that transplanted German. This placed a rather mediocre ruler, George III, among the gods—rather like a long string of Roman emperors. Foreign astronomers found Herschel's patriotic gesture a bit much. Some would have preferred the name Neptune, but eventually Uranus held sway. Uranus was father of Saturn, as Saturn was father of Jupiter. We are staring back through the paternal bloodline of gods.

SILENT UPON A PEAK

Keats preferred the Petrarchan sonnet almost exclusively, early in his work. Its octet and sestet require a complex intertwining of logic and

rhyme (here *abba abba cdcdcd*)—the Shakespearean sonnet can be satisfied with three examples and a homily. Keats's octet closes with the
crescendo of Chapman's speech. The sestet opens upon an excitement
scarcely contained—contained only by comparison to the watcher of the
skies who, after long and fruitless waiting (Herschel had spent months
methodically examining the sky sector by small sector for double stars),
sees something passed over by all watchers before; and to the conquistador who, on thinnest rumor, has slogged through nearly impassable
jungle and swamp in search of a will-o'-the-wisp. Keats asks us to give
name to their reactions.

The Isthmus of Panama was then known as the Isthmus of Darien.
At the moment of discovery, this Cortez—rapt, enraptured, what you
will—stares in wonder. He has entered avant la lettre that mise-en-scène
of the Romantic sublime, the sight from a precipice over a distant realm,
a view no European had seen. Wonder does not need words or does not
have them. Indeed, the sea needed only one word, since what startled
the first Europeans was not just the sea's unexpectedness, or its vastness,
but its apparent dead calm—hence the name with which Magellan christened it, the Pacific. That is an apt name for the pure serene.

The new planet glides in silence through another pure serene. Keats
forces us to imagine the astronomer's surprise, excitement, gratification;
but while Cortez, his fictional Cortez, gazes out upon the new ocean,
his men look wildly at one another, as if unsure what to say, or without
the need to say a thing. Perhaps they slowly realize what this discovery
must mean—gold. When Clarke remembered that night, he recalled
Keats's "teeming wonderment."[118] The acts of seeing with which the
poem began—the "many goodly states and kingdoms seen"—are united
with the discoveries of the eye in the new planet and in Cortez's over-
look of the Pacific. Chapman, in a nice turn, had to be heard to be seen—
the words on the page were not enough.

I am taken with Helen Vendler's notion that Keats's tropes represent
his "active search for the right simile," his "wrestling with experience";
but I'm not convinced that Cortez is therefore the more adequate
symbol, that Keats simply replaces the watcher of the skies, who is "too
passive, too isolated, too impotent."[119] She underestimates the long
nights, the impatient hours, the deep frustrations of the astronomer
(Keats knew the anxiety of anticipation)—the poet, like the astronomer,

works in solitude. Had Keats laid the tropes down in reverse order, the effect might have been equally striking. These are not images competing, one summarily dropped in favor of the other, but collaborative, offering discovery divided against itself: the night versus the day, the solitary versus the group, looking up into the overwhelming emptiness of the heavens versus looking out upon the vacancy of the sea (Keats's title is "On First Looking Into . . .").

Keats knew Homer's words spoken aloud, loudly, but he found his words describing silence—the silence, in a way, enjoyed on his long walk home, contemplating all he had heard. In another minute, Cortez's men may have begun to shout in excitement; but the poem closes, decrescendo, on the sublime moment of revelation, the silence yet unbroken.[120] The sonnet was the young poet's first major poem, written before Keats was Keats. (Leigh Hunt later remarked that it "completely announced the new poet taking possession"—it would be tempting to say, like a conquistador, or a man granted a fiefdom by Apollo.)[121] Despite its flaws, we read it tainted by foreknowledge of all the poems that followed.

There is a last irony, pointed out long ago by Keats's biographer Aileen Ward. The line that so entranced Keats, "The sea had soakt his heart through," is not Homer.[122] Indeed, the heavily layered description Keats adored was sometimes just George Chapman. Homer's grasshoppers were not "cold spinie"; his Neptune did not make the city of Aegae (Aegas, in Chapman) shake "with his drad entrie"; nor, in the description of the wreck of Odysseus, is there mention of a woman's birth pangs. Even the gate of ivory may lead to invention. Chapman could on occasion out-Homer Homer.

Donald Justice, "Henry James by the Pacific"

The American Scene, that itinerary of his brilliantly melancholy return to America, took Henry James through New York and New England, down into the cities of the Eastern Seaboard, and as far as Palm Beach. He left the journey where in a sense it left him:

> There was no doubt, under the influence of this last look, that Florida still had, in her ingenuous, not at all insidious way, the secret of pleasing, and that even round about me the vagueness was still an

appeal. The vagueness was warm, the vagueness was bright, the vagueness was sweet, being scented and flowered and fruited; above all, the vagueness was somehow consciously and confessedly weak. I made out in it something of the look of the charming shy face that desires to communicate and that yet has just too little expression.[123]

James in his fiction was the master of such characterization, captured almost in the act of becoming present and vivid to his own imagination, "vague" because the impressions from which character might be "built up" had not coalesced, or solidified, or congealed. (That the character is here the state of Florida suggests how far toward fiction James's journey had taken him.) The passage is a reminder that James's style itself depends on a beguiling, willful vagueness, one extraordinary in how much it reveals while seeming to wind candy floss around a paper core.

There, a sentence or two later, the book ended, at least in its American edition, published in 1907. The British edition pressed on for a few pages, where James ruminated, thoughtfully, lugubriously, over what he had discovered. He had seen an immense swath of country, or as much as the Pullman cars could show him through the "great square of plateglass."[124] However much the train's "great monotonous rumble" seemed to boast, "See what I'm making of all this—see what I'm making, what I'm making!" James could answer only, "I see what you are *not* making, oh, what you are ever so vividly not."[125] The America he saw was a solitude ravaged:

You touch the great lonely land—as one feels it still to be—only to plant upon it some ugliness about which, never dreaming of the grace of apology or contrition, you then proceed to brag with a cynicism all your own.[126]

Tocqueville was no more eloquent in his admiration or despair.

James's journey did not end with the book—after his return north, he pressed westward to Chicago, to Los Angeles and San Francisco and Seattle, then back east through St. Paul. *The American Scene* was meant merely as an introduction. Though it had been his intention to offer a sequel on his western visit, seeing the vast continent he had previously only imagined, events overtook him. The San Francisco earthquake in April 1906, less than a year after James sailed back to England, disturbed him so much that he ended his American reveries. As his nephew Harry later recalled, "He felt it as an event so stupendous and sensational that it must throw what he had to say into the shade."[127]

It was perhaps this sense of incompletion, this invocation of the artistic idea conceived, toyed with, and reluctantly abandoned, that drew Donald Justice to that western journey. James's impressions survive only in stray letters and a few pages in a notebook, but from their incomplete matter and their troubled grandeur Justice wrote a sonnet as sad and knowing as any in American literature.

HENRY JAMES BY THE PACIFIC

In a hotel room by the sea, the Master
Sits brooding on the continent he has crossed.
Not that he foresees immediate disaster,
Only a sort of freshness being lost—
Or should he go on calling it Innocence?
The sad-faced monsters of the plains are gone;
Wall Street controls the wilderness. There's an immense
Novel in all this waiting to be done,
But not, not—sadly enough—by him. His talents,
Such as they may be, want an older theme,
One rather more civilized than this, on balance.
For him now always the consoling dream
Is just the mild dear light of Lamb House falling
Beautifully down the pages of his calling.[128]

The sonnet was collected (as "Epilogue: Coronado Beach, California") with three brief preambles under the title "American Scenes (1904–1905)."[129] There the poet drew from James's journey for portraits, each just two quatrains, of Cambridge houses, a railroad junction south of Richmond, and an old cemetery in Charleston. That is how the poem appears in his *Collected Poems*, though Justice had originally published the sonnet separately[130] and later published it alone once more, under the title above.[131]

The poem begins almost whimsically, with a sidelong allusion to Poe, whose "kingdom by the sea" has been reduced to a modern hotel-room, the sort to which James resorted after those deprivations and inconveniences that were a tax on his patience through much of his travels. (He called the hotel a "synonym for civilization.")[132] The pathos-heavy verses of "Annabel Lee," its lovers parted by death, read now like a popular song composed for the fashionable morbidity of the 1840s (the poem was indeed adapted in that vein just before the Civil War).[133] The constriction and the absurdity of the hotel room—its rented comforts, its transient occupation—seem the wrong casement for that Jamesian brooding from which his rare, rarefied art so often hatched. In a hotel, he was no better than any other tourist. The poem's first provocation lies in the title—who would imagine James, that denizen of the parlor, that habitué of New York and London, having anything to do with the Pacific? He is out of his ken.

James, however, loved Southern California: "The days have been mostly here of heavenly beauty, and the flowers, the wild flowers just now in particular, . . . fairly *rage*, with radiance."[134] We would think ill of the novelist had he known nothing of nature; we should not think ill because he was no camper, no lover of the discomforts a hotel's comfort might make bearable. Here at the start, Justice has made a small protest against Thoreau, against the Romanticism that would never truck with hotels—the contemplations of art do not require for their setting the "Rocks, caves, lakes, fens, bogs, dens, and shades of death" of *Paradise Lost*.[135] The sublime may be purchased on hire, in other words, and at a remove.

That lost freshness is the freshness of the whole country, a century or more after the end of the Revolution. The American experiment always seemed tenuous, perhaps more so to those who had long lived abroad. (Who within a country has ever seen it plain?) There were disasters immediately ahead—the San Francisco quake, the Panic of 1907—but none worse than the disasters behind: the Civil War, the Panic of 1873, and the Year of the Locust the following year. Still, every freshness is ground down by history; and James's great theme is the loss of innocence, dramatized most brutally where the innocent meets a Europe wiser and more cunning and fatal. (The distinction is not subtle—freshness is lost gradually, minute by minute, but innocence is lost once for ever.) The reader cannot ignore that, for the aging novelist now in the shadows of his career, the freshness lost is personal as well. *The Age of Innocence*, by James's friend Edith Wharton, would not be published until after his death—but it was set in that Gilded Age James knew well.

Sailing to America after an absence of more than twenty years, the novelist sought signs of the life he had abandoned. (He would have titled his book *The Return of the Native*, he wrote in a letter, "if Thomas Hardy hadn't long ago made that impossible.")[136] Perhaps the saddest short story of his late career is "The Jolly Corner" (1908) in which an expatriate returns to New York after an even longer lingering abroad, returns repeatedly to his large old-fashioned house, now closed up, where he is haunted by a figure glimpsed briefly, flittingly, at the end of a vista of rooms or half concealed in the gloom, a figure with the face of a stranger and a mutilated hand. Only at the end of the tale does the exile realize that this compound ghost is the self he would have become, had he remained. The fiction possesses a rueful substrate for an author long dispossessed. James visited the family home in Boston, the house on Ashburton Place where he had lived during the late years of the Civil War, and was so moved that weeks later he came once more, only to find the building razed and the ground naked and bare, "as if the bottom had fallen out of one's own biography."[137]

No wonder James often found solace in his rented rooms. He wrote from a club in Chicago, just before the push west,

> I am already . . . rather spent and weary, weary of motion and chatter, and oh, of such an unimagined dreariness of *ugliness* (on many, on *most* sides!) and of the perpetual effort of trying to "do justice" to what one doesn't like. If one could only damn it and have done with it! . . . This Chicago is huge, *infinite* . . . ; black, smoky, *old*-looking. . . . Yet this club (which looks old and sober too!) is an abode of peace, a benediction to me in the looming largeness; I *live* here, and they put one up . . . with one's so excellent room with perfect bathroom and w.c., of its own.[138]

If even Paradise benefits from a Paradise to escape to, how much more important that Hell should. (The charming rumbling and rambling of

James's letters might remind us that his brother, William James, coined the phrase "stream of consciousness.")

It may not be surprising that James felt this loss of freshness just where freshness achieved so much amid so little, in that California spring where a man could dine like an Adam. ("I live on oranges and olives," James remarked in delight, "fresh from the tree.")[139] That is the Eden for which this Adam had perhaps unknowingly been searching, yet it casts further into darkness all that James has seen and disliked in the hideously altered cities along the way. Paradise may be regained, but never innocence.

The second quatrain of the sonnet suggests what might be made of those American losses—the exile is always seeking to turn into gold his portion of straw. In view of that alluring emptiness of the Pacific, James, the poet's James, contemplates the inner vacancy of the country he has crossed. Arriving in Los Angeles after a tiresome journey on the Southern Pacific, the real James reported that he had "reached this racketing spot . . . many hours late, & after an ordeal, of alkali deserts & sleep-defying 'sleepers' drawn out almost to madness."[140] From all that muddled, middling emptiness, something, perhaps.

The "sad-faced monsters" had been slaughtered nearly to extinction by hide and tongue hunters (pickled buffalo tongue was once a delicacy). Much of that Jamesian sense of a future foreclosed falls into the simple, discomfiting sentence, "Wall Street controls the wilderness." This was the end Frederick Jackson Turner had foreseen, or worse than the end.[141] The possibility of infinite American expansion, one that contemplated the eventual annexation of Mexico and Canada, with further annexations abroad, was no longer possible. The escape within, the movement ever west, had died with the closing of the frontier. Wall Street owned the wilderness because Congress had deeded it away. To build a railroad across that vast country known as the Great American Desert, transcontinental railroad companies had been given generous land grants along the track—land greater in area than the state of Texas. The very comforts James enjoyed in his posh Pullman were purchased from those destroying the wilderness, yet given what made James James he could have seen that landscape only by train.

The great novels of the Master (as his disciples called him, perhaps not always without teasing) were now behind him—*The Golden Bowl* (1904),

The Ambassadors (1903), *The Wings of the Dove* (1902), and more distantly *The Portrait of a Lady* (1881). Only recently behind, the greater of them, but behind nonetheless. Ahead lay the tedious gathering and finicky rewriting of the New York edition, with its tortured, artfully ambitious introductions; but his triumphs would now be rare, dominated by mishaps and failed projects. Apart from those introductions and half-a-dozen mostly mediocre stories, his finished work would be reduced to his refined memoirs of childhood and the end of youth. It was perhaps James's fear of what lay ahead at sixty-one that drew Justice at sixty to contemplate the artistic crisis every artist may eventually face.

There might have been a Jamesian novel of the West, a novel that encapsulated the American character—its industry, its careless ambition and go-ahead nature, its heedless desire for profit. It would have been unlike any novel the Master had written. He had often set the American character in the frame of Europe, where in mutual incomprehension the American sometimes lost more than innocence. ("Innocence," with its brute capital, is where the poem leaves the freshness offered by youth—the novelist aging as well as his country—and enters the realm of Adamic innocence and the loss of Paradise.) There seems no evidence in his letters or journals that James ever contemplated such a novel, but Justice uses the idea to broach the real subject, the artist's recognition of his own limits, and of his eventual extinction. Justice, who never wrote a poem of major length, and except once or twice never a love poem, filled his late work with gestures of valediction, often in poems of quiet refusal.

It is a terrible moment, when a man realizes that he no longer possesses a reflexive understanding of his own country. On his belated return to America, James found once familiar cities he hardly recognized, like Boston and New York (as well as a few, like Philadelphia, that came as a relief). "The Jolly Corner" suggests that to have stayed would have been an invitation to tragedy; but of course James could not know what novels he could have written, what triumphs he could have endured, had he not moved to England. That might have been a melancholy thought.

The terms in which Justice casts that knowledge are those of talent. The word, in its modern sense, derives from the parable in Matthew 25, where before a long journey a man divides his treasure among three servants—five to the first, two to the second, and a single one to the last, each according to his merits. On his return, when asked how they employed their "talents," the first two servants boast that they had doubled his money by using it for trade. (It would be profitable to know what sharp practice or Yankee cuteness the servants used.) The gold or silver talent, weighing sixty-five pounds, was no mean amount of money. The last and lowest servant confesses that, fearing his master's wrath, he had buried his only talent. The master has him cast "into outer darkness." The parable, of course, looks toward those gifts granted by God— what we now, following the parable, call talents. If we do not use God's gifts, the burden of the parable implies, we shall be cast out as well. It also implies that, however lavish or mean the gift, we are expected to use whatever we're given.

One of the stray amusements of Justice's sonnet is the poet's care with words—the rhyme between *talents* and *balance* that calls up the money-changer's balance, the alliteration tying *Wall Street* grotesquely to *wilderness*, the brute conjunction of *Master* and *disaster* (used to very different effect in Elizabeth Bishop's villanelle "One Art"). From the moneychanger's balance we have acquired our sense of an account in balance. When Milton wrote, "To serve therewith my Maker, and present / My true account" in the sonnet "When I consider how my light is spent,"[142] the word refers both to financial accounting and to the account rendered to God at the Day of Judgment—it may also be the tale the poet feels impelled to write. Such small pleasures, such small recognitions of pleasure, are those any good poet scatters by the way. Though they may be bound to meaning, they are not necessary to it; yet they come with such frequency in Justice's poem that a reader may be tempted to look deeper, to find perhaps in those vanished sad-faced monsters a reminder of the vastation James's father faced in midlife, a year after his son's birth—or of those devastations, those terrible epiphanies, James forced upon his major characters.

Perhaps, at the outer edge of affection and allusion, *Innocence* bears hidden ties to *immense*, partly because *Innocence* has been conditioned by the previous *lost* (what is greater than lost innocence?), which sits menacingly above it at line end, like the warning Dante saw over the gates of Hell. *Immense* is dramatically and seductively enjambed with *Novel*—the line might have continued, "There's an immense / Tragedy" or "Sadness" or "Relief." The play among these collusions is intricate, and not just because James was often drawn in his novels, immensely, to the theme of lost innocence. Though I resist critics who find meaning in the physical—often accidental—placement of words, had I written the poem I would not have been displeased by the accident. In his sonnet, Milton too uses the parable of the talents. The line "And that one talent which is death to hide" swings Janus-like between Matthew and our modern usage, which predates Milton by two centuries. Milton's crisis is his blindness—how can he continue to write afterward? If a man fails to use God's gift, will he be cast, in this case, from an inner darkness into an outer one? What lay before the poet was the epic of lost innocence, *Paradise Lost*, the work (really the long novel of a different day) that looms in the background of this closing of the frontier.

The minor pleasures extend to meter—Justice's pentameter is canny enough to absorb the juddering of the third line, where the poet has probably invoked the rare privilege of an initial anapest: "Not that HE foreSEES." (Otherwise the line would be trochaic pentameter—or even hexameter.) The tenth line is similarly difficult, and would require an odd emphasis ("SUCH as THEY MAY be"—trochee-spondee—when the phrasing seems to ask for "SUCH as THEY may BE"). That stress on "may" introduces a fine hesitation to James's thinking that, given his manner, might be perfect here. The anapests sown through the poem are otherwise naturally inserted, so never assertive; and, because of the sharp caesura, the reader might not notice that the seventh line could be scanned as an alexandrine.

The sonnet is a form with certain debts that must be recognized and paid. Justice was a poet who rarely worked in form without testing it a little—he trusted that a good artist could get away with things a bad one cannot. It is by such pressure on convention, by such slight fractures of the expected, that a reader is made sensitive to the artist's finesse—the finesse evident, for example, in the mimicry of the final line, where the initial trochee allows a fall brought up short, amusingly, by the word "down" (the fall begins with "falling" in the previous line). A reversed first foot is the most common variation in iambic pentameter; but it's unusual to find in meter the echoes of meaning, or at least ones the least interesting.

A man who knew nothing but civilization might have found a novel on the wilderness, or what wilderness yet remained, a bad idea. Twain perhaps reached a similar impasse when he came to write the sequel to *Huckleberry Finn*. On the Mississippi, he was in his medium—the world where he had grown up, the river he had traveled as a cub pilot during the great days of the steamboat. The sequel was titled *Huck Finn and Tom Sawyer Among the Indians*,[143] and after some fifty pages Twain abandoned it. It's one thing to imagine a Connecticut Yankee in King Arthur's court—such a novel can dine on secondhand medievalism—but the American wilderness was to Twain both too close and too far away. He was out of his element, and he knew it.

The sonnet ends with a dying fall, a couplet using feminine rhymes. *Falling/calling* echoes the feminine rhymes of *Master/disaster* and *talents/balance*, among the most galvanizing rhymes in the poem. The consoling dream for James can no longer be of the elsewhere, of America unseen or America abandoned—both are now lost to him; and he is driven back to Lamb House, his beloved home in Rye, where he had written the three extraordinary novels of the early century. The consoling dream may be a retreat, as the poet must have realized—in its first printing, the line read "recurring," which feels darker, more burdened, a spectral possession like that in "The Jolly Corner." Justice meant the dream to be comforting, no doubt, for a James so far from home. "Consoling" secures the warmer, less psychological reading.

The return to Lamb House feels like a defeat, however, a defeat only partially rescued by that falling light—falling handsomely, but still falling. "Fall" is a charged word after so much talk of innocence. Adam and Eve were ejected from their kingdom—but in a sense James has withdrawn to his own paradise, there to live out his days like Prospero in retirement. The word that ends the poem, however, is "calling." Milton quarreled with himself about how to use those God-given talents; he found his answer, not in Matthew 25, but in the parable of the vineyard in Matthew 20:1–16, where men hired in the morning complain when those hired later in the day are paid the same amount. "God doth not need / Either man's work or His own gifts," Milton is informed by Patience. Though not one of the seven cardinal or theological virtues, Patience was mentioned as the "fruit of the Spirit" by Paul in Galatians 5:22, along with love, joy, peace, and other virtues. It was translated in the King James Version as "longsuffering," hence Milton's "They also serve who only stand and wait." (James knew patience as a devil—he remarks in his brief notes on California, "I can only invoke my familiar demon of patience, who always comes, doesn't he?, when I call.")[144] Milton must wait, in other words, for the call. We still use that word, in the sense of artistic calling, though we know it better by its Latin equivalent, vocation.

At the end of the poem, James is called back to his calling, to those words he puts down so masterfully—and the reader should not ignore the quiet, almost religious gesture, neither to be mocked nor really to be believed, of the English light falling onto the page (an illuminated manuscript!) like the light of the Annunciation. In this ending, the artist has been summoned to his gifts once more, called by whatever figure we wish to name (God, the Muse, one's private demon of artistic necessity). It is perhaps a sly touch that those late novels had been composed by what might also be called a calling—beginning in 1897, at least at Lamb House, a secretary typed out James's sentences as he dictated them.

A reader of more religious temperament might discover in the name Lamb House a hint of passivity and sacrifice. Indeed, James could be seen, if not a lamb led to ritual slaughter, then as the passive recipient of those gifts—but the retreat to Rye does suggest that no longer will James take on a major challenge in the novel. (Indeed, apart from an adaptation he never finished another.) He will merely write bad plays, thumbing through his life in his autobiographies, and his art in the New York edition, waiting for the end. The name of the house makes an accidental but severe contrast to those monsters of the plains, shot down in their thousands and tens of thousands for that most American of religions, commerce. (All for pickled buffalo tongues, winter coats, and lap robes.) Though that calling back was in some ways a failure for James, it was not for Justice, whose late poems were among his most gorgeous and most darkly revealing.

Justice drew heavily from *The American Scene* and the attendant notebook for the sets of paired quatrains that preceded the sonnet in "American Scenes (1904–1905)." In "Cambridge in Winter," for example:

Immense **pale houses**! **Sunshine** just now and **snow**
Light up and pauperize the whole brave show—

Each fanlight, each veranda, each good address,
All a **mere paint and pasteboard paltriness**!

These **winter sunsets are the one fine thing**:
Blood on the snow, some last impassioned fling,
The wild frankness and **sadness of surrender**—
As if our cities ever could be tender![145]

The original lines in the notebook read:

The **snow**, the **sunshine, light up and pauperize** all the wooden
surfaces, all the **mere paint and pasteboard paltriness. The one
fine thing are** the **winter sunsets**, the **blood on the snow**, the pink
crystal of the west, **the wild frankness**, wild **sadness** (?)—so to
speak—**of** the **surrender**.[146]

You must cast an eye upward from these lines for the phrases con-
densed and formed into the initial exclamation: "the **immense** rise in
the type and scope and scale of the American **house**, as it more and
more multiplies." The poet has adjusted the syntax, tightened the prose
here and particularized it there (to pointed effect in the third line), and
allowed the rhymes suggested in James to drive to the surface some of
the themes he chose to leave buried. The scene of the houses is so
resplendent that the reader who fails to give due weight to "pauperize"
and "paltriness" may not realize how much James detested new American architecture.

Justice had less material for the California scene—or, more likely, he
conceived of the sonnet differently, as a portrait of James, not an invocation of the Master's observations of the here or there. The only debt the
sonnet owes to *The American Scene* lies in the penultimate line—James
had remarked in his notebook, "These things are all packed away, . . .
till I shall let in upon them the mild still light of dear old L[amb]
H[ouse]."[147] There were probably other Jamesian sources—note a passage from early in his unfinished *The Middle Years* (1917):

Youth is an army, the whole battalion of our faculties and our fresh-
nesses, our passions and our illusions, on a considerably reluctant

march into the enemy's country, the country of the general lost freshness.[148]

Here the pressure and attention of the sonnet is felt in fine.

The sonnet may have an even more obscure source, however—"On First Looking Into Chapman's Homer." The poems each concern discovery of a land often rumored but never visited. Lack of ancient Greek kept Keats beyond the borders of Homer's domain, as no doubt sheer discomfort had for James when thinking of California—the transcontinental railroad was not completed until he was in his mid-twenties, and it offered only miserable comfort for years thereafter. Balboa (to correct Keats's error) reached the shores of the Pacific after a slog through sixty miles of jungle and swamp, a journey of some twenty-five days.[149] James could have traveled from Chicago to Los Angeles—two thousand miles or better—in less than three, though delays made him late.[150] Swaddled in the absurd comforts of a Pullman car, he would have been provided with a chef and a stock of good wines. (He mentions in a letter from Chicago that he believes the train equipped with "barber's shops, bathrooms, stenographers and typists.")[151] Recall that according to William Robertson in *The History of America* (1777), when Balboa reached the Pacific with his cohort of men,

> as he beheld the South Sea stretching in endless prospect below him, he fell on his knees, and, lifting up his hands to Heaven, returned thanks to God. . . . His followers . . . rushed forward to join in his wonder, exultation and gratitude.[152]

This was the version Keats knew—he too wrote from books. Balboa stood alone, looking out at his discovery, knowing that history had changed. Beyond the horizon lay other lands to conquer and the great trading entrepôts of Asia. He had found the realms of gold.

Keats too was changed. Having been introduced one night to Chapman's translation of Homer, he wrote his sonnet rapidly and fluently the next morning—it was the first poem of genius he produced. Having come the immense distance, James—the James that Justice partially invents—takes stock of himself, looking back over the country so rapidly compassed. It is a retrospective of a life unlived—he sees the great themes a novelist might gather in force, the life of the country to which he had been born. He knows he must abandon them, as he had abandoned the country itself twenty-odd years before. For James, that country, his own country, must remain unwritten. He would turn homeward, having found at the far reaches of the New World, not possibilities opened, but possibilities finally and forever closed.

Each poet has used a great literary figure as the medium of self-discovery—these are poems in part about the rewards of reading. Keats casts his discovery in terms of conquest. Having written the sonnet, he embarked upon his brief, radiant career. For Justice, his career nearing its end, the question is whether age makes the artist impotent. If the later sonnet is a peculiar inversion of "Chapman's Homer" (James's observation on youth's "reluctant march into the enemy's country" provides the military link), each is also a performative act whose writing resolves an artistic crisis. Keats felt denied the greatest poet of the Western world by his ignorance of ancient Greek. Chapman's translation opened the borders, and the poet responded by showing what his gifts could accomplish. Justice considered whether the aging artist could continue to write, whether age emasculates the artist—the beauty of the sonnet proves the anxiety premature. In "When I consider," Milton also found the answer to a question—whether, though blind, he could still exercise his magnificent gifts.

Henry James stayed at the Hotel del Coronado when he visited San Diego—the conquistadors who possessed Keats left their mark on James as well. (George Sand, he once wrote, "found her gift of improvisation . . . by leaping—a surprised *conquistador* of 'style'—straight upon the coral strand.")[153] The hotel, built in 1888, still stands, grand or grandiose as ever. I once asked Donald Justice whether he had recognized the odd, subterranean links between "Chapman's Homer" and "Henry James by the Pacific." He seemed surprised, then gratified. After thinking for a moment, he said, "Not at all."

6. Shakespeare's Rotten Weeds, Shakespeare's Deep Trenches

WILLIAM SHAKESPEARE, SONNET 2

When fortie Winters shall beseige thy brow,
And digge deep trenches in thy beauties field,
Thy youthes proud liuery so gaz'd on now,
Wil be a totter'd weed of smal worth held:
Then being askt, where all thy beautie lies,
Where all the treasure of thy lusty daies;
To say within thine owne deepe sunken eyes,
Were an all-eating shame, and thriftlesse praise.
How much more praise deseru'd thy beauties vse,
If thou couldst answere this faire child of mine
Shall sum my count, and make my old excuse
Proouing his beautie by succession thine.
    This were to be new made when thou art ould,
    And see thy blood warme when thou feel'st it could.[1]

About the early history of the sonnets, we know almost nothing. The first reference comes in 1598, when Shakespeare already had a reputation on the stage—the plays behind him included *A Midsummer Night's Dream, Romeo and Juliet, Richard II, Richard III,* and *The Merchant of Venice.* That year Francis Meres praised him in *Palladis Tamia* as the "most excellent" English playwright, like Plautus and Seneca the master of comedy and tragedy.[2] Shakespeare had first come to attention as the author of a popular pillow-book, *Venus and Adonis* (1593), in whose dedication he looked forward to "some graver labour," probably *The Rape of Lucrece* (1594).[3] Meres remarked that the "sweete wittie soule of *Ovid*

> VVHen fortie Winters fhall befeige thy brow,
>   And digge deep trenches in thy beauties field,
> Thy youthes proud liuery fo gaz'd on now,
> Wil be a totter'd weed of fmal worth held:
> Then being askt,where all thy beautie lies,
> Where all the treafure of thy lufty daies;
> To fay within thine owne deepe funken eyes,
> Were an all-eating fhame,and thriftleffe praife.
> How much more praife deferu'd thy beauties vfe,
> If thou couldft anfwere this faire child of mine
> Shall fum my count,and make my old excufe
> Proouing his beautie by fucceffion thine.
>   B·   Thi⌐

> This were to be new made when thou art ould,
> And fee thy blood warme when thou feel'ft it could,

William Shakespeare, Sonnet 2 (1609 Quarto).
Source: STC 22353, *Shake-speares sonnets: Neuer before imprinted.* Leaf B1,
recto and verso. By permission of the Folger Shakespeare Library.

lives in mellifluous & hony-tongued *Shakespeare*, witnes his *Venus* and *Adonis*, his *Lucrece*, his sugred Sonnets among his private friends, &c."[4] (There's an unwritten history in that "&c.") The sugared sonnets were eventually published in quarto as *Shake-speares Sonnets* (1609).[5]

Who those private friends were and what they possessed has been subject of speculation ever since. If not an outright liar, Meres was close enough to that circle to have heard of these private verses. Perhaps he had seen a few—"sugared" sounds like firsthand acquaintance, not gossip. In the surviving manuscripts over the next century, there are almost 250 copies of Sidney's poems, nearly 800 of Jonson's, and over 4,000 of Donne's.[6] Of Shakespeare's sonnets there are only twenty-six, almost all dating to the 1630s or later, none probably earlier than 1620.[7] Either Shakespeare's private circle was very small, or its members guarded the sonnets closely.

We can't appreciate what it would have been like to receive one, written in secretary hand perhaps on an octavo leaf, folded and sealed, delivered by messenger or slipped from a pocket ("I think I haue his Letter in my pocket," *All's Well That Ends Well*).[8] The poems were probably untitled and for the most part unpunctuated, like Shakespeare's contribution to *The Book of Sir Thomas More*.[9] Seeing the manuscript sonnets scattered through miscellanies is probably as close as we can come.

In 1599, possibly late the year before, two sonnets appeared in *The Passionate Pilgrime. By W. Shakespeare*.[10] Of the score of poems included in this slight octavo volume, probably only five were his—three from the 1598 quarto of *Love's Labour's Lost* and two of the Dark Lady sonnets, 138 and 144.[11] (The attribution and sham piecing-out suggest public interest.) Differences between these and the versions published in the Quarto (Q) imply that Shakespeare later revised the poems. Revision and rearrangement of sonnet sequences—for instance, by Samuel Daniel and Michael Drayton—were not unusual.[12] Though a good number of Shakespeare's surviving manuscript sonnets derive from printed versions, those for sonnet 2 contain marked variants.[13] Of the thirteen manuscripts, twelve appear closely related.[14]

Heminge and Condell, in their preface to Shakespeare's First Folio, claimed that "wee have scarse received from him a blot in his papers."[15] Ben Jonson replied in *Timber: or, Discoveries* (1640), "Would he had blotted a thousand."[16] In his prefatory poem to the Folio, as John Kerrigan has observed,[17] Jonson offered a more reasonable judgment about his "gentle Shakespeare": "he, / Who casts to write a living line, must sweat / . . . and strike the second heat."[18] That would mean revision. (Jonson also wrote that Shakespeare outshone the tragic and comic playwrights of ancient Greece and Rome—the remarks are lavish, even for elegy.) We know from various passages in the plays that Shakespeare must have revised his work; and his additions to *Sir Thomas More*, however fluent, have blots enough.[19] Such changes give us a glimpse of Shakespeare in the workshop. Do the dozen manuscripts preserve sonnet 2 in an early form? Since Gary Taylor's closely argued article "Some Manuscripts of Shakespeare's Sonnets," published in 1985,[20] reactions among editors of the sonnets have been mixed: Duncan-Jones against; Kerrigan and G. Blakemore Evans in favor; Burrow, though skeptical, not prepared to dismiss the idea.[21]

It's impossible to tell beyond doubt whether the manuscripts preserve the rewriting of cloth-eared copyists, the improvements of some smart aleck, or an older version of lines Shakespeare later revisited. The conservative meter and echoes from plays of the 1590s tell us the sonnets were started early in his career; but, however sophisticated modern stylometric analysis, which suggests that many were written or revised in the following decade, how much he touched them up, if at all, is a question almost beyond answer. Sonnet 2 may be the rare case where something hidden is revealed. I have nothing to add to the historical arguments; but I wish to compare the two versions poetically, judging the gains and losses.

> When forty winters shall beseige thy brow
> And **trench** deepe **furrowes** in y^t **louely** feild
> Thy youthes **faire** Liu'rie so **accounted** now
> **Shall** bee **like rotten weeds** of **no** worth held
>   Then beeing askt where all thy bewty lyes
> Where all y^e **lustre** of thy **youthfull** dayes
> To say within **these hollow** suncken eyes
> Were an all-**eaten truth**, & **worthless** prayse
>   **O** how much **better were** thy bewtyes vse
> If thou coudst **say** this **pretty** child of mine
> **Saues** my **account** & makes my old excuse
> **Making** his bewty by succession thine
>   This were to bee new **borne** when thou art old
>   And see thy bloud warme when thou feelst it cold.[22]
>
> (Westminster Abbey, MS.41, f. 49)

I have used Taylor's transcription of what is apparently the best copy,[23] dropping only his title, "Spes Altera," which he borrowed from a different group of manuscripts.[24] (The Westminster manuscript was given the title "To one y^t would dye a Mayd.") He has made an interesting but not convincing case that the title is Shakespearean: the phrase, from the *Aeneid*, means "another hope," or, if you will, "another chance," appropriate for the subject here. The differences in the manuscript text (hereafter, W) have been highlighted in bold.

The argument of sonnet 2 in Q goes something like this: "At forty your fair skin will be wrinkled, your once-fine clothes ragged. If someone

Manuscript version of William Shakespeare, Sonnet 2.
Source: Ms. 41, f.49, courtesy of the Library, Westminster Abbey.
Copyright: Dean and Chapter of Westminster.

asks where all that beauty has gone, you'll answer that there's a little left in your eyes—but you'll feel ashamed. Use your beauty, have a boy, be able to say he's inherited your good looks. Then you'll feel young again."

STANZA I

The sonnet opens with a long prospect of the future, the destruction of beauty over forty winters, a phrase more dirgelike and elegiac than a hopeful "forty springs." Duncan-Jones objects that the manuscript's "trench deep furrows" (instead of "dig deep trenches") "substitutes a clod-hopping metaphor of ploughing furrows in a field" for an image of siege war and "introduces associations with seed-sowing and eventual harvest which are wholly inappropriate."[25] Perhaps it's not so simple. Though furrows derive from the art of farming, not the art of war, "trench" is a violent verb: in its earliest uses, "to cut; to divide by cutting, slice, cut in pieces; . . . to cut one's way," as the *OED* has it. You can see it doing military service for Caxton in 1485—"[He] gaf hym a stroke vpon his helme so sharply that he trenched moo than vc maylles," that is, more than ninety-five rings of mail (*OED*).

Trenching, in its oldest meaning, required sword or blade. Shakespeare used a boar's tusk for the task ("The wide wound, that the Boare had trencht / In his soft flanke," *Venus and Adonis*)[26] but employed it of love in *The Two Gentlemen of Verona*: "This weake impresse of Loue, is as a figure / Trenched in ice" (a drawing scratched or cut into ice, presumably not figure skating).[27] Despite its domestication early in the sixteenth century for digging up ground, the verb remained slightly brutish: "The place . . . so broken dygged or trenched" (*OED*, 1541). "Trench" was a military noun from the first, but never just that—its uses for war lie uneasily against uses in peace. The swords were also plowshares.

By Shakespeare's day, "trenches" could be merely a synonym for "furrows" ("Thy garden plot lately, wel trenched & muckt" [*OED*, 1573]), so "digge deep trenches" was little more than "trench deepe furrowes"— little more, except that Q conjures up age's long siege against the face, while the manuscript looks across beauty's furrowed fields ("Witnes these trenches made by greefe and care" can be found in *Titus Andronicus*).[28] We still speak of someone "furrowing" his brow. If the line alluded to old ridge-and-furrow plowing, furrows would have been much deeper than on modern farms. Shakespeare saw that loss of beauty wasn't just farm husbandry; it was a war only age could win.

Why alter one phrase for the other? By the middle of the fifteenth century, a trench was a "long, narrow ditch dug by troops to provide a place of shelter from enemy fire and observation." Trenches would have caused more damage to beauty, retaining associations with wounding or scarring. The trenches in Q reinforce the metaphor of war, but "besiege" doesn't have to overwhelm the poem with violence—it was already modulating toward more ironic or comic uses: in *Foole vpon Foole* (1600), by

Robert Armin (Shakespeare's fool after Will Kempe), a man "snatcht the Hawke, and hauing wrong off her necke begins to besiedge that good morsell."[29]

War's trenches savagely mimic plowed fields. Still, the manuscript version cruelly undermines the very purpose of farming—sowing and harvest. The furrows are prepared year by year but never seeded. The implications of "seed" (child, semen), a word implied though never invoked, go back centuries earlier. Duncan-Jones prefers a field scarred by military trenches;[30] the first thoughts of the manuscript have the field cut by furrows that never bear a crop, insulting in its mockery of husbandry (a buried pun is not impossible—note the appearance of "husbandry" in sonnets 3 and 13). The deeper sense is that the furrows of age are destructive only if we do not seed a new generation, our ruined brows reborn as their smooth, unmarked ones.

It's tempting to dismiss the manuscript's "louely feild" as unimaginative, though for Shakespeare "louely" wasn't a watered-down synonym for "beautiful" or "attractive" but a word that could rise to something more robust: "Lovable; deserving of love or admiration" (*OED*). If the Quarto version is an improvement, the advantage lies partly in the shift to "thy beauties field," the Fair Youth becoming landowner of beauty, a characterization more dramatic than just calling the brow lovely. The manuscript, however, cannot easily be dismissed as incompetent rewriting. Those trenched furrows are a visual effect. Beauty's face, beauty's field—yet "field" in heraldry is the surface or background of a shield. Here it might seem part of a coat of arms, something else inherited—an inheritance that for a noble youth would have, like beauty, duties and responsibilities.

To a modern ear, "faire Liu'rie" seems pallid compared to Q's "proud liuery"; but our ears need a slight adjustment to hear what the Elizabethans heard. Modern usage has been denatured. In Old English, "fair" meant beautiful or pleasing to the eye, a sense retained in phrases like "fair weather." Meanings exclusive to women ("fair sex," for instance) come only in the fifteenth century. The sense of beautiful language or speech ("polished, elegant; eloquent") is very early, again Old English, and gave rise to the distinction between fair copy and foul papers. The main modern definition, "free from bias, fraud, or injustice" or "honest, just; reasonable," was applied to conduct in the late fourteenth century and to people only in Shakespeare's day; but we're mistaken to let uses dominant now overwhelm the earlier meanings embedded in "fair livery." "From fairest creatures we desire increase," Shakespeare wrote in sonnet 1, and it might not have been accidental that "fair" was still in mind. That the sonnets in Q were arranged in the order composed is unlikely, but poems intimately tied may have been written about the same time.

Kerrigan has privately made the point that, if we accept the manuscript as an earlier version, the revisions would have been conditioned by sonnets written later.[31] However the Quarto came to be, it's not likely to have begun as a sequence—the order, apart from the marriage sonnets (1–17), is too haphazard. (It's little wonder that so many critics have wasted time trying to reorder the sonnets or defend their received order.) Any revisions would have been affected by the unfolding relation between the two men and by whatever occurred between them in the years between inspiration and revision.

To take one instance, the shift from "faire Liu'rie" to "proud liuery," stronger poetically, seems even stronger if we read the change in light of the difficulties between the men that enter into what seem later sonnets. Had there been some estrangement, the revisions might have mirrored this alienation of affection by slight alienations of language. The tone does seem to cool between W and Q, and it should be remembered that by 1609 whatever passions had once existed had perhaps long been exhausted.

The phrase "faire Liu'rie," then, is not mere filler, not merely equivalent to "nice clothes," though it doesn't have the reach and implication of Q's "proud liuery." There the transferred epithet creates a tiny vignette of a youth proud of his clothes (or the clothes are the source of pride— "Of publike [public] honour and proud titles bost [boast]," sonnet 25.) No one is threatening to disinherit the boy, but his failure to continue the bloodline is itself a disinheritance. The appeal is to his vanity—when his beauty is as ruined as his old clothes, he'll have nothing to show for it if he doesn't have a child. The livery stands metaphorically for the young man's outer figure. (Though "livery" at this period had the specific sense of the "characteristic uniform or insignia worn by a household's retainers or servants" or the "distinctive dress worn by the liverymen of a Guild or City of London livery company" [OED], the more general sense was a "characteristic garb or covering; a distinctive guise, marking, or outward appearance.") What is beauty but skin deep? "Proud" at base suggests the clothes are "stately, magnificent, imposing, or splendid"— and perhaps, as poetically used of animals, "spirited, fearlessly vigorous; moving with force and dignity." (Hence, a pride of lions, originally a medieval term.) Clothes are a person's skin or hide.

The dense layering of ideas is not entirely absent from "faire Liu'rie," especially when drawn near "accounted." A man's clothing was listed in any inventory, especially one made after death. ("Account" meant "audit" from the early sixteenth century—note "What acceptable audit canst thou leave?" [sonnet 4].) You might say, if the revision was Shakespeare's, that in the draft he courted the eye in "faire," in revision shifting the gaze to "gaz'd on." "Thy youthes faire Liu'rie so accounted now" would imply, not just reckoned ("told," in the bank teller's sense), but explained or justified—"so accounted now" might mean clothes often remarked on, judged beautiful, subject of tales told by telltales; but it looks toward the reckoning that age shall make. Through the metaphor of keeping books, "so accounted now" prepares "of no worth held"—its reversal in the following line—while in Q "so gaz'd on now" and "of smal worth held" have smaller claim on each other. When he softened the accounting, Shakespeare was almost required to give more weight to the livery.

A "totter'd" reed (Q) is tattered or tottering. Weeds were of course clothing, a usage that survives only in "widow's weeds" (survivals are often found in case-hardened phrases). The use of "rotten" (W) began in decomposition of man or beast—beneath the idea of rotten clothing lies rotten flesh ("The sweete War-man is dead and rotten," *Love's Labour's Lost*).[32] The poet associated the ideas often enough, using "dead and rotten" three times, "rotten death" once. Death is always at the edges of the sonnet but never grasped. The "hollow suncken" eyes, the truth "all-eaten"—these are marks of corpses as well as old age.

The idea of rotten haberdashery was not new (silk is particularly prone to dry rot). A sermon of 1388, possibly by Wycliffe, argues that "mo clothes be rotten with the rych then with the poore."[33] The idea reeks of decay (Shakespeare used it comically in *As You Like It*: "You'l be rotten ere you bee halfe ripe").[34] A weed whether tottered or tattered, rather than rotten, might seem merely to trade like for like—but perhaps in revision Shakespeare was determined not to let death overplay its role. "Fortie Winters" keeps the luxury of hope—if the youth died young, his only memorial would be his child. John Dover Wilson in his edition of the sonnets noted that mourners wept at the funeral of Sir Philip Sidney because he had not produced a son.[35]

Shakespeare exploited here the ambiguity of "weed." Some flowers in gardens are weeds in the wild; or, put another way, a weed is only an unappreciated flower. Q's "totter'd" is usually corrected to "tattered." Tattered clothing is familiar, but to allow the alternate spelling brings the senses into tension. (Just because the clothes have become ragged doesn't mean the youth is still wearing them.) Kerrigan has the mixed richness right: the submerged sense of unwanted plant is "drawn out by *beauty's field* (with its echo of *beauty's rose* in Sonnet 1, as though that flower became, after *forty winters*, an aged and torn hedgerow pest)." The original spelling "implies not just ragged disorder but the slumped unsteadiness of a plant past its prime."[36] That would be a flower perhaps rotting on the stalk. There is also, from the original sense of "totter" as swinging to and fro, a specific use in the sixteenth and early seventeenth centuries—to be hanged on the gallows. The spectral idea drifts back toward the underlying presence of death. We have here, not Shakespeare correcting, but Shakespeare rethinking. It's hard to imagine a writer of such coiled and instantaneous invention not looking over old lines and finding new weights and measures. The early version is coarser and dramatic, the later subtler; but it has lost little and gained more in translation.

STANZA 2

The second quatrain is a mean bit of wit. The youth, grown old, when asked where his beauty lies, because he's childless could say only, "In my deep sunken eyes" (Q). Kerrigan is probably right that "all the treasure of thy lusty days" quietly invokes the parable in Matthew 25, where a lord who must travel "into a far country" entrusts his wealth to his three servants, wealth in the form of talents.[37] (A talent could be gold or silver. The royal Babylonian talent, according to the *OED*, weighed about sixty-five pounds.) The senior servants both invest the money and double it; but the lowliest, given a single talent, buries it in the earth to keep it safe. He is cast "into outer darkness" on the lord's return. The Fair Youth, if he has no children, will eventually bury his beauty in the grave. (Compare sonnet 6, "thou art much too faire, / To be deaths conquest and make wormes thine heire.") The "deepe sunken eyes" also seem buried—in the face.

"Thy beauties vse" must cast the pearls of beauty before the next generation (some early notion of genetics did not escape the Elizabethans). The very idea of "treasure" is something stored up—hence, "treasure hunting," "treasure trove." Duncan-Jones sees "treasure" and thinks "semen,"[38] but her ear is too keenly tuned to sexual innuendo. She has probably gotten the idea from Eric Partridge's *Shakespeare's Bawdy*, but Partridge is catch as catch can. His sole example, from *Othello* (Emilia speaks: "It is their Husbands faults, / If Wiues do fall: [Say, that they . . . powre (pour) our Treasures into forraigne laps]"), is not wholly persuasive.[39] "Lap" could on rare occasion mean "embrace" (the use is most often verbal) as well as "pudendum" (*OED*). Emilia could be talking about jewelry. The suggestiveness (not just of "treasure," but of "use") is hard to pin down, as in sonnet 20: "But since she [Nature] prickt thee out for womens pleasure, / Mine be thy loue and thy loues vse their treasure." Say that Shakespeare's filigree of teasing play is the delight of frustration, or that the evasion of impropriety is the acknowledgment of impropriety.

The manuscript variant, "all yᵉ lustre of thy youthfull dayes," seems to have influenced Shakespeare's choice of Q's "lusty," containing much the revision does not—"lustre," as the *OED* has it, means "shining by reflected light; sheen, refulgence; gloss." Early uses are associated with the radiance of gems (which might have suggested "treasure" in revision), thence eyes—in the plays, the word compliments lips or eyes. Taylor notes that, when Gloucester is blinded in *Lear*, Cornwall asks, "Where is thy luster now?"[40] Perhaps the use in the manuscript suggests that the quality could refer to young skin, moist with newness, while the aged are lucky still to have luster in the faint glisten of their eyes.

The example is typical of Shakespeare's impaction, meanings not collaborating so much as crushed together, laid down leaf by leaf like coal. Again, the earlier version of the line seems more vivid. "Treasure" is vaguer, though tied to deeper meanings in the new-made sonnet—the use of one's inheritance, beauty now bound more firmly to things (talents, say) that must be accounted for, not just in the sense of tales told but of sums brought to judgment. One generation's treasure must be tallied before it can be inherited by the next—and one way of accounting is to admit such things exist to be passed on. Beauty would be a kind of treasure.

In this fantasy of interrogation, the manuscript allows the youth to speak directly twice, the Quarto only once, the first exchange reported as indirect discourse. The shift is not large, the loss of immediacy considerable compared to the manuscript, where the exchange has been jotted down like testimony in a legal deposition. The force of argument here is telling—the friend has turned inquisitor, or dramatized the inquisition the youth must one day undergo. Linked to the speech in the next stanza, this exchange is like a fragment of a play, with commentary, the sort directors sometimes give actors who want motivation.

Probably the words in manuscript should be read, not as a compound, "hollow[-]suncken," but as coordinate adjectives, "hollow[,] sunken eyes," though here Shakespeare's usual underpointing (if it is his) allows the readings to strain at each other. "Sunken" suggests depth, the way the eyes of the elderly seem to recede into the skull; but "hollow" draws in emptiness, blankness—perhaps not actual blindness, since that would be too ruefully comic. (The idea that eyes grow hollow with age was a commonplace.) It's no doubt accidental that "hollow" follows "lustre" so neatly; but, had Shakespeare known the word's old meaning as "cave," "hollow" might have suggested itself, at least subconsciously. "Hollow" is resonant and terrifying, with death at the edges, "deepe" merely descriptive—the revision has lost some of the bitter edge of the manuscript.

It's possible that "sunken" suggested "treasure" in Q, a reference to well-known tales of sunken galleons. Shakespeare wrote in *Henry V*, "As rich . . . / As is the Owze [ooze] and bottome of the Sea / With sunken Wrack, and sum-less Treasuries"[41] (the first quarto has "shiplesse treasurie"), and, in *The Rape of Lucrece*, "Who feares sinking where such treasure lies?",[42] so he had the association in mind, as least by the time he revised the sonnet. Perhaps he was guilty of a little self-plagiarism. The phrase "sunken treasure" may be owed to such quotations.

An "all-eaten truth" (W) is presumably a truth devoured, eaten up like wool by moth larvae, truth once beautiful, now just a rag (perhaps carrying forward the metaphor of rotten clothes)—that, or merely a truth all must eat eventually, however galling. The line renews the "glutton" image in sonnet 1. Everyone loses his beauty, and for the youth in age to say there's still a bit of the old luster in his eyes is "worthless" (the undercurrent of money and accounts surfaces again)—that is, unprofitable, of no value. The shift from manuscript to Q—let me continue to call these changes revisions, for ease—is often subtle even when radical. Truth is judged by manners or mores outside oneself ("Time devours all," as Duncan-Jones reminds us),[43] but shame something felt within. Instead of suggesting that the Fair Youth will come to know a truth all must know, a truth worse for wear, Q holds out the unlovely portrait of the youth in age, ashamed at not having taken advantage of early gifts. As manipulative psychology it's masterful, if we take the sonnet as having real motive.

Q's "All-eating" may seem difficult to parse, but Colin Burrow suggests it merely a synonym for "all-consuming," a phrase that comes into English about the time of the sonnets. (The implication, he proposes, is "universally destructive.") "All-eating shame" is no doubt the cousin of our contemporary idiom, in a guilt culture, "eaten up with guilt." Shakespeare wrote a similar idea into *Othello*: "I see sir, you are eaten vp with passion."[44]

"Worthless prayse" (W) is clear enough—Shakespeare had already used the phrase in *Titus Andronicus*.[45] Those who think the manuscript not an early version are forced to believe that some reader of the sonnets who possessed a nearly eidetic memory for the plays (probably read rather than heard) decided to improve sonnet 2 by translating "thriftlesse praise" into something more comprehensible. ("Worthless" appears in sonnets 80 and 100.) The manuscript line is not deaf, however, to other uses of "worthless"—"destitute of moral character, contemptible" (when used of people) and "unworthy." These trouble the simple meaning, especially when linked so firmly to the metaphorical strain of money, gemlike things, accounts. It's not a great distance from calling someone "of non acompte" (as John Gower had)[46] to calling praise worthless, when the person bestowing it on himself is bankrupt of sensibility. Perhaps

Shakespeare didn't calculate what happens when you bring the subject of sex close to that of payment—or perhaps he did.

Q's "Thriftlesse praise" would be praise, as the *OED* makes it, "not thriving or prosperous; unsuccessful; unfortunate"; maybe better, "unprofitable, worthless, useless" (there are "thriftlesse sighes" in *Twelfth Night*)[47] or "wasteful, improvident, spendthrift." Already in *Richard II* Shakespeare had compounded ideas of shame and money related to fathers and sons ("He shall spend mine honour, with his shame, / As thriftles sonnes, their scraping Fathers gold").[48] The unworthy son in the play becomes the unworthy son in the sonnet, since failure to pass on your own beauty is a slap against your parents. The various forms of "thriftless" may seem subtler as it drifts through these opening sonnets— "vnthrifty louelinesse [loveliness]" (sonnet 4), "an vnthrift" (9), "none but vnthrifts" (13). They secure the sense of selfish prodigality.

"Shame" in Q shifts the line from a sad acknowledgment of truth to disgrace. This sort of deepening is typical of Shakespeare's second thoughts. As in the parable of the talents, the Fair Youth conceals that vanishing beauty in his own aging flesh, eventually to be buried in wrinkles—beauty's furrowed fields ("wrinkles" are picked up again in sonnet 3)—rather than let the bounty renew itself and blossom once more. "To sow wild oats," already a well-known phrase in the 1570s ("That wilfull and vnruly age, which . . . [as wee saye] hath not sowed all theyr wyeld Oates," *OED*), seems early to have suggested sexual profligacy. The *OED* citations come from Thomas Watson's *Passionate Centurie of Loue* (1582) and Middleton's and Dekker's play *The Honest Whore* (1604). The idea would be cold comfort to anyone wanting the Fair Youth to marry, but it testifies to the nearness of bearing crops and bearing children. Wild oats are anyone's crop—only marriage lets you claim the harvest. The Earl of Pembroke, one of the main candidates for the Fair Youth, knew this when he refused to marry the pregnant Mary Fitton, one of Queen Elizabeth's maids of honor.

STANZA 3

On his return from the far country, the lord in Matthew 25 "reckoneth" with his servants, scolding the one who hid the single talent—"Thou oughtest therefore to haue put my money to the exchangers, and then at my comming I should haue receiued mine owne with vsurie." If you don't use beauty—as you'd use money, employing it to make more—you won't increase it and deserve no praise. "Beauties vse"/"bewtyes vse" (W/Q) must be beauty's usury (both derive from the Latin *usus*) because beauty has only declining value. The Fair Youth is called a "profitles vserer [usurer]" in sonnet 4; but in sonnet 6 the poet argues, "That vse is not forbidden vsery [usury]," that is, the use of beauty to make beauty. (No longer illegal, usury at this period was still considered a sin.) Sex also lurks there—"use" was synonymous with copulation (*OED*).

The manuscript's *worthless* praise prepares this notion more keenly— the other meaning of *thriftless*, that is, want of thrift, which sits ill at ease with Matthew 25, implies overspending rather than failure of investment. "Cast yee the vnprofitable seruant into outer darkenesse," says the lord. We use "talent" now for a gift from the Lord, which we must use, lest we make Him angry—Shakespeare has not dragged theology into the waste of beauty; but the idea lies beneath the surface, simply assumed, as duty to God often was.

"O how much better were" (W) has the directness of a first draft; but Q is an improvement, repeating "praise" emphatically from the previous line. In tone this is reasoned, but either line would allow an unreasoned or frustrated reading like "Isn't it blindingly obvious that . . . ?" At this point the speaker has exhausted all his forceful rhetoric—the likeness of the Fair Youth ravaged by age, almost begging him to compare his older friends to portraits or miniatures made in youth; the shame of being asked why he's now so ugly, when he must answer pathetically that what little beauty remains lies in his eyes. Surely no one would be so impolite—Shakespeare is only suggesting what people will be thinking. This might be a moment when the speaker has had enough. What youth ever listened to rational argument? The turn of the sonnet offers the way out, but the speaker could be forgiven for allowing himself a hint of desperation: "Can't you see, looking around, the best use of beauty is letting a child inherit it?" Perhaps, though the poet does not say, the best use of a man's beauty and wealth would be to marry a beautiful woman, making beauty a double inheritance.

We should not discount the possibility that the argument is mendacious. Dover Wilson suggested that sonnets 1–17 might have been commissioned by lord or lady for a wayward son—and that the seventeen sonnets might have been presented on the young lord's seventeenth birth-day in 1597.[49] The idea is intriguing, if no more than that. Had Shake-speare been approached to write these sonnets, the Fair Youth's parents would not have worried about the waste of beauty, just what would hap-pen to their estate if he died without issue. Using beauty would have been merely the rationalization. Though any parent might want to be a grand-parent, one with estates has deeper worries. Inheritance is a question scarcely less fraught now. The identity of the Fair Youth might be found in an only child or eldest son—Southampton was one, Pembroke the other.

The Q reading seems more wheedling than the manuscript, more artistically deployed, argument without the same tremor of feeling. It's the choice of an artist who no longer feels the same passion. The manu-script sonnet could of course have been touched up in the 1620s or 1630s[50] by someone steeped thoroughly in the sonnets—the manuscript line is sober, more homely, perhaps inferior—but the difference in intensity, the falling away of emotion into rhetoric, seems more likely the product of revision when passions have cooled.

The possibility that some years elapsed between writing the original and revising it for publication might also explain the shift from the famil-iar "this pretty child" to the more ornamental "this fair child," from the plain "say" to the more rhetorical "answer." "Pretty" originally meant "cunning," then "clever, skilful" (*OED*), which would be far from the meaning; but not quite so far is "artful, well-conceived," which might even be a buried pun. From the fifteenth century, however, the word also meant what we mostly mean now, "good-looking, esp. in a delicate or diminutive way," usually used of women or children. "Pretty" suggests intimacy, not with the child, who is only imagined, but with the Fair Youth. Perhaps it was only the poet's desire to use "fair" here that led him to change "fair livery" to "proud livery" in line 3—it's one thing to reuse a word for emphasis, another to betray a niggardly vocabulary.

The lines given to the Fair Youth continue, so we should imagine him prospectively saying, in the manuscript, "This pretty child of mine / Saues my account & makes my old excuse." This too would be a richer and more spirited presentation of what might happen—though the subjunctive is used in both versions, in the manuscript the youth grown old tells us what this future child actually does ("Saues my account"), Q what the child shall do. Perhaps this difference is much of a muchness; but the manuscript seems more personal, more a concerned friend making an argument than a Cicero pursuing his cause. The first has the controlled urgency of a man with a private stake, the second the demeanor of a man before a public audience.

Long ago the scholar T. W. Baldwin heard echoes in these opening sonnets of a letter by Erasmus printed in Thomas Wilson's *The Arte of Rhetorique* (1553), a standard grammar-school text Shakespeare seems to have known. Particularly marked are the lines, "You shall haue a pretie litle boye, runnyng up and doune youre house. . . . You shall seme, to bee newe borne. . . . What man can be greued [grieved], that he is old, when he seeth his awne countenaūce . . . to appere liuely [lively] in his sonne."[51] "Pretty" and "to bee new borne" in the manuscript lie closer than Q to the original, as Gary Taylor pointed out.[52] This is the most compelling argument that the manuscript is Shakespeare's draft. Kerrigan notes the resemblance of sonnet 3 to another line in the letter ("What punishement is he worthy to suffer, that refuseth to Plough that lande, whiche beyng tilled, yeldeth childrē"),[53] but the line may also lie beneath the plowed ground here.

Both "account" and "count" were synonyms for financial reckoning, so the shift must have been for meter or for the words' different nuances. Q's "Shall sum my count" is fairly obvious. ("Count" means "account" here—"And summ'd the accompt of Chance," *Henry IV, Part II*.)[54] When the Fair Youth must provide the reckoning of his days, his fair child balances the books, wiping out any deficit—the gradual debt, for example, incurred as beauty is depleted over time. In sonnet 1, the "glutton" youth was accused of eating the "worlds due," namely, offspring, like a Cronus. The loss of children would be another liability of his selfishness.

"Sum" might mean to total a column of figures or to "sum up," to provide a narrative summary—here, of a life. (Perhaps Gabriel Harvey in *Pierces Supererogation* [1593] comes close: "He summed all in a briefe, but materiall Summe; that called the old Asse.")[55] "Account" and "count" could both mean (though the latter was somewhat old-fashioned in this sense) a narrative, the story of a life. Surely this reading is at least as important—the money and accounting metaphors are mere figures, as it were. What a man often leaves behind as his accidental bequest is not the tally of his sums and sins, his getting and spending, but the tale of his days—and of course his children.

As for the manuscript, Christian theology defined "account" (W) as the "final reckoning at the judgement seat of God" (OED). Hence, "to go to one's account." "Saues [saves]" (W), too, is theological: "to redeem from sin, bring salvation to," that is, to save from Hell. The words smuggle in religion; but the revision has pushed it out, leaving the meaning—perhaps regrettably—limited to accountancy and tale-telling. (Possibly the revision gives insight into Shakespeare's developing feelings about Christianity.) The manuscript retains the Shakespearean habit of letting meaning grow weedlike—the version in Q shows a more considered but more limited approach, which suggests, not that Shakespeare had lost his touch, but that he was calculating his effects.

"Make(s) my old excuse" is difficult. The line may be read as "justify, when I am old, the consumption of the beauty expended during my life" (Stephen Booth),[56] or less likely as the "excuse I make when I am old" (Colin Burrow).[57] Booth admits the problem forthrightly, suggesting that we take "old as an ellipsis for 'when I am old'; the context demands that the phrase be understood by synesis, i.e. as meaning what it must mean rather than what its syntax would otherwise indicate ('make my usual excuse')." Though Shakespeare's language often confounds the reader, the phrase was altered in a number of manuscripts to ease the sense—indeed, it's the phrase most varied. That the W reading survived in Q (except for "makes" becoming "make") suggests that Shakespeare was happy with the wording. Accusations of simplification in the manuscript founder here.

The shift from "Making" (W) to "Proouing [proving]" (Q) in the last line of the quatrain secures the legal metaphor in "succession," linked to the metaphor of the accounting necessary to settle an estate. If it's a second thought, it's chosen to turn aside the religious undercurrent of the quatrain. (The echo of "makes"/"Making" in W is similar to repetitions in other sonnets and would not by itself have asked for revision.) To "prove" at this period meant, not just "to demonstrate the truth of by evidence or argument," but "to establish the genuineness and validity of" (*OED*)—we still prove a will. "Succession" in both versions works well enough for the normal replacement of parent by child, but in Q beauty provides the legal proof for the boy to inherit his father's estate. This stronger sense is the "occupation or possession of an estate, a throne, or the like" or the "act or fact of succeeding according to custom or law to the rights and liabilities of a predecessor." "Making" (W) is more constricted—there succession has no obstacles to overcome. The general thought in Q is clear: the boy is both "proving his beauty" (demonstrating it by his face, more metaphorically through some legal procedure in which resemblance—genetics, again—clinches the argument) and "proving his beauty by succession thine" (showing his beauty is the rightful successor to the father's own).

COUPLET

The couplet in many Shakespearean sonnets is almost superfluous—and the same couplet, probably repeated through mishap, works perfectly well in sonnets 36 and 96. Here the couplet makes a difference. It's cast in conditional language, so the benefits cannot accrue if the Fair Youth fails to take the advice. Should he marry, the pretty child of the manuscript will make him "new borne." It's hard to avoid the pun on "newborn" here. The first use in the *OED* is of a child (early fourteenth century), the second of Christ; but already by the date of the sonnets Sidney had used it for sighs and Spenser in the sense of being regenerated, probably the primary meaning here, though still leaning toward the original, literal sense. Perhaps that's the sense Shakespeare wished to avoid in Q ("new made" is a feeble phrase), because though it's a radical leap—the father is the child of the child—it does confuse matters. Still, the sense of Christian resurrection, elsewhere alluded to, is plain, and plainly banished in Q.

The poem ends in a probable allusion to the story of David in 1 Kings, when he had become "olde, and striken in yeeres, and they couered him with clothes, but hee gate no heate." His servants brought him the young damsel Abishag. The Fair Youth needs a wife, then a son. Shakespeare's point might be that, with a beautiful child to inherit all else you possess, the feeling will so warm you no Abishag will be necessary.

The sonnets bear the marks of poems written obsessively, probably in gouts—singly, by pairs, perhaps little runs, but not all at once with the focus of arrangement. When he came to collect them (Duncan-Jones suggests he was impelled by the closure of the theaters in 1603–1604 and 1608–1609),[58] many may have been a decade or more old, written during the sonnet craze of the nineties. Perhaps he had written some after, as whim or feeling dictated. How thoroughly he revised we cannot say; but the evidence of the plays, like the evidence of the stray pages in *Sir Thomas More*, argues that he couldn't keep his hands off a text when it lay before him. If he did revise, the original might have looked like the manuscript of sonnet 2. Taylor has a convincing list of Shakespearean echoes in the manuscript, especially from plays of the 1590s, particularly those before 1596–1597.[59]

Burrow notes the signs of confusion in Q that might have been caused by manuscript copy, either through misreading (as in the three sonnets with an unrhymed line—26, 69, and 113—and in the many where "their" ought to be "thy"), mistakes or failures of revision (perhaps the repeated couplet in 36 and 96), or revisions tentative or poorly marked (sonnet 99, with fifteen lines).[60]

A poet may make a poem worse in revision, may soften effects that give it the wrong conviction and finish when required for a chain of sonnets. Shakespeare likely had written the poems from immediate impulse, as his friendship with the Fair Youth developed, stumbled, had consequences. There was no need to polish them—they were private. He passed a few to friends, which tells us little more than that he had friends. The Earls of Pembroke and Southampton, the main rivals for the role of Fair Youth, were still alive in 1609—they both married and outlived Shakespeare.

Sonnet 2 seems to follow directly from the first sonnet, with its pretty opening. If Shakespeare had a hand in the arrangement, as some have argued, the whole sequence derives from the argument announced in "From fairest creatures we desire increase, / That thereby beauties *Rose* might neuer die." The sonnets were almost certainly not written in the order we have; but these two come from the same source, whatever prompted them, and the second after the first. Some metaphorical strains in the first seem recollected or teased out by the second, so that "riper" in the first is complemented by metaphors of field and weed(s) in the second; and "bright eyes" become the "hollow suncken" or "deepe sunken" eyes. Perhaps the idea of "famine where aboundance lies" is echoed in those weeds—fallow fields or fields that no longer produce may be overgrown with such trash. "Thy selfe thy foe" may have been extended into the second sonnet's "beseige," and spring in the first becomes the winters of the next. The closing accusation of sonnet 1, "else this glutton be," is in W turned into Truth, which all must eat, but in Q becomes the glutton Shame, the Fair Youth's shame, which shall eat him up.

I understand the argument that the differences in manuscript are not beyond some meddling reviser. As Duncan-Jones has it, "Collectors of poems in this period frequently introduced readings which could in some sense be called improvements, and may have taken a pride in doing so."[61] We must look, not backward from Q, however, but forward from the manuscript. The differences are perhaps, not degradation from published text, but improvements from manuscript with the stamp of Shakespeare's mature mind. We must take notice of what was lost, because the manuscript is not without its own delicacies of meaning. The phrasing in Q has been cooled (*pretty* to *fair*) or redirected (*truth* to *shame*), generally made more complicated. What was more highly tempered has been composed. Note too how the metrical position of some words has quietly been adjusted, not just "how much" in line 9, "This" in 10, and "my" in 11, but "liuery" in 3 (two syllables in W, three in Q). Such alterations seem, not the work of an eager stranger, a would-be Shakespeare, but second thoughts of a man of forty-five reviewing his raw, youthful, emotional sonnets for print, tinkering to make them more of a piece, the way the revision to "thriftless" ties it more deeply to other sonnets early in the sequence.

A critic sharpened by such thoughts would look at what is revealed when "trench" is changed to "digge," "rotten" to "totter'd," "lustre" to "treasure," "hollow" to "deepe," "say" to "answere," "saues" to "sum," and "borne" to "made." The manuscript is in places more aggressive, rougher, more intense, while Q is artful and calculated, poised in greater subtlety. If warmth had become coolness, the changes in Q, some of them, might be admissions of regret. The former directness, the rich conversion of feeling to verse, might have been just what an older

Shakespeare would eliminate when about to publish such poems. Detachment makes them slightly more fictional, perhaps just the note he wanted. The changes, to push the idea further, might have been caused, not just by regret, but by embarrassment.

Was Shakespeare the boy with small Latin and less Greek, the adolescent deer poacher, the May in a May-December marriage, the rural schoolmaster, the horse minder at early theaters, the traveling player, the lawyer's clerk, old King Hamlet's ghost, Greene's hick actor and "upstart crow" (a "Tygers hart wrapt in a Players hyde"), the playwright who never "blotted a line," the canny part-owner of the Lord Chamberlain's Men, the prickly seeker after a coat of arms ("Non sanz droict"), paterfamilias of the Stratford mansion, the real-estate investor, the country conservative in favor of enclosing common land or the country sentimentalist who hated the idea, the sociable lush, the secret Catholic, the husband with a roving eye for women and men alike, or all of these, or none?

Reading the private life as if it too were a work of art can be claustrophobic as well as illusory, a will-o'-the-wisp. The temptation is always to look for hints and clues that explain the words on the page (private prejudices, past sins, haunted dreams, ragged desires), when often what the poet was trying to do was to escape the burdens of the life. That doesn't mean the life isn't there in cryptic form.

We're unlikely ever to know who Shakespeare was, he was so many. Even were a chest of his papers to surface tomorrow in some lumber room in Warwickshire, the biographies would lie only a little closer to the poet whose shape shifts with every reading. We know more about Shakespeare than about many another Elizabethan playwright—Kyd, say, or Webster. Yet Shakespeare's language, darting like a water strider now here, now there, ignoring the dark currents it rides on while courting the toothy monsters below, could only have been written by a man difficult to grasp. A biography of a thousand pages, every fact tacked down like a piece of upholstery, could not tell us enough about Shakespeare; but every poem, packed like an overstuffed cloak-bag, tells us too much.

7. Pound's Métro, Williams's Wheelbarrow

EZRA POUND, "IN A STATION OF THE METRO"

As he recalled it,

> I got out of a train at, I think, La Concorde and in the jostle I saw a beautiful face, and then, turning suddenly, another and another, and then a beautiful child's face, and then another beautiful face. All that day I tried to find words for what this made me feel. That night as I went home along the rue Raynouard I was still trying. I could get nothing but spots of colour. I remember thinking that if I had been a painter I might have started a wholly new school of painting. . . . Only the other night, wondering how I should tell the adventure, it struck me that in Japan, where a work of art is not estimated by its acreage and where sixteen syllables are counted enough for a poem if you arrange and punctuate them properly, one might make a very little poem which would be translated about as follows:—

> "The apparition of these faces in the crowd :
> "Petals on a wet, black bough."[1]

Early in March 1911, Ezra Pound arrived in Paris. By late May he had moved on. The specters in the Métro obviously haunted him. The lines were finished by fall the following year, when he sent *Poetry* a batch of poems that, he hoped, would "help to break the surface of convention."[2] When these "Contemporania" were published at the head of the April 1913 issue, the poem appeared in this fashion:

IN A STATION OF THE METRO

The apparition   of these faces   in the crowd :
Petals   on a wet, black   bough .[3]

The first thing striking about the couplet is the subject—beauty discovered underground. (The magazine altered the title's full caps in Pound's manuscript, where the small doings underground seem overwhelmed by the massive sign above, to small caps, the magazine's house style for parts of a sequence. Pound had put "Metro" in quotation marks.) The previous century, Turner in *Rain, Steam and Speed—The Great Western Railway* (1844) and Monet in his views of Gare Saint-Lazare (1877) had brought the railroad to painting; but it would be hard to call the results traditional. Turner's oil is a little terrifying—a rabbit flushed from cover dashes ahead of the locomotive—while Monet's frontal portraits of iron-clad leviathans are steamy visions. The works resemble fever dreams, suggesting how difficult it is for the artist to venture outside the approved list of salon subjects. To do so is to court rejection—but not to do so lets art fossilize the taste of the past.

The material culture of poetry often lags a generation behind the world outside. The shock of modernity in Pound's couplet has faded, but it's jarring to compare what he was writing before that fateful encounter in the Métro. In *Ripostes* (1912): "When I behold how black, immortal ink / Drips from my deathless pen—ah, well-away!" and "Golden rose the house, in the portal I saw / thee, a marvel, carven in subtle stuff."[4] A smattering of modern diction seeps in elsewhere, but Pound's imagination had been steeped in Victorian vagaries, with a weakness for the long-baked poeticisms of "'twould" and "'twas," of "hath" and "'neath" and "ye" and "thou," the language of Nineveh reconstructed from torn-up pages of the King James Version. Pound's English resembles the appalling translations of Gilbert Murray, which should have killed off interest in Greek tragedy forever.

The most dramatic poem in the book is Pound's faux-barbarian version of "The Seafarer"—rough-hewn, archaisms for once used to effect, the weatherbeaten rhythms of alliterative Anglo-Saxon smuggled into a premodern English that never existed. The poem looks forward to

Pound's experiments with Chinese translation in *Cathay* (1914), which inaugurated the idiom in which he did his best work—no longer burdened by nineteenth-century haberdashery, he found a verse line adequate to his rough inflections.

It was at the end of *Ripostes*, in his prefatory note to "The Complete Poetical Works of T. E. Hulme," that Pound coined the term "Les Imagistes."[5] Innocent readers may have thought Hulme just as much a figment of imagination as Hugh Selwyn Mauberly, Pound's later alter ego. We probably owe to the Englishman (and not just to his example of plain speech, graven image) Pound's interest in Japanese and Chinese verse. The spring after the American arrived in London in 1908, he joined the Poets' Club—Hulme, the secretary, reminded Pound of a Yorkshire farmer. F. S. Flint later remembered that members had written "dozens" of haiku "as an amusement. . . . In all this Hulme was ringleader."[6]

Hulme, who died in the war, helped bring the American's medievalism up short. (Ford Madox Ford was another bluff influence. On reading Pound's *Canzoni* [1911], he rolled about the floor, presumably howling the while at the preposterously stilted English.)[7] We should also not underestimate the effect of reviewers, who wrote things like, "If Mr. Pound can find a foreign title to a poem, he will do so. Queer exotic hybridity!"[8] Pound was sometimes slow to change—after 1920, there was an increasing refusal to change—but during a crucial decade he could be goaded into brilliance.

Beginning in 1909, Pound became a frequent visitor to the Print Room at the British Museum. There he was probably exposed to the extraordinary collection of *ukiyo-e* prints gathered by the curator, his friend Laurence Binyon.[9] From such accidents and oddments, such stray collisions, Pound manufactured his new style. Only the month before "In a Station of the Metro" appeared, his fellow traveler Flint had contributed the article "Imagisme" to *Poetry*, a manifesto for the new poetry Pound was promoting:

1. Direct treatment of the "thing," whether subjective or objective.

2. To use absolutely no word that did not contribute to the presentation.

3. As regarding rhythm: to compose in sequence of the musical phrase, not in sequence of a metronome.[10]

Pound added dicta of his own, "A Few Don'ts by an Imagiste," which elaborated the orders of battle, among them:

Use no superfluous word, no adjective, which does not reveal something.

Don't use such an expression as "dim lands of *peace*." It dulls the image. It mixes an abstraction with the concrete. It comes from the writer's not realizing that the natural object is always the *adequate* symbol.

Go in fear of abstractions. Don't retell in mediocre verse what has already been done in good prose. Don't think any intelligent person is going to be deceived when you try to shirk all the difficulties of the unspeakably difficult art of good prose by chopping your composition into line lengths.

Use either no ornament or good ornament.[11]

The minor vogue and rapid extinction of Imagism, a movement whose influence we still feel, has been hashed over by literary critics for a century. Its rehearsal here is merely to bring the poem into focus within the slow progress toward the densities of language, the images like copperplate engraving, that made Pound Pound.

When you read Pound's early poems book by book, his transformation is the more remarkable. In *Personae* (1926), which collected poems published before *The Cantos*, he pared his apprentice work of many of its embarrassments, almost a hundred of them. The poems absent are rarely as good as those he chose to keep, though the latter have the young Pound's same brash overreaching; the varnished diction ("Holy Odd's bodykins!" "a fool that mocketh his drue's disdeign");[12] the curious tone with contrary modes of sapheaded ardor and bristling hostility; and the contempt for modern life, cast into antique dialect. (No other modern poet started as a contemporary of Chaucer.) The worst of the discarded are deaf to their own high comedy: "Lord God of heaven that with mercy dight / Th' alternate prayer wheel of the night and light," and "Yea sometimes in a bustling man-filled place / Me seemeth some-wise thy hair wandereth / Across my eyes."[13] It took a long while for Pound to practice his preaching—he saw the direction for English poetry before he could follow it. Though he never entirely shook off the archaic trappings and the high romance of the troubadours, Imagism taught him to focus on image and let it whisper meanings he'd been shouting, Sturm und Drang fashion, with a bushel of exclamation marks attached.

The mechanics for change were in place. Then came the occasion, a letter from Harriet Monroe, editor of the newly launched *Poetry*: "I strongly hope that you may be interested in this project for a magazine of verse and that you may be willing to send us a group of poems."[14] Pound initially gave her a couple of poems lying on his desk, but the opportunity was too tempting to squander. Monroe was a dreadful poet and a conventional editor, but Pound saw the advantage of being the magazine's house cat—he immediately granted her exclusive rights to his verse and agreed to become *Poetry*'s foreign correspondent.[15] Monroe gave him a toehold among American literary magazines; he in turn provided access to the avant-garde abroad. The literary cities of the day were still Boston and New York. A magazine devoted only to poetry and founded in the uncultured heartlands not far from the Great American Desert was a novelty. (Think of the *New Yorker*'s scorn for the old lady in Dubuque even a decade later.)[16]

The best things in *Poetry*'s first years were the poems by Pound, Eliot, Frost, and Yeats, as well as Pound's hammer-and-tongs prose— Pound brought the others into the fold. In the fall of 1912, only a couple of months after the letter, he offered Monroe the job lot of "Contemporania." (That he briefly considered calling the series "March Hare" pleads an intention both whimsical and provocative.)[17] In March came the articles on Imagism, the theory. Then at last, the next month, "Contemporania."

"In a Station of the Metro" is the rare instance of a poem whose drafts, had they survived, might retain the relic traces of a complete change of manner, from gaslit poeticism to the world of electric lighting and underground rail. "Contemporania" showed Pound's first acquaintance with the modern age, with the deft gliding of registers, the slither between centuries of diction, that made virtue of vice: "Dawn enters with little feet / like a gilded Pavlova," "Like a skein of loose silk blown against a wall / She walks by the railing of a path in Kensington Gardens," "Go to the bourgeoise who is dying of her ennuis, / Go to the women in suburbs."[18] (In American poetry, it has never hurt to knock the suburbs.) His embrace of the modern is not a rupture with the past—there is antiquarian fussiness enough—but an acknowledgment that the past underlies the present, that present and past live in sharp and troubled relation. "In a Station of the Metro" is the final poem of the group.

At the beginning of his most productive years (roughly 1912 to 1930), Pound might as well have been a medieval troubadour yanked into the modern world. When he describes the woman in Kensington Gardens, he remarks, "Round about there is a rabble / Of the filthy, sturdy, unkillable infants of the very poor"[19]—it's not clear whether this judgment betrays her prejudice or his Swiftian realism (or not so real, since infants of the poor died in droves). Already a certain chagrin clung to the earlier poems. Addressing them, he admits, "I was twenty years behind the times / so you found an audience ready."[20]

Pound's biographer Humphrey Carpenter called "Contemporania" a "blast to announce the appearance of a new circus-act," the poems "written in a hurry and to fill a gap." Pound referred to their "ultramodern, ultra-effete tenuity"—and these "modern" poems, as he called them elsewhere, were quickly parodied by Richard Aldington, among others.[21] Pound must have thought better of them, because he included a few in his *Catholic Anthology* (1915) and all but one in *Lustra* (1916).[22] It would hardly have been the first time a writer, lashing out against his contemporaries, found the way forward. Pound's genius, when he was young, was as restless as Picasso's. Ambition is gasoline.

"IN A STATION OF THE METRO"

A title is not usually the first line of a poem. It may exist in tenuous or digressive proximity to what follows, at times merely the equivalent of an easel card propped to one side of the stage or the placard flourished by a bikini-clad model between rounds of a prize fight. The title may tell us merely where we are, or how far along. Here it flows seamlessly into the first line; but its status, like so many features of the poem, remains ambiguous. "In a Station of the Metro" was, as a title, a challenge to an aesthetic that would not have seen as poetry a poem set in such unromantic surrounds. The history of poetry has repeatedly been the march of the unpoetic into the poetic.

After the title, the first presence is almost an absence—apparitions are neither here nor there but halfway between two worlds, between seen and unseen, appearance and disappearance. The link to the supernatural is as old as the word—"apparition" first described a ghost, employing a term used in Latin of servants, whose presence could be summoned. The degrees of meaning spread from the reappearance of a star after occultation to the appearance of the infant Christ to the Magi, also called the Epiphany. These faces call up the shades of the *Odyssey*, where the dead Elpenor is referred to by the Greek word "eidolon," a specter or phantasm. The dead there lived in darkness; if you attempted to hold them they faded from your hands, insubstantial, "like a shadow / or a dream."[23]

Pound's recollection of the Métro would have been more or less vivid when recorded for *T.P.'s Weekly* in June 1913. Setting down that moment a year later for the *Fortnightly Review*, he added new details:

> I wrote a thirty-line poem, and destroyed it because it was what we call work "of second intensity." Six months later I made a poem half that length ; a year later I made the following *hokku*-like sentence :—
>
> > "The apparition of these faces in the crowd :
> > Petals, on a wet, black bough."[24]

(The indentation seems to have been the magazine's choice, not Pound's.) Pound was enough of a classicist, and a showman, to know the advantage of arriving in medias res—indeed, there is scarcely another way to start when the end is almost the beginning. Those passengers drifting by are not revenants, but they rise from the gloom of the underground station. The old-fashioned spaces before semicolons and colons affect the text of the poem. (Such spaces have been removed from Pound's prose below.) Note the introduction after "petals" of a comma soon to vanish again.

The Métro had opened scarcely a decade before, during the Paris World Fair—or Exposition Universelle—in the summer of 1900.[25] The trains ran on electric motors, and the electric lighting on the platforms provided artificial daylight. London's underground stations had been choked by the steam and sulfurous coal-smoke of engines that scattered cinders on the waiting crowds. One traveler remarked on the "smell of smoke, the oily, humid atmosphere of coal gas, the single jet of fog-dimmed light in the roof of the railway carriage, which causes the half-illumined passengers to look like wax figures in a 'Chamber of Horrors.'" *Wax figures!* An American, aghast at the "sulphurous smoke" that left the London stations "filled with noxious fumes," reported that "leading medical experts" believed the Underground responsible for a "large number of new diseases," "ailments of the heart or lungs," "headache and nausea."[26] Those wax figures give us an idea of what Pound saw.

Paris was lighter and cleaner. Still, standard bulbs were weaker then, and houses brightly lit compared to the days of candlelight and gas jets would seem a miasma now. An early photograph of the Gare de Lyon station shows a shadowy realm barely interrupted by the faint glow of ceiling fixtures (the scene is probably lighter than normal because of the photographer's flash).[27] There is a witness. In September 1911, a few months after Pound's visitation, another traveler came to Paris and recorded in his diary that "in spite of the electric lights you can definitely see the changing light of day in the stations; you notice it immediately after you've walked down, the afternoon light particularly, just before it gets dark."[28] This was Franz Kafka. Had the day been rainy, the station would have been even darker.

A crowd is the city's signature, especially for those from the country. Recall Wordsworth in London, a century before:

> How oft, amid those overflowing streets,
> Have I gone forward with the crowd, and said
> Unto myself, "The face of every one
> That passes by me is a mystery!"[29]

This is nearly the experience of "In a Station of the Metro"—but recall, too, Eliot's Dantesque London a few years after: "A crowd flowed over

Paris Métro, Gare de Lyon, 1900.
Source: Collection of Julian Pepinster—DR.

London Bridge, so many, / I had not thought death had undone so many."[30] Pound's vision occurred in a "jostle," he says; but the poem is all stillness, a freeze frame as static as haiku.

The interiors of most early stations, including La Concorde, were lined with chamfered white tiles, highly glazed—these dispersed the light and in later photographs give the interior a watery look.[31] Pound's poem depends on the daylight above the darkness below, not least because a visit to the underworld is a visit to the dead. Readers would have known the journey of Odysseus in *Odyssey* 11 (the *Nekuia*), or of Aeneas in *Aeneid* 6. The ritual slaughter of sheep, whose blood drew the dead to Odysseus, must already have been ancient when Homer composed his verses.

The comparison to petals is stark; but the gists and hints go deeper, as well as the sense of loss. The classic haiku demands a reference to season taken from a time-honored list—perhaps Pound knew that much. (How well he knew Japanese verse is moot, since he apparently believed haiku required, remember, sixteen syllables and punctuation.) However the scene occurred in the lost longer drafts of the poem, through the

Paris Métro, reflective lighting.
Source: Collection of Julian Pepinster—DR.

juxtaposition of painterly images he may have come to this brief form—
it might very simply be translated into Chinese. Pound's construction of
the series was fluid and contingent, but on one point he told Monroe he
was adamant: "There's got to be a certain amount of pictures to ballance
[*sic*] the orations, and there's got to be enough actual print to establish
the tonality."[32]

The intention of the image is plain—beyond the strewn blossom lies
transience. In his reminiscence in the *Fortnightly Review*, Pound says he
"saw suddenly a beautiful face, and then another and another, and then
a beautiful child's face, and then another beautiful woman."[33] The beauty
of petals—roughly oval, like faces—lasts but a week; the faces in the Métro
are like those of the dead, the lives however long too short in retrospect.
Indeed, the dead never age. In the underworld, young women remain
beautiful; children, children.

Despite the faint tincture of the classics, Pound's petals seem immediately present. In the Paris spring, these might have been the palest pink
of cherry blossoms or the rouge-tinted white of plum. Cherry trees may
have been blooming in the Jardin des Tuileries above the station. "A wet,

black bough": *bough* here, therefore probably a tree, though "boughs of roses" is not unknown. In a minor poem from *Exultations* (1909), "Laudantes Decem Pulchritudinis Johannae Templi," Pound praised the "perfect faces which I see at times / When my eyes are closed— / Faces fragile, pale, yet flushed a little, like petals of roses."[34] The image was in the warehouse.

Pound would have left the Métro in sight of the giant red-granite obelisk erected in the long octagonal square by King Louis-Philippe in 1829, less than forty years after it had served as the site of the guillotine. There Louis XVI, Marie Antoinette, Robespierre, and Danton met their fates. Known as la place de la Révolution during the Terror, the square was afterward renamed, not without the luxury of irony.

Blossoms wither and fade, lives wither and fade. Those visions in the Métro, so casually encountered, might have been at the peak of a beauty that death, like art, would arrest, had arrested. The poem depends on the electric shock of seeing the bloom of such faces in the murk underground. That's the point. Beauty rises here from the sordid darkness, a motif familiar from Aristotle's notion that life emerged spontaneously from rotting flesh. Had the lighting been better, the faces would not have been so striking. These are faces *in* the crowd, so he is probably ignoring some in favor of others—his eye was drawn to beauty.

The poem works that ground between nature and civilization, country and city, pastoral and metropolitan. (We should be disconcerted by the pastoral image materializing in the unfeeling world of the machine.) The dunghill versus harmony. The *Georgics* versus the *Aeneid*. Pound built the image out of the clash of prejudices. Paris of course had its own underground city of the dead—the Catacombs, whose entrance lay on what had been known as Hell Street (rue d'Enfer). The poet stayed at a pension no great distance away when he arrived in Paris in 1911.[35]

Pound noted in "A Few Don'ts" that "An 'Image' is that which presents an intellectual and emotional complex in an instant of time. . . . It is the presentation of such a 'complex' instantaneously which gives that sense of sudden liberation; that sense of freedom from time limits and space limits; that sense of sudden growth, which we experience in the presence of the greatest works of art."[36] Pound was unusual in being able to examine, almost with calipers, what he was doing—and what he intended to do. The poem here is theory writ small, or theory is the poem writ large. The poem is an interleaving of juxtapositions—not just the image of the faces versus that of the petals, but the acuteness of a title so casually and harshly modern versus the ghostly faces and blown petals after. The simplicity of the poem lives above a confusion of staccato confrontations.

The conjunction of images binds the worlds together as much as it holds them apart. This is Pound's *phanopoeia* at its most basic. The beauty exists in eternal confrontation with the squalid, but it is beautiful in part because of that squalor. After Pound, there was not a poet who could requisition the power of such images until Geoffrey Hill. Pound's crucial critical idea of the period, applied directly to translation, was the distinction between *melopoeia*, "words . . . charged, over and above their plain meaning, with some musical property"; *phanopoeia*, a "casting of images upon the visual imagination"; and *logopoeia*, the "'dance of the intellect among words.'"[37] This first appeared in "How to Read, or Why" (1929), but he was using the terms *melopoeia* and *logopoeia* at least as early as 1921.[38]

The image, however exact physically, trembles with ambiguity. Do the faces look wet in the liquid light of the Métro? Was it raining above, the passengers having rushed into the darkened station from a shower? (That Pound mentions only women and a child among the faces suggests that this might be late afternoon, the women having spent the day in the gardens above, perhaps driven into the subway by the rains.) Are the petals from blossoms torn apart by spring rain, stuck to the wet bough, to fall when the sun returns? Or are they blossoms freshly opened in clusters along a branch? Pound's familiarity with *ukiyo-e* prints might indicate sprays of cherry or plum blossom (Hokusai and Hiroshige contributed important examples),[39] but seeing one face after another suggests solitary petals. Pound likely had a single thought in mind, not two—such minor puzzles the reader must hold at bay. Some of the disconcerting play rooted in the poem lies between the static and dynamic terms of the image: petals pasted in stillness or clusters buffeted by a breeze. If the exact date mattered, as it does not, amid the usual showers of early spring in 1911, Paris had two prolonged periods of heavy rain, March 12–18 and April 27–29.[40] (The end of the Paris cherry or plum blossoms is usually mid-April.) The dates are merely idle speculation; but idle speculation is not the worst way to attack a poem, so long as it's no more than that.

What of the black bough? Perhaps the gloom suggested it. (The thicker the crowd, the fainter the light.) The atmosphere, dark enough already, would have been filled with the smoke of men indulging in pipes or cigarettes.[41] Yet the original Métro cars were made of dark varnished wood. Though some still ran on other lines, those no longer passed through La Concorde. The new metal-clad cars, however, had been painted brown (later deep green) in imitation of the wooden models; it's not clear if Pound could have seen the difference in the Stygian darkness of the station.[42] (Kafka: "The dark colour of the steel sides of the carriages predominated.")[43] That might have been enough, had Pound seen the faces against the dark backdrop of the wooden cars, or what he recollected as wood.

Aeneas's descent into the Underworld through the wide-mouthed cavern of Avernus in *Aeneid* 6 might also lie behind the image of Pound's half-lit station.[44] The Art Deco entrances built for the Métro, of which many remain, feature two tall curving posts like spindly flower stalks, each topped by a small red lamp. Mark Ovenden remarks in *Paris Underground* that these lamps "were said to look like the Devil's eyes at night; the steps of Hades down his throat leading to the belly of the beast!"[45] Unfortunately, Ovenden cannot recall the source; and Julian Pepinster, perhaps the most knowledgeable historian of the Métro, does not think the comparison ever made. It is suggestive but, alas, likely unhistorical.

One entrance at La Concorde did not possess these spiry posts—it also served as an exit. It was scarcely less gloomy, however. In a photograph of 1914, this entrance appears as a shadowy arched mouth cut into a stone facade along the border of the Tuileries, the sign METROPOLITAIN capped by five small bulbs, probably red, to cast light upon it through the dark. This wide-mouthed stone entrance is the only one that might have provoked classical thoughts in Pound. There, if we take him at his word, he would probably have emerged from the underworld.[46]

The poet, given his turn of mind, might have recalled another passage in the *Aeneid*—where Aeneas rode Charon's ferry across the Styx. The trains come and go, as endlessly as the ferry of the dead. Perhaps Pound recalled the sulfurous atmosphere of the London Underground,

Paris Métro, La Concorde, 1914.
Source: Collection of Julian Pepinster—DR.

not completely electrified even then. Until bridges and subways were built, the ferry remained the common carriage across water in all river cities—London, Paris, New York. If we take the journey of the dead further, the pale-faced figures would be the newly dead rushing to board— Pound saw them pressing toward him, as Aeneas saw the crowds on the bank of the Styx. Other myths muscle in, especially the eternal return of Persephone (invoked in Pound's Canto 1, a reworking of the *Nekuia* episode). Surely, had the Métro traveler a tutelary goddess, it would be she.

Pound's tone is nondescript, almost clerical, a notation of image complex in demand and reservation. There's something of the awe beauty disposes, or abandons in its wake—his transfixion has been transferred to the petals. They have a hypnotic bloom. The anonymous *flaneur* explains nothing (he gives no motive for his appearance, because the moment does not require motive)—if you didn't sense the ghostly quality of these presences (ghostly, not ghastly), his remark would not be far removed from forensic. He's merely the medium of impression, the words that give voice to image. One of the poem's quiet gestures is that it lets the title establish the surrounds. Pound's longer recollection registered the stir and arrest of this accidental scene: "In a poem of this sort one is trying to record the precise instant when a thing outward and objective transforms itself, or darts into a thing inward and subjective."[47] Eliot's idea of the objective correlative, which bears a filial relation, was not mentioned until his essay "Hamlet and His Problems" in 1919.[48]

The neutrality of voice perhaps owes something to Pound's stray reading of Oriental translation, though his deeper interest in Chinese poetry came only in the fall of 1913, when the widow of the scholar Ernest Fenollosa gave his papers to the eager young poet. Still, Pound had arrived in Europe toward the end of half a century of Japonisme ushered in by Commodore Perry's expedition of 1853–1854. That the poet spent time looking at *ukiyo-e* prints was no odder than his taste for painters like Whistler, that chronic bohemian, on whom the Japanese influence was marked. One of Pound's friends thought the poet's outlandish dress and irritating manner mimicked the painter as well.[49] "You also, our first great, / Had tried all ways," Pound wrote of Whistler in 1912, nailing his flag to that mast.[50]

Translation accounted for the simplicity and directness of Imagism. The poet had in effect thought in an alien language, a tongue he did not know, and translated back to English.

RHYTHM

In the *Fortnightly Review* memoir, after remarks similar to those on "spots of colour," Pound added: "It was just that—a 'pattern,' or hardly a pattern, if by 'pattern' you mean something with a 'repeat' in it. But it was a word, the beginning, for me, of a language in colour."[51] He was not referring to rhythm here, but his thoughts on rhythm align in rudimentary form with this moment. (*Melopoeia*, as he says in *ABC of Reading* [1934], is where "language charged with meaning" succeeds in "inducing emotional correlations by the sound and rhythm of the speech.")[52] He continues, in the expanded reminiscence, "I do not mean that I was unfamiliar with the kindergarten stories about colours being like tones in music. I think that sort of thing is nonsense. If you try to make notes permanently correspond with particular colours, it is like tying narrow meanings to symbols."[53] There he rejects the relevance of Baudelairean synaesthesia.

Pound certainly had rhythm in mind when he typed out the poem for Harriet Monroe.

> The apparition   of these faces   in the crowd :
> Petals   on a wet, black   bough .[54]

These spaces might be called phrasal pauses, except the last, which provides emphasis or suspense after "black." Monroe must have questioned Pound about rhythm, because he replied with a salvo: "I'm deluded enough to think there is a rhythmic system in the d[amned] stuff, and I believe I was careful to type it as I wanted it written, i.e., as to line ends and breaking *and capitals*."[55] Recall the odd comma after "petals" in the version Pound published in *Fortnightly Review* in 1914. The phrasal pauses are gone, but he couldn't quite let go—that comma is the last remnant of a missing space.

The spaces before colon and period might be thought similar to pauses in reading at the end of a line or a sentence (you cannot hear punctuation, not accurately, with perhaps one exception, the question mark). These spaces, however, had no significance—they are simply an artifact. Pound was following an old typographer's-convention throughout the manuscripts and typescripts of "Contemporania."[56] Perhaps Monroe was so cowed by Pound's reply she didn't realize that the terminal spaces of "In a Station" were unnecessary. The other poems lost such spaces in print, but this was the only poem in the group with phrasal pausing in addition. ("Line ends and breaking" referred to enjambment, not spaces before punctuation—but obviously he confused her.) The convention had not entirely vanished in print—you see spaces before all major stops except comma and period in the first edition of *Gaudier-Brzeska* (1916), as in the *Fortnightly Review* article that preceded it.

Such rhythms would have been more difficult to enforce before the invention of the typewriter—the typewriter was Pound's piano. He liked to think of himself as a composer, though his work in that line was not a success—he had a tin ear and a tin voice. His longest composition, the one-act opera *Le Testament*, is an agony of droning and caterwauling.

Pound added, in his salvo, "In the 'Metro' hokku, I was careful, I think, to indicate spaces between the rhythmic units, and I want them observed."[57] ("Hokku" was the common name until the end of the previous century.)

Pound's colored "pattern" has only a sidelong reference to music. Still, there he came as close as anyone to a definition of free verse: free-verse rhythm, too, is not a "pattern," not something with a "repeat." (A pattern without a repeat, Pound might have said, meant that poetry should not look like wallpaper.) We are returned to Flint's notes on Imagism: "As regarding rhythm: to compose in sequence of the musical phrase, not in sequence of a metronome." Pound's disruptive idea of rhythm almost demanded that he break the phrasing after "black"—he could not require this without spacing, but when he printed the poem in *Catholic Anthology* (1915) he gave up trying to bully the reader. The spaces vanished.[58] That he had such a rhythm in mind tells us about the poem; that he was willing to abandon the notation tells us about Pound.

The analysis of rhythm does not often consider the length of words or the shift in parts of speech. To chart these things and superimpose them must be clumsy, but if we include the title the map might run:

$$\underline{x} \quad x \quad \underline{N}\text{-}N \quad \underline{x} \quad x \quad \underline{N}\text{-}N$$

$$x \quad \underline{N}\text{-}N\text{-}\underline{N}\text{-}N \quad \underline{x} \quad x \quad \underline{N}\text{-}N \quad \underline{x} \quad x \quad \underline{N}$$
$$\underline{N}\text{-}N \quad \underline{x} \quad x \quad \underline{A} \quad \underline{A} \quad \underline{N}$$

where x = articles, prepositions, pronouns, demonstrative adjectives; A = adjectives; and N = nouns. (Polysyllables are hyphenated, metrical stress underlined.) What can we learn from the lines' DNA? That most nouns appear in the strong positions at the beginning and end of lines, their force amplified by the string of monosyllables at line end, like a series of drum beats. The monosyllabic nouns are more dramatic, and more dramatically placed, than those longer. The rhythm of meter is augmented by the rhythm of syllables. (The meter of the final line mirrors but truncates the meter of the title.)

In *Lustra* (1916), the poet replaced colon with semicolon.[59] (That even here a space precedes the punctuation at the end of the first line of "In a

Station" should not be taken as a sign that Pound cared. The space was not lost in *Personae* (1926) until the revised edition of 1990, long after the poet's death.)[60] The colon surrenders the pale faces to the petals; the semicolon juxtaposes them in equal and trembling rapport. The colon is a compass direction; the semicolon a long rest, a musical notation. (Call it the difference between an equation and an encounter—or a traffic accident.) Pound considered the images superimposed ("The 'one image poem' is a form of super-position, that is to say[,] it is one idea set on top of another. I found it useful in getting out of the impasse in which I had been left by my metro emotion.")[61] Call it a jump cut at its sharpest, at its gentlest a dissolve, that technique so beloved of early cinema—Pound's era. He was thinking of film in that later reminiscence: "The logical end of impressionist art is the cinematograph"—that is, the motion-picture camera. "The cinematograph does away with the need of a lot of impressionist art."[62]

As Pound says about the moment of discovery, in the *Fortnightly Review* memoir, "I do not mean that I found words, but there came an equation . . . not in speech, but in little splotches of colour."[63] He must have felt in the early version of the poem that he had to direct the reader's eye from one thing to the other. Later, he was satisfied to nestle the images side by side. The lack of a verb leaves the tenor and ratio of comparison to the reader, as in haiku. The virtue of the sentence fragment is the unease produced when the verb is denied—however this seems to those fluent in Japanese, in English the verb is the absent guest longing to appear. Elijah.

To think of the petals as notes lined up along the musical staff of a bough takes the metaphor beyond its bounds; but, had the words scattered along the line struck Pound as a series of notes, the spaced phrases completed the rhythm of notation. The spacing perhaps prevents the reader from recognizing both lines as iambic, an alexandrine followed by acephalic tetrameter. The tension between iambic rhythm and the rhythm of phrasing gives the poem its motive tension. (The device was frequently used by Frost.) The iambics continue; the phrasings interrupt and stutter. When the poem appeared last in the series of "Contemporania," the pauses at line end must have seemed more emphatic, lingering, final.

The stamp or impression of "In a Station" would not remain so vivid without indirection. The best of Pound's early work lies, not in medieval ventriloquism or harangue, but in his new taste for implication. The best example of the method comes from *Cathay* in "The Jewel Stairs' Grievance," his translation of a poem by Li Po (now usually Li Bai):

> The jewelled steps are already quite white with dew,
> It is so late that the dew soaks my gauze stockings,
> And I let down the crystal curtain
> And watch the moon through the clear autumn.[64]

Working from Ernest Fenollosa's notes, Pound called the poet Rihaku, as he was known in Japan. (Fenollosa had studied the Chinese poems with Japanese teachers.)[65] The poem seems slight; but, as he did for no other poem in the short pamphlet, Pound added an instruction manual.

> Note.—Jewel stairs, therefore a palace. Grievance, therefore there is something to complain of. Gauze stockings, therefore a court lady, not a servant who complains. Clear autumn, therefore he has no excuse on account of weather. Also she has come early, for the dew has not merely whitened the stairs, but has soaked her stockings. The poem is especially prized because she utters no direct reproach.[66]

The cunning is worthy of Sherlock Holmes. (Even Pound felt so—when he analyzed the poem in his essay "Chinese Poetry," he remarked, "You can play Conan Doyle if you like.")[67] The original poem is not in code; but it depends on knowledge of Chinese poetry, including, as Wai-lim Yip notes, the genre of court poetry it imitated. (If Pound did not recognize the genre, Yip argues, he made inspired guesses.[68] Holmes, again.) The inductive method, placing the necessities of interpretation entirely upon the reader, had been crucial to "In a Station of the Metro." This is undoubtedly part of what Pound meant by *logopoeia*—the "'dance of the intellect among words.'"[69]

The claims of implication, of mysteries deciphered, were developed in even scrappier fashion in "Papyrus," Pound's interpretation of a bit of parchment containing fragmentary remains of a poem by Sappho. Pound used only the beginning three lines:

> Spring. . . . . . .
> Too long. . . . . .
> Gongula. . . . . .[70]

Gongula (more accurately, Gongyla) is a woman's name.[71] The Romantic idea of the fragment, the partial whole (recall "Kubla Khan"), found purchase here, though Pound's translation of the first two fragmentary lines has been sharply disputed.[72] The question is not, is this a love poem, but does a love poem require more?

There remains the mystery of what provoked Pound, bedeviled by the scene in the Métro, to the comparison. In "Piccadilly" (1909), he'd written of "beautiful, tragical faces," "wistful, fragile faces," and "delicate, wistful faces"—he was drawn to beauty like a pre-Raphaelite dauber.[73] (In "How I Began," Pound complains, "I waited three years to find the words for 'Piccadilly,' . . . and they tell me now it is 'sentiment.'")[74] More than a little of the pre-Raphaelite survives in *Lustra*. Consider, among many examples, "discovering in the eyes of the very beautiful / Normande cocotte / The eyes of the very learned British Museum assistant" ("Pagani's, November 8")—another louche charmer, another chance encounter.[75] After complaints by the printer and publisher, this and other poems thought scandalous had been dropped from the original British edition.[76]

Was there any shade who might have tormented him during the long revision of the poem? Perhaps. On an earlier visit to Paris in 1910, he had met Margaret Cravens, an American bohemian who became his patron.[77] She killed herself with a revolver in June 1912. Her death long troubled her friends, and some mistakenly believed that she had been in love with Pound.[78] He wrote an elegy for her, later titled "Post Mortem Conspectu," intended for the group of "Contemporania," though he withdrew it and published it elsewhere.[79]

The incident in the Métro occurred over a year before Cravens's suicide, but we know from his accounts that Pound revised a long while before his revelation that the inciting moment in all its affliction could be compressed to two images. (The "*hokku*-like sentence" occurred to him as early as the spring before her suicide.)[80] This Parisian ghost might have stalked Pound while he was whittling away the original version. Like Ajax turning from Odysseus in the Underworld, nursing his old grievance, the figures in the Métro do not say a word: "'So I spoke. He gave no answer, but went off after / the other souls of the perished dead men, into the darkness.'"[81] Kafka remarked, "Métro system does away with speech; you don't have to speak either when you pay or when you get in and out."[82]

Years later, Cravens's death is recalled in Canto 77 ("O Margaret of the seven griefs / who hast entered the lotus"), where Pound invoked the land of the dead, later mentioning the lotus again, the flower associated with her in his elegy. Then: "we who have passed over Lethe."[83] (His father showed Aeneas the river Lethe, where the dead promised a second body drank to forget.) There was much to forget. It might be tempting to recall the myth of Orpheus and Eurydice—another journey to the underworld to rescue someone dear, and a failure. That presses the possibilities too far. The archeology of image is difficult; and the critic can do little more than strew a few suggestions relevant to the poet's state of mind, insofar as such a transient thing can be explored at all. The poem does not need Cravens to conjure up the passage through the underworld. If the ghostly faces are the faces of the dead, they steal a little beauty from the petals. If they are the faces of the living, they borrow transience. As apparitions they could be both living and dead.

There may have been a more lingering cause for Pound to be thinking of the dead. One evening in 1903, a fire caused by a train's short-circuited motor filled the tunnels and Couronnes station with smoke. The lights were extinguished; passengers wandered in darkness, dying along the platform and at a neighboring station. Eighty-four were killed. Pound had visited Paris in 1906, when memory of the fire would still have been fresh. Perhaps he had heard of it. The pale faces crowded along the platform might be an eerie reminder of those who had died underground.[84]

The apparition of these faces in the crowd;
Petals on a wet, black bough.[85]

WILLIAM CARLOS WILLIAMS,
"THE RED WHEELBARROW"

As he recalled it,

> The wheelbarrow in question stood outside the window of an old
> negro's house on a back street in the suburb where I live. It was pour-
> ing rain and there were white chickens walking about in it. The sight
> impressed me somehow as about the most important, the most inte-
> gral that it had ever been my pleasure to gaze upon. And the meter
> though no more than a fragment succeeds in portraying this pleasure
> flawlessly, even [as] it succeeds in denoting a certain unquenchable
> exaltation—in fact I find the poem quite perfect.[86]

So, William Carlos Williams, having been asked which of his short poems
he would like posterity to know, if it could know only one.[87] He chose
"The Red Wheelbarrow":

> so much depends
> upon
>
> a red wheel
> barrow
>
> glazed with rain
> water
>
> beside the white
> chickens[88]

Published first in *Spring and All* (1923), this may be among the earliest
paeans to modern poetry's aesthetic particular, the everyday object
dragged into the marble galleries of art. The poem's Shaker English has
proved its most unexpected—and telling—contribution to American
verse. Anyone might have written in that humbling severity, the poetic
equivalent of Grant Wood's *American Gothic*. Readers have long been

moved by poems anyone might have written—however terrible, however good, such shreds of homespun are often the most deeply loved. You could say "The Red Wheelbarrow" is a Georgic lost in New Jersey.

The scene has been rendered in the plainest Wordsworthian style, the free verse not free but nearly lifeless, a flat, abrupt string of words shaped to its lack of ornament. The eye takes in the scene, but scene must seduce the eye—that is the dual condition of the visual: the charmer charmed, the sorcerer ensorcelled (call it vision if you require the taint of religion). Binocular vision is moral; but perspective is invented in surfaces, whether retina, canvas, or paper.

Rarely has a poem of banalities attracted such sustained close reading. The opening is based on a rhetorical trick, a question left hanging. "So much" of what? The phrase is old, or old enough. So much depends "upon the character of the clergymen" (1832), or "upon servants making fires" (1797), or "upon the man behind the cow" (1916). "Marriage is the most sacred, since so much depends upon it" (1720). So much depends "upon the individual temper of the particular judge" (1902), or "on the nature of the soil" (1828), or "upon the purity of the gold" (1823), or "upon the House of Commons" (1826). "So much depends upon the teacher, and so little upon the text" (1884). "So much depends upon the testimony furnished by the physician" (1825). So much, indeed, "depends upon the eyes of the reader" (1815).[89]

"So much depends upon circumstances" (1833) is the general way of putting it, yet the philosophical general is as devoid of circumstance as the circumstance of "The Red Wheelbarrow" is devoid of anything else.[90] So much depends on this, or that, or something more, but the stakes are absent—we are presumed to know already, yet we know that we don't know, or know only that "so much" too vague to know. So much of our lives? So much of the world? Williams's gesture has fueled much later poetry, often suffering lapses into sentimental vagary. There's nothing more dangerous in rhetoric than the unsaid.

"So much depends . . ." The thought is fragmentary but not a fragment. The *OED* says of "much" as a noun, "The word never completely assumes the character of a noun" and "can be modified by adverbs like *very, rather.*" The phrase "so much" has adjectival and noun uses dating to the early thirteenth century, and as a noun phrase meaning a "certain unspecified amount" it is almost as old, reaching back at least to the late fourteenth century. Its early appearance in the Wycliffite Bible reads, "Womman, seye to me, if ye solden the feeld for so moche?" "So" is one of those words that does duty in the dirty corners of English where formal grammar doesn't quite hold. It's doing so still, modifying willy-nilly in fresh turns of phrase: "Fuchsia was so last year," "You're so out of here."

The poem would have been very different phrased as a question and more intelligible had Williams written "so little"—given the trivial details, the shudder of meaning comes only because it *is* "so much." (Charting the entanglement of "so much" and "so little" would require phase switching or a two-state quantum system, depending on the measure of irony.) Williams records the force of intention: "The sight impressed me somehow as about the most important . . . it had ever been my pleasure to gaze upon." Where the poet proposes and the reader disposes, intention does not limit the poem's latent meanings. Indeed, by not answering the implicit question, Williams has given the reader free rein; but a reader is usually less interested in the variety of possible response than in what the poet had in mind. Interpreting a poem is like deciphering a message incomplete, with a key partly corrupt.

Critical tactics often reveal the critic more than the poet—and a poem so spare invites overattention. Many critics, like Hugh Kenner, have felt obliged to quarrel with the etymology of "depends":

> "Depends upon," come to think of it, is a rather queer phrase. Instead of tracing, as usage normally does, the contour of a forgotten Latin root, "depends upon" ignores the etymology of "depend" (*de* + *pendere* = to hang from).[91]

Or Charles Altieri:

> How resonant the word "depends" becomes, when we recall its etymological meanings of "hanging from" or "hanging over." The mind acts, not by insisting on its own separateness, but by fully being "there": by dwelling on, depending on, the objects that depend on it.[92]

Such arabesques ignore the appearance of the modern meaning as early as the sixteenth century, not long after the word made its way into

English. Williams was unlikely to be thinking of any flutter of ambiguity in the Latin. (A brief scan of the entry for *dependeo* in Lewis and Short would have shown that the ancients were already familiar with the modern usage. The literal meanings were "to hang from *or* on" and "to hang down," not "to hang over.") You might as well try to squeeze out meaning by saying that "upon," as the *OED* reminds us, once implied "elevation as well as contact" or that "rain" seems to have no history before cognates appear in Germanic languages—and therefore might have been of interest to Tacitus, that close student of empire.[93] If there were a drop rather than a leaning, it would be found only in the physical relation of three prepositional phrases, "upon" descending from "so much depends," each seeming to cling vertically to the one before. In the blood relations of grammar, however, "with rain water" modifies "glazed," while "glazed" and "beside the white chickens" separately modify "barrow." A sentence diagram would display the relations clearly.

Readers new to "The Red Wheelbarrow," if not hostile, sometimes become a little giddy on learning that such simple lines can be called a poem. Part of the pleasure derives from its violation of the "poetic," part from how much the opening promises and how little the poem delivers. (The reader's longing for meaning is used as an Archimedean lever.) So much depends because of the assertion, but assertion is not argument—"so much depends" is a riddle without revelation, leaving a void where the conclusion should be. The wheelbarrow, the glazing rain, and the chickens may do nothing for the reader; Williams claims no more than that they are obscurely momentous to him. A revelation is a privacy whose interior we are never likely to visit. The poet can render only the aftermath—the rest may remain a mystery even to him. Other readers, other epiphanies: a dog lying on a burnt carpet, an old book left open with a single word circled, red snow drifting across an empty lot. The poem is a Rorschach blot.

The history of painted wheelbarrows is long and cryptic. Had the color been unusual, Williams might have been startled only by the oddness of the scene. Barrows in the twenties were often still made of wood, which unpainted or unvarnished would soon rot if not kept under cover. Painted wheelbarrows must have been common. A novel from 1841, *Rollo at Work*, mentions a blue wheelbarrow, as does *Leslie's Monthly Magazine* in 1905; the now nearly forgotten Thomas Bailey Aldrich wrote in 1889 in

Scribner's Magazine that "few men who were boys in Portsmouth at the period . . . but will remember Wibird Penhallow and his blue wheelbarrow."[94] Green wheelbarrows appear in the magazine *The Garden* of 1904 as well as in *The Flag of Truce*, a novel of 1878; and a yellow one in *Arthur's Illustrated Home Magazine* of 1875, while a 1907 issue of *Geyer's Stationer* ("A Weekly Devoted to the Interests of the Stationery and Kindred Trades") reports that a certain hardware-store owner "paints his store front yellow, he paints his wagons yellow, he paints his push-carts yellow, and uses a yellow wheelbarrow. He uses yellow stationery and yellow envelopes."[95] As for red wheelbarrows, they can be found in the *National Magazine* of 1908, the *New-Church Messenger* of 1918, and the *Saturday Evening Post* of 1920.[96] In this period, the English advice columnist Charlotte Eliza Humphry remarked that a woman at Ascot had worn "almost enough rouge on her face to paint a little wheelbarrow."[97] That would be a red wheelbarrow.

The 1897 Sears catalogue advertised four types of wheelbarrows, including what was called a tubular-steel miners' barrow, which with its steel "tray" comes closest to what we call a wheelbarrow now.[98] The miners' barrow cost nearly three times as much as the Handsome Lawn Wheelbarrow, which had high, flat wooden sides—the better to carry grass clippings, garden waste, or chicken manure—as well as steel-spoked wheels and "two coats of brightest and best vermillion [*sic*] paint."[99] This is probably the sort of barrow Williams saw. The slightly more expensive Clipper Garden Wheelbarrow ("nicely painted and striped") seems too fancy for a working garden, and the two inexpensive railroad-wheelbarrows tipped to the side (made for handling dirt and used in the construction of railroads and canals). The catalogue for 1912 offered six wheelbarrows, four of hardwood and two with steel trays.[100] The cheapest garden-barrow, apart from one for boys, was made of hardwood and also painted red. Montgomery Ward's catalogue of 1922–1923 had similar wooden garden-barrows; though "well painted," the color goes unremarked.[101] The metal wheelbarrows may have been left unpainted.

Vermilion was a brilliant scarlet red containing mercuric sulfide, obtained from ground cinnabar. Used for rouge by the whores of Shakespeare's day and on our continent in the Indian's war paint, it was the painter's preferred red into the twentieth century. By the twenties,

Barrows.

This wheelbarrow is well made. Has full sized tray Wheels 16 inches in diameter. When packed for shipment wheel is bolted on inside of tray and legs are folded on side of handle. Can be easily set up by any one

No. 18300. Half bolted railroad Wheelbarrow, with wood wheel. Each...................................**$1.00**

No. 18301. Half bolted railroad Wheelbarrow, with steel wheels. Each...........................**$1.10**

No. 18302. Clipper garden Wheelbarrow is strong, well made and nicely painted and striped. With steel wheel. Price..**$2.50**

No. 18303. Tubular steel miners' Barrow. Size No. 6. Tray made of No. 14 steel. Capacity, 3 cubic feet of dirt. Weight, 80 lbs. Price, each...................................**$5.82**

We can give you rock bottom prices on mining or contractors' supplies. Send us your specifications for prices.

Our $2.10 Handsome Lawn Wheelbarrow.

No. 18304. This is the handsomest and best Lawn Wheelbarrow made. This wheelbarrow has finely shaped handles, braced with steel; two coats of brightest and best vermillion paint; one coat of high grade varnish; sideboard staples are riveted, non pull out. It is the best mortised wheelbarrow on the market. These barrows are fitted with the neatest steel wheels, 18 or 20 inches. In this feature they are incomparable. There are few barrows on the market having wheels larger than 16 inches. These wheels are constructed on the latest improved model of the bicycle, and are remarkably light and substantial broad tired wheels. Our special price for this wheelbarrow...................................**$2.10**

Sears, Roebuck and Co.'s Handsome Lawn Wheelbarrow, 1897.

however, bright commercial reds were usually made of iron oxides (one writer in 1913 estimated that half the paint coming from paint factories was red). American vermilion, also called chrome red, was a scarlet red chromate, the favorite of barrel makers, wagon makers, and the makers of cabooses.[102] There's a good chance the red wheelbarrow was painted that red.

Between wheelbarrow and chickens, in these pendant particulars, comes the medium, the glazing rainwater. The glazing is no more than distantly related to the varnish the painter applies, as a last touch, to the canvas. (Williams usually lacked such subtle calculation, to his benefit.) Still, the scene was observed through a frame, a window frame; and the restless movement of the eye from one particular to another mimics—perhaps even enacts—the eye's passage from object to object in landscape painting. Landscape invites the eye to travel the path of the painter's reckoning, but the poet in his more limited realm is more ruthless. He judges precisely how the scene will be ordered and read. The poem is an act of managed perception, the visual mechanics conditioned by formal pattern, the parts partial until the whole is grasped. Indeed, "The Red Wheelbarrow" focuses on fragments of a larger scene. It's perhaps not irrelevant that the eye may be drawn to a dash of red in pastoral, as Constable knew—and hunters of antelope. The still life is not quite, as it were, a *nature morte*. It's the *nature morte* within an invisible *nature vivante*.

In 1888, five breeds of white chicken—Dirigios, White Javas, White Minorcas, White Plymouth Rocks, and White Wyandottes—were recommended for recognition by the Committee on New Breeds of the American Poultry Association. Three were admitted: the Minorcas, the Plymouth Rocks, and the Wyandottes.[103] (One early breeder of White Plymouth Rocks claimed to have been inspired by his boyhood encounter with the white Roc in the *Arabian Nights*.)[104] Other white breeds had long been familiar—the first volume of the association's *American Standard of Excellence* in 1874 mentions at least half a dozen.[105] The admission of so many new white varieties at once, however, touched off a fad for white chickens.[106] These breeds—or one later recognized, like the Rhode Island White, admitted in 1922 to *The American Standard* (by then renamed *The American Standard of Perfection*)[107]—are the likeliest candidates for the fowl stepping blithely through the rain around that wheelbarrow. None of the white breeds dominated, but the White Plymouth Rock was among the most popular. No doubt the owner of those backyard chickens was looking for good layers.[108] Chickens of the day were smaller than factory-farmed chickens now.

Everything in the poem exists within the gravity of that wheelbarrow, in the little world introduced by "so much depends / upon . . ." The mystery of the scene lies in the poet's casual intensity—he saw the objects as never before. (The early saints experienced such moments of radical vision.) That the extraordinary may be found in the ordinary, the magnificent within the everyday, is a commonplace of scientific discovery, from the barnacles and finches contemplated by Darwin to the melted chocolate-bar that led to the microwave. Late in life Newton is said to have said, "I seem to have been only like a boy playing on the sea-shore, and diverting myself in now and then finding a smoother pebble or a prettier shell than ordinary, while the great ocean of truth lay all undiscovered before me."[109]

It was crucial, however, that the poem remain an exotic—that it never be repeated. Just as Marcel Duchamp in 1917 faced the law of diminishing returns when he followed his porcelain urinal, the first "ready-made" he attempted to exhibit, with a coat rack, Williams would have destroyed the epiphany had he later written that so much depended on a blue barber's-chair or an alligator suitcase.[110] When Heraclitus declared that you can't step into the same river twice, he went beyond a lesson about getting your feet wet. The first example of the new is revolutionary, the next is shtick.

THE STRUCTURE OF WHEELBARROWS

The poem must find a form equal to its revelation. We know "The Red Wheelbarrow" not just through the words but through the visual arrangement—what lies beyond syntax in the shape of the poem itself. The four unrhymed couplets, varying in their variations, have been stealthily organized, three words laid like a lintel upon one. Syllabic forms, to which this form bears filial affinity, don't always call so much attention to themselves—when they do (as in Marianne Moore's poems, to which we're indebted for the modern syllabic), indentation usually stamps the visual pattern across stanzas. Though it never became part of Williams's armory, the form of "The Red Wheelbarrow" was almost certainly inspired by the principle of word count in classical Chinese poetry.[111] The three-word verses of the *Three-Character Classic*, which Williams had read a few years before in *Chinese Made Easy*, had perhaps lodged in his head.[112]

As a thought experiment, the poem might be rearranged into four-word lines:

so much depends upon
a red wheel barrow
glazed with rain water
beside the white chickens.

The losses of emphasis cannot be offset. The same words are not at all the same poem. In poetry, form matters, as does the sequence of information. The distinctiveness of the original might suggest—even if we knew nothing of Williams's tastes—the geometric torsion of the Cubists, word count and enjambment making the syntax accountable to angles and surfaces. How unlikely the poem would have been had so much depended upon "the white chickens / beside // a red wheel / barrow // glazed with rain / water." That might have been titled "The White Chickens" before being instantly forgotten. Had so much depended, however, upon "a red / Duesenberg // glazed with rain / water // beside the snow / weasels," the poet could have been an even greater hero of the avant-garde.

The visual strategy of the original depends upon violent enjambment to frustrate the stale, flat, unprofitable prose. "Upon // a red wheel /" could have continued, "chair // glazed with rain / water"—just as "beside the white /" might have completed the idea with "Russian" or "collar" or "egret." (Enjambment always invites a mob of ghosts.) The first and last couplets sever a humdrum phrase, the colloquial "depends / upon" and the matter-of-fact "white / chickens." In the case of such familiar words, momentary shock is more refreshing than examination afterward. The reader's eye registers the breach—but isn't more humor packed into such deceits when the stakes are so small?

Rainwater and *wheelbarrow*: the middle couplets violate compounds that first appeared in English not as pairs but as single words, "rainwater" during the Old English period and "wheelbarrow" in the fourteenth century. The butchery makes the familiar strange again. Words severed by the eye are joined again in speech, as the magician rejoins the lady sawn in half—the shattered portrait is itself a form of revelation. It's hard not to see here the fracturing influence, the aggressive art of perception, of Juan Gris's collage *Roses* or Marcel Duchamp's *Nude Descending a Staircase, No. 2*, Cubist art Williams knew well. (Duchamp met Williams in the fall of 1915 and visited him at Rutherford the following spring.)[113] The eye must consider the elements independently, just as mounting an old shop-sign on a gallery wall or a urinal on a pedestal asks that the object be seen afresh, torn from its usual surroundings.

Williams was working in a tradition, whether he knew it or not. Jonson had enjambed "twi- / Lights," Milton after him "Mile- / end Greene," and Hopkins, more ludicrously, "ling- / ering" and "as- /tray," all for the sake of rhyme. The breach of manners works better as comedy, as in Lewis Carroll's "two p / ennyworth only of beautiful Soup." Such nods and winks turn up decades after Williams in Bishop's "Glens Fall // s" and Lowell's "duck / -'s web- / foot," again for rhyme.[114] Elsewhere in *Spring and All*, Williams enjambs the line "That sweet stuff / 's a lot of cheese."[115] The delay is a rimshot. The execution in "The Red Wheelbarrow" is calculated (no hyphen eases the pain), but so is the understanding that the drama is empty: Williams chose not the Miltonic tease ("yet from those flames / No light")[116] but an anti-Miltonic pratfall, which reveals with a flourish of classical gesture the vacancy of Romantic pastoral. "The Red Wheelbarrow" is an antipoem in more ways than one.

Too much can be made of such things. In the centuries after their appearance, "wheelbarrow" and "rainwater" often as not appeared divided or hyphenated, those engagements through which word pairs usually pass on their way to marriage—the premature wedding was long disputed. They're still found divided or hyphenated, and even Williams was inconsistent: "our drinking water was rain water," he wrote in *Autobiography* (1951). "Rainwater" in the story "A Descendant of Kings" was reprinted two decades later in *Make Light of It* (1950) as "rain water."[117] The poet had suffered a heart attack and a stroke by then, so perhaps he didn't notice or care.

In many of Williams's less successful poems, a scene is exposed and developed like a snapshot (the metaphor comes from hunting). The wheelbarrow and chickens, however, have been set at the distance of art while seeming to possess no art at all. The preamble is also an editorial (or, if you will, a framing device): "so much depends" gestures vaguely then lands with a thud upon "upon." The couplets that follow perfected modernist enjambment, in which a quiet, unassuming phrase is broken dramatically at line end—only for the next line not to be dramatic at all. It's like barreling along a highway and seeing, too late to avoid the abyss, a "Bridge Out" sign—except there is no abyss, just a terrifying drop of six inches. The short lines afterward place an object in isolation—barrow, water, chickens—even as syntax knits them together. We might expect a final line-break as cold-blooded as those in the inner stanzas, but Williams has wrong-footed the reader again. Readers enjoy being wrong-footed.

The poem was left untitled until anthologized in William Rose Benét's *Fifty Poets*. (Williams perhaps missed the tremor of meaning when he wrote "unquenchable exaltation"—as if the rain had poured down hosannas.) A year later, in 1934, the poet confirmed the title in *Collected Poems, 1921–1931*.[118] As a title, "The Red Wheelbarrow" is shrewd in its effects. First, it pushes the later break of "wheel / barrow" into the deliberately theatrical, though earlier readers, used to seeing the word in various forms, might have thought the amputation not all that daring. Second, the definite article promotes the indefinite wheelbarrow to feature attraction—what had been generic gets top billing. A title often thrusts to the fore the dominant subject or symbol, focusing the eye before the eye sees—the title anticipates the effect it in part creates. Last, the emphasis of "the" suggests that "so much" means a "very great deal" rather than "not all that much" (i.e., "so much and no more"). Either that is not just any wheelbarrow, or any wheelbarrow might have such an effect—but that particular one did for Williams.

The minute adjustments and implications of poetic form seem to reveal the world's organizing pattern, or merely the pattern the poem takes within the chaos of the ordinary. Consider the unbalanced couplets of "The Red Wheelbarrow," the first line always three or four syllables (in order, 4–3–3–4), the second a word of two syllables. All but the first disyllable are nouns (the unbalanced arrangement is unlikely a metaphysical point that existence teeters atop essence). One of the things the eye is most alert to is symmetry; and here the poet has produced, not just symmetries in words where there are none in the scene, but local asymmetries within larger symmetries. Syllabic patterns are interesting as far as they go, but they explain few of the poem's effects. At best, counting syllables reveals some tarry residue of the poet's workshop; but a poem read aloud almost never gains from a count almost impossible to hear. The sculptural structure, however, forces the inchoate into visual form.

Many critics have labored to detect patterns in sound, which might seem to betray a method of composition bordering on the aesthetic. In practice the repetition of *e*'s or *d*'s or *w*'s matters little. At worst the reader is subjected to tone-deaf analysis, as in the delightful mishmash of Barry Ahearn's *William Carlos Williams and Alterity*:

> The first and second stanzas are linked by the long "o" in "so" and "barrow" and by the short "uh" in "much," "upon" and "a." "L" and "r" interlace the core stanzas (the second and third); these two sounds, however, are not in the first and fourth stanzas. . . . The central stanzas are mellifluous, the frame stanzas choppy. Then again, however, the honeyed and the choppy are linked in the third and fourth stanzas. They are joined by means of a parallel construction; the long vowels in "gl*a*zed with r*a*in" match those in "bes*i*de the wh*i*te."[119]

Any aspect of a poem can be made to bear meaning, but not all bear meaning particularly well. In most poems written by a poet with an ear, the sound has been braided; yet the noise the poem makes, melodic or not, rarely calls for meticulous planning. It would be tempting to invoke the Duchess's advice to Alice, "Take care of the sense, and the sounds will take care of themselves"—but things are rarely that simple.[120] Williams once admitted that his "Lovely Ad" was an "inconsequential poem—written in 2 minutes—as was (for instance) The Red Wheel Barrow [*sic*] and most other very short poems."[121] (The statement was taken from a transcript of his remarks, so the variant title has no significance.)

Much criticism of "The Red Wheelbarrow" consists of observations true but not interesting, observations far less crucial than those interesting but not true. Critics have a talent for overreading matters usually ignored—indeed, things the poet may have done whimsically, carelessly, or without knowledge of the consequences. The early reviewer in *Poetry* who thought the poem "no more than a pretty and harmless state-ment"[122] is preferable to the later critic who argued himself from design to cornball insight:

> The wheelbarrow is one of the simplest machines, combining in its form the wheel and the inclined plane, two of the five simple machines known to Archimedes. Just as civilization depends on number, civili-zation depends on simple machines. . . . "So much depends upon" the wheelbarrow in its service not only through the centuries, but as a form whose components are indispensable to the functioning of a highly industrialized civilization.[123]

"Yeah, yeah," as the philosopher said. That doesn't mean minor or acci-dental choices don't condition meaning.

The form drives the perceptions of "The Red Wheelbarrow" toward a pacing and pointing they would not have as a line of prose:

> So much depends upon a red wheel barrow glazed with rain water beside the white chickens.[124]

The metrical shape of the poem wrestles against syntax. William has cast the sentence into accentual couplets, with two beats in the first line, one in the second. The technical analysis of meter, unhappily, too often leads to hair-raising sentences of the sort in Kenneth Lincoln's *Sing with the Heart of a Bear*:

> This third line is composed of two spondees enjambed toward an inverted foot, a trochaic "*bar*row," which serves as the wheeling reverse pivot, indeed, of the second line.[125]

It's easy to go too far with meter and lose sight of the forest, the trees, and anything sitting on the branches. (Finding two spondees in the third line is impossible.) There is nonetheless something to be said for meter here. If the poem had been cast not in four couplets but two lines, the meter might have been more uniform:

$$— \quad ' \quad — \quad ' \quad —\, '$$

so much depends upon

$$— — \quad ' \quad — — \quad ' \quad — \quad — \quad ' \quad — — \, ' \quad — \quad — \quad ' \quad —$$

a red wheel barrow glazed with rain water beside the white chickens.

The iambic regularity of the opening assertion would be followed by five anapests and a feminine ending, a rhythm disrupted in the original by enjambment and stanza break—as well as by the tendency of some readers to pronounce the word, once broken, as "wheel BARrow," instead of "WHEEL barrow." (Williams's own matter-of-fact reading, in the two recordings I've heard, was WHEEL / barrow." He also said "rain / WATer," rather than the usual "RAIN / water.")[126] The rhythmic alternation of lines long and short creates minor dramas within the beautiful stutter of enjambment. This is not to suggest that meter so occult fails to give musical underpinning to the whole.

In *Fifty Poets*, Williams described the meter as "no more than a fragment." Perhaps he thought the poem too brief to establish meter—more likely, in his inexact way, he simply meant the rhythm had been cut short. The reader may discover various emotional cognitions and recognitions in rhythm, recognitions that might be no more than chance—yet how carefully Williams has deployed and interrupted meter here, keeping the regularity dormant. His calculation is no less cunning than that of Ezra Pound when he introduced the long spaces into early printings of "In a Station of the Metro." Free verse is often a way of troubling the reader's hearing, of refusing uniformity in favor of unpredictable rhythmic variety—jazz, in other words.

SPRING AND ALL

"The Red Wheelbarrow," so famous in isolation, was not intended for isolation. It first appeared in the long sequence *Spring and All* (1923), where Williams tried to give his work aesthetic ground by interspersing untitled poems with off-the-cuff critical musing. Williams felt indignant, as he remembers in *Autobiography*, that Pound and Eliot had crippled American poetry:

> Out of the blue *The Dial* brought out *The Waste Land* and all our hilarity ended. It wiped out our world as if an atom bomb had been dropped upon it and our brave sallies into the unknown were turned to dust. . . . I felt at once that it had set me back twenty years. . . . Critically Eliot returned us to the classroom just at the moment when I felt that we were on the point of an escape.[127]

Williams was a raggedy thinker, and through *Spring and All* the aesthetics have been scattered according to some shotgun technique. After a preamble, the reader is confronted by Chapter 19, then Chapter XIII (its title printed upside down), Chapter VI, Chapter 2, Chapter XIX, sections III, Chapter I, then sections III–XXVII, with section VII missing or unnumbered. ("Chapter headings are printed upside down on purpose," he recalled in *I Wanted to Write a Poem* [1958], "the chapters are numbered all out of order, sometimes with a Roman numeral, sometimes with an Arabic, anything that came in handy.")[128] The book is a fossil of the avant-garde sensibility of the flapper era. Shock repeated wears into tedium, yet this hurrah's nest, stuffed with rubbish like "Wrigley's, appendecitis [*sic*], John Marin: / skyscraper soup— // Either that or a bullet!,"[129] contains three of Williams's most extraordinary early lyrics: "By the road to the contagious hospital," "The pure products of America go crazy," and "so much depends."[130]

Biographia Literaria might have been such an *omnium gatherum* of critical whimsies had Coleridge possessed no plan and suffered a course of opium emetics. Williams gives a Cook's tour through the muddle of his imagination, often not bothering to finish his sentences ("It is the imagination that—").[131] "The prose is a mixture of philosophy and nonsense," he later admitted.[132] The remarks trailing "The Red Wheelbarrow," which must be considered linked to it, try to parse the difference between prose and poetry:

Poetry has to do with the crystallization of the imagination—the perfection of new forms as additions to nature—Prose may follow to enlighten but poetry—

"There is no confusion," he ends these thoughts, "only difficulties."[133] What such reflections omit is the extraordinary way Williams sculpts the threadbare sentence into a sharp-witted poem. Compare the bathos of the previous poem in the sequence, also in couplets:

one day in Paradise
a Gipsy

smiled
to see the blandness

of the leaves—
so many

so lascivious
and still.[134]

It took another decade, until "This Is Just to Say" ended "so sweet / and so cold," for Williams to give warmth to such blowsy rhetoric.[135] On the rare occasions when he came close to reproducing the form of "The Red Wheelbarrow," in poems like "To a Mexican Pig-Bank," "Between Walls," and two or three others, the writing collapsed into slack lines and high-school banality.[136]

Does *Spring and All* mean "Spring and the Universal All," "Spring and Everything That Follows," "Spring Miscellany," or, say, "Spring and All That Nonsense"? Only the last would pay real homage to the American demotic. ("I write in the American idiom," Williams once remarked—or boasted.)[137] The title goes at least this far: spring is present in fructifying possibility, with hints of resurrection and the defeat of death. "The Red Wheelbarrow" would be very different had the sequence been titled *Winter and All*. The scene would have become an abandoned barrow, chill rains, chickens soon to meet their fate, a world of dreariness and decay. Symbols are weathervanes—they point where the wind blows. Laid back into the sequence in which it appeared, the poem looks more didactic, achieving its depths through surface comprehensions.

THE RIFLING OF SOURCES

Williams's imagination was so permeable to the influences of the period, it's impossible to trace the exact sources that formed the peculiar provenance and complex of properties, the sealing of affectations, that formed "The Red Wheelbarrow." A poem is often the sole record of the particular incident or private meditation that moved the poet to speech; the relation between figure and ground is necessarily complex. Teasing out the strands of invention that have implication for the words on the page cannot provide the critic with an easy answer, only a more difficult set of questions.

As with all discussions of influence, the critic investigates long after the crime has been committed; without the poet's sworn testimony (leaving, like all testimony, ample room for forgetfulness, wishful thinking, and the plain fib), these can be only hints and misses. A poet can bear witness to his intentions, so far as he recalls them, but not to those meanings that struggle or bully in unawares. The roll call of influence here is long, or longish, but the core would include:

The Ezra Pound of "In a Station of the Metro" and *Cathay* (1915) (all the matter and canter of Imagism)—Pound's attempt to purge poetry of Georgian lacemaking and gingerbread, focusing the line through the indelible image in the belief that, if exact enough, if hemmed in with enough implication, plainspoken American would possess the brute vigor of Elizabethan English.

Classical Chinese and Japanese poetry, largely through translations by Arthur Waley and Pound, as well as the latter's imitations.[138] The influence is already apparent in some short poems in Williams's *Sour Grapes* (1921): "The Soughing Wind," "Spring," "Lines," "Memory of April," "Epitaph."[139]

The avant-garde artists of the day (particularly Duchamp and Williams's favorite painter, Juan Gris).[140] Most influential were their attempts to make everyday objects into art, and their desire to distort or disrupt the tired mechanics of seeing. Not to be ignored are phenomenology, already influential before World War I, and the photographic movement toward seeing the immediate without ignoring that it *is* being seen, from which came Alfred Stieglitz.

The longing for a true American poetry, which can be traced back to Emerson's essay "The Poet" ("We have yet had no genius in America, with tyrannous eye, which knew the value of our incomparable materials. . . . Our logrolling, our stumps and their politics, our fisheries, our Negroes, and Indians, our boa[s]ts, and our repudiations . . . are yet unsung").[141] Eliot and Pound were apostates here. Williams was willing to use Pound's methods against him.

Williams was an amateur painter, in his twenties immersing himself in the New York art scene.[142] His closeness to gadabout avant-gardists like Duchamp and Charles Demuth (*Spring and All* was dedicated to the latter) was crucial to his poetic identity. Influence traveled both ways—Demuth's painting *I Saw the Figure 5 in Gold* (1928), now considered a precursor of Pop Art, was a lively response to Williams's poem "The Great Figure."[143] The critic can make too much of such accidents of friendship, but there's a sense in which "The Red Wheelbarrow"—through the medium learned in Pound's Imagist poems (Williams had known Pound since 1902)—attempted something painterly. The window frame and the brightly separated objects might be enough, or nearly enough, to secure the case, at least in the case of an amateur painter.

Williams recorded in *Autobiography* his startled reaction to the Armory Show of 1913:

I went to it and gaped along with the rest at a "picture" in which an electric bulb kept going on and off; at Duchamp's sculpture (by "Mott and Co."), a magnificent cast-iron urinal, glistening of its white enamel. . . . The "Nude Descending a Staircase" is too hackneyed for me to remember anything clearly about it now. But I do remember how I laughed out loud when first I saw it, happily, with relief.[144]

Alas, memory played him false. He never attended the show.[145] (Nor did the show include Duchamp's urinal, conceived four years later only to be rejected by the Independents' Exhibition.) Perhaps the poet so wanted to claim its influence that he came to believe he'd been present.[146] More likely, decades after, he conflated the show with seeing the urinal in Duchamp's studio, or in the Alfred Stieglitz photo—that would be a mistake delightful to Dada (as perhaps would Williams's persistent misspelling "Du Champs" in the prologue to *Kora in Hell* [1920]).[147] It would be tempting to detect in the faulty memory of that "glistening," that almost watery glazed porcelain surface, the glazing rain of "The Red Wheelbarrow."[148]

In *Autobiography*, Williams says of his encounters with other artists of the period:

> It seemed daring to omit capitals at the head of each poetic line. Rhyme went by the board. We were, in short, "rebels," and were so treated. . . . Whether the Armory Show in painting did it or whether that also was no more than a facet—the poetic line, the way the image was to lie on the page was our immediate concern. For myself all that implied, in the materials, respecting the place I knew best, was finding a local assertion—to my everlasting relief. I had never in my life before felt that way. I was tremendously stirred.[149]

So, Rutherford. So, wheelbarrows. Williams the small-town doctor made poetry of the local, and he was a man so local he died in the town where he was born.

He found the contretemps over *Fountain* amusing. Late in 1917, he wrote that the *Blind Man*, the magazine where Duchamp defended the piece (and which contained Stieglitz's photograph), "likes to reach out of the cabinet and grab whatever it touches and to imagine it has hit upon a new thing."[150] Duchamp's own remarks seem telling. Writing anonymously there, he argued that R. Mutt (Duchamp's brief nom d'artiste) "took an ordinary article of life, placed it so that its useful significance disappeared under the new title and point of view—created a new thought for that object."[151] In no shallow or incomplete sense, the red wheelbar-row is Williams's reply to Duchamp's urinal.

Emerson's dicta were the source of divergent impulses. Whitman hauled poetry into the American tongue, opening the verse line to the hard-worn and resistant slang of American speech, but not inoculating the poem against those foreign words he loved, the bizarrerie of lan-guage that left his poetry a gallimaufry of competing and clashing tones. Like the country itself, Whitman welcomed immigrants. His peacock display was very different from Williams's self-imposed auster-ity, the paring away of the foreign influence and classical learning that afflicted Pound and Eliot (*Spring and All* was published the year after *The Waste Land*). The classical and arch European focus of so much of their poetry gave Williams his chance, while driving him toward a plain, denuded version of the demotic—compare his poems to *Huckleberry Finn* or *The Red Badge of Courage*, much less *Leaves of Grass* or the sailor talk in *Moby-Dick*, to have a sense of what greater things the American vernacu-lar could do, if asked.

This is an old battle in poetry, one whose tensions draw poetry back toward the colloquial whenever it strays too far. Shakespeare knew the allure of songs Bottom could grasp, as well as the power of rhetoric whose lushness Bottom could feel, even if he could not appreciate its refinements. The songs of Burns and Blake, the dark roil of the border ballads, all have their place—in this skirmish at least, poetry is not either/or.

Take these influences individually or in company, boil them down to the haunting image, to speech so barn-door plain it could be read by chickens, to stiff-necked chauvinism (not far removed from that of nativ-ists in the decades before the Civil War—there was another burst of nativ-ism in the 1920s), to things that provoked American sentiment (no doubt some critic has suggested red wheelbarrow, white chickens, blue—well, gray-blue—sky), and you have the approximate conditions from which "The Red Wheelbarrow" arose, as well as the form in which ambi-tion was cast. There, at least, Williams succeeded, if we accept the terms of that ambition.

The present tense can never be true. There's always a gap between the seen and the written. This is not a scene confronted, but a scene perhaps almost immediately reframed. The stark bucolic objects of the poem have their American charm, which could be read as cloying kitsch, partly because Williams fended off context. The complex provocations that led to that backyard have been suppressed, the moment stripped to still life, mediated by the contemplation buried in "so much depends . . ." Here is the root of Williams's most famous aesthetic statement, "No ideas but in things" (*Paterson: Book I*).[152]

In a poem, motive and surroundings are almost always absent—we can investigate and perhaps inhabit them, but we must rely on intuition and inference when outside sources remain unavailable. Williams's statements are extrapoetical and can be shrugged off, but the critic must judge whether such sources force us deeper into the mystery of the poem. Would we refuse to credit Shakespeare's sworn assurance, were he available for interrogation, that he wrote "this too too sullied flesh" or "a' babbled of green fields"? Could we ignore, should he recall it, his source for the seacoast of Bohemia?[153] Though such questions sidle beyond the imprint on the page, they aren't impertinent. If we would reject such evidence, we must spurn Williams's recollections because they lie behind the plane of the poem and therefore have no more relevance than a triangle's understanding of a solid.

The poem risks parody in its simplicity, yet almost no reader has taken "so much depends" ironically—perhaps because elsewhere Williams relates his most trifling experience so earnestly. (Sentiment in poetry, especially the sentiment of vision, sells at a price higher than cynicism.) Still, there are whispers of sarcasm in Williams. Referring to "The Great Figure," he once reproached a friend, "You missed the irony of the word *great*, the contemptuous feeling I had at that time for all 'great' figures in public life compared with that figure 5 riding in state."[154] This is impossible to detect in the poem. Like many a work of art, "The Red Wheelbarrow" would benefit from the suspicion of acerbity, even if ruined by it. Only Williams's reminiscence prevents that suspicion.

Text is all, except when context is more than all. By providing little in the poem beyond a few painterly notes toward some scene never to be fully rendered—the way Edward Lear sketched his landscapes, scribbling the necessary colors on rocks and trees—Williams left a large blank where meaning should be. He may not have intended this, but action overwhelms intention. Here the poem's inadequacy becomes a kind of adequacy, because the reader abhors a vacuum.

The opening of the poem is a conspiratorial wink—Williams's humaneness, his love of the minutiae of existence, made him the warmest of the great moderns, if also the most mawkish and at times the most insubstantial. How chilly the others were—Eliot in his religious asperity (later a more essential part of his nature than the rollicking pub-scene in *The Waste Land*); Pound in his permanent tedious lecture (the pompousness of his "Ezuversity," as others called it, scarcely left room for self-mockery); Stevens in the abstractions that substituted for emotion (that was perhaps how he kept a slightly moony nature in check); and Moore in her bemusement, acting as if her path had been crossed by more pangolins than tender feelings. Even Frost, however human the poems, however deep his gaze when turned on his fellow men, had a curious, cruel reserve—the poems that lapse into codswallop and lard often hint at bitterness beneath.

We see in a poem only what we're permitted, or prepared, to see (poetry wears blinders beyond the margins of the page). There may be little gained by speculating about the invisible accoutrements of "The Red Wheelbarrow"—whether beyond sits rotting garage or whitewashed shed, or nothing but a chicken coop. Still, the history of a poem has its uses. Williams's memory could prevent various bad readings—some critics, for instance, have assumed that the poem takes place in a barnyard. John Hollander supposed that the "freshness of light after the rain . . . is this kind of light which the poem is *about*, although never mentioned directly."[155] The poem, however, never reveals what Williams made clear in *Fifty Poets*, that the rain was still falling (perhaps there was a hard sunshower with enough light for that glazing). It makes a difference whether we're observing a scene in the rain; in the broken light after rain; or at the moment after, when light falls like revelation. Chickens pecking about in falling rain might say something about endurance or survival. Williams is not responsible for readings that find only something straightforward and doltish—that, for example, water and wheelbarrows and chickens are, well, important (or that the stanzas look like miniature wheelbarrows). The poet is rather more metaphysical.

The point, if the point matters, is that this is not a true pastoral—it's a pastoral of the New Jersey suburbs. The urban bucolic's desire for something absent (when Horace was in Rome, he longed for the farm) here becomes an argument that revelation may descend upon a back street. The epiphany of Archimedes also occurred in an inconvenient place. To know such things, we have to go beyond the page.

MR. MARSHALL

Decades later, Williams supplied more information. "The Red Wheel-barrow," he recalled in *Holiday* magazine in November 1954,

> sprang from affection for an old Negro named Marshall. He had been a fisherman, caught porgies off Gloucester. He used to tell me how he had to work in the hold in freezing weather, standing ankle deep in cracked ice packing down the fish. He said he didn't feel cold. He never felt cold in his life until just recently. I liked that man, and his son Milton almost as much. In his back yard I saw the red wheelbar-row surrounded by the white chickens. I suppose my affection for the old man somehow got into the writing.[156]

The 1920 census for Rutherford records that Thaddeus Marshall and his son Milton D. lived at 11 Elm Street. (The census taker wrote Grove Street by mistake, as later and earlier censuses make clear. Elm was a block northwest.)[157] Thaddeus, a widower, then sixty-nine, owned the house. He had been born in South Carolina, his mother's home. His father was a Cuban who spoke Spanish. Milton at thirty was a railroad porter. A decade later he was listed as a Pullman porter—the Rutherford train sta-tion was only half-a-dozen blocks away.[158]

A black couple named Patrick and their daughter Cecil (possibly Cecile) rented part of the house from the Marshalls. The father was a tailor who owned his own shop. Though the neighborhood was predominantly white, black families lived next door at 9 Elm and up the street at no. 25. The Mt. Ararat Baptist Church, marked "Negro" on the 1917 Sanborn insurance map, was three houses up from the Marshalls.[159] Everyone in the black families could read and write. The only brick house on the block stood on the southwest side of Marshall's property, owned by a retired German whose daughter was a warper at a silk mill. Part of that house, which featured a large and fancy corbeled frieze-board, was rented

Thaddeus Marshall.
Source: Courtesy Teresa Marshall Hale.

1920 U.S. Census, Rutherford, N.J.

to a Polish-speaking Russian family—the father worked as a machine operator in a button factory. Occupations among the black families were various and more lowly: servant, laborer at a foundry, laundresses to a private family. The one anomaly is a boarder at no. 25 who was a stationary engineer at a tire factory. Unlike a locomotive engineer, a stationary engineer operated or tended large fixed machines—it was perhaps a job with a future. Henry Ford began as a stationary engineer at an Edison generating plant.

On Washington Avenue, which intersected Elm a block southwest, the census listed a long series of white neighbors, most born in New Jersey or New England, though a few were immigrants from Sweden,

Thaddeus Marshall's House, Rutherford, N.J.
Source: Courtesy Meadowlands Museum of Rutherford, N.J.

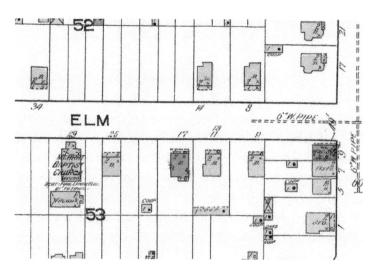

Sanborn Insurance Map of Rutherford, N.J., 1917.
Source: Courtesy of Princeton University Library.

Denmark, Holland, Hungary, and Ireland. (The great majority had immigrant parents.) Their occupations, like their houses, were a little fancier. There were a mason and a carpenter who worked as contractors, a restaurateur, a chauffeur for a private family, a statistician, a printing-house salesman, a civil engineer, a nurseryman, clerks for a coffee importer and a cold-storage company, two sales girls at a dry-goods store, and the owner of what was likely a small factory. A tailor's presser and a laborer at a tire factory, however, lived around the corner on Elm.

According to the 1880 census, though the identification is uncertain, a Thaddeus Marshall was a waiter in Atlantic City. This might have been before or after Marshall worked as a fisherman. By 1900 he had moved to Rutherford, where he had a wife and five children, and was employed as a store porter. His oldest son, also called Thaddeus, worked as an elevator boy in a hotel.[160]

Marshall's house stood at the less attractive end of the street. A couple of lots away, the block ended at Morse Avenue, from which one could pitch a stone onto the railroad tracks that ran south to Hoboken. Marshall's block, its lots then less than half filled in, was in no way poor—the two-story frame houses were small but not mean, though the Baptist church was not much larger than the houses. On the corner of Elm and Morse stood a substantial store of ornamental concrete-block, vacant in 1917 but a few years later occupied by an Italian bootblack. The wealthy, older part of town—Dr. Williams's neighborhood—lay in another direction.

The most striking feature of Marshall's home, filling the entire rear boundary of the property, was a massive chicken coop. Half the houses nearby, the Sanborn map shows, had coops in the backyard; but this was three times as large.[161] (The coop must have been a fairly recent addition. The 1909 Sanborn map shows only an outbuilding at the corner of the property.)[162] Marshall probably appears in an earlier poem, "St. Francis Einstein of the Daffodils":

there are both pinkflowered
and coralflowered peachtrees
in the bare chickenyard

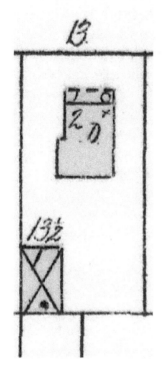

Sanborn Insurance Map of
Rutherford, N.J., 1909 (detail).
Source: Courtesy of
Princeton University Library.

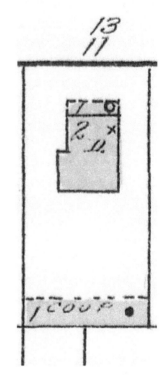

Sanborn Insurance Map of
Rutherford, N.J., 1917 (detail).
Source: Courtesy of
Princeton University Library.

of the old negro
with white hair who hides
poisoned fish-heads
here and there
where stray cats find them—
find them—find them.[163]

If this is the old fisherman, we have a sense of his practicality and cunning. The poison would have protected the chickens. In the 1910 census his occupation was listed as street huckster.[164]

Marshall must have had an egg business then, and he might have sold live or dressed chickens as well, including those whose laying was done.

If we trust the St. Francis poem, in season he could have peddled fruit from that small orchard. To such speculations (and they are no more than that) another might be added. A street huckster needs something to haul his wares. Flats of eggs and a cage of chickens would have been too unwieldy without something like a wheelbarrow to carry them.[165] Nearby Elizabeth, like other New Jersey cities, had ordinances licensing "every cart, wagon, dray, wheelbarrow or any vehicle used for the purpose of hawking, huckstering, peddling or vending vegetables, fruits, berries, fish, oysters, general produce, wood, coal, ice, or any wares or merchandise."[166] The huckster could not sell on street corners or before shops offering the same products, but the ordinance did not apply "to farmers or gardeners selling the produce of their farms or gardens."[167] If he sold, Marshall apparently escaped official notice, as Rutherford's similar ordinance declared that no hawker or peddler "shall be required to take out a license . . . to sell produce of his farm."[168] If he sold, he most likely sold door to door.

Marshall's house still stands, much altered, but not the chicken coop. Williams lived at 9 Ridge Road, some nine or ten blocks to the south. Why the doctor felt as he did about the scene must forever remain obscure. We don't know if one of the Marshalls was his patient. (Williams might have gone that day for fresh eggs, or to treat the twelve-year-old daughter of the Patrick family, or merely because he liked the company.) We don't know if something occurred that in memory gave this vision the same varnishing glaze as the rain. Did Williams see its importance in some blinding flash, like Saul on the road to Damascus, or was the meaning more gradually revealed? ("The sight impressed me somehow" soft-pedals the moment, but "about the most

1910 U.S. Census, Rutherford, N.J.

important, the most integral that it had ever been my pleasure to gaze upon" suggests something ravishing and even terrifying.) Hacking at words—he said he wrote the poem at speed—did he scribble lines about chickens and a wheelbarrow, then realize that the scene would cut deeper left alone? Brevity is the claim to implication. He was known to write poems on prescription blanks.[169]

We have to deal with the made object; the making is too often a side-show, false to what has its own perfection, by whatever crooked path achieved. A poet is surprised when a few trivial, unconsidered lines that took no time to write come to define him. It's the critic's job of work to show why this is so—why the simple lives in complexity, why beneath the surface of the words lies matter perhaps only briefly considered, if considered at all. Richard Eberhart often complained that he didn't know why "The Groundhog" had been anthologized so often, when a poem written the same day had never been anthologized at all. In a different aesthetic world, one that loathed wheelbarrows, Williams's poem about the gypsy, Paradise, and the bland leaves might have been the one memorized and set to music.[170] Or used in Paris to name an English-language bookstore.

"The Red Wheelbarrow" implies that being initiated into the vision will allow us to understand—that's the logic of the phrasing. Abandoned in the physical realm, we seek meaning elsewhere. For all his interest in art, Williams dresses his objects in the equivalent of house paint—not scarlet or vermilion, cream or eggshell, but barber-pole red and white. That kind of happenstance seems calculated. Nothing in the objects makes them worthy of attention but the cruel fact of their plainness. Another poem in *Spring and All* makes similar claims. Seeing an old man, a laughing woman, and a boy staring at the man's watch chain—all this observed from a car—the poet remarks, "The supreme importance / of this nameless spectacle // sped me by them / without a word."[171] At such overwritten moments, all Williams's successes seem mistakes.

"The Red Wheelbarrow" reveals a silent affinity to Van Gogh's paintings of old shoes. (Williams's biographer Reed Whittemore noticed this.)[172] The epiphany encompasses, not just the majesty of trivial things, but the life those things drag behind. To call the wheelbarrow and chickens the trappings of honest work injects more political philosophy than the poem can bear. It's unlikely that the ghost of Marx hovers in the background (Williams, though a leftist, was fiercely anti-Marxist); but a previous poem in the sequence mentions Tolstoy, whose embrace of peasant life fits the vision here.[173]

Even torn from its place, removed to the rugged exigencies of art, the wheelbarrow retains the trace of labor, that honest toil so easy to romanticize if you never get your hands dirty. The number of American farms and farmers increased decade by decade until 1935, but the percentage of farmers among American workers began to decline not long after the Revolution, falling in little more than a century from over 80 percent in 1810 to barely 20 percent in 1940.[174] The humdrum objects represent a world of pastoral labor pushed further and further from town life but still present on this back street, where an old man perhaps earned a living selling eggs. That the reader cannot know this, can discover it only by reading the margins, makes the vision more compelling. Without these historical particulars, these secrets art ignores, it's hard to believe that the objects—and therefore the poem—could have meant so much to the poet. In this the poem still gratifies the protocols of Dada—think of Duchamp's "so that [the object's] useful significance disappeared."

Marshall listed no occupation in 1920, so perhaps by then he had given up the business (he could still have sold to the neighborhood). The barrow might have stood for a way of life recently vanished. Williams long felt underrated as a poet. This goes too far, but the wheelbarrow could be taken as a symbol of an occupation grasped; even if eventually abandoned, it got a man through life. Whether that would be doctoring or poetry, only the doctor would know.

The memorable part of the poem is the utter humility, even barrenness, of what follows the teasing words of the opening. Those three words remain an enigma; the contrast between metaphysical confidence and the pastoral particulars offers a key. Critics armed with the tools of New Criticism have knocked at the soundness of line lengths, counted syllables on fingers and toes, examined as if with a microscope the curious enjambment of "wheel / barrow" and "rain / water." The Byzantine nature of the critical enterprise looks a little ridiculous compared to the poem's homely objects and pedestrian drabness. (Williams might not have been displeased by the spectacle of critics lost in labyrinths of their own making.) The provocations lie in the absence of meaning—a conscious artlessness, a faux naïveté, as artful as art. The poet is reading something into the scene he can't quite say, can grasp only through the epiphany that for the reader forms, not an explanation, but a symbolic action.

The philosophy of the red wheelbarrow is invisible. Complex philosophy is rarely stripped to such bareness (like the Elgin marbles, summoning new aesthetics when the lurid coats of paint were removed). The electric charge of Duchamp's *Fountain* is present only if we remember that the work of art is also a urinal (phase-switching again, or Schrödinger's cat). The wheelbarrow is no different—the utilitarian object has been turned into art, but it must remain that workman's object if we're to recover the shock. The argument, if there is one, is that the omphalos at the center of the world is just an ordinary red wheelbarrow. It is wrapped in another argument, that unpoetic language is the proper medium of American verse.

CODA

Two related paintings, usually similar in size, are called pendants—portraits of man and wife, views of a single landscape, two interpretations of a classical motif. Such paintings say more together than they do apart. (The first use, according to the *OED*, was for a pair of ribbons—and some dangling objects, like pendant earrings, continue to come in pairs.) Hung in the adjacent alcoves, such works supported what was once called a chimneypiece, a picture above the fireplace—or were paired either side of a larger painting on a wall. The latter arrangement is still found in museums.

"The Red Wheelbarrow" and "In a Station of the Metro" are in some ways pendants—as well as poems violently antithetical by two opposed temperaments. The differences of these poems possess a power beyond affinity: New Jersey versus Paris, life versus death, New World disorder versus Old World order, town versus city, animal versus human, outside versus inside, ground versus underground, the commonplace world versus the classical vision, one poem almost without history and the

other drenched in it. Even Williams's lack of punctuation lies opposed
to Pound's fussy semicolons and colons—his contrived diction and syntax criticizing Williams's (as Marianne Moore put it) "plain American
which cats and dogs can read."[175] Yet epiphanies come as they will, and
Williams's point could not have been made had the vision been the least
unusual.

Originally embedded in a sequence, each poem escaped sequence.
Pound and Williams wrote these Imagist poems largely in the same style,
yet with different manners and to different ends. The controlled image
in each is juxtaposed haiku-style with a second; yet Pound's poem presents the images in a tension that must be negotiated, while Williams
offers clichés of the barnyard—here merely a small-town backyard where,
as once was common, chickens were kept. There's a critical difference in
what these poets desired from image. Pound asked for depths to be
sounded, Williams only that a nerve (sometimes a very small nerve) be
struck.

We learn a lot about the taste of the age from the poems that become
food for anthologies. Consider that peculiar volume of 1933, quoted earlier: *Fifty Poets: An American Auto-Anthology*. The editor asked the "best
fifty poets in America"[176] to choose "one of their shorter poems by which
they would like to be remembered." A few poets, including Eliot, politely
declined. (Benét "deeply relished," he said, "Portrait of a Lady" and "Bur-
bank with a Baedeker, Bleistein with a Cigar.")[177] Pound, approached by
letter and cable, to his credit replied in vituperative fashion, claiming the
anthology would "aid in further muddling the critical sense (if any) of
the pore bloody ole public." The anthologist was forbearing, to *his* credit,
and recommended Pound's poems despite being told that he was "pre-
serving mildew" and "falsifying critical standards."[178]

Pound was not wrong about the mildew. Apart from the other great
moderns, all present—and a few poets who, though rarely read, still
deserve reading (Robinson, Masters)—the table of contents is a dire
reminder of what American poetry looked like in the 1930s. If readers
took seriously William Ellery Leonard, Lizette Woodworth Reese, Anna
Hempstead Branch, Grace Hazard Conkling, Charles Erskine Scott
Wood, and many another, the worse for readers. The editor did not fail
to place himself among the "best fifty." I doubt a similar anthology

published today would look any better come the next century. Frost offered "Birches"; Stevens, "The Emperor of Ice-Cream"; and Moore, with characteristic quirkiness, "A Grave" (another poet had suggested it). Frost and Stevens in their late fifties knew enough to judge as well as any future anthologist.

Williams chose "The Red Wheelbarrow," which represents his occasional grace and innumerable vices. You could begin a lot of perfectly trivial poems, I once proposed, with "So much depends" or "This Is Just to Say," and make something almost meaningful. Williams's problems came when he pressed too hard for meaning, not too little. ("This Is Just to Say" may be the most passive-aggressive poem in English, yet few poems have portrayed so nakedly the quiet battle between husband and wife.)[179]

Pound's poem asks to be read historically, in part because the time and place have import—the specific circumstance and disposition of the Métro affect the reading. We have to know what the Métro smelled and sounded like, what the atmosphere of the stations was, in order to understand how much of the image is mired in history and how much in Poundian fancy—Pound was the sort of poet to have a vision of ghosts because he'd read both the *Aeneid* and the *Odyssey* (the latter only in Latin). Williams's pastoral image, however, would have been ripe for Norman Rockwell Americana any date after the landing of the Pilgrims. Chickens were probably among the passengers on the Mayflower.

Both "In a Station" and "The Red Wheelbarrow" live in the slipstream of Cubism and Dada; but Pound comes to such art on equal terms (one can imagine his poem hanging next to "Nude Descending a Staircase"), while "The Red Wheelbarrow" refuses the call of "art." It's like a caption to a lithograph advertising chicken feed or an amateur daub of a barnyard, though it's not a barnyard. Yet Williams's poem could be placed next to a black-and-white photograph and offer something to the exchange, while next to a photograph Pound's world might seem over-imagined. That tells us something about the difference between arts, and something more about poems. Williams is informed by the art of seeing, however casual; Pound by history, however immaterial. Or the ghosts of history.

The attraction of these poems lies partly in their extreme brevity (both poets were later given to modernist length, Williams trying to outdo Pound; Pound, Dante), partly in the difference of composition—Pound patiently, painfully, paring away before the sudden insight (fixing the image like a photograph, with salts); Williams dashing the poem off in careless abandon. Their methods cast a raking light across the imaginative act. And perhaps each poem is really about rain.

8. Dickinson's Nerves, Frost's Woods

EMILY DICKINSON,
"AFTER GREAT PAIN, A FORMAL FEELING COMES"

After great pain, a formal feeling comes—
The Nerves sit ceremonious, like Tombs—
The stiff Heart questions 'was it He, that bore,'
And 'Yesterday, or Centuries before'?

The Feet, mechanical, go round—
A Wooden way
Of Ground, or Air, or Ought—
Regardless grown,
A Quartz contentment, like a stone—

This is the Hour of Lead—
Remembered, if outlived,
As Freezing persons, recollect the Snow—
First—Chill—then Stupor—then the letting go—[1]

STANZA I

"Not born" yourself, "to die," you must reverse us all.
—to Samuel Bowles, about 1875

Not surprisingly for a poet in love with reversals, Dickinson began with syntax head over heels. To launch so rhetorically confesses that the lines were scribbled after deliberation—and calculation. Since the Romantics, many poems sound as if the poet had written in the heat of passion—emotion not recollected in tranquility, as Wordsworth had it, but before the tears had stopped. That is a lie agreed upon.

English often gains traction by inverting normal word order. Other languages have different rules of engagement—the German verb, that bane of simultaneous translators, often straggles along at the tail of the sentence; and it's not out of order for the *Aeneid* to begin, "Arma virumque cano." Inversion in English is the rhetorical signal that rhetoric is present, so a certain formality noses in even before "formal" has been whispered. Inversion of syntax does not reveal, as some critics have it, an inversion of theme, feeling, or argument. That's not the way writers usually think.

The task of the poet is, not to succumb to rhetoric, but to take advantage of it. Even a good poet might not have been aware of an opportunity beforehand—or troubled to analyze the profit, knowing subconsciously the choice was right. Milton recognized the power of delay when he began *Paradise Lost*, "Of man's first disobedience, and the fruit," an extended prepositional phrase that prevented him from getting round to subject and verb until the sixth line. (Call it acting out the speech act, or purpose by design—drama delayed is the promise of style.) Dickinson began over one hundred and fifty poems with prepositions, as many as begin with "I."

Her inversion resolves a problem in syntax: "A formal feeling comes after great pain" would have destroyed the pentameter line, as well as any resistant energy the line might have had. When poets compose in brief forms, rhythm is ever-present (Dickinson's iambics vary here from trimeter to pentameter). Had the phrase "a formal feeling comes" occurred to her first, she'd have realized without thinking that "after great pain" could not follow. The inversion makes peace with the meter and restores chronology—it's appropriate that the poem start with pain.

Though minute investigation of the dramaturgy of meter is better kept to a minimum, it would be hard not to notice the pitch forward of the inverted first foot, the monumental stolidity of the spondee "great pain" that follows, and the tripping light-footedness of "a formal feeling comes." Whatever music meter grants is underscored here by alliteration, the more emphatic the shorter and closer the words. The device's musical qualities depend on other factors and may require more distance. A sensitive ear should detect the falling quality of fore-stressed words like "formal" and "feeling," casting the line downward in contrast to the rising iambics, as if formal feeling were decrescendo after pain. To work line by line toward the choreography of emphasis and velocity would stress too minutely what is better experienced, like a fireside tale—or a joke. The affect of meter always triumphs over intention. Still, there are moments when analysis proves by no means negligible.

Taxed with grave thoughts, Dickinson might have recalled the passage from the opening of *The Winter's Tale*, another fiction touched by cold: "the reverence / Of the grave wearers. O, the sacrifice! / How ceremonious, solemn, and unearthly."[2] "Ceremonious" is sometimes used disparagingly for outward form rather than inward feeling. The rituals of etiquette after a death inform grief while assuaging it; indeed, ritual is the formal repetition that consecrates marriage, baptism, *rites de passage*, coronation, and the sanctification of the dead. Here, though, emotion seems unassuaged, though the stages of freezing to death are also treated as invariant rite—chill, stupor, submission. The speaker doesn't know if the Hour of Lead can *be* outlived, and in the ritual of poetic form creates a symbolic death.

This social, stoical metaphor counterfeits the century's obsequies of mourning. When the grieving gathered at the house of the dead, the corpse was laid out in the parlor, while mourners kept nightlong vigil nearby. The custom was recorded in *Huckleberry Finn* (1884):

> I peeped through a crack of the dining-room door, and see the men that was watching the corpse all sound asleep on their chairs. The door was open into the parlor, where the corpse was laying, and there was a candle in both rooms.[3]

And in this New York recollection of about 1830: "The hall and rooms being filled, I stood upon the piazza, which opened by a large raised window into the parlor where the corpse lay in a coffin, clad in graveclothes."[4] (The older tradition of mourners surrounding the deathbed was fading out by the mid–nineteenth century.)

The dead whom Dickinson had known were buried or entombed. Banned by the Catholic Church until 1963, banned still by the Eastern

Orthodox Church, cremation was long considered pagan and sacrilegious. A grave is a metaphorical tomb—aboveground tombs were usually reserved for the rich, who could afford to build them. Though Dickinson's tombs are abstractions, the world of her nouns is largely abstract, like that of Shakespeare's sonnets. Still, she knew more of tombs than the tombs in books. In a letter of 1855, while visiting her father in Washington, her farthest trip from home, she wrote to friends, "Hand in hand we stole along up a tangled pathway till we reached the tomb of General George Washington."[5] The overgrown path may have led to the Old Tomb, a simple crypt faced with plain brick. The bodies of the general and his wife had been moved two decades before, however, to the much grander New Tomb, for which he had left a bequest. This mausoleum stands across from a pair of stone obelisks, as if he were a pharaoh.

Dickinson would probably have seen the Amherst town tomb in West Cemetery. Built a few years before the poem was written, it stored bodies democratically through a hard New England winter, when frozen ground could not be broken. The low, gloomy granite-fronted vault, covered in sod, lay not far from her house, the only tomb in the graveyard where the poet, her sister, and her parents were later buried. (Her white coffin was carried, at her request, out the back door of her home and across the fields.)[6] Dickinson's poems live in abstraction, but abstractions may be fleshed.

The trappings of the poem recur in lines probably written a year later,

No Bald Death—affront their Parlors—
No Bold Sickness come
To deface their stately Treasures—
Anguish—and the Tomb.[7]

The "Sweet—safe—Houses— / Glad—gay—Houses—" that open the poem are caskets—caskets "Sealed so stately tight— / Lids of Steel—on Lids of Marble," hiding lavish interiors, "Brooks of Plush—in Banks of Satin." The parlors are the parlors of the dead, where death can no longer visit. (For such houses of the dead, recall "Safe in their alabaster chambers," with its "Rafter of satin, and roof of stone.")[8]

In the opening stanzas of "After great pain," the speaker's body is dissected and personified, as if Heart and Nerves and Feet had become independent realms of the senses, no longer alive in coordinate passion. Many know the dissociation of grief—the poet must gather the limbs of Osiris, if they can be gathered at all. (The rendering of the terrible aftermath gives this poem the immediacy of experience, not innocence.) In this autopsy of numbness, the precise sense of "Nerves" is vague because the word was often an amalgam. The meaning draws partly from anatomy, partly from the medical condition ("disordered or heightened sensitivity; anxiety, fearfulness, tension, nervousness. . . . Freq. in *attack of nerves*," *OED*). The irony endured here is that the nerves have been anesthetized—what would normally carry feeling sit dead as a tomb. Embalmed in the formal hour, they no longer transmit sensation.

The idea of tombs—stolid, mute, imperious—sitting inside the house might be taken as graveyard wit, were the idea not so lurid and Gothic. (Dickens might have made high comedy of the simile.) The scattered nerves have become a crowd of mourners—such a scene could take place only before a funeral. Though the grieving might later return, they'd no longer be obliged to the solemn manners of ceremony.[9]

This strange vision might have been part of a formal elegy, had Dickinson not directed our attention elsewhere. She could have begun, "After great deaths," making the funeral arrangements tediously literal. The poem is not a portrait of the hours of mourning but an extended metaphor for the aftermath of an event only alluded to. It's less an allegory than a mimesis of suffering for the embattled Heart, Nerves, Feet (three cardinal virtues for knight or saint, perhaps). The tableau might be mistaken for the stage set of a morality play. Dickinson forces us to imagine what could have caused a pain so overwhelming that mourning the dead seems the only comparison. Tombs perhaps rose to her mind unbidden, a horror that could not be warded off, because what was dead was hope. And not just hope.

The poet had a particular dread of funerals, as she mentions in a late letter: "When a few years old—I was taken to a Funeral which I now know was of peculiar distress, and the Clergyman asked 'Is the Arm of the Lord shortened that it cannot save?' He italicized the 'cannot.' I mistook the accent for a doubt of Immortality and not daring to ask, it besets me still."[10]

A stiff heart, like the deadened nerves, has lost the living impulse. The *OED* reminds us that *stiff*, applied to the body, means "unable to move without pain." That's only a short distance from another sense, "rigid in death." Not long before the poem was written, the noun had passed into slang for a corpse.[11] Dickinson was an archeologist of the strata of meaning—the word here absorbs the lesser senses of unbending manners or style without grace. Why not a *heavy* heart, which would be unable to beat without pain, just alive enough to question? The poet has rescued the cliché by avoiding it, but the phrase goes back at least as far as *Venus and Adonis* ("Heavy heart's lead, melt at mine eyes' red fire!").[12] The reader who heard the suppressed allusion, if it was an allusion, would understand both the condition—Venus longs for death—and Dickinson's skillful withholding of "lead" until near the end of the poem. The poet was member of a Shakespeare Club at a time when Shakespeare unexpurgated was considered too indecent for women or children.[13]

What is the heart's question, however? The usual notion, found in the nuanced reading eighty years ago by Cleanth Brooks and Robert Penn Warren in *Understanding Poetry* (1938),[14] is that He must be Christ, that the Heart in pain cannot remember who bore the cross, or when. Yet the revelation must be, not merely that the Heart is bewildered, but that the pain is unbearable. The shock lies in implied recognition, as if the speaker had said, "The pain happened yesterday, but it feels as if I've suffered for centuries."

The interpretation aligns with the standard Christian piety of capitalization; but the ambiguity of syntax festers a bit, since the antecedent of "He" would be absent. In her letters, Dickinson doesn't capitalize personal pronouns referring to Christ, though in poems she inserts the capital about half the time. Where she personifies "Heart," however, the pronoun is never capitalized. If her capitals were not accidental, merely inconsistent, the reading must be Christian.

Critics have long been hobbled by the failure of early editors, including Thomas H. Johnson in his variorum edition (1955), or in the reading edition that followed (1960), to include the single quotation marks

Dickinson used to set off these questions.[15] Though she was perfectly capable of mislaying quotation marks, she didn't throw them in unwittingly. The direct quotations might have been rendered more clearly,

> The stiff Heart questions, 'Was it He that bore?'
> And 'Yesterday, or Centuries before?'

Like most of her editors, I have kept her single quotations marks. Had the Heart questioned the duration of its *own* sorrow, the psychology might have been more intense; but then the Heart should have asked, "Was it I that bore?" (R. W. Franklin restored the quotation marks in his now standard edition of her poems [1998].) Still, some sort of amnesia follows the speaker's fracturing of identity. The measure of devastation, of grief-stricken distraction, is the Heart's failure to recollect when the major event in Christian faith occurred—or, if that goes too far, then the Heart's willingness in extraordinary grief, the loss still so fresh, to believe Christ might have died the day before. The loss has canceled the labor of time.

The speaker states, not "My pain is Christ's," but "I can think of no pain so severe except His on the cross" or "I feel as if I had been crucified myself." William Empson remarked in *Seven Types of Ambiguity* that he "usually said 'either . . . or' when meaning 'both . . . and.'"[16] There are limits, however, to the generosity of ambiguity.

For the zealous, pain is the most aggressive form of devotion. It wasn't blasphemous for the faithful to believe that in torment they were reliving Christ's pain—so martyrs consoled themselves. The Heart's assumption of Christ's agony is an extraordinary appropriation of Christian myth, especially if, like the speaker, the Heart is female. The speaker gains neither the saintliness of martyrdom nor the assurance of resurrection, only the record of an intensity of anguish beyond measure. It is the condition of great loss always to be immediate.

As so often in Dickinson, the slippery syntax, helter-skelter layering of image, and meanings barely whispered become a powerful method not of statement but, if there were such a word, of *suggestedness*. (There *is* such a word, coined by Jeremy Bentham and rarely heard since, except from the mouths of philosophers.) A particular word goes unmentioned here. As it made its way to English through French and Anglo-Norman, "Passion" referred to the sufferings of Christ upon the cross. The use in English for overpowering emotion, the *OED* reveals, came only late in the fourteenth century, and for love probably only with Spenser. The link is through suffering, not faith—but beneath the suffering, even when the word was only hinted at, ever after lay the veiled pun of romance. There's a rare romantic acuteness in borrowing the Crucifixion so baldly for the mortal pain of love.

Dickinson was suspicious of the organs of religion. She may have fled Mount Holyoke Female Seminary, where she lasted just a year, because her classmates were so given to proselytizing. (The school ranked the faith of students—Dickinson was among those classed as "impenitent," pigeonholed with the "No-hopers.")[17] Even at home she was surrounded by those far more pious. The Connecticut River Valley still bore the thunderous inheritance of Jonathan Edwards's preaching a century before. The poet would have witnessed the decline of the Second Great Awakening in the 1840s and remembered the shock, during the Great Revival of 1850, when many close to her, including her father and sister, had converted to evangelical Christianity. (Her mother had been saved shortly after Dickinson's birth.)[18] "I am standing alone in rebellion," she wrote.[19] Her brother, Austin, followed the others a few years after.[20] At school Dickinson could not accept Christ as her savior ("I regret that last term," she wrote from Holyoke, ". . . that I did not give up and become a Christian. It is not now too late, . . . but it is hard for me to give up the world").[21] By thirty she no longer went to church.

Even could the overwrought invocation of the Passion be ignored, the repetitions of pain and paralysis—the ceremonious nerves, the heart in rigor mortis, the mechanical feet, the quartz contentment, the hour of lead—overdo the theatrics to a considerable extent. In reverse angle, however, exaggeration to the point of melodrama expresses the extremity of the speaker's despair. (One can imagine how the matter would have been handled on the nineteenth-century stage, with weeping and gnashing of teeth.) Though couched in abstraction, the agony is not abstract. Dickinson has presented in four lines an autopsy of traumatic pain—the speaker has become one of the living dead. Such torment is death itself.

STANZA 2

The Feet, mechanical, go round—
A Wooden way
Of Ground, or Air, or Ought—
Regardless grown,
A Quartz contentment, like a stone—

Dickinson apparently suffered a crisis late in 1861, though with a woman so elusive critics might learn more by consulting the shapes of clouds. She was private even within her family. In her thirties she gradually withdrew from company, speaking to rare visitors from the top of the stairs or behind a half-closed door; yet once she'd been eager to join evening society next door at the Evergreens, home of her brother Austin and his wife, Sue, then Dickinson's closest friend. Stray reminiscences report the delight the poet gave, even in her own kitchen, reciting her poems in a matter-of-fact way.[22]

What loss could have been so traumatic it would feel like a death, the pain comparable only to Christ's martyrdom? In April 1862, Dickinson had begun to correspond with Thomas Wentworth Higginson, who had written a lead article in the *Atlantic Monthly* for young authors, "Letter to a Young Contributor."[23] (As the article was unsigned, it's unclear how she knew to write "T. W. Higginson. / Worcester. / Mass.") She asked, "Are you too deeply occupied to say if my Verse is alive?"[24] Years after her death, he recalled that her handwriting was "so peculiar that it seemed as if the writer might have taken her first lessons by studying the famous fossil bird-tracks in the museum of that college town."[25] She left the letter unsigned, concealing her name on a card slipped into a small envelope. Higginson added, "Even this name was written—as if the shy writer wished to recede as far as possible from view—in pencil, not in ink."[26]

Dickinson enclosed four poems. His reply was cautious. "It is probable that the adviser," he later wrote, "sought to gain time a little and find out with what strange creature he was dealing. I remember to have ventured . . . on some questions, part of which she evaded . . . with a naïve skill such as the most experienced and worldly coquette might envy."[27] She had answered, "You asked how old I was? I made no verse—but one or two—until this winter—Sir."[28] This went beyond shyness to the bald-faced lie. By her editor R. W. Franklin's estimate, she had already finished more than two hundred and fifty poems, having written seriously for four years.[29] It would be charitable to imagine that she didn't consider the earlier work poetry, but more likely she didn't want Higginson to know she was already past thirty—his article, after all, was for "young" contributors.

Dickinson needn't have gone further, but what she wrote next was odd:

> I had a terror—since September—I could tell to none—and so I sing,
> as the Boy does by the Burying Ground—because I am afraid—[30]

Higginson reflected, "The bee himself did not evade the schoolboy more than she evaded me."[31] What "terror" could have been the proximate cause of her poetry? A boy sings (or whistles) past a cemetery to give himself courage, to pretend he's fearless. (Dickinson's house, remember, lay not far from a burying ground—from an upper window she could see funeral processions enter the gate.)[32] That her mind leapt immediately to the graveyard suggests the near occasion of death—her own, someone else's, the death of something. There's no sign, however, that she had been mortally ill or that anyone close to her had died, apart from the first Amherst boys to fall in the Civil War.[33]

Perhaps she hoped that Higginson would believe her poems incited by some tragic event. Her letters are full of feints and sleights of hand. It's hard to believe that the "terror," whatever it was, could be the sole reason she was writing poetry, yet she had no reason to concoct some mortal panic. The closer to truth, the less prone she was to exaggeration:

> My Mother does not care for thought—and Father, too busy with his
> Briefs—to notice what we do—He buys me many Books—but begs
> me not to read them—because he fears they joggle the Mind.[34]

For a letter that ignores so much, the bantering surface and wincing coyness cannot hide the resentment, even rage, within.

> When a little Girl, I had a friend, who taught me Immortality—
> but venturing too near, himself—he never returned—Soon after,
> my Tutor, died—and for several years, my Lexicon—was my only
> companion.[35]

Recall her later testimony of unease at what she had taken as the clergyman's doubts about immortality.

Dickinson can't always have seen the ambiguities trembling beneath
ambivalence. The friend only *ventured* near—but near to immortality or
to Dickinson herself? If the latter, he rejected her. Immortality would be
one way to describe a love match—made in Heaven, we say. (She brooded
over immortality, Christian immortality, using the word in more than
forty poems.) Dickinson doesn't mean that after the Tutor's death she was
locked in a room with a dictionary, just that she was reduced to words
for company. She closed the letter, which had covered so much ground,
having cheerfully avoided the direct questions, "Is this—Sir—what you
asked me to tell you?"[36] Perhaps Higginson had asked how she came to
write poetry. Disingenuous might be the word.

It's unclear how fervent or abiding Emily's youthful dalliances were,
if there were dalliances at all. Her brother and sister both claimed she
was no stranger to romance.[37] Dickinson had the romantic spirit. A
valentine she wrote in 1850, when just nineteen, is flirtatious and
high-strung:

> Sir, I desire an interview; meet me at sunrise, or sunset, or the new
> moon—the place is immaterial. . . . And not to *see* merely, but a chat,
> sir, or a tete-a-tete, a confab, a mingling of opposite minds is what I
> propose to have. . . . We will be David and Jonathan, or Damon and
> Pythias, or what is better than either, the United States of America.[38]

This delightfully giddy manner goes on a long while. After the piece was
published in the Amherst College literary magazine, one of the editors
remarked, "I wish I knew who the author is. I think she must have some
spell, by which she quickens the imagination, and causes the high blood
'run frolic through the veins.'"[39] Her identity could not have been
much of a secret, as she'd let slip the name of her dog, Carlo, a black

Newfoundland who would have been well known to neighbors.[40] The favorite candidate for the recipient of this literary skirmish, the first of her publications, is an impoverished Amherst student named Gould.[41]

There were other possible suitors in her circle—a young man named Newton reading law in her father's office; an Amherst student named Emmons; and the brothers Howland, one a tutor and the other also reading law with her father—yet little sign, however deeply drawn these friendships, of what hopes she sustained.[42] Courtships of the period seem like signals between ships buried in fog. Newton is probably the tutor mentioned to Higginson. After his early death, she called him her "grave Preceptor" as well as an "elder brother."[43] Any romance is unlikely. Her next letter to Higginson, six weeks later, added, "My dying Tutor told me that he would like to live till I had been a poet, but Death was much of Mob as I could master—then."[44] This is a remark about the common life—the missing "as" and the word "mob" without article introduce more confusion than necessary. (This usage was falling out of fashion—Addison had spoken of a "cluster of mob," and Chesterfield said that "every numerous assembly is *mob*," *OED*.)

Dated probably to the fall of 1862, some months after she wrote Higginson, "After great pain" is one of a clutch of poems that seem—cryptically, elusively—to rake over the coals of an unhappy love affair. The feelings, the nerves, the stiff heart (all in the aftermath of a loss so enormous it seems like death) make it hard to imagine any loss with so great a torment—any loss but love. Speculation among biographers has been drawn almost entirely to two men, but her life is so occluded they are no more than ghosts of possibility.

Returning from the visit to her father in 1855, Dickinson had stopped for two weeks with family friends in Philadelphia.[45] It's imagined that one Sunday her hosts invited her to hear the charismatic minister Charles Wadsworth at the old Arch Street Presbyterian Church. There's no evidence they met; but Dickinson's later references to him and a single stiff-necked, undated letter to her—misspelling her last name and responding to what was apparently a request for counsel or consolation—imply that their letters were later destroyed. (After her death, her correspondence was burned, as she desired. This stray, which mentions an "affliction" and her "trial," as well as her "sorrow," may have escaped because unsigned.

Absence of evidence may be the evidence.)[46] Dickinson could be secretive about correspondence—she used two neighbors to forward some of her letters, and a New York couple, possibly, for letters to Wadsworth in the 1870s.[47] The latter story came from their granddaughter. Twenty years later, she insisted she "must have made it up."[48]

Wadsworth had been devilishly handsome when young, bushy browed though rapidly balding. Called a "new lion" by one of the New York papers, he was compared to Henry Beecher, the most celebrated preacher of the day.[49] Wadsworth's sermons, which read like the worst sort of Christian bombast now, became so wildly popular that a concealed trapdoor, cut through the floor behind the pulpit, let him enter the chancel like some ham actor.[50] We know almost nothing of his interest in Dickinson except through letters she wrote after his death to his friends the Clark brothers.[51] Though Beecher's numerous infidelities are an example of pastoral bad behavior, Wadsworth was happily married and lived hundreds of miles from Amherst. He was also sixteen years her elder. He visited Dickinson once in 1860 and again decades later, two years before his death in 1882.[52]

There's no reason to believe that Dickinson exaggerated when she claimed to have enjoyed an "intimacy of many years" with him. She called him her "Shepherd from 'Little Girl'hood" and "My Philadelphia." Indeed, he may have confided in her—she referred to him as a "Man of sorrow," a "Dusk Gem, born of troubled Waters," and said that he was "shivering as he spoke, 'My Life is full of dark secrets.'"[53] There is also the curious story, passed down by Martha Dickinson Bianchi, Emily's niece, that on that trip south Dickinson had "met the fate she had instinctively shunned," a love "instantaneous, overwhelming, impossible." After she "fled to her own home for refuge—as a wild thing running from whatever it may be that pursues," the man followed her to Amherst.[54]

Unfortunately, there's no record of such a visit. Parts of Bianchi's story align with what we know of Wadsworth—that, for example, he moved to the West Coast—but he did not abandon his profession, as she maintained; his departure did not occur a "short time" after meeting Dickinson; and she did not press a woman to name her son Charles. The tale may be family tattle, passed along in mutilated form. (The source was Bianchi's mother, Sue Dickinson.)[55] Still, there's a hint of something deeper in the poet's recollection of their final meeting. She was in the garden, she wrote, "with my Lilies and Heliotropes," when her sister announced a visitor, the "'Gentleman with the deep voice.'"

> "Where did you come from," I said, for he spoke like an Apparition.
> "I stepped from my Pulpit to the Train" was my [*sic*] simple reply, and when I asked "how long," "Twenty Years" said he with inscrutable roguery.[56]

Is this roguery the bantering of an old friend or a confession of regret?

The same month Dickinson wrote Colonel Higginson about her "terror," Wadsworth answered the call of a Presbyterian church in San Francisco and moved west with his family. If his looming departure caused her alarm, he must have written her the previous September. (Philadelphia papers reported his intention in January—he may have known earlier.)[57] That, at least, is the assumption.

There's a nearer recipient for her affections, Samuel Bowles, editor and owner of the *Springfield Republican*. Lively, opinionated, apparently inexhaustible, greedy for company, sometime after her brother's marriage he began regular visits to the Evergreens.[58] Eventually he published most of the very few poems Dickinson allowed into print.[59]

Bowles is a restless, attractive figure, part of a stratum of American nineteenth-century ambition—the go-ahead sort, eager for the fray, intimate with politics, a gregarious and magnetic striver who eventually worked himself to death. His marriage was bitterly unhappy. His wife suffered from various ailments, not all physical—jealous, oversensitive, a bit of a termagant, she made his life a misery.[60] That he found solace in spirited conversation with intelligent women no doubt made a wretched bond more wretched. He had many women friends, and there were rumors that a few were more than friends.[61]

Bowles became a mainstay of Evergreens society before Emily had begun her long withdrawal ("my crowd," she once called Susan and Austin).[62] He was only four years older, though frequently indisposed by his own list of complaints—headaches, insomnia, and sciatica among them.[63] In April 1862, as he prepared to sail to Europe for his health, the poet wrote an anxious letter pleading with him, on behalf of the

Dickinson coterie, to make a last visit (*"Please* do not take our *spring—away—*since you blot Summer—out! We cannot *count—*our tears—for this—because they drop so fast"). This he did.[64] The "terror" could have been his decision the previous September to take the voyage, presuming that she had heard of it.[65] When he returned in November 1862, she declared that she could not see him—she was ill, perhaps, or overwhelmed by the prospect. Or he had rejected her. Soon after his return, her private letters to him stopped for a dozen years.[66]

It was not a complete break or breach, though afterward he came more rarely to the Evergreens—the letter to Austin that heralds his withdrawal is tortured.[67] Some fifteen years later, the year before he died, Bowles arrived in Amherst, and Dickinson again refused to see him. He apparently called up the stairs, "Emily, you damned rascal! No more of this nonsense! I've traveled all the way from Springfield to see you. Come down at once." Her sister Lavinia said that she "never knew Emily to be more brilliant or more fascinating in conversation than she was that day." The anecdote emerged half a century afterward courtesy of a Dickinson cousin, who claimed that Bowles had begun, "Emily, you wretch!" Thomas H. Johnson, however, editor of her correspondence, justified the revision by noting that a letter Dickinson probably sent soon after is signed "Your 'Rascal,'" with a postscript: "I washed the Adjective."[68] Much of what we know about the poet comes filtered through the prejudice and fading memory of others; much of what we know from her is confused, ambiguous, perhaps equally unreliable.

Dickinson and Bowles found each other captivating, though he seems to have been equally taken, or perhaps a bit more, with her sister-in-law. (Town gossip was town gossip.) Over the years Dickinson sent him some fifty poems, most of which he apparently failed to understand; those he published were the most adapted to the taste of the day.[69] Her own taste in literature was conservative and often sentimental. She wrote Higginson, "You inquire my Books—For Poets—I have Keats—and Mr and Mrs Browning." That seems to have been as much Mr. as Mrs., though she apparently adored *Aurora Leigh* and had a taste for romantic drivel much worse. (It was Mrs. Bowles whom she pressed with a name for her son—but Robert, after Browning, not Charles.)[70] She hung a portrait of Mrs. Browning in her room. "You speak of Mr

Whitman—" Dickinson wrote as well, "I never read his Book—but was told that he was disgraceful."[71]

Any speculation about the poet's hidden romantic life, if there was such a thing, must inevitably be bound to three letters to the unknown man she addressed as Master, letters found only in draft, two of them much amended and revised. Dickinson apparently roughed out her letters before making fair copies, though few such drafts exist. No doubt most were lost in the holocaust.[72]

Though it's not clear that the Master Letters were ever sent, their tone is very like the provocations and insulations of her letters to Bowles. In one of their comic exchanges, he became Dick Swiveller from *The Old Curiosity Shop* and she the Marchioness.[73] It's worth remembering that the Marchioness was a lowly maidservant who in the end married Swiveller. Franklin, the scholar most schooled in her handwriting, dates the first letter to the spring of 1858, the others to the first half of 1861.[74] Though the gradual changes to certain letter forms in her hand may be almost as good as carbon dating, the science is not exact—and even carbon gives only a range.

Critics who thought Dickinson incapable of passion called the letters fantasies. Had they been mere caprices, there should have been clues elsewhere in her work—her imagination was disturbed, but not in quite that way. Reading her poems suggests that, like T. S. Eliot, beneath detachment lay the turmoil of a mind always under intense pressure of the real.

In the second Master Letter, for example, the abject abasement makes uncomfortable reading:

Oh' did I offend it—~~Did'nt it want me to tell it the truth~~ Daisy—
Daisy—offend it—who bends her smaller life to his <its'>, meeker
<lower> every day—who only asks—a task—~~who~~ something to do for
love of it—some little way she can not guess to make that master glad—
A love so big it scares her, rushing among her small heart—[75]

"Its'" was meant to substitute for "his"—Dickinson sometimes used her pronouns thus, as she does later in the sentence, as well as in a poem dispatched to Bowles and dated by her writing to "about early 1861," the possible date of this Master Letter. The poem was pinned around a pencil stub and seems to beg him for a word: "If it had no pencil, / Would it try mine— / Worn—now—and *dull*—sweet, / Writing much to thee."[76] (*Dull* is a pleasant bit of self-judgment.) The plea—comic, pathetic— hints that he had kept her waiting for a reply.

There is also the extraordinary poem, dated perhaps to the fall of 1862, that opens,

> If I may have it, when it's dead,
> I'll be contented—so—
> If just as soon as Breath is out
> It shall belong to me—
>
> Until they lock it in the Grave,
> 'Tis Bliss I cannot weigh—
> For tho' they lock Thee in the Grave,
> Myself—can own the key—
>
> Think of it Lover! I and Thee
> Permitted—face to face to be—
> After a Life—a Death—we'll say—
> For Death was That—
> And This—is Thee—[77]

The anguish, the separation from the lover in life, the fraught wish for love after death—it's hard not to place such a poem and others like it in the complex of attraction and rejection that forms the Master Letters.

Clues to the recipient are frustratingly ambiguous. In the third letter, however, Dickinson writes, "If I had the Beard on my cheek—<like you> . . . "[78] Wadsworth, at least in surviving photographs, had no beard. Bowles did.[79] There's another telling reference:

> The prank of the Heart at play on the Heart—in holy Holiday—is forbidden me—You make me say it over—I fear you laugh—when I do not see—but "Chillon" is not funny.[80]

This is not the only time she refers in her letters to the story of the prisoner of Chillon, which she probably knew from Byron's sonnet and verse tale, very loosely based on the imprisonment of the monk and Geneva patriot François Bonivard. In the tale, when the prisoner is at last released (Bonivard spent four years in a dungeon), he has become so accustomed to his chains, he declares, "It was at length the same to me, / Fetter'd or fetterless to be, / I learn'd to love despair."[81] To Bowles she wrote, in a damaged letter of early 1862, "My Love is my only apology. To the people of 'Chillon'—this—is enoug[h]."[82] Who are these "people"? Others who share her predicament, perhaps, of not wanting freedom from her chains.

Dickinson's memory of Byron is imperfect. If "people" meant a town, she has forgotten that Chillon was an island castle. Two years later, she wrote her sister, "You remember the Prisoner of Chillon did not know Liberty when it came, and asked to go back to Jail."[83] Byron's prisoner did not ask to return, but it's revealing that she recalled the ending that way. If the meaning is clear, that she was a prisoner of love (or had, like the prisoner, "learn'd to love despair"), her distorted memory is touching. Freed, she'd ask to be shackled again. It seems far likelier that Chillon represented that love whose imprisonment she longed not to leave rather than the incarceration suffered when later her eyes went bad; but metaphors, like letters of credit, may be negotiated over great distances.

There's also the mutilated evidence of that 1862 letter, torn along the edge with the loss of some writing. In both Master Letters that year, Dickinson repeatedly calls herself Daisy, a nickname chosen or given. The letter to Bowles is similarly apologetic, and there she also refers to herself as Daisy—perhaps. Unfortunately, the crucial word is now incomplete: "To Da[isy?] 'tis *daily*—to be gran[ted]." Richard Sewall, her best biographer, interprets it so (certainly she might have delighted in the grace note of wordplay in *Daisy/daily*).[84] The pencil poem she sent Bowles ended, "If it had no word— / Would it make the Daisy, / Most as big as I was— / When it plucked me?"[85] The meaning is almost impenetrable, even after substituting "he" for "it," as seems necessary in context. Perhaps, very roughly, if he doesn't write, would she wither like the plucked daisy? Or shrink back to what she was before she *was* Daisy? Or would he at least make her his boutonnière? Or. Or. (The sexual meaning of "plucked" presumably went unheard, as it had fallen out of use the previous century.)[86] The stub of a pencil might be considered a stalk plucked of its flower. The hints are teasing at best—but her intentions might not have been so hidden from him. She writes as if he would understand.

Much depends on the dating of the third Master Letter and the meaning of "Could you come to New England—this summer—could Would
you come to Amherst—Would you like to come—Master?" Johnson
dated this "about 1861," which is little help, though by early December
Bowles was staying in New York, just outside New England. Franklin
redated it to the summer of 1861, months too early for that trip.[87] It's possible that she took so long to mail a fair copy—if one was ever mailed—
that she crossed out "summer" in draft because the season had passed.
(Dickinson sometimes procrastinated with letters.) On its current dating, the passage might be read to favor Wadsworth.

A number of the poems Dickinson sent to Bowles can be read as
explicit confessions of her feelings, especially the poem beginning "Title
divine—is mine! / The Wife—without the Sign!"[88] It's not clear that he
had the wit to read them so—a man may be a blockhead in such matters,
or in kindness pretend to be. Dickinson was not a woman who risked all
by saying all. Even so, many poems that year make all but plain that she
was devastated by something. She described herself in the second Master Letter, "Daisy—who never flinched thro' that awful parting—but held
her life so tight he should not see the wound."[89]

The secret lives of the nineteenth century have never been adequately
revealed—we still misread the lack of manifest sign. (It was most of a
century after the poet's death that the torrid infidelity between Austin
Dickinson and Mabel Loomis Todd emerged from the shadows.)[90]
Early writers sometimes thought Dickinson bloodless, immune to
anything that stank of emotion. That was the later family view, at least
in public.[91] Her propriety was worn like her white dress, immortally
laundered—but, if Dickinson were not writing *in propria persona*, she
was giving a good imitation. "After great pain" first appeared in *Further
Poems of Emily Dickinson* (1929), subtitled *Withheld from Publication by
Her Sister Lavinia*—that is worth remembering.[92] A cluster of poems
of similar direction—one probably from 1861, also not published until
Further Poems—began, "A wife—at Daybreak I shall be," and ended,
"Master—I've seen the face before."[93] Even so, other readings remain
possible, or a layering of conflicted readings, as always with a poet with
more to conceal than reveal.

Wadsworth lived too far away and was happily married; Bowles may
not have known Dickinson until a few months after the first Master

Letter—neither problem is insuperable. Critics have made much of the kinship of image and vocabulary between the Master Letters and Wadsworth's sermons or her letters to Bowles. Each candidate has his passionate advocates. The Master of the first letter and the Master of the others might even have been different men—in her love, at different hours, she might have served different masters. The arguments are circumstantial, the circumstances impossible to reconstruct.

A humdrum explanation for her "terror" has sometimes been proposed, something she would have been more likely to mention to a stranger like Higginson. Two years later, Dickinson suffered prolonged eye-trouble. Her friend Joseph Lyman transcribed a passage from a letter not preserved: "Some years ago I had a woe, the only one that ever made me tremble. It was a shutting out of all the dearest ones of time, the strongest friends of the soul—BOOKS." She had endured, she reported, "eight weary months of Siberia."[94] That may refer to the first of two long spells of treatment in Boston, each about seven months; but an even earlier attack might have driven her to poetry at the thought she was about to go blind. Recall, though, that this was a terror "I could tell to none."[95] That sounds deeper than eye trouble.

The "terror," whatever it was, came near the outset of five years in which Dickinson wrote more than half her poems, over nine hundred. (If you drop the hundred or so that can't be dated by her handwriting, she apparently wrote two-thirds of her poems between 1858 and 1865.) Unfortunately, there's no evidence of a previous attack—we have nearly forty letters from the seven months after the "terror," while scarcely two dozen for the more than two years when her eye problems were acute. The poems declined sharply during the attack in 1864 but—if the dating can be trusted—were not much affected by that of 1865. Terror comes in many forms, and the difficulty with her eyes does not foreclose a romantic disaster that provoked the poems linked to pain and parting.

All this is a long way around the barn, but it's crucial to keep these letters and these shadow relations in mind, even when the difficulties cannot be resolved. Virtually everything in this précis of romantic love can be quarreled with. With her eccentricities, her catastrophic reserve, her niggling and unearthly brilliance, Dickinson was the oddest of odd ducks—her strange manner taxed the patience of acquaintances.

The Master Letters are so personal and specific (one implies that the recipient knew her dog), they were almost certainly written to someone; and we know Dickinson a little better if we consider that both likely candidates were beyond reach. To read her as a woman apart cannot be sustained when the life lies so close to the surface of the words. The modern idea of romantic passion comes from the sufferings of troubadours over a beloved already married. For Dickinson, male and female could easily have been reversed.

FEET

Returning to the second stanza, we're faced with the extreme condition of Dickinson's ambiguity. She lived her life in code (a key word in her poems is "circumference"), her equivocations guarding privacies even from those with whom she corresponded. The ambiguities of the poems and letters are of a piece—puzzling then, puzzling still. In the sort of ambiguity familiar to readers, one meaning radiates into suggestive alternatives, or two readings lie superimposed and entangled. In Dickinson's work, it's often hard to decipher the central meaning; the reader is left with two, or three, or four equally plausible variations.

Nerves have long been a symbol of bravery, calm in battle, sensitivity; the Heart of steadfastness and love (they're metonymies of feeling); but Feet are pathetically grounded in the physical. The nerves and the heart, apart from Christian use of the latter, have no place in art except in anatomy texts; but drawing legs and feet was a necessary part of the classical artist's training—Rembrandt was rare in never learning to paint legs convincingly.

"The Feet, mechanical, go round"—every movement labors here, and what might have been conscious act becomes the numbed motion of the machine. ("Going through the motions" would be the modern phrase, but it was current in Dickinson's day.) Many machines are rotary in action—something goes round. Dickinson would have seen washing machines and sewing machines and locomotive engines enough. A well-oiled machine is soothing and reliable, but it runs without will or thought or feeling. A poem from the same period, late 1862, begins, "From Blank to Blank— / A Threadless Way / I pushed Mechanic feet— / To stop—or perish—or advance— / Alike indifferent."[96] The numbed condition was on her mind. The lines bear contradictory relation to Tennyson's "That nothing walks with aimless feet"—Dickinson's feet have lost sense of purpose. (Tennyson's poem begins, "Oh yet we trust that somehow good / Will be the final goal of ill.")[97]

In the nineteenth century, a mechanic was anyone who worked with his hands—a carpenter or blacksmith, even a manual laborer. Though the meaning later narrowed, there remained the sense, recorded in the *OED*, that things "mechanical" were vulgar. At the start of the century, the essayist Vicesimus Knox had inveighed against the "literary madness of the trading and mechanical orders"—that is, shopkeepers and laborers who had the insolence to become authors.[98] The prejudice further taints the slogging movement, as if the feet were condemned, not just to brute labor, but to labor unworthy. Dissociation preserves but also protects. A life nerveless, stiffened, routine need never be examined—some suffering prevents suffering. There are also irrelevant or subordinate meanings to which syntax makes the lines vulnerable. In English idiom, "go round" means to pay a visit ("I can do no better than go round to Jenny's," *Bleak House*), as well as to travel indirectly or aimlessly ("If they could only go round towards the City Road," *Dombey and Son*).[99]

What on earth is the wooden way? Either the feet go round *in* wooden fashion, wherever they tread (though we might expect "*in* a wooden way," and the feet are unlikely to be both wooden and mechanical), or they take a path made of wood. Boardwalks in cities and towns were still a sign of civic improvement—in 1850 San Francisco, the "sidewalks were made of barrel staves and narrow pieces of board." There's no evidence Amherst had plank walks then, but other towns did. Even as late as 1895, they could be found in a similar college town, according to *Godey's Magazine*: "From the Bryn Mawr station a boardwalk, which sometimes proves full of pitfalls for the unsuspecting stranger, leads along a level road, past attractive houses." A few years after Dickinson's visit, a soldier noted the "old plank walk" that led to Washington's tomb.[100] The combination on that trip of a tomb, a wooden way, and Wadsworth is only a cheerful accident.

The way could be a plank bridge, which lies *over* ground, or air, or ought—the ought that is a river, say—but it isn't made *of* those things. The old plank roads (American plank roads boomed in the 1840s), or a belfry's plank flooring (where one could walk round the bells), or a house's porch or floors (many a worrier has paced a room)—all are possible, and none is quite convincing. The wooden way in "I stepped from Plank to Plank" seems to be a pier or a seaside boardwalk.[101] (The poem has a furtive relation to "From Blank to Blank.")

The problem lies in the construction of the passage itself. As it stands in manuscript, the stanza is very odd. The original reads:

> [1] The Feet, mechanical, go round—
> [3] Of Ground, or Air, or Ought—
> [2] A Wooden way
> [4] Regardless grown,
>   A Quartz contentment, like a stone—[102]

Dickinson numbered the first four lines for rearrangement. It's not clear if she changed her mind as she wrote or simply made a copying error. (Her eye might have caught "Ground" as she wrote "round," and she just thoughtlessly continued.) To "go round— / Of Ground, or Air, or Ought" is bizarre English, even for Dickinson. There are rare locative uses where "of" may mean "on" or "in" (*OED*), but the meaning would still be crippled—and there's no parallel for this sense anywhere in her work.

Though her punctuation was altered, the first appearance of the poem, in *Further Poems*, took account of her reordering, rendering the lines as "The feet mechanical go round / A wooden way / Of ground or air or Ought, / Regardless grown, / A quartz contentment like a stone." (Later collected editions made them, for no good reason, a quatrain with lines ending *mechanical/way/grown/stone*.)[103] Johnson in his influential variorum edition placed the reordered stanza in a footnote, but the poem as printed followed the manuscript.[104] Franklin's now standard edition (1998) transposed the lines as Dickinson directed:

> The Feet, mechanical, go round—
> A Wooden way
> Of Ground, or Air, or Ought—
> Regardless grown,
> A Quartz contentment, like a stone—

Manuscript of Emily Dickinson, "After great pain, a formal feeling comes."
Source: MS Am 1118.3 (26c), Courtesy of Houghton Library, Harvard University.

Unfortunately, the corrupt stanza, unhappily the version in Johnson's one-volume reader's edition (1960), still appears in anthologies and even critical works.[105]

The second line of the manuscript stanza ("Of Ground, or Air, or Ought") disrupts her couplet rhyme, and the whole destroys the quatrain pattern; but Dickinson's stanzaic forms were frequently irregular, sometimes radically so. (Higginson noticed and did not disapprove.)[106] Even reordered, the stanza is difficult to interpret. Critics, if they don't simply ignore the lines, usually tear out their hair trying to explain what the "Wooden way / Of Ground, or Air, or Ought" ought to be.

The confusion is unnecessary if Dickinson's directions for recasting the stanza were meant only as an aide-mémoire. The terminal punctuation of the second and third lines might always have been in the right place—it was just the two lines themselves she mixed up. And perhaps while concentrating on her task, realizing something was amiss, she put an unnecessary dash after the first line. She never treated punctuation as fixed, altering it manuscript to manuscript, sometimes bending toward convention, sometimes dashing the poem to pieces. On occasion she misplaced punctuation, but she grumbled only once when a mark was changed in print.[107] It was not the least consideration against remaking fair copies willy-nilly that the laid or wove paper she used for her fascicles was expensive.

The numbers clearly mean that the stanza should be recast. If we keep Dickinson's punctuation in place (removing, for this exercise, the unnecessary dash at the end of the first line, though frequently she interrupted syntax this way), the meaning becomes plain:

> The Feet, mechanical, go round
> A Wooden way—
> Of Ground, or Air, or Ought
> Regardless grown,
> A Quartz contentment, like a stone—

The wooden way is no longer composed of ground or air or something; rather, on this path the speaker is insensible to anything around her. The stanza could just as easily appear as a quatrain, fully restoring the couplet rhymes and iambic meter.

> The Feet, mechanical, go round
> A Wooden way—of Ground,
> Or Air, or Ought regardless grown,
> A Quartz contentment, like a stone.[108]

Cutting off the list at the end of the line would not be unusual in her work (compare "the sound of Boards / Or Rip of Nail—Or Carpenter," "Of Amplitude, or Awe— / Or first Prospective—or the Gold").[109] Dickinson was not beyond breaking her lines for emphasis, however, or shortening or lengthening her meter. In the irregular version, however, sense perhaps more gracefully follows the line, which seems her intention.

One of the main uses for "wooden way" just before Dickinson's day was for pre-steam railways, which often ran on wooden rails.[110] There's another possibility. Riddles occupied many a parlor of an evening— "What is a wooden way of ground, or air, or ought?" might at that day have been answered, "Treadmill." (More than one critic has already suggested this.)[111] The mode of punishment later suffered by Oscar Wilde was constructed as a paddle wheel set above the ground but, because each step was open, above air as well. It was the endless staircase that, for many prisoners, led only to death. Introduced in some New England prisons in the 1820s, it proved inefficient at milling grain or pumping water.

The treadmill would expose the speaker's sense of being punished— she must serve her sentence. (The Crucifixion was a punishment.) It would be pretty to think that a buried pun on "sentence" would have occurred to Dickinson, given the patched-together, dash-happy nine-line extravaganza with which the poem ends. The poem never achieves release—it ends on an interminable dash, a continuation not quite declared an ending. Such a sentence can never be outlived—surely the aftermath of a death feels that way. The idea is too ingenious, unfortunately, like the notion, pursued by Helen Vendler among others, that the disordered stanza reveals a disordered mind.[112]

None of this can tell us for certain what Dickinson intended by the "wooden way." Through the nineteenth century the phrase could also mean a bridge approach, a track leading from the ground to scaffolding, and, after her death, more than one type of elevated railway. Indeed, there's a thin chance that she employed the word as a synonym for "wooded" (this American usage persisted only through the nineteenth century) and that the wooden way is no more than a path through woods. The business of the stanza is to show the speaker, in the stupor of grief, reduced to an automaton walking she knows not where. It's to the credit of critics that none, so far as I know, has imagined the great pain as merely physical—say, that of a broken leg.

Dickinson often had some ground for her metaphors, but the shadows of her poems lie in the guilts of ambiguity or in simply not caring how easily the reader might be led astray. If her private readers made her aware of the snarls and tangles, they were not snarls and tangles she chose to unravel. (She sent very few friends, only half a dozen or so, more than a handful of poems.)[113]

"Ought" is the variant spelling of "aught," that is, "anything whatever." Given the license of Dickinson's language, there's the sidelong possibility that in punning fashion she meant the noun "ought," duty or necessity (George Eliot, "The will supreme, the individual claim, / The social Ought" [1874]; and Gladstone, "The two great ideas of the divine will, and of the Ought, or duty" [1878], OED). I'd dismiss this as a stray implication if the poem didn't seem a little short of duty but a little long on necessity. Within the mist of such metaphors, there are shapes but no clear figures. About the best one can hope for with Dickinson's metaphors is to establish a range or grid of potential meaning within which the real meaning has been embedded. Dickinson hedged her meanings, but hedging at times reveals more than clarity, just as her revisions show the movement of mind toward the opacities of brilliance: in "Blazing in gold and quenching in purple," the "kitchen window" became "oriel window" and at last "Otter's Window."[114]

Presumably it is the Feet that have grown regardless, personified like Heart and Nerves, embodied though only fractions of the body. Distracted, unconscious of walking but still walking, they have fallen into the contentment of the inanimate. An underlying meaning of "regardless,"

just passing out of fashion, was "slighted; not worthy of regard"—
that would be an attractive whisper of meaning, even were the other
ascendant.

QUARTZ

Ceremonious nerves, stiff heart, mechanical feet grown regardless of their
path—the benumbed state of grief is summed in two metaphors: "Quartz
contentment, like a stone" and "Hour of Lead." As a girl, Dickinson had
studied geology at Amherst Academy, which she entered aged nine. Students of the academy were allowed to attend lectures at Amherst College, including those by one of the eminent geologists of the day, the
Reverend Edward Hitchcock. (Harriet Martineau saw the young girls
there some years before Dickinson was a student.)[115] A copy of his textbook *Elementary Geology*, which became one of the most widely adopted,
lay in the family library. It was also, perhaps unsurprisingly, the geology
book assigned at Mount Holyoke.[116] Though she didn't stay long enough
to take up the subject there, Dickinson did write her brother—it shows
her bristling enthusiasm for the sciences—that she was "engrossed in the
history of Sulphuric Acid!!!!!"[117] Hitchcock's influence appears in later
poems like "On a Columnar Self."[118]

Dickinson knew enough geology to realize that quartz is a crystal, not
a stone; but "quartz stone" was a phrase often used, and Hitchcock repeatedly refers to "quartz rock."[119] Some varieties are considered semipre-
cious gemstones, and pure quartz is almost as hard as hardened steel. The
contentment, then, would be obdurate—but perhaps like pure quartz
translucent or transparent, easy to see into.

To press the reading further, and even too far, "Quartz contentment"
is a striking metaphor for feeling crystallized within. Of all the miner-
als, Dickinson chose the one then considered, by Hitchcock among
others, the most common (in fact, feldspar predominates).[120] When the
quartz crystal stops growing, it has reached a state of what might be
called contentment—frozen at least metaphorically—but that contentment is a hard, beautiful thing without feeling. "The Dew— / That stiff-
ens quietly to Quartz," she wrote in another poem, within days or weeks,
the word's only other appearance in surviving poem or letter.[121] Lost in

the subterranean arguments and silent treaties of language, "Regardless *grown*" almost becomes the promise fulfilled in grown quartz—just as a spire of quartz crystal might, by its resemblance to an icicle, prepare the frozen death to come.

The main ingredient of sand, quartz glitters—indeed, the unmentioned glittering may anticipate the snow implicit in the ending. A snowflake, too, is a crystal. In Dickinson's day, contentment could mean, not just ease of mind, but the very action of becoming satisfied, a meaning later lost (Arthur Helps, "With no contentment to the appetites of the hungry" [1851], *OED*). The flicker of appetite would be disturbing. The metaphor marks the speaker's ruthless patience, with perhaps a touch of fatalism. A stone has the capacity to wait without change, for eons if necessary. (It would be wrong to assume that contentment requires passivity—a quartz contentment could be read as the grip of obsession, or of near madness.)

Dickinson's contentment was rarely content. There is, not just "Tell it the Ages—to a cypher— / And it will ache—contented—on" ("Bound—a trouble"), and "A perfect—paralyzing Bliss— / Contented as Despair" ("One Blessing had I"), but more disturbingly "A nearness to Tremendousness— / An Agony procures— / . . . // Contentment's quiet Suburb— / Affliction cannot stay / In Acres" ("A nearness to Tremendousness").[122] Contentment can be a frozen despair, a serenity not the least serene.

STANZA 3

This is the Hour of Lead—
Remembered, if outlived,
As Freezing persons, recollect the Snow—
First—Chill—then Stupor—then the letting go—

The machine-like walk is the first hint of the circumstance of the last stanzas—a death march through extreme cold, the body on automatic, numbed within and numb without, mechanical because near exhaustion, moving because stopping is sleep and sleep is death. ("Death march" was a phrase first found in this sense less than two decades before; as the alternative to "dead march," the march of a funeral procession, it had been in the language for a century [*OED*].) It's as if Dickinson remembered the cold before the poem could mention it. Had she been recalling the town tomb, she was already thinking of frozen bodies.

If "Quartz contentment" summarizes the plodding of the feet (meditation by walking in circles is not uncommon), the "Hour of Lead" is the collapsed figure for the state of grief that governs the poem—it returns to formal feeling with a vision of the dull, inertial aftermath of trauma. Apart from uranium, lead is the heaviest naturally occurring element. (Though discovered by a chemist at the time of the French Revolution, uranium had little use beyond glassmaking or photography until the twentieth century—it went unmentioned in Hitchcock's *Geology*.) "Heavy as lead" is a phrase at least as antique as Burton's *Anatomy of Melancholy* (1621).[123] The heart or soul "as heavy as lead" was a customary formula.

Shakespeare took the qualities of the metal beyond the heartsick metaphor in *Venus and Adonis*. "Like dull and heavy lead" (*Henry IV, Part II*) and "Is not lead a metal heavy, dull, and slow?" (*Love's Labour's Lost*)[124] are confirming instances of the mental dullness and heavy-footed pace intimate with the Hour of Lead. "Leaden"—what is the Hour of Lead but leaden?—has an acute semantic range here, as the *OED* reminds us: "heavy, dull, benumbing," and, of the limbs, "hard to drag along."

It's no more than an amusing coincidence, given the possible connection to the Master Letters, that the next line in *Love's Labour's Lost* is "*Minime*, honest master, or, rather, master, no." The exchange is part of an elaborate quibble between Don de Armado and his page, Moth. There's a slow-gaited ass, a message to be delivered, and a promise to be "swift as lead"—when his master remonstrates, Moth replies, "Is that lead slow which is fir'd from a gun?" Recall the third Master Letter—"If you saw a bullet hit a Bird . . ." The reader can cut too deeply, but—whatever connection to Shakespeare, little or none—the lines remind us that any mention of lead may bring up bullets, and that Dickinson, no mean quibbler herself, was perfectly capable of thinking of hardness and perhaps translucency when she wrote "quartz" and then heaviness and stupor, or perhaps brute violence, when she thought of lead. She began a poem, "My Life had stood—a Loaded Gun."[125]

I FELT A FUNERAL

Months before, probably, Dickinson had written what may be a trial piece.

> I felt a Funeral, in my Brain,
> And Mourners to and fro
> Kept treading—treading—till it seemed
> That Sense was breaking through—
>
> And when they all were seated,
> A Service, like a Drum—
> Kept beating—beating—till I thought
> My mind was going numb—
>
> And then I heard them lift a Box
> And creak across my Soul
> With those same Boots of Lead, again,
> Then Space—began to toll,
>
> As all the Heavens were a Bell,
> And Being, but an Ear,
> And I, and Silence, some strange Race
> Wrecked, solitary, here—
>
> And then a Plank in Reason, broke,
> And I dropped down, and down—
> And hit a World, at every plunge,
> And Finished knowing—then—[126]

"After great pain" appears here in nascent form, or rather through the looking glass. Both open with a funeral—something has died. We have mourners eventually "seated" versus nerves that "sit ceremonious," "treading—treading" versus the mechanical feet, "My mind was going numb" versus "Chill—then Stupor," "Boots of Lead" versus "Hour of Lead," "Plank in Reason" versus "Wooden way," and Brain and Ear versus

Nerves and Heart. "Dropped down" and "Finished knowing—then" become "Stupor—then the letting go." Even the critical appearance of "then" betrays a similarity of dramatic construction. There are differences—the mechanical round of the wooden way is enacted in the earlier poem by the relentless *ands*, a baker's dozen of them (an anaphora of them, as it were). Half the lines start there, emphasizing the leaden treading and the beating, beating of the funeral service.

The images form a cluster like those in Shakespeare: funeral, mourners, treading, sitting, parts of the body, numbness, silence, lead, solitude, obliteration—and perhaps even verbal echoes like "Wrecked" / "recollect." (Shakespeare's clusters are more disconcerting and almost irrational—dogs and candy, for instance, and geese, disease, and bitterness.)[127] Though Dickinson's images derive mainly from the trappings of a funeral, the echoes can't quite be argued away—her funerals lack a preacher, for instance. The elements of "After great pain" are not exact equivalents—"Hour of Lead" is not "Boots of Lead"—but when lead is invoked, for example, walking or treading lies near. (The latter phrase has some age to it. William Drummond of Hawthornden wrote an epigram about Charles I that included the line "In boots of lead thrall'd were his legs.")[128]

There's a similar cluster in a poem written late in 1862, "A Prison gets to be a friend," a poem so infused by "The Prisoner of Chillon" it might have been spoken by the prisoner himself. There are parts of the body ("face," "Eyes," and, amusingly, the "Cheek of Liberty"); "Content" versus "Quartz contentment"; and, most tellingly, "We learn to know the Planks— / That answer to Our feet," the image of the prisoner circling in his cell, a "Demurer Circuit— / A Geometric Joy" (later, "The narrow Round—the stint— / The slow exchange of Hope").[129] Perhaps the "Wooden way" also had intimations of such a circuit—certainly that phrase and the "Plank in Reason" have some association with imprisonment and loss of hope. The dominant feeling is loneliness and the passive acceptance of hard fate.

Return to "I felt a Funeral." "I heard them lift a Box"—this must be a coffin, a "box of boards," as Dickinson wrote in a letter that year.[130] The old euphemism was frequently heard in the nineteenth century. (A Gold Rush miner wrote in 1849, "They take a poor fellow when he does happen to die, and put him in a rough box, clothes and all, and chuck him in a hole.")[131] "Box" was not pure slang, as the *OED* has it, but figurative at times for a lowly coffin resembling a long packing crate—at times it *was* a packing crate. Dickinson's use of the word may therefore be calculated—there's more of the plain terror of death in being pitched, like candles or twists of tobacco, into a miserable box. The poem, like "After great pain," is about a loss that drives the speaker nearly mad—the cause is likely the same.

The mourners tread in the brute, steady way of mechanical feet. They sit during the service, where the words batter the speaker into numbness. Do they beat like the drum of a dead march? As pallbearers, the mourners lift the coffin and walk across her soul in their "Boots of Lead." The heavens toll like a church bell, probably the slow, steady knell of the funeral bell. All being becomes just a passive state of listening, of being forced to hear. The speaker and Silence are shipwrecked (Dickinson usually uses "wrecked" of shipwrecks), a "strange Race" together—it's hard not to see an allusion to *Robinson Crusoe* here. Are they "strange" because they do not speak in a world where everyone else can't stop talking, or because she is now so estranged from the living? Her growing discomfort with company is perhaps shadowed here.

The speaker is not describing her own funeral—the funeral is "in my Brain." Still, great loss makes the living feel that something inside has died. The poem may be a literal version of the idea. When the mourners tread across her soul (Dickinson originally wrote "across my Brain," probably forgetting she had used the word in the opening line), that is all figurative—but the poet writes as if someone had just walked over her grave. Again, the line seems the literal version of a commonplace. The shuddering in the usual phrase goes back at least to Swift.[132] There is a death to answer a death.

Should we be reminded of that nineteenth-century horror, being buried alive? Poe was obsessed by the idea. His stories "The Premature Burial" and "The Fall of the House of Usher," among others, are the most famous examples; but the fear was widespread. Dickinson once wrote Higginson, "Of Poe, I know too little to think"[133]—but that doesn't mean she knew nothing. The line, as so often, is cunningly evasive.

The horror of life in death lies not far from the death in life beneath both poems. Dickinson continued, after her remark on Poe, "Hawthorne appalls, entices." Did she know "The Minister's Black Veil" from

Twice-Told Tales (1837),[134] where a village parson appears one Sunday in a black veil, causing consternation among his congregation and leading his betrothed to break their engagement? He continues to wear it all his life, refusing to remove it even at the point of death. The Recluse, as Bowles once called Dickinson, might have had a moment of recognition—of enticement—after being appalled. She wrote a poem about a veil, after all, that opens, "A Charm invests a face / Imperfectly beheld— / The Lady dare not lift her Vail / For fear it be dispelled."[135] Reticence has its responsibilities.

Reason breaks down, but where is the "Plank in Reason"? Is it just an imaginary plank across the great reach of the Heavens? Cynthia Griffin Wolff, in her biography of Dickinson, offers a telling emblem from the book *Religious Allegories* (1848), showing a gentleman crossing a plank that bestrides a dark abyss. The man holds a radiant book that must be the Bible, the plank is carved with the word "FAITH," and a shining mansion awaits his crossing.[136] Dickinson's "Plank in Reason" would be quietly critical. Other senses of "plank" seem not to apply.

If the speaker feels buried, is the plank the bottom of a board coffin from which her corpse plummets into whatever realms lie below? "And Finished knowing—then—": the speaker vanishes into unknowing and the poem ends in dissolution, just as "After great pain" ends in . . . in nothing. Dickinson considered changing "Finished" to "Got through" but perhaps felt the ambiguity would have promised survival.[137]

FREEZING

The last line of "After great pain" is a death not quite death. "If out-lived" introduces the species of doubt that secures the magnitude of pain. The effects of extreme cold were familiar—Dickinson's knowledge of death by freezing could have come from many sources. There may have been some local incident (Samuel Bowles suffered severely from sciatica after a harrowing sleigh ride to Amherst early in 1861);[138] but, throughout this period, there are scenes in tales like "The Christmas Letter" from *Godey's Lady's Book* (1856):

> She is so very weary, and the stupor is returning. So, feebly brushing off the snow from a felled tree lying by the wayside, she sits down.

She grows colder, more lethargic, more numb; minute by minute goes by, yet still she sits. She is just sinking into unconsciousness.[139]

The most notorious incidents of freezing to death, however, occurred half a century before on the retreat of the French army from Moscow and more recently during the Arctic expeditions.

In *The United States Grinnell Expedition in Search of Sir John Franklin* (1854), Elisha Kent Kane, who served as ship's surgeon to the first Grinnell Expedition, quoted from his own "scrap-book":

"I will tell you what this feels like, for I have been twice 'caught out.' Sleepiness is not the sensation. Have you ever received the shocks of a magneto-electric machine, and had the peculiar benumbing sensation of 'can't let go,' extending up to your elbow-joints? Deprive this of its paroxysmal character; subdue, but diffuse it over every part of the system, and you have the so-called pleasurable feelings of incipient freezing. It seems even to extend to your brain. Its inertia is augmented; every thing about you seems of a ponderous sort; and the whole amount of pleasure is in gratifying the disposition to remain at rest, and spare yourself an encounter with these latent resistances. This is, I suppose, the pleasurable sleepiness of the story books."[140]

Can't let go. Here is the numbness of the "formal feeling" and "Hour of Lead," here the incipient freezing, the inertia of the mechanical feet ("Regardless grown") and "Quartz contentment" and "Hour of Lead." Here, in short, is the memory of someone freezing to death. Kane is adamant that the feeling is not sleepiness—and nowhere does Dickinson mention sleep. This may be the very passage that informed the poem, the details reworked, perhaps even the "letting go" suggested by the bizarre tingle of the "magneto-electric machine."

Kane had prefaced the account by saying, "I felt that lethargic numbness mentioned in the story books." I've been unable to find any book that answers the surgeon's reference: *Frankenstein* (1818) will not do, nor *Symzonia* (1820), nor *The Narrative of Arthur Gordon Pym* (1838).[141] Perhaps *The Rime of the Ancient Mariner* (1798/1834) comes closest among imaginative speculations about the frozen north or south, with "The ice was here, the ice was there, / The ice was all around," the "Night-mare

LIFE-IN-DEATH," and the "gentle sleep" the Mariner enjoys. At times Coleridge approaches Dickinson's own nightmarish vision. When the Mariner wakes, he recalls,

> I moved, and could not feel my limbs:
>   I was so light—almost
> I thought that I had died in sleep,
>   And was a blessed ghost.[142]

The numbness is there, and the fall into sleep that may be a falling out of life; but the connections are weak.

"Storybook" had increasingly come to mean a collection of children's stories. There are tales of the cold in Grimm and Andersen, but none relevant to Kane's memory. One novel within range is Fenimore Cooper's *Sea Lions* (1849), toward the end of which a man almost freezes to death in the snow. His companions rub his limbs and give him a dose of brandy, followed by coffee:

> After a swallow or two, aided by a vigorous friction, and closely surrounded by so many human bodies, the black began to revive; and the sort of drowsy stupor which is known to precede death in those who die by freezing, having been in a degree shaken off, he was enabled to stand alone.[143]

Drowsy stupor. But perhaps we don't need to know what books or stories Kane referred to. He recorded in *Arctic Explorations* (1856) his later experiences leading the second Grinnell Expedition:

> I was of course familiar with the benumbed and almost lethargic sensation of extreme cold; and once, when exposed for some hours in the midwinter of Baffin's Bay, I had experienced symptoms which I compared to the diffused paralysis of the electro-galvanic shock. But I had treated the *sleepy comfort* of freezing as something like the embellishment of romance. I had evidence now to the contrary.[144]

The "embellishment of romance" suggests that he wasn't thinking of children's stories. Two of his men "came begging permission to sleep":

Presently Hans was found nearly stiff under a drift; and Thomas, bolt upright, had his eyes closed, and could hardly articulate. . . . The floe was of level ice, and the walking excellent. I cannot tell how long it took us to make the nine miles; for we were in a strange sort of stupor, and had little apprehension of time.[145]

Benumbed, lethargic, extreme cold, diffused paralysis, sleepy comfort, freezing, stupor. Emily's father's copy of the 1857 printing of *Arctic Explorations* was in the Dickinsons' library.[146] This immensely popular book stayed in print for half a century and eventually sold over 150,000 copies.[147] If Dickinson were not recalling Kane's first book, the second would have done—and perhaps she knew both.

A lost traveler making endless circles appears in Charles Francis Hall's account in *Arctic Researches and Life Among the Esquimaux* (1865) of the search for a lost shipmate: "The tracks turn again in a circle. Now they come in rapid succession. Round and round the bewildered, terror-stricken, and almost frozen one makes his way."[148] Such aimless circling is much like that of the prisoner in his cell. During the 1860s, references in her poems to the polar regions show that the poet had read of the search for Sir John Franklin. The lines "When the lone British Lady / Forsakes the Arctic Race" (in "When the Astronomer stops seeking") refer to the end of Lady Franklin's search for her husband.[149] In "Through the strait pass of suffering," Dickinson makes the expeditions north a figure for suffering martyrs ("The Martyrs—even—trod"), intent to the point of death on their search for grace:

> Their faith—the everlasting troth—
> Their expectation—fair—
> The Needle—to the North Degree—
> Wades—so—thro' polar Air![150]

The "even—trod" through the "strait pass of suffering" echoes the numbing round of the feet in "After great pain," as well as Christ's journey through the Stations of the Cross. Dickinson sent this poem to Bowles, adding meaningfully, "Because I could not say it—I fixed it in the Verse."[151]

Looking again, it's possible to see the figure of cold creeping backward into the second stanza. The "Quartz contentment" is a figure for cold-heartedness, the inner stiffening for which "icicle" had been a metaphor for two centuries (Herrick: "Shall I go to Love and tell, / Thou art all turn'd isicle?")[152] Could the "going round" be that compassless wandering of the lost, freezing traveler, another perhaps unconscious preparation for the cold to come? Or was it conscious? If "Quartz contentment" is implicated by the inner chill, then "stiff Heart" may be as well.

Anyone living in a clapboard house in New England, as the Dickinson family did for fifteen years, knew how cold the cold was.[153] In Robert Frost's "Snow," the preacher Meserve says, "This house is frozen brittle, all except / This room you sit in."[154] (It's midnight, and his hosts have been roused from bed. Probably they're in the kitchen, with the fire in the stove stirred up.) Lying alone in bed on a frozen winter night when the fire has gone out, lying under a dead weight of quilts, too cold to risk moving an inch, even a woman not a poet might imagine she knew the touch of the Arctic, and a little of death to come.

IF OUTLIVED

The poem occurs after the inciting pain and before pain has been outlived. The doubt in "*If* outlived" offers neither solace nor proportion—letting go would be letting go of life, not putting the past behind (the poem is too despairing for that), though the latter exists as a ghost reading. Ghost readings have reason but not probability; they lurk below the surface as a contradictory palimpsest or "*drama* of Reason," as Coleridge called his parenthetical remarks.[155]

Elsewhere during these months, Dickinson used "let go" for the end of life ("Looking at Death, is Dying— / Just let go the Breath," "You'll find—it when you try to die— / The easier to let go"), but also, a year later, for renunciation ("Renunciation—is a piercing Virtue— / The letting go").[156] Perhaps that's how long renunciation took. The immediate layer of meaning is governed by the metaphor of the freezing victim, letting go of consciousness, not yet life itself. "Letting go" occurs rapidly in the poem, but such a death would have been slow.[157] The ending serves not as catharsis but as a record of exhausted surrender. It may reveal, not a longing to die, only a longing not to feel or think.

If agony is the condition, death would be a cure. Some in great pain, Dickinson would have known, choose death by freezing. (Cold was sometimes employed as an anesthetic—it's not too much to hear through this, from a lover of Keats, "My heart aches, and a drowsy numbness pains / My sense." Hemlock was the sedative.)[158]

THE DASH

Many of Dickinson's poems end with a dash, which here acts like an ellipsis, the gradual lapse into oblivion—or a flourish, the end of things. She ended more than half her poems thus, in one version or another. Often where there are two versions, one ends with a dash and the other with an exclamation point. A dash also suggests that there might have been more to say—or rather something that remains unsaid. Her punctuation has driven critics slightly mad. Shakespeare, like other Elizabethan authors, left his stops to the printing house; and letter writers of her century often slapped down one dash after another (Austen and Byron, for example, Keats and Whitman). It can be difficult to tell whether one of Dickinson's marks is period, comma, dash, or a stray dot where her pen rested. Punctuation in all printed versions of the poems must therefore be provisional—the precision of the editor conceals the guesswork.

Though her punctuation often seems intuitive, Dickinson was not obliged to clarify the poems for anyone but herself, not even the friends to whom they were sometimes sent. A poet does not have to revel in such discretions to take advantage of them, or to put off the labor of making decisions necessary for the printer. When she left only these sketchy notations toward the pauses that delay our run-on words, the poems preserved their original privacy. Or perhaps something closer to dignity.

END

"After great pain" is the memoir of a Lazarus not yet dead, by a speaker who does not even say she *wants* to survive. She's merely reporting how the experience would feel—peaceful, that is—from the rare accounts of survivors. If such pain can be outlived, only those who have returned from the cold of the tomb can speak with authority. The Resurrection surfaces here, given the way Christ's exemplary act of suffering stands at the edge of the first stanza. That would deepen the speaker's degrading torment—Christ was never more a man than at the moment His faith gave out upon the Cross. He rose from a tomb, of course.

Beneath signs of claustrophobic horror and deathlike formality, beneath the mechanical walk and inner paralysis, the poem lives in the aftermath of shock. The speaker has passed beyond chill ("formal feeling" perhaps introduces the idea) into stupor ("Hour of Lead"). "Formal feeling" doesn't mean absence of pain—only numbness to it, and the wish to be numb is proof of its severity. The poem describes the period after terrible loss when the feelings insulate themselves—such grief is a climate that may continue for months or years. Reading too much Dickinson is like suffering an attack of claustrophobia—no later poet produced that feeling so oppressively until Sylvia Plath.

There are crowds enough in this poem—nerves, mourners, freezing persons—but at center a speaker who never refers to herself. The "I" has been erased in radical solitude—despair lies beneath what seems a valediction. The poem leaves the matter of survival in doubt. That is the horror. There's no better poem about dying alone, whether physically or emotionally—yet, if this is a poem of obliteration, Dickinson has written with unnerving detachment. The most extraordinary aspect of this moving narrative, this narrative of movement, is that despite the great pain the speaker does *keep* moving. A traveler cannot freeze to death until he stops.

Dickinson's poems of love denied are some of the most extraordinary documents of American passion. Though she sustained her cryptic privacies, it's surprising how raw the emotions remain. In her refusal of recollection and tranquility, the poems resist consolation—their furies lie just beneath the surface, sometimes not even that deep. In this she was a modern poet, not just *avant la lettre*, but *avant la naissance*. She died, as did Whitman, as a new generation was born. Her surface meters perhaps made it difficult to recognize that she was a poet out of her time. The occasional corruptions of meter and rhyme therefore seem, whether a mild sloppiness of craft or the extremity of calculation, the sign of naked pain breaking through. Sonya in *Uncle Vanya* says about love, "Uncertainty is better. At least with uncertainty there is hope." "After great pain" occurs when there's no longer any hope.

ROBERT FROST, "STOPPING BY WOODS ON A SNOWY EVENING"

I fear I am not a poet, or but a very incomprehensible one.
—Robert Frost to Susan Hayes Ward, 1896

STOPPING BY WOODS ON A SNOWY EVENING

Whose woods these are I think I know.
His house is in the village though;
He will not see me stopping here
To watch his woods fill up with snow.

My little horse must think it queer
To stop without a farmhouse near
Between the woods and frozen lake
The darkest evening of the year.

He gives his harness bells a shake
To ask if there is some mistake.
The only other sound's the sweep
Of easy wind and downy flake.

The woods are lovely, dark and deep.
But I have promises to keep,
And miles to go before I sleep,
And miles to go before I sleep.[159]

For a long while, Robert Frost was a failure with a vague longing for poetry. At eighteen, after one semester at Dartmouth College, he'd left out of boredom. Five years later he lasted three semesters at Harvard before abandoning college for good. Frost's wife was then heavily pregnant with their second child, and the scapegrace began to complain of mysterious pains and chills. Thinking that the young man suffered from nervous illness or tuberculosis, the family doctor told him to work outdoors. As a boy in San Francisco, Frost had raised chickens, so he decided to become a poultryman.[160]

Though squeamish about the art of butchering, Frost soon owned a large flock of Wyandottes at a house and barn rented in Methuen, thirty miles north of Boston. In 1900, a year along, his three-year-old boy had died of cholera, his own health was still precarious, and the landlady couldn't wait to bid good riddance to the poet and his white fowl. His grandfather, William Prescott Frost, bought him a farm some fifteen miles farther north in Derry, New Hampshire, though the old man held back the title deed and, apparently without asking, arranged for his ne'er-do-well grandson to board a hired man—Frost's good friend from high school, Carl Burell.[161] Leather cutter, harvester, hotel handyman, assistant to a mill gatekeeper: as a young man Frost had been no stranger to hard work.[162] After Dartmouth, he'd drifted from job to job, teaching at first, then becoming a guardian for his future wife's older sisters (he tried to induce an abortion when the eldest, unhappily married, showed up pregnant). He had briefly managed a hack Shakespearean actor, and before returning to teaching spent months replacing arc-lamp filaments at a woolen mill.[163] That his grandfather was so indulgent is remarkable. Frost nonetheless was offended by the arrangement. He also apparently never paid the Methuen landlady for several months of rent.[164]

The Magoon Place, as the Derry farm was called, offered pastures, an apple orchard, a grove of hardwoods, and a hayfield. The bay window of the clapboard farmhouse overlooked the Londonderry Turnpike; the three bedrooms upstairs proved suitable for the Frost family and the hired man, as well as Burell's aged grandfather. A west-running brook ran through the thirty acres, and to the south a stone wall kept the Magoon apple trees from the neighbor's pines. Thickets of berries lay by the barn, with a few pear, peach, and quince trees elsewhere.[165]

Frost's grandfather died the following summer, in July 1901, bequeathing the dumbstruck poet, who thought the man despised him, the farm rent-free for ten years, after which he would be handed the deed. The legacy came with a $500 annuity, increasing after a decade to $800. Grandfather had torn up grandson's promissory notes, of which there were more than a few. (Old Mr. Frost was an antique progressive who washed the dishes, cooked, and cleaned with his wife, an early suffragette.) The poet, who received far more than his sister, managed to resent what his grandfather left to charity.[166]

Frost was no farmer. Burell and his grandfather did most of the farm work, while their boss kept the chickens. The two boarders made the farm efficient and for their industry were repaid with Frost's petty bickering. By the spring of 1902, Burell's grandfather was dead and Burell was gone. It's no wonder the farm started to decline—Frost didn't even know the proper way to milk a cow. By his own admission, he rose late, milked at noon and midnight, and preferred writing to biblical day-labor. His neglect meant there was little outside income.[167]

The would-be poet had usually spent his annuity long before the check arrived. In debt throughout the town, he made matters worse by buying a high-strung dapple-gray mare named Eunice, then in 1905 a red sleigh and a dashing sulky. For four years after Burell's departure, Frost straggled along, helped each summer by the annual check, which aroused some jealousy among his impoverished neighbors.[168] Life on the Derry farm might have made a screwball comedy in the thirties (a local theater advertised "moving pictures" as early as 1908),[169] but they were very dark years for Frost. No longer young, he was writing poems and getting nowhere.

Toward the end of a lecture at Bowdoin in 1947, a student from the University of Maine asked Frost to name his favorite poem. The poet, then in his seventies, declined rather brusquely. Afterward he called the young man to the podium:

"I'd have to say 'Stopping by Woods on a Snowy Evening' is that poem. Do you recall in the lecture I pointed out the importance of the line 'The darkest evening of the year'? . . . Well—the darkest evening of the year is on December twenty-second—which is the shortest day of the year—just before Christmas."[170]

The student, N. Arthur Bleau, wrote down his recollections three decades later, so their accuracy can't wholly be trusted. He paraphrased the rest of Frost's answer:

> It was a bleak time both weatherwise and financially. . . . It wasn't going to be a very good Christmas unless he did something. So—he hitched up the wagon filled with produce from the farm and started the long trek into town.
>
> When he finally arrived, there was no market for his goods. . . . He finally accepted the fact that there would be no sale. There would be no exchange for him to get a few simple presents for his children's Christmas.
>
> As he headed home, evening descended. It had started to snow, and his heart grew heavier with each step of the horse in the gradually increasing accumulation. He had dropped the reins and given the horse its head. It knew the way. The horse was going more slowly as they approached home. It was sensing his despair. There is an unspoken communication between a man and his horse, you know.
>
> Around the next bend in the road, near the woods, they would come into view of the house. He knew the family was anxiously awaiting him. How could he face them? What could he possibly say or do to spare them the disappointment he felt?
>
> They entered the sweep of the bend. The horse slowed down and then stopped. It knew what he had to do. He had to cry, and he did. I recall the very words he spoke. "I just sat there and bawled like a baby"—until there were no more tears.
>
> The horse shook its harness. The bells jingled. They sounded cheerier. He was ready to face his family. . . . Not a word was spoken, but the horse knew he was ready and resumed the journey homeward.[171]

However approximate Bleau's memory, Frost's daughter Lesley confirmed that her father had told her the same story "so closely, word for word."[172] The poet's tale is not particularly revealing, because the elements not in the poem—the failed journey to market, the unbought presents, the horse's decision to halt (which would change the implication of the title), the tears—are not necessary. Rather, they provide to the tone and tenor of criticism Frost's shrewdness in knowing what to leave out.

WHOSE WOODS

Whose woods these are I think I know.
His house is in the village though;
He will not see me stopping here
To watch his woods fill up with snow.

"Stopping by Woods on a Snowy Evening" begins so casually, it hardly seems to begin at all. The opening inversion delays our perception of the line's intent, while recording the reflections of the traveler who has brought his chilly journey to a stop. The line is the very imitation of musing—the tacit question must have been asked before the poem had begun. The present tense is not the first act of artifice.

The title is "Stopping by," not "Stopping in," because the traveler sits on a road with a lake on the other side. He's not in the woods; he's outside looking in. "Stopping by" of course means to pay a visit, but implicit in stopping by is that eventually you must go. You say hello, bring a gift, offer condolences, return the hammer. You stay the period dictated by local etiquette, then make your excuses and push off. Frost has managed the brief incident as if stopping by were the neighborly thing to do. In a sense, it is. The traveler is paying his respects.

Few poems in English literature begin with "whose," perhaps none before the seventh song in *Astrophil and Stella*:

Whose senses in so evil consort, their stepdame Nature lays,
That ravishing delight in them most sweet tunes do not raise.[173]

Later examples occur in Herrick, Burns, and Hardy; but the gambit is rare—perhaps unduly so, as it's a strategic way to begin in medias res, by an act of possession or inquiry. The poem opens with Frost's traveler mildly dismayed—he has asked himself a question he cannot answer with confidence. Something caused him to halt the slow journey home. Knowing Frost's account at Bowdoin, the reader must proceed divided. What does the poem say for itself, and how does the tale alter or adjust what the poem reveals?

The overwhelming despair Frost later remembered is absent, at least from the opening—and the tone is not the least despondent. The traveler stops, it seems, only to puzzle over the property map; but the following lines make clear he may have deeper motive. Why does he wonder about the owner? Because he doesn't want to be observed. (That's one of many hints his state of mind is not plainly disclosed.) "I *think* I know"— it's almost dark or dark already, the man knows the place roughly, may have heard who owns woods thereabouts but cannot be sure. *His house is in the village though*—so the traveler need not worry about him. Introducing a species of doubt so early creates a tremor of unknowing through the whole. The traveler's uncertainties are never resolved—and he may be mistaken.

The cleanest reading of "Stopping by Woods" is lighthearted and whimsical. The seven sentences fairly gallop along in tetrameter—the poem has to be read slowly to prevent it from bouncing. The jaunty meter (tetrameter so regular always cozies up to doggerel) and homely diction (only one word beyond two syllables, the lead plumb of "promises") welcome the puckish sensibility rejected at the end with little more than a shrug—if you choose to read the end that way. Why would a man worry about being seen on an empty road at dusk, unless he had stolen the horse? Why would he worry, unless stopping to watch the woods was a most uncountry-like thing to do—impractical, lazy, pointless? Such unease would cut deeper if the traveler already had a reputation for not being a local, not one of them, not a true Yankee.

At winter solstice, the sun sets in Derry at roughly a quarter past four p.m., so it would be pitch black well before five. "Evening" reaches from the first shadows of night to blind dark—winter light doesn't linger. As it's snowing, when dusk fades no stars would be visible and probably no moon. In such conditions, no one fifty yards distant could identify traveler or horse. The longer you ponder the lines, the more they seem pitched against the sober-mindedness of the Yankee farmers who took such a dim view of Frost's farming. (The stereotypical Yankee was flint-hearted and penny-pinching—businessman first, businessman second.) Traces of Frost's bemusement at his neighbors linger in "Mending Wall," "The

Code," "Snow," and other poems. Even the practical horse can't see the point. The man who doesn't want to be observed doesn't want to be observed observing, because the snow-dusted woods are beautiful—or, in the word that fired the Romantics, sublime.

Watching was a rejection of everything Frost had come to dislike about mill towns and hardscrabble farms. For all the homely wisdom embedded in the poems, he was a man who by then loathed hard labor and avoided it, while sniping at those with a Calvinist faith in honest work. The pastoral is more appealing if you don't have to slave dawn to dusk.

The opening byplay about the owner briefly distracts the reader from any suggestion that the traveler has stopped merely to watch falling snow and filling woods. (You might have thought he was going to praise the owner's taste—or his good fortune.) The syntactic inversion also rescues the metronomic tetrameter from sounding like an advertising jingle: the poem might have begun, "I think I know whose woods these are. / I've watched them from my touring car." (A man drove a Pierce-Arrow through Derry in December 1906.)[174] Such lines would rush helter-skelter toward meaning, comically betraying the intent. Instead, the opening gradually reveals the thoughts whose development drags through the stanza.

Frost was canny to raise the question of ownership, the old quarrel concealed at the center of the poem. Who owns the woods? From the days of Jamestown and Plymouth (or, further back, the lost colony at Roanoke), the untamed forest, home to the Indian often a mortal enemy, had been cut down for timber or cleared for farms. In the country from which early settlers came, Sherwood Forest and the Forest of Arden were mythic antecedents—how strange it must have been for such pilgrims to disembark in a land of trees unending. The forest was that darkness all colonists fear, the darkness that had to be destroyed to establish civilization in the New World. What Auden wrote of the sea applies equally to the forest: it is "that state of barbaric vagueness and disorder out of which civilisation has emerged and into which, unless saved by the effort of gods and men, it is always liable to relapse."[175]

Woods usually have a collar of settlement around them, while forests remain deep enough, broad enough, to conceal a hidden realm. Often just remnant forest, woods preserve a scrap of wildness within civilized

bounds. No man without good reason bothered to fence his woods—
that wasn't the purpose of fences. It would have been unneighborly. In
what is perhaps the first draft of the poem, Frost wrote, "Between a forest and a lake."[176] He had to struggle toward the difference.

Early settlers of New England had little idea that the glacial soil was
poor and thin, especially in upland farms. Even farms with better soil
were often too stony. Almost all the old growth in New Hampshire had
been chopped down for farms before 1800—not many generations later,
land laboriously cleared of boulders, which became the boundary walls
sometimes called stone fences, was abandoned when the ground played
out.[177]

Worse, not long after the Civil War, growing grain for flour proved
no longer economical in the East—the railroads could deliver it more
cheaply from the Midwest. Farms failed by the hundreds; trees sprang
up again in deserted fields. Wheat prices in the 1890s had fallen to as little as a quarter of what they'd been after the war, and during the first
decade of the new century they were not much higher. (In constant dollars, bushels brought only slightly more than 40 percent of their price
three decades before.) Even at the pre–World War I peak, in 1910, the cost
of a bushel was a little over 80 percent of what it had been in 1866.[178] By
1900, only one man of fourteen in Derry was a farmer full-time, most
working for other farmers.[179] In much of New England, the new woods
were crisscrossed by the stone walls of derelict farmsteads. There were
long discussions of the consequences.

Vermont, 1871: "Here are huge stone walls inclosing nearly all the
fields, standing now after their weight has pressed the earth for more than
half a century, as high as a man's shoulders. And like heavy old fences
[they] enclose the old roads that wind up the hill—old roads never to be
traveled more."

Maine, 1891: "Very many of the abandoned farms are well fenced with
good stone walls, while many of them have nice stone walls dividing
fields, where trees are thickly growing."

New England, 1901: "Where once were 'mowings' and 'plowings' are
now wild and free stretches of woodland. Dilapidated stone walls ramble through the woods and are heaved by the roots of great trees. Here

and there is the ruin of a foundation, with trees growing inside and the tiger lilies still persisting at the border. . . . Roads that once were clean from wall to wall are now narrowed to mere wagon trails."[180]

In "The Generations of Men," Frost mentions a "rock-strewn town where farming had fallen off, / And sprout-lands flourish where the ax has gone." Echoes of this abandonment can be heard in "The Wood-Pile" and "Directive" ("There is a house that is no more a house / Upon a farm that is no more a farm"—with later mention of "forty cellar holes").[181] "Stopping by Woods" could be considered a side effect of the skirmishes between large landholders and impoverished labor. The man who could let his woods lie idle was a convenient target for the quiet fury, or exhausted resignation, that lay beneath the surface of small American towns.

In an 1873 survey of New Hampshire town selectmen, those in Londonderry, just west of Derry, responded, "There are very few if any farmers who are making money. . . . There are men who style themselves farmers, but who have made their money by some kind of business or speculation such as lumbering, and return to the old homestead to spend their days and live by farming, but in reality live upon their income."[182] The young found their jobs in Derry's shoe factories.

The owner of the woods, however, is a blank. He could be rich enough not to live on his land, or just a man who had moved to the village for work. (He has a house there, so he isn't merely boarding.) Were these maple woods, they might have been used once a year when the sap was running, otherwise appearing neglected.[183] The owner may have moved because he was elderly, or because he possessed far more than he had use for, or because he needed a woodlot. Perhaps he just enjoyed owning a stretch of trees. We cannot say he was wealthy enough not to use them, like a great patron who scarcely glances at the art he's purchased—a Hearst, say, or Browning's duke in "My Last Duchess." Though he lives in the village, the owner cannot represent a simple opposition between capital and poverty, philistine and philosopher.

Frost grew up during a series of economic catastrophes that stretched from the Panic of 1873, the year before he was born, through the Panics of 1893 and 1896, two decades sometimes called the Long Depression.

Sharp falls in business and trade were more devastating than any the country had experienced, even worse than during the Great Depression to come. The standard of living declined by more than half between 1865 and 1898 and was not much better by 1905.[184] During such deflation, farmers did poorly, paid on the barrelhead only what little their crops were worth, while laborers—those still in work, whose wages stayed fairly steady—benefited from the drop in prices. Despite his annuity, Frost was barely scraping up a living. Had he gone to the local grocers to sell eggs or apples, the worse for him.

The traveler reins in his horse. We can read the woods then as no longer the absentee owner's, but briefly the traveler's own. He takes the woods at their honest value. Were Frost writing of himself, the lines open to a psychological turn where the woods stand for an abandon he must control if not suppress. The poem would then read more fiercely as an act of imaginative trespass and reparation. Could Frost have felt a touch of envy when he looked at woods owned by a man who could afford to live elsewhere? Who could afford, perhaps, not to work?

The guilty violation might give a little thrill. If the traveler felt that sense of trespass, though he isn't yet trespassing, he needn't worry—unless the fictive Melmotte were particularly disagreeable, he'd have been unlikely to take offense. Forty years ago, it was still local custom in northern New England not to lock a house in winter, in case someone needed to come out of the cold; and any land not posted was open to hunters. Some Yankees still live that way.

MY LITTLE HORSE

My little horse must think it queer
To stop without a farmhouse near
Between the woods and frozen lake
The darkest evening of the year.

He gives his harness bells a shake
To ask if there is some mistake.
The only other sound's the sweep
Of easy wind and downy flake.

In this winter's tale, the traveler drives home in the dark under steady snowfall. Otherwise the woods would not fill up. He's alone except for the horse, which provides comic relief. The harness makes clear the man is riding in something—buggy, sleigh, sulky, wagon, all of which Frost owned. Downy flakes fall gently. It's not a blizzard—only someone addicted to irony would describe a blizzard as a snowy evening. It's nothing like the weather in "Snow."

A New England road quickly becomes impassable in the snow, even a mild wind causing drifts. If a storm were threatening, the wagon would have been the best choice for the task the poet recalled at Bowdoin. Unlike the other vehicles, it had room for a load of eggs and other produce. When Frost wrote "horses" in the first draft, he was certainly thinking of a wagon, with a dash lamp and perhaps side lamps to light the way. He wouldn't want to wander off the road in the dark. (The wagon could have been drawn by one horse, like buggy, sleigh, or sulky.)

We're not required, however, to draw Frost's life into the poem. Indeed, if we untether ourselves from his recollection, the drama of the scene becomes more interesting. Had the traveler halted on a snowy road in buggy or sulky, he might never have reached home. Stopping to watch the woods fill up does not imply the ground was bare, making the sleigh impossible, though empty woods thickening with snow would be dramatic.

The traveler is simply going somewhere, and he stops. For all the poem cares, he could be traveling away as easily as traveling home. It's difficult to talk of the relation between life and art in Frost, because the life was entirely in service to the art, as it was in confessional poets like Lowell and Plath. (Nothing they confess, however, should be taken on trust.) Frost often ignores the binding constraints of his life—the harness, if you will—when he turns to poetry. The scene in a poet's mind, it must also be remembered, may be very different from the scene in the reader's.

The weather would have been below freezing. Downy flakes are the familiar flat, usually hexagonal snow crystals, forming between 32° and 25° or between 14° and −8° Fahrenheit.[185] (Snow between those ranges is shaped like small needles or prisms.) In such temperatures, a man might freeze to death, an exhausted traveler even more likely to succumb.

Return to the interior of Frost's tale: the poet owned a democrat wagon, a light flatbed farm wagon (in "Blueberries" he mentions a "democrat-load / Of all the young chattering Lorens alive").[186] The horse seems endowed with good sense—a go-ahead sort, without the dreaminess, the romantic wistfulness, of the traveler, without the sense of failure or deprivation. Many of Frost's characters resemble Frost, or what he imagined himself to be. During the years at Derry, he aged through his mid-twenties long into his thirties, no closer to his design of becoming a poet, burdened by family, mourning the death of his boy.[187] The man who wrote "Home Burial" probably lived those scenes. The world at times tumbles in on such a man.

The traveler doesn't halt in the woods, but beside them. Readers often forget, because of the title, that the road passes between woods and an ice-bound lake—the traveler is caught between two potential deaths. The woods and lake lie in the empty quarter between small towns, small-minded societies claustrophobic with the cares and woes of American character. (*Babbitt* was published in 1922, the year Frost wrote the poem.) In northern New England, that distance may stretch ten miles or more, a long way to travel even if you pass the occasional farm. It's hard to convey the desolation of those spaces, the sense of absolute isolation of such woods—and such farms. Full of old quarrels with myth and death, such vacant expanses are the glass plate on which to expose dark tales of the id.

An icy lake would have required days of temperatures below freezing. Wind off the lake, even easy wind, would have made the night still colder, in what now is called wind chill. The sound suggests a wind stronger than the traveler admits—he may be softening the bitterness of the weather. Or, to press the reading a little far, he only half hears the wind because he's mesmerized by the loveliness. Though the snow-covered lake might have been just as lethal as the woods, the traveler doesn't seem drawn there. Perhaps since the famous scene in *The Prelude* no lake has offered much by way of revelation.[188]

Sometime in these years, Frost wrote "Despair," a poem about suicide by drowning. He chose never to publish it. The speaker compares himself to a dead diver in lake or pond ("He drank the water, saying, 'Oh let me go— / *God* let me go'"), but at the end the speaker also seems to drown. The sonnet ends hauntingly, "I tore the muscles from my limbs and choked. / My sudden struggle may have dragged down some / White lily from the air—and now the fishes come." Lawrance Thompson, in his biography of Frost, used the poet's handwriting to date the sole copy to 1906.[189]

Such a poem didn't fit with the poet Frost became, but it seems to derive from that same bleak period. Thompson notes that "each time [Frost] drove from his farm with his old horse and wagon along the back-country road to Derry Depot for provisions, he passed an isolated pond deep enough for drowning." The poet told Elizabeth Shepley Sergeant that he and his family "sometimes took drives on forgotten Derry roads that had forgotten farms." There was one "with a black 'tarn' beside it (for convenient suicide) and what a pang it cost the poet not to have chosen it!"[190] Probably he was joking.

"The darkest evening," Frost said, was the winter solstice. A similar phrase had been used half a century before by Alexander Smith, a poet once as beloved as Frost. In 1920, a contributor to the *Atlantic* mentioned *Dreamthorp* and *North of Boston* among books suitable for kitchen reading—"utterly sincere,—simple and candid,—caring nothing at all for the shams and pretensions of life but everything for its realities."[191] Consider the opening of part 3 of Smith's "A Boy's Poem":

A dark hour came, and left us desolate:
Then, as a beggar thrust by menial hands
From comfortable doors, doth wrap his rags
Around him, ere he face the whistling wind
And flying showers that travel through the night,
We gathered what we had; and she and I
Went forth together to the cruel world.
O we were bare and naked as the trees
That stand up silent in the freezing air,
With black boughs motionless against the sky,
While midnight holds her lonely starry sway.[192]

The setting is probably Glasgow; but note the "dark hour," the "whistling wind," the cold, the hard travel, then the simile "bare and naked as the trees / That stand up silent in the freezing air," the motionless branches, midnight. In European folklore, the woods were often a place of danger or refuge.[193] Some two dozen lines later, the speaker recollects his birth:

> Red Autumn died unseen along the waste,
> The soundless snow came down in thickening flakes,
> And Poverty, who sat beside our hearth,
> Blew out the feeble fire, and all was dark.
> It was the closing evening of the year,
> The night that I was born.[194]

The closing evening of the year. Though the scene in "Stopping by Woods" is different, the trappings and themes are eerily similar, especially if Frost had never read Alexander Smith. There were poems by Smith, though not this poem, in Frost's well-thumbed copies of *The Oxford Book of English Verse* (1900) and *The Oxford Book of Victorian Verse* (1912).[195]

It's curious that two stanzas in "Stopping by Woods" are given, more or less, to the horse—this clever displacement concentrates on the trivial while the poem ignores what lies beneath. If his thoughts were dark, a man might think the horse had sensed his despair; but even were that merely projection he would feel no less devastated. There's a similarly willful horse in "A Hundred Collars," where a college professor, having missed his train, must share a room in a small-town hotel. The man already in the room is a subscription agent for the Bow *Weekly News.* The professor is right to be wary—such agents were often suspected of jiggery-pokery. (Frost had sold magazine subscriptions as a boy.)[196] The paper was apparently fictitious; but the annual subscription cost the same dollar charged by the *Derry News,* the village weekly.[197] The agent is an easy-going sort:

> I take the reins
> Only when someone's coming, and the mare
> Stops when she likes: I tell her when to go.
> I've spoiled Jemima in more ways than one.

She's got so she turns in at every house
As if she has some sort of curvature,
No matter if I have no errand there.[198]

"The mare / Stops when she likes." The horse in "Stopping by Woods" tells the owner when to go. They're both in charge.

Frost had no illusions about horses—he says the horse "must" think the stop queer, which is some way short of saying that the beast does, or could. It seems at first yet more projection. Horses are so easily trained, however, compared to undomesticated equids like zebras, that disrupting their routines makes them uneasy. In the following stanza, the traveler interprets the shake of harness bells as impatience, not a stray shiver. Horses adapt to cold, growing a longer coat when the days begin to shorten. Though the solstice comes fairly early in a New England winter, the horse should have had its full coat.[199] Besides, the horse doesn't share the man's fears—if they *are* fears—or his hypnotic fixation. The horse, which no doubt just wants to get home to his stall and his feed, is the animating devil that draws the traveler back to his conscience. That the traveler is saved more or less by accident, whether by shiver or shake, may be part of the dry comedy.

The harness bells deserve a moment. There's no evidence of a New Hampshire law requiring the driver of a sleigh to fit his horse with bells, though such laws had been enacted in Michigan, Wisconsin, and Massachusetts. A reference in an 1833 Nashua newspaper is probably to a local ordinance.[200] Sleighs, because almost silent, could be dangerous to pedestrians—a creaking wagon would hardly have needed bells, and the only examples I've found of wagon horses decked out so come from Europe. Unless Frost were the only man in New Hampshire to put bells on a wagon horse, the bells reveal a crucial fracture between the poem and the tale. Though Frost says "harness bells," the term was often used for "sleigh bells." "Harness bells" fits the meter. Perhaps Frost in his draft changed back to a single horse because the sleigh was more appealing. That he never specifies wagon or sleigh is an ambiguity the reader must bear.

Why would the horse think it queer? Because it must be used to stopping at farmhouses. This halt beside the woods on a freezing night is out of character for the traveler. Whatever caused him to draw back the reins must have been an impulse perhaps never succumbed to before. The traveler's explanation touches on the whimsy that would make light reading of the poem—the horse represents, as a farcical touch, the social world that judges dreamers and romantics, or perhaps protects them from themselves. Still, a traveler so affected by the sight of woods under snow, so susceptible to the message nature might write, would not be immune to reading irritation—or warning, or criticism—in a shiver.

As a young poet, Frost once admitted he had a sweet tooth for the "traditional cliches"; but his lazy phrasing may sometimes deceive a modern ear.[201] Frost never tried too hard to give the language tension—his interest was always deeper, in the torsions of meditation or the conflict between people. "Easy wind" might seem difficult to salvage; but the range of "easy" has encompassed, as the *OED* reminds us, "freedom from pain or constraint," "comfortable, luxurious, quiet," "free from mental anxiety, care, or apprehension," "indolent," and, when used of motion, "not hurried, gentle." (Dickinson had "easy Sweeps of Sky.")[202] The very peacefulness of the scene conceals the threat—and freedom from pain is precisely its fatal allure. An easy road could be traveled without hindrance. An easy burden was no burden—and burdens are the underlying theme. (In Frost's tale, produce unsold, presents unbought.) In the more ominous reading of the poem, ease is what the traveler cannot feel—and ease at this period offers the sharpest and unhappiest contrast to what Frost knew.

"Downy flake" seems trite now, but in Frost's day the reader would have heard more acutely the old meaning—soft as goose or duck down. Chaucer spoke of the down of doves, and there were down beds as far back as the fourteenth century (Robert Greene, before 1592: "Mars lies slumbering on his downy bed," *OED*). Feather pillows were a luxury when many farm pillows were filled with corn husks or hay (Spanish moss was a little fancier). The link here is to the desire to sleep, always a hazard to a traveler stranded in the cold. Still, "downy flake" was not a new phrase—it had been used by Cowper and Thomas Moore, as well as in an early eighteenth-century translation of Oppian ("While downy Flakes lie scattered on the Ground").[203] Frost raised chickens. Only a couple of months after he moved to Derry, an ad appeared in the *Derry News*:[204]

> Breeding Cockerels
> ## WHITE WYANDOTTES
> I have for sale a number of thorough-
> bred Cockerels from a strain of first class
> layers at $1.00 apiece.
> R. L. FROST, Magoon Place,
> Or Lock Box, 140, West Derry.

A man who had plucked a few would know, not just that drifting snow is soft as feathers, but that the air filled with flakes looks like an explosion in a hen house.

"The woods are lovely" also doesn't take the language very far from the surface. The adjective seems more English than American, but Frost had spent two and a half years in England between 1912 and 1915. The phrase can be found, among other places, in *The Journal of Horticulture* (1880) and in a poem of 1827 from the *New-York Mirror, and Ladies' Literary Gazette* ("The woods are lovely in their gorgeous train"). Southey in *Madoc* (1805)—"Thy summer woods / Are lovely"—comes near.[205]

Of course the adjective was broadcast—in *Rokeby* (1813), Walter Scott has, not just "lovely woods," but a lovely heir, vale, glade, road, maid, land, sight, as well as a "lovely child, a lovelier wife."[206] Most early meanings of the word have died out (loving, amorous, friendly, lovable); but this vague synonym for "attractive," first for people, then for things, remains. ("Attractive" has itself almost lost touch with its origins, as have "rapture" and "charm," "captivate" and "enchant.") Other phrases in the poem, like "dark and deep," are found more often than one might imagine ("The rising world of waters dark and deep," *Paradise Lost*)[207]—as are "I think I know," "must think it queer," "there is some mistake," "miles to go," "before I sleep." Frost constructed something memorable from phrases anyone might have picked up by the way. "Stopping by woods," however, and "promises to keep" (in the sense of having them) are rare or nonexistent before the poem was published.

THE WOODS ARE LOVELY

The woods are lovely, dark and deep.
But I have promises to keep,
And miles to go before I sleep,
And miles to go before I sleep.

The lighter reading comes easily enough. However alluring the woods, their darkness and depth can't safely be explored on such a night. (Their mystery inhabits an enchantment.) The traveler's duties beckon, so with a shake, or a shiver, and a recollection of how far he has to travel, he rides away. The power of the poem lies in how deviously, how hauntingly, a darker reading lurks beneath the lighter one. Only gradually does something lethal seem concealed within the shadowy woods.

It's not impossible that the poem was meant to be somewhat droll, that "the woods are lovely, dark and deep" is no more than aesthetic appreciation. The description, coming where the traveler is almost obliged to offer an explanation for tarrying, must be followed by qualification or rejection, if he's not to stay. The traveler doesn't consider the description for long before being roused to himself—his promises cancel out those bewitching trees almost immediately. Frost's later tale was a recognition of all those things he found troubling to admit. Traveling slowly in such temperatures can be risky. The drowsy numbness should remind us of Keats.

The woods represented everything wrong with disorderly nature, a patch of wildness within civilized bounds. Was Eden garden or forest? "Paradise" came from the Persian word for walled garden, and "Eden" probably from an Aramaic word meaning "fruitful"; but artists have at times—Cranach the Elder in *The Garden of Eden*, Brueghel and Rubens in *The Garden of Eden with the Fall of Man*—interpreted it as a jungle of wild animals that would have gratified both Rousseau the painter and Rousseau the philosopher. From Creation to Expulsion lasts but a few score verses.

James Fenimore Cooper and Henry David Thoreau might be called the tutelary spirits of the American hinterland. The American sublime depended on American landscape; and by the later nineteenth century that came to mean, through painters like Thomas Moran, Albert Bierstadt, and Thomas Hill, the untrammeled spaces of the American West. The exotic realms of these artists who began in or near the Hudson River School originally lay in the forests of New York and New Hampshire. The founder of that school, Thomas Cole, made his own version of the Garden of Eden look like the Hudson Valley or the Catskills, with palms added and what might be the Matterhorn.[208]

In readings both light and dark, the woods become seductive—dark beauty cuts both ways, toward fulfillment or destruction. Even if the speaker pulls away at the end of the poem, that doesn't mean the enticement is lessened or won't call again, some dark night on the road. To be powerful, the lines must leave the polarities unresolved. Perhaps they're not truly opposed—for the traveler, peril is submerged in a terrible beauty.

Are the woods "lovely, dark and deep," as Frost's original punctuation had it? Or are they "lovely, dark, and deep," as his posthumous editor, Edward Connery Lathem, revised the line in *The Poetry of Robert Frost* (1969), long the standard edition?[209] (Lathem's frequent alteration of Frost's punctuation has been much deplored.) Frost's absent comma left loveliness defined as "dark and deep," while the editor's revision gave the three qualities equal weight. Perhaps the poet was insensitive to the difference or entertained by the ambiguity, but his choice must have been deliberate. Frost knew very well how to use the Oxford comma ("measured against maple, birch, and oak," "I'd summon grouse, rabbit, and deer").[210] Despite the encroaching dark, the traveler can see something under the cloud cover—snowfall and ground snow scatter light effectively, making the evening lighter. He cannot see far into the dark woods, but he knows or senses that they're deep.

The scrupulous Library of America edition of Frost's poems (1995) removed Lathem's comma after "dark." It failed to restore the period after "deep," however, which ended the line in all early printings. The period was present through the first printing of *Collected Poems of Robert Frost* (New York: Henry Holt, 1939); but the piece of type became worn, as is evident in the printing of September 1941. By the printing of July 1945, the type had eroded so badly the period had vanished, except for a faint smudge. *Complete Poems of Robert Frost* (New York: Henry Holt, 1949) was apparently set from one of the later printings of *Collected Poems* (1939), with the period missing. Frost didn't notice when he corrected the proofs, but someone else afterward inserted a comma.[211]

The period stops the cold contemplation cold, as if the traveler had to think hard at that moment, as if the only right choice were to stay and walk into the woods. The "But" that follows then comes with a tortured heave. The comma makes the shift from contemplation to resolution entirely too easy. The case for the period—critically, not forensically— would be that the tetrameter runs along so fluently Frost realized it had to be brought up short at this moment of decision. The traveler has halted, been woken to himself by the horse's bells, and taken a last long look at the woods. Then, after the pause the period demands, he gives himself excuse to move on.

The poem first appeared in the *New Republic* of March 7, 1923 (reprinted the following month in the British magazine *Chapbook*).[212] The version was slightly revised for his book *New Hampshire* later that year, where Frost changed "The little horse" of the draft to "My little horse," which established a stronger bond between man and beast. Responsibility is the shadow of possession—the traveler might have been more likely to heed the animal's warning. Curiously, the thirteenth line in the *New Republic* read, as it did in the draft, "The woods are lovely dark and deep," with no internal punctuation at all.[213]

Is the traveler thinking of suicide? It's possible that from the start he saw not just allure, or the emptiness of terror, but escape. The woods are beckoning—enchanting, perhaps—yet nothing before that crucial "but" implies that the traveler can't look, appreciate, and quietly depart. That he has halted long enough for the horse to shake suggests he has lingered. Does beauty always wear a shroud? It was with their beguiling song that the Sirens lured sailors to destruction—and there's a mini-*Odyssey* in this journey from nowhere, from a past not recounted to a home at increasing distance. Indeed, if we take this traveler's tale as the epic writ small, the attraction of the woods makes sense—beauty can be as fatal as other poisons. Odysseus was waylaid by beauty, indeed, overcome by just a song. Whether the Sirens sang in Greek or just warbled indecently remains unknown.

A man who thinks about walking into the freezing woods could as easily walk onto the lake, if the ice were thin. Recall the miller's wife in

Edwin Arlington Robinson's "The Mill," who after her husband's suicide walks to the millpond:

> Black water, smooth above the weir
>   Like starry velvet in the night,
> Though ruffled once, would soon appear
>   The same as ever to the sight.[214]

That was one method of a quiet country death.

A number of critics have proposed that the dark woods and frozen lake place the traveler between Dante's *selva oscura* and the lake of Cocytus—that would leave the man at both ends of Hell. It's an ingenious reading (Hell with no Virgil except the horse), but like many such readings perhaps overingenious. Still, on this night the traveler has the chance to begin his own *Commedia*, his own journey through Hell; and he doesn't take it. Perhaps he's already aware of the icy lake of traitors at his back.

The traveler's longing to enter the woods, if we choose to read the poem so, is very different from a desire to walk out onto the unknown blankness of the lake. Unless the lake were pocket-sized, it might look, covered in snow, with snow falling, like the endlessness of the Arctic. The woods are inviting because they seem a kind of home, a refuge where a man can hide from responsibility—that's what makes them hazardous. At least since the days of Robin Hood, if not the Christian hermits, men have headed to the woods to escape the burdens or iniquities of the world. Loners, criminals, the monster of Frankenstein—all found a place where they could isolate themselves without choosing to die. Thoreau wrote in *Walden* of the virtues of being lost in the woods:

> Often in a snow storm, even by day, one will come out upon a well-known road and yet find it impossible to tell which way leads to the village. Though he knows that he has travelled it a thousand times, he cannot recognize a feature in it, but it is as strange to him as if it were a road in Siberia. . . . Not till we are completely lost, or turned round, . . . do we appreciate the vastness and strangeness of Nature.

Thoreau saw self-knowledge there—"Not till we have lost the world," he wrote, "do we begin to find ourselves."[215]

The trees may offer knowledge to some, solace to others; but on a snowy night, the temperature below freezing, they contain nothing for a man without shelter or fire—nothing but extinction. The traveler must know this, but no doubt the certainty of death and the loveliness of the woods are part of the attraction. The power of that desire is made clearer by how near he might have come to staying. What if the horse hadn't jingled its bells?

The feelings in "Stopping by Woods" were not so rare in Frost. The mise en scène closely resembles "Into My Own," the opening poem of *A Boy's Will* (1913), the poet's first book, published not long after he had taken his family to England in 1912.

> One of my wishes is that those dark trees,
> So old and firm they scarcely show the breeze,
> Were not, as 'twere, the merest mask of gloom,
> But stretched away unto the edge of doom.
>
> I should not be withheld but that some day
> Into their vastness I should steal away,
> Fearless of ever finding open land,
> Or highway where the slow wheel pours the sand.
>
> I do not see why I should e'er turn back,
> Or those should not set forth upon my track
> To overtake me, who should miss me here
> And long to know if still I held them dear.
>
> They would not find me changed from him they knew—
> Only more sure of all I thought was true.[216]

The wish to disappear into those dark trees (*old*, so perhaps remains of ancient forest), the woods both dark and deep (where one might never find farmed land or highway again), perhaps the slightly arrogant touch of the ending—these are announcements of a disposition.

"Stopping by Woods" is darker. Frost touches there on the American dread, so common in northern and western states, of freezing to death.

It was a genuine fear, since in a blizzard (the word that shortly before the Civil War came to mean a severe snowstorm) a traveler could easily lose his way. The poem might seem too complicated in its slants and affirmations to be read simply, but there's something darkly tempting about those woods—and a man in the depressed mood to which Frost confessed might have seen such a death as peaceful. He was highly offended, however, when John Ciardi, in a provocative 1958 article,[217] argued that the traveler had a death wish: "I suppose people think I lie awake nights worrying about what people like Ciardi of the *Saturday Review* write and publish about me . . . ," the poet grumbled. "He makes my 'Stopping By Woods' out a death poem. . . . It's hardly a death poem." Frost continued, "No mystery about it. . . . These people can't seem to get it through their heads that the obvious meaning of a poem is the right one."[218]

Frost was not a man comfortable with his fears. At a lavish dinner for his eighty-fifth birthday, the critic Lionel Trilling called him a "terrifying poet."[219] The poet seemed disconcerted by the remark. He usually rejected the bleaker reading of his lines, but with "Stopping by Woods" he had already admitted his utter despair to his daughter, as well as to the young man at Bowdoin. The poem revealed, or at least permitted, a reading too close to the truth—it's hard to imagine Frost plucking the story from thin air, just for the sake of sympathy.

What exactly were those promises? If we keep to the narrow track of Frost's tale, duties to family, obligations explicit in marriage (ceremonial vows having legal consequence), and those stray professions and trivial promises to wife and children that are burdens only when a man cannot fulfill them. Frost resisted the pure autobiographical, so the unnamed traveler might have made promises to God, state, man, woman, employer, stranger. We should not forget his implicit promise to the horse, which if abandoned might freeze to death. The poem opens itself to all the burdens that constitute a life: social contracts met easily or by hard graft, business matters that leave a weary trail of paper, old resolutions unkept. Frost's poems often open out this way, whatever the autobiographical seed-corn. That's the matter of poems when narrow experience is adjusted into art.

AND MILES TO GO

The most striking turn in the poem—what makes it memorable—is the closing repetition of "And miles to go before I sleep." It displays, perhaps, the fatigue, the reluctance, the beaten-down condition of the traveler—he has surrendered to the demands of the world he has almost forsaken. The same exhaustion might have made him give up, had he been seduced just a little more. Something draws him back, and not something as abstract as "promises." These must be specific promises, ones that may conflict with those he has made to himself.

The ending is even starker when we recall that what the woods have offered and the traveler has refused is sleep, the sleep of freezing to death. The snow's comforting but lethal embrace seems gentle. Travelers who burrow deeply enough may even survive the night—there's more than one reason to call it a "blanket" of snow. "Sleep" has a dark ambiguity here—the traveler comes close to sleeping forever in those woods. For Frost, the day would have been long, farmers on market days usually rising long before dawn. The disappointment has at last caught up with him. We might wonder, if not for the poet's habit of rising late, why he spent so long getting to and from a village scarcely two miles away.

The lines possess a rather sprightly rhythm for a poem about suicide contemplated and rejected, but "sleep" is the word that retrospectively sends the poem toward the funereal and melancholy. The traveler wants to sleep, but he cannot sleep *there*. It was not by accident that the German chemist's apprentice who first extracted an active alkaloid from the opium poppy named it morphium, after the god of sleep. We know it as morphine—to "fall into the arms of Morpheus" was the nineteenth-century euphemism for nodding off. Frost's story at Bowdoin reveals that just such bleak thoughts lay beneath the poem—and that, even if edited out, they remained lodged there for *him*. If you call the underlying distemper of the poet's tale merely recognition of a failure terrible and complete, the black longings overlie reasons the finished poem has suppressed.

Had the invitation been any stronger, the traveler might not have been able to resist the call of the snowy Sirens. (It would push things too far to say the wind was their song.) Still, it's possible that his first hesitation was the compelling one, that these were not his woods and he had no right to enter them, not that such a worry would stop a man who really wanted to die. If he were doubtful, however, the embarrassment of his corpse being found on someone else's land might have been enough.

What should we call the tone of the final lines? The promises form the standing debts recalled only after the horse's reminder. At the end we have the denial of art and longing, of beauty and desire, for the burden of promises very different from the burden of promise Frost felt as a young artist. The tone could be touched with sadness (at having to abandon a beautiful place), resignation (that his liabilities to the world loom larger than his attraction to the woods), frustration or regret, irritation, anger, fatigue, self-castigation, consolation, determination, rueful acknowledgment, relief, even love. All suggest themselves, even were the lines tossed off nonchalantly. Nonchalance may be the deepest road into the self. If sleep is a metaphor for death, for the easing of great pain, the poem's traveler is admitting that his life has some distance to run—that may be a burden as well.

Frost's poems are often an excellent mirror of the reader's ambivalence. The tone of the ending could be, could have been intended to be, a sort of harrumph, a Yankee's "Well, I must be getting on. No more nonsense, now." Perhaps the poet did not see all the possibilities, which put every reading of the poem at hazard from some silent alternative. The second time the traveler says the line, it might even have been in a different tone. In *Pale Fire*, Nabokov's scholar Charles Kinbote calls "Stopping by Woods" "one of the greatest short poems in the English language." Kinbote believes "And miles to go before I sleep" is "personal and physical" the first time, "metaphysical and universal" the second.[220]

FORM

In Vermont, one evening the summer of 1922 (Lawrance Thompson says July, then June), Frost worked through the night writing the title poem of *New Hampshire*, a poem that must have made some readers think they'd been wrong about the poet.[221] This satire of manners was no doubt meant to conjure up Horace, but Horace Greeley on a bad day could have done no worse. There are poets like Auden who can write as public men, then retreat to the privacies of genius. Frost was a disaster as a public man, his jokes so leaden you wonder how he could think them funny ("Lately in converse with a New York alec / About the new school of the pseudo-phallic . . .").[222] The cornball sophistry of his state-of-literature poem that was also a state-of-the-nation poem might leave you sorry to be within a mile of his opinions.

Having finished the draft of this disaster at sunrise, Frost wasn't ready to sleep. "Stopping by Woods" was written "with one stroke of the pen," he later remarked.[223] He made a similar remark about a number of poems. Frost told Thompson,

> there was something more that he wanted to write. Tired as he was, he sat down, and heard the old sound of the voice speaking words clearly. Half asleep, and without any consciousness of ever having thought of the idea before, he continued to write steadily until the short poem was done.[224]

This slightly spooky autodictation went a little far toward the mythology of self in which Frost delighted. Perhaps he said such things just to see if someone would believe him. John Ciardi was one of many who heard a version: "Time and again I have heard him say that he just wrote it off, that it just came to him, and that he set it down as it came."[225]

There's no reason to disbelieve Frost, however, when he claimed that the poem "just came." What may be the first draft has survived, as mentioned—but only the last three stanzas, which show many changes, some radical. It's almost impossible for a poem to appear all at once without second thoughts. The revisions may have rushed like a millrace, may have been no more than the immediate recasting poets often do in their heads—here we simply have the record. It might have seemed to Frost that the poem was born complete, without the long wrestling and spilled ink, the third thoughts and fifth thoughts, that frequently attend a poem's birth. Even so, except where he inserted revisions the hand shows no hesitation at all—it's the fluent writing of a fair copy, not a draft.

The form Frost chose has been called an "interlocking Rubáiyát," taking the Rubáiyát stanza (*aaba*) and using the unrhymed third line as the base rhyme for the stanza following (*aaba bbcb ccdc*). In 1898, Frost had written "The Rubaiyat of Carl Burell"[226] (the friend later his hired man)—the poem was fashioned in limericks, but Frost almost certainly knew Edward FitzGerald's translation of *The Rubáiyát of Omar Khayyám* (1859).[227] The interlocking form, however, was probably Frost's invention.

THE DRAFT OPENING

The draft page shows how difficult simplicity can be. We don't have a sheet with the opening stanza, so perhaps Frost spoiled a whole page on alternatives or started scribbling on a scrap now lost. (His ruled notebook paper fit three quatrains almost exactly.) First he wrote, "The steaming horses think it queer / To," then canceled it. Having interviewed the poet in the early 1940s, John Holmes reported—in Charles W. Cooper's *Preface to Poetry* (1946)—that Frost "began with what was the actual experience of stopping at night by some dark woods in winter, and the fact that there were two horses. He remembered what he saw then. 'The steaming horses think it queer.'"[228] Holmes had a copy of the draft before him when he questioned the poet. As Frost never owned a pair of horses, already he had edged into fiction. Bleau recalled his talking of only the single horse. The disparities in the poet's tales offer their own commentary.

The next line appears roughly as follows:

> Horse Must
> Little ~~xxxx will~~
> The ~~horse begins to~~ think it queer

The poet had started again, "The horse begins to think it queer," probably then deleting "begins to" while adding "little" and "will," then crossing out "horse" and squeezing in a word now illegible ("xxxx" above, probably a one-syllable synonym, possibly "mare")[229]—at last restoring "horse" and replacing "will" with "must." (The handwriting seems to indicate that these last two revisions were almost simultaneous.)

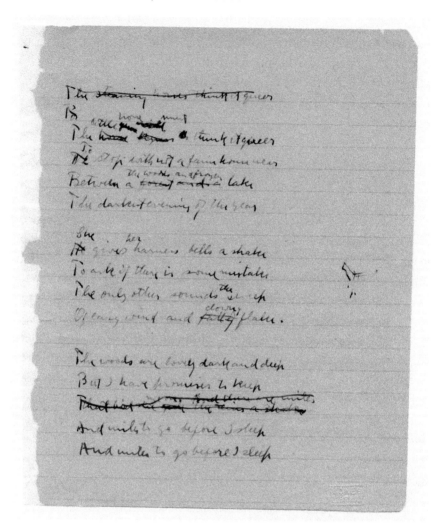

Draft of Robert Frost, "Stopping by Woods on a Snowy Evening."
Source: Courtesy of Special Collections, The Jones Library, Inc., Amherst, Mass.

The line looks set, "The little horse must think it queer"; but he started the next line "We stop," only to return to his original idea, "To stop." Queried by Holmes, Frost replied,

I launched into the construction "My little horse must think it queer that we should stop." I didn't like omitting the "that" and I had no room for "should." I had the luck to get out of it with the infinitive.[230]

That isn't exactly what the draft shows (he didn't make the change to "My" until its printing in the *New Republic*); but, except for altering "a forest and a lake" to "the woods and frozen lake," the stanza was otherwise finished and almost unpunctuated, as was common in his drafts.

The third stanza begins, "He gives harness bells a shake." Frost must have been writing so rapidly he failed to put pronoun or article before "harness bells," making a similar error two lines later, before "sweep." Then he changed the horse from male to female, so the draft read, "She gives her harness bells a shake." This must have been almost immediate, probably when Frost first read the line over, because he caught the missing word and put "her," not "his." Had "mare" been the word scratched out above, he might have tried to sneak the idea into this line, or gone back to the opening only later to replace the unnecessary word with the earlier version, "horse." The change to a mare might have drawn the poem closer to life, since from early 1902 to early 1906 the only horse he owned was Eunice, the small high-stepping mare, preceded by a large roan gelding named Billy and succeeded by another large roan gelding, also named Billy—or Billy-the-Second.[231] The incident was most likely to have taken place in the years he owned Eunice, if it took place at all. By the time he published the poem, he had changed the horse back to a gelding (stallions being unsuitable). Later in the stanza, he replaced "falling," the redundant adjective, with "downy."

No one seems to have pointed out the obvious, that "Stopping by Woods" may originally have started, "The steaming horses think it queer." So long as he had the title in mind, or one similar, the poem would have made perfect sense. The eventual opening, providing the anxiety crucial to the psychological complication and moral depth—the traveler enters as a man with guilts—could have come belatedly. (A single horse would have a more defined and intimate relation to this lone traveler.) Frost might have thought he'd finished the poem, hence, even with the hesitation and revision at the top of the page, this near-fair copy of a three-stanza version.

THE DRAFT CLOSE

There's no way of halting Frost's interlocking Rubáiyát without leaving a line unrhymed, except by adding a line to pick up the hanging rhyme, as Dante did at the end of his terza rima cantos. In "Stopping by Woods," Frost might instead have rhymed this odd line on "ō," the base rhyme in the first stanza, making a cycle of the whole, though the echo would have gone unheard. He found a third way, breaking the form by continuing the stanza rhyme through the third line, providing closure by repeating an entire line. Such a master stroke, leaving no line unrhymed, became all but a signature—it can never be borrowed without imitating Frost. Here is a transcription of the draft stanza:

> The woods are lovely dark and deep
> But I have promises to keep
> ~~me on. And there are miles~~   [". A" written over ", a"]
> ~~That bid me give the reins a shake~~
> And miles to go before I sleep
> And miles to go before I sleep

The poet admitted in a letter to Charles Madison, published in the revised edition of Brooks's and Warren's *Understanding Poetry* (1950), that the ending had raised hell. Initially he'd written the third line

> in such a way as to call for another stanza when I didn't want another stanza and didn't have another stanza in me, but with great presence of mind and a sense of what a good boy I was I instantly struck the line out and made my exit with a repeat end.[232]

The draft stanza's first lines read, "The woods are lovely dark and deep / But I have promises to keep / That bid me give the reins a shake." It's not clear whether he continued immediately to the fourth line or, as he said, stopped to reconsider. ("Stopping by Woods" could have ended with the peripeteia "But I have promises to keep," making an un-Shakespearean Shakespearean sonnet.) A new rhyme-sound would have been left hanging, so bringing the "āk" rhyme down from the third stanza could have been intentional. The echo of the third stanza's base rhyme would have been unorthodox, but more pleasing than leaving the line unrhymed. Frost must have forgotten, however (this is another sign the poem was, then or originally, written headlong), that he'd just used "shake"—it would have been rattling around in his head. Changing the rhyme to "awake" would not have been impossible.

The poet instead revised the third line to "That bid me on and there are miles" (altered briefly to "That bid me on. And there are miles . . ."), which may accidentally have provided the solution. "That bid me on" is weak as motivation or transition—the poet realized that if he dropped the line the poem could find a more troubling register. The usual notion, found in John Holmes's remarks, is that once "miles" gave Frost the clue he quickly wrote the pair of repeating lines.[233] This is certainly plausible, but the intermediate version of the stanza may instead have been:

> The woods are lovely, dark and deep
> But I have promises to keep
> That bid me on, and there are miles
> And miles to go before I sleep.

That seems more probable, however Frost recalled it decades later. The draft can't reveal whether he started to revise the third line before or after writing the next. If he'd already written the last line or had it in mind, he'd have seen that the syntax of "But I have promises to keep / That bid me give the reins a shake / And miles to go before I sleep" is ambiguous—it's not immediately clear whether "miles" is governed by "have" or "give." "Miles" here might have suggested "miles" for the line before, the internal rhyme providing a sort of closure—perhaps that was consolation enough.

The mistaken repetition of "shake" may have given him the idea of repeating a word in closure—or, no, a whole line, resolving the discord with the unexpected return, which he called a repetend. (When base or crown molding cannot be continued into a wall because it would look awkward, the molding is "returned," folded into itself at a ninety-degree angle.) Sensing the failure of the third line in either version, Frost might at last have seen in "miles to go" a far better line and decided to repeat it, bringing the poem to its unexpected close.

In a letter to Sylvester Baxter, the year after the poem was drafted, Frost recounted his struggle with rhyme:

> What [the repetend] does externally is save me from a third line promising another stanza. . . . A dead [e.g., unrhymed] line in the last stanza alone would have been a flaw. I considered for a moment four of a kind in the last stanza but that would have made five including the third in the stanza before it. I considered for a moment winding up with a three line stanza. The repetend was the only logical way to end such a poem.[234]

The three-line stanza would presumably have been "The woods are lovely dark and deep. / But I have promises to keep, / And miles to go before I sleep." He might have seen, in other words, that the draft third line was superfluous, seen too that he could bring the last line up and end there. His brilliance was in realizing that if he repeated the line, the poem had found a satisfying and unexpected close.

There were a number of logical ways to end the poem. Drafts can't always speak. Frost may even have considered repeating the last line as a flourish after closing the poem with the Rubáiyát stanza, but the five-line stanza would have been unwieldy. If that's how we should read the palimpsest of the draft, Frost saw its wordy inadequacy. Crossing out the third line, he achieved that rare thing in poetry, a *coup de theatre*.

FROST'S TALE

A poem may possess an autobiographical germ, the infection or inflection of a life; but once freed of circumstance its meanings become open to negotiation. Frost's later tale of despair in the snow has its limiting attractions, but how far can the critic reasonably go beyond that? Until Occam takes back his razor? What if the owner were God, whose house, His church, stands in the village? This has been proposed.[235] The woods would then be protected, holy, a place where a man might wander or meditate distant from the roils of the fallen world. (The identifying pronoun in line 4 is in lowercase. Frost capitalized the divine pronoun uniformly in the masques but only once in a poem, and then in his first book.)[236] However lovely the scene, the traveler has made promises and must abandon those sacred woods until he owes less, perhaps, to the world. Such woods would align with Romantic notions of Nature, the embodiment of a Deistic universe that offers man the sublime, whether or not he has faith. Edmund Burke saw the particular attraction of sublime wilderness: "In nature dark, confused, uncertain images have a greater power on the fancy to form the grander passions than those have which are more clear and determinate."[237] It is only a mild irony that Frost's woods would almost certainly have been second growth, so only the imitation of wilderness.

Take a different reading that stretches the bounds of the probable. The villages of East Derry, Derry, and West Derry (the last, through which the railroad passed, also called Derry Depot) run east to west along the old road traveling southwest to Nashua. Born by the Pacific, Frost had come of age in eastern mill-towns when not dropping in and out of college. Apart from his brief misadventure in Methuen, the outskirts of these villages, which together form the town of Derry, were the first place he had lived among farmers. Say he had two selves, a village self and a country self (a pastoral version of Henry James's "The Private Life"). The village self would have been a man like his grandfather, a farmer who became overseer of a cotton mill, a man of money and good sense, living in town but with property elsewhere—that is, the Derry farm.[238] The owner of the woods in this fantasy of selves would have been the village Frost. This practical Frost would never see his dreamy country self stop by the woods. With village manners and village proprieties, the village Frost would never succumb to the rich enticements of dark trees and falling snow. Such a man couldn't imagine doing the unexpected. These two views of the world mark the inner division, the tension, between the two Frosts. He almost became a village Frost when he moved to town in 1909.

The Frost who stops is the poet, who must risk the encounter in order to survive it. One of Frost's poetic virtues is that he could court the darkness within himself (in "Desert Places," among other places), then draw back, divided between the pragmatic self and the self taken by nature and beauty. This reading of Frost as his own dark twin is mildly fanciful; but many men are divided against themselves, and only a man like the doppelgänger would stop on such a chilly night, against reason, against the instinct of the horse, against the promises that eventually draw him home. I doubt Frost would have been upset by either reading, since both avoid intimations of the death wish he was so eager to reject. The lighter reading, toward wildness and art, is pulled by the darker toward escape from obligation and failure.

The poet once claimed he'd like to follow "Stopping by Woods" with "forty pages of footnotes"—whether his or his critics', he didn't say.[239] (He probably meant endnotes, like Eliot's for *The Waste Land*.) He also remarked to an audience, about the meaning of his verse, "I'll take credit for anything you find."[240] Would the criticism stand criticism, however? With symbols so free-floating, it's difficult to bring the poet's life strictly to bear—the conditions of the life offer only hints, not strictures. Shadings, not clean lines.

Can we determine the precise date of Frost's dark night of the soul? He knew his calendar: during the years in Derry, the solstice occurred December 22, though when he was growing up it was almost always the twenty-first. The year could have been as early as 1900, when the *Derry News* noted on September 28 that the Magoon Place had been sold "to R. Frost of Lawrence, Mass., who will take immediate possession." He moved in days later.[241]

According to Lawrance Thompson, Carl Burell and his grandfather were soon "helping to pack eggs in boxes and load live 'broilers' into crates," arranging to buy, with old Mr. Frost's money, a Jersey cow and the democrat wagon. Apples were picked and shipped to Boston. Still, the hired man was working under a sharecropping arrangement that gave him most of the fruit and vegetables.[242] Apart from the year Carl Burell left, Frost didn't pick apples—he sold them from the tree, according to the Derry historian Richard Holmes.[243]

Frost arrived at Derry in debt, perhaps debt even beyond the promissory notes held by his grandfather and the rent never paid to his Methuen landlady—he had no spare cash, we know from an incident not long after, so nothing for store-bought presents. On the other hand, local merchants would probably have extended credit to a newcomer, a man who apparently owned a farm. (Merchants of the day were often liberal with a customer until they learned better.) Frost's budget must also have been tight in 1901, because he tried to get an advance from his grandfather's trust.[244] When the Frosts moved, however, their daughter Lesley, then only a year old, was their only surviving child. Their son Carol was born in 1902, so Frost could not have worried about "children's" presents before then. The Frosts had a third child the following year, a fourth by Christmas 1905.[245]

In the summer of 1902, the poet received his first annuity check not long after arranging a sizable investment loan from a friend.[246] Frost did not repay the full amount, if he ever paid back a cent. (The loan was worth almost 40 percent of the value of the farm.) He continued to spend beyond his means, given to lavish purchases like the red sleigh and the handsome sulky. Though unable to pay his bills, in 1903 Frost took the family for a month of sightseeing in New York. In 1905, the year he impulsively bought sleigh and sulky, he owed money to the local butcher and probably other merchants.[247] The longer he pretended to be a farmer, the worse his finances must have become. He took out another large private loan in the spring of 1906, using as collateral the farm he didn't yet own. He was already teaching part-time and by that fall could count on a steady teacher's-salary.[248] Though the family stayed on the farm until 1909, for the last three years Frost's income—apart from the spring of 1907, when he was ill with pneumonia—came almost entirely from the annuity check and his teaching. His neighbor Napoleon Guay in the later years sharecropped the farm, taking care of the cow and the chickens.[249] Frost sold the Magoon Place in 1911, after he had been given the deed.

Hard evidence for Frost's version of events must come from the weather. Good snow records exist for Concord, twenty-five miles north; Nashua, ten miles southwest; and Lawrence, fifteen miles south. (The records for Manchester, which lies closer than Concord, are incomplete.) Unfortunately, snowfall can vary greatly even within a New England town—a heavy snow of over six inches in Concord on Christmas Eve, 1901, produced less than half an inch along the river nearby.

1901	December 24	Concord	6.2"
1904	December 18	Nashua	2.5"
1905	December 21	Concord	2.6"
	December 21	Concord River	2.6"
1906	December 22	Nashua	4.0"
	December 23	Concord	5.5"
	December 23	Concord River	6.0"
	December 23	Manchester	8.0"
1908	December 18	Concord	4.0"
	December 18	Concord River	4.0"
	December 18	Nashua	4.0"

The table shows the only significant snowfalls the week before Christmas during Frost's farm years.[250] (More than a week before the holiday or after Christmas Eve and Frost's solstice-and-presents story falls apart—heavy snows earlier and later are not helpful.) The storm of 1901 did not come soon enough. Merchants were unlikely to buy produce late on Christmas Eve—Frost should have known this. Had the failed trip occurred that afternoon, he would likely have mentioned it in the telling. His trials would have been more pathetic as a Bethlehem journey. The produce was probably eggs and poultry, the eggs wrapped in hay, though after Burell left there might have been vegetables.

Heavy snows in 1902 and 1903 fell on or after Christmas. The snows of 1904 and 1905 (the latter almost at the solstice) seem too paltry. In her journals, published as *New Hampshire's Child* (1969), Lesley Frost listed the children's presents for 1905: "a horn . . . and a little table and a little chair for a doll and a little play house and some strore berry [strawberry] and three crismas books with picshers in them and a stove handle and some stove covers."[251] That doesn't seem a mean Christmas for a farmer's family. Though Lesley was six, the other children were only three, two, and a babe in arms. The Derry historian thinks this the hardest year for Frost financially, because he lost his egg contract; but Thompson, who doesn't give an exact date, implies that the contract was canceled after the new year. Even then, Frost could sell eggs to the local dairy H. P. Hood and Sons, if not advantageously.[252] John Evangelist Walsh, in *Into My Own: The English Years of Robert Frost* (1988), also believes 1905 the year of the snowy evening; but he mistakenly thinks that was the only Christmas Frost owned Eunice.[253]

The town historian points out that Lesley's diary entry for the 1905 presents was made a month before Christmas ("It will be fore weeks before crismas will be here and irma and carol and i are to have these things.") This looks like something the mother has confided in her daughter, however—and Lesley seems to record a trace of their conversation ("Downt [don't] you thingk all those things will be nice 'yes very nice[']").[254] The list is in any case so specific (were the strawberries a jar of preserves?), it seems hard to imagine that, for example, "three crismas books with picshers in them" were not already at hand. There's no entry after Christmas expressing misery, and Lesley's much later recollection of the holiday betrays no disappointment—indeed, she thinks she received a new composition book in which she almost immediately wrote half-a-dozen little anecdotes, as all are dated 1905.[255] Had Frost not brought the promised presents, had the children suffered a joyless Christmas, there should probably have been evidence in the aftermath.

In the fall of 1906, Frost began receiving a regular teacher's salary, so that Christmas was even better:

> There was a christmos tree with candles on it. . . . Carol had an atomobeel and and some tules [tools]. ~~And~~ Irma some some dishes and the noars [Noah's] ark. And i had some dishes and we both had dolls. ~~And~~ I had a go-go and a trunk.[256]

(A go-go may have been a child's toy, but it could have been Lesley's mishearing of "go-cart," a baby's walking frame.) The solstice snow that year would otherwise be very promising; but Frost no longer owned Eunice, the little horse. He would have had barely any produce to trade. (The sharecropping would have given him enough milk, eggs, and broilers for the family, not much more.) From 1906 until Frost left the farm, he spent weeks away each summer.[257] After he started teaching full-time that fall, it's hard to imagine that he could have raised more

vegetables than the family needed. Though the poet was ill the following spring and lost his salary for the term, the Christmas of 1907 was
even better:

> There was a rocking chair and doll and a dog with a little bell tied
> around his neck and pichures for Irma, and there was a train of cars
> and and a pig and a pig's trogh and a pig pen and a little boat and a
> ball and some pichures for Carol and a ball and a doll and a rocking
> chair and a kitty and some pichures for Marjorie and some dominos
> and some dice and a ruler and a little tracing and drawing book and
> two dolls and a rabbit for me, and there was a blackboard and some
> candy for all of us together.[258]

Lesley left no record in her journal of Christmas 1908, though by then
Frost's salary had made the family financially more secure. Snowfall in
Derry must remain speculative.

In short, the first two Christmases (1900–1901) Frost had just one
child, so young she probably would have thought a potato a fine present. The next four (1902–1905), there isn't a snowstorm that obviously
answers the description, and in 1905 the children apparently did not do
without. In 1906 and 1907, the children received a cornucopia. The last
three Christmases (1906–1908), Frost was scarcely involved with the farm.
Apart from 1901, 1906, and 1908, during the nine Christmases the family spent on the Derry farm no snows beyond a dusting fell within a few
days of the solstice. By the "darkest evening," Frost might have meant,
though he said otherwise, a night of the new moon near the solstice.
In the farm years, that could only have been 1903 (December 18), 1906
(December 16), or 1908 (December 21)—none, according to the snow
records, a likely year for Frost's journey.

Curiously, when Lesley Frost confirmed N. Arthur Bleau's story, she
wrote,

> I find there was at least one other to whom [my father] vouchsafed
> the honor of hearing the truth of how it all was that Xmas eve when
> "the little horse" (Eunice) slows the sleigh at a point between woods,
> a hundred yards or so north of our farm on the Wyndham Road.[259]

She hadn't read the account carefully, since Frost recalled that he was driving a wagon and that the night was the solstice. This could not have been the same story, "word for word." Her "Xmas eve" might have been approximate, covering the week just before the holiday—but, at the Christmas Eve snow in 1901, Lesley was the only child, and the horse could not have been Eunice, bought months later.[260] The distance to the house was much farther than one hundred yards, and she may have forgotten the name of the road—the Frost farm sat beside the Londonderry Turnpike, though in the family the pike might have been known as the Windham Road, as it did run more or less toward Windham. (The official Windham Road lay half a mile west.) There were problems with Lesley's memory as she aged. In a 1963 *Redbook* article about the Christmas of 1907, she recalled a metal train-set her older brother Elliott received on Christmas seven years before, when she "must have been going-on-two, and he was four."[261] Though she was twenty months old that Christmas, he had been dead almost six months.

The factual world of the poem continues to fray. Remember, however, that Frost started his rough draft with two horses, made them a single male, then at least for a time a mare. He might, in other words, already have drifted from fact into the compromises of art. The fluidity of this single detail suggests that from the beginning the description of the snowy evening was poetic. Frost did not have "miles to go," because the farmhouse was just down the road—according to his tale, almost in sight. "To stop without a farmhouse near" was an exaggeration. There were a couple of houses at the corner, at least one a farmhouse, though none on the drive down the pike home.[262] Emptying the landscape of people made the night more ominous. The poem, in the writing, forced itself toward cunning—but poems are rarely transcriptions of life. They worship at a different altar.

That the details of the poem cannot be made to align with the supposed origin should serve as a sober reminder that a poet's obligation does not extend to any shallow adherence to facts. Poems are fictions, but origins may be fictions, too. It's far more important that the poem pay homage, say, to physics. The only part of "Stopping by Woods" that seems less than fanciful is the frozen lake. During the years 1900 to 1905 the *Derry News* mentions skating or ice cutting in the weeks before

Christmas except in 1902 and 1904, and the temperatures recorded in Nashua then were as cold or colder. In 1906, it reported on December 28 that the Hood company had started cutting ice—that might have been before the holiday.[263] Each element in Frost's tale probably derived from life in Derry; but it's unlikely that the failure to sell produce, the lack of money for presents, the snowstorm, and the stop by the woods all occurred one year at the solstice.

Frost's route, when he sold produce, can be followed along the roads from West Derry. Frost probably drove along Broadway, the main street, visiting the likely markets. The village grocers listed in the *New Hampshire Register, Farmer's Almanac and Business Directory* for 1901 included Morse and Tenney, the Annis Grain Company, G. W. Sargent, and G. B. Smith. E. Nelson dealt in fruit; and Benson and Morse sold meat, fish, and groceries. Other merchants in town offered shoes, clothing, dry

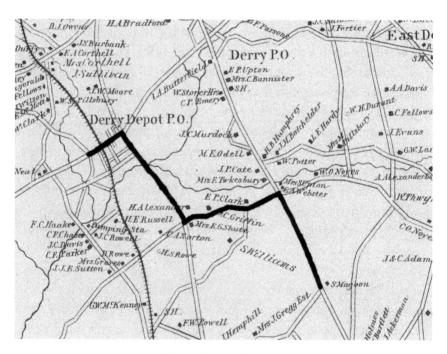

Map of Frost's journey.

Source: From *Derry, Rockingham Co. Seabrook, Rockingham Co. . . .*
(Boston: D. H. Hurd, 1892), courtesy of David Rumsey Map Collection,
www.davidrumsey.com.

goods, stoves, hardware, coal, coffins, meat, drugs, stationery and tobacco, furniture, jewelry, and millinery. There were also a baker; two laundries; and H. P. Hood and Sons, which sold milk, cream, and butter.[264] Postcards show West Derry as a thriving town by the time the Frosts arrived, Broadway crowded with brick blocks and clapboard stores, the large shoe factories just out of sight.

Failing to sell his goods, the poet drove home, crossing the tracks in the center of town, turning south off Broadway down Birch Street, then east at Shute's Corner onto Rockingham Road (labeled Island Pond Road on the endpapers of Lesley Frost's journal, though that lay beyond the next crossroads), and after another half-mile or so turning south again at Webster's Corner onto Londonderry Turnpike. From the corner the road ran straight to the Magoon Place, half a mile further south. Frost was mistaken in his recollection—you can't see the farm until you crest a rise. He pulled up, according to Richard Holmes, just past the corner to watch the snow fall on Nat Head's Woods—the woods ran along the west side of the turnpike from Webster's Corner down to Berry Road, which entered the pike across from the farm.

Frost's daughter told Lawrance Thompson "that there was a family legend . . . that the pond regularly passed by [my father] on his drive from the farm to West Derry was the one he had in mind, and mentioned as a 'frozen lake,' in 'Stopping by Woods on a Snowy Evening.'"[265] Holmes says that just northwest of the crossroads, along West Running Brook, lay a now vanished millpond.[266] Had Frost drawn up at the "bend in the road" and the "sweep of the bend," as he says, he'd have been between the woods and the pond just above the crossing. Lesley Frost's memory that her father mentioned a stop between woods is interesting; but there would have been woods in all directions, rising as well beyond the millpond. The scene on that snowy evening of course doesn't have to make sense according to Derry's geography—it only has to make sense according to the poem's. Frost was forever turning anecdote to allegory. If a poet is not on oath when he writes, he's certainly not on oath when he confides his inspiration.

Nathaniel Head owned a large house at Glidden's Corner in East Derry. Frost should have known of the man, because decades before he had built the Magoon Place.[267] It's common in New England to name,

West Broadway, West Derry, N.H., c. 1910.
Source: Author's collection.

Broadway, Looking West, West Derry, N.H., c. 1908.
Source: Author's collection.

not just houses after their owners, but woods and other landmarks. Names continue long after the owners are dead. Magoon was three owners back—but the Magoon Place eventually became the Frost Place.

The reader of the poem is not told the traveler is a farmer, that he has a wagon of unsold goods, or even that he's driving a wagon. Frost's mood, his longing, his despair—none enters the poem directly. They can be only conjectures lying above a psychology deeply buried. Were the tale true, approaching home on that miserable ride brought on the crisis of failure. Were the tale true, Frost might have flinched from being observed, not just because watching the woods was odd, but because he was weeping. Such a man passed between two worlds—commerce in town and family at home, failure behind and before, like the Charybdis of the cold forbidding lake, from which the traveler implicitly turns, and the Scylla of the tall and welcoming woods. (Snow falling on a frozen lake might, to a different man, have been just as beautiful and beckoning.) The poet, by his own account, chose instead the failure that is life.

Frost was often guilty of self-mythologizing, and the poem was written more than a dozen years after he left the farm. He was a Yankee fabulist, known to stretch a blanket, his myths carefully nursed, elaborated, curated. The harrowing Christmas tale—the drive through heavy snow with what were probably unsold eggs (Frost's "revulsion" at butchering, as Thompson calls it, makes dressed chickens less likely),[268] the empty pockets for presents, the mad weeping before the woods—would have been laughed out of Hollywood; but Frost's story, Christmas and failure and weeping and all, is the ghostly descendent of *A Christmas Carol*, just as it's the ghostly ancestor of *It's a Wonderful Life*. Was the tale a fiction cobbled up for his daughter, a fireside yarn that made Frost a heroic and vulnerable father? The geography is probably the geography of Derry, source of so many of his poems; but the weather records reveal a tale that might have come from whole cloth. Lesley said that her father asked her not to repeat it, because he feared being pitied—yet he told the same story to a gullible stranger.

There's another possibility. Before his grandfather purchased the Derry farm, Frost had agreed to rent a farmhouse in Pelham.[269] After he moved to Derry, the Pelham farmer threatened to sue. Frost had run through his grandfather's cash and had to return to the old man, hat in hand, for thirty dollars in settlement money. The poet was rebuked even more roundly than he'd expected. He believed, according to Lawrance Thompson, "that his grandfather was saying under his breath, 'Good riddance. Go on out and die'":

> During the drive from Lawrence to Pelham, a bleak wind began to blow fine flakes of the year's first snowfall, and Rob could feel the chill penetrating to his bones so ominously that he imagined his grandfather's unspoken wish might be carried out before the day was over. It was nearly suppertime before he reached Pelham, and his enemies there were so hostile to him, even after he had paid the $30, that he was glad to get out of their house in the dusk and start the long drive back to Derry. As the darkness settled in[,] the wind-blown snow felt like fine sand against his face. Snow began to pile and drift in the road just enough to hinder the tired horse and threaten serious difficulties. Rob lost his way in the dark, had to stop at a farmhouse to ask for directions, grew more and more miserable as he got closer to home, and finally drove into his barn near midnight sick with rage and disgust.[270]

This was no easy ride—more than fifteen miles down to Lawrence, ten miles northwest to Pelham, then ten miles home. (The situation, a man stopping at a farmhouse during a blizzard then pressing on into the storm, was used later in "Snow.") The long drive, the bitter cold, the exhausted horse, the heavy snow, the lack of money, the disgrace—these come very close to a rough draft of Frost's tale. Which was the better story to tell his daughter? Frost's Derry version of Dickens offered the resolution of abject failure in simple homecoming, and quiet nobility in weeping over the presents he could not buy.

Frost's humiliation before grandfather and angry farmer leaves the origin of the poem with rough edges and without consolation, a grubby account of money borrowed and money owed, rage against his grandfather, rage against everyone who had done him wrong. Rage seems the chief furniture of Frost's discontent. Of course a critic must be wary, as the Pelham tale must also have come from Frost—but it's much less prettified than the stories Frost liked to tell.[271] The snow in 1900 did not come early. At the end of November a few inches fell in Nashua and Concord; but on December 4 Concord reported one of the worst storms of the period, almost fifteen inches. Curiously, Lawrence and Concord River received almost nothing, and Nashua only a few inches the next day.[272] Still, the fourth might have been the evening of that snowy drive Frost later transposed to a mythical solstice ride.

"Stopping by Woods" was his "best bid for remembrance," Frost wrote Louis Untermeyer in 1923—and, he added at Middlebury College decades later, "all I ever knew."[273] The years on the Derry farm were responsible for most of the poems that made Frost Frost. The physical geography of the Magoon Place and the roads and woods nearby became the settings for, not just "Stopping by Woods on a Snowy Evening," but "Mending Wall," "After Apple-Picking," "West-Running Brook," "Birches," and many another. ("To a large extent," Frost said, "the terrain of my poetry is the Derry landscape, the Derry farm.")[274] When you drag in narrative poems short and long about his neighbors or his hapless life as a farmer, the foundation of his greatness lies in the half-dozen years when he failed once more: "The Code," "A Hundred Collars," "The Black Cottage," "The Ax-Helve," "'Out, Out—,'" "Snow," among many others, are Derry poems. Frost's economy of means was part of his necessary laziness.

Had Frost's grandfather not taken a rough liking to his prodigal grandson, had Frost gone straight from chicken farming in Methuen to the schoolroom, most of his characteristic poems would never have been written. He had been born in San Francisco. The Yankee farmer and cracker-barrel philosopher so knowing in country ways was the invention of those brief years off the Londonderry Turnpike. The further Frost got from that farm, the lesser the poems were. They lost their sense of place.

CODA

In the aftermath of some private devastation, Dickinson adapted the experience of Arctic traveler to the New England nightmare of freezing to death. The loss was local, the unease local; but the alien source answered something in the far-flung nature of the original desire, desire for a man himself a kind of Arctic—distant in place, remote in feeling, never to be considered a home. Assuming, of course, that the poem was personal.

There was torment in or near "After great pain" and "Stopping by Woods." It should not be surprising that two poems buried so deeply in the American character drew on the lethal conditions of snow. Such poems, though we scarcely think of it, were limited by geography—they would probably not have been written by poets below, say, the fortieth parallel. They require felt knowledge of the deep snows of the northern states or the blizzards of the Midwest. Frost's snow is gentle, but a traveler on the open road had to seek shelter—a little more snowfall, a little more wind, and the roads would have become impassable. In a severe storm, a man could die between his house and his barn.

Frost was a boy of eleven when his widowed mother moved east in 1885.[275] He'd have had no real experience of snow before then, but the snows of 1886–1887 killed millions of cattle across the West and ended the era of the open range. Had the Frosts stayed in San Francisco, they'd have seen nearly four inches fall downtown, still a record. Frost would have been almost fourteen when the Great Blizzard of March 1888, struck the Northeast, drifts up to forty feet high covering New England. A sudden blizzard two months earlier, known as the Schoolhouse Blizzard, killed over two hundred people on the Great Plains.

Dickinson was dead by then; but when she wrote her poem she'd have remembered the Cold Storm of 1857, which left ten-foot drifts around Washington. Though New England was not as severely affected, a few days later temperatures there dropped to minus forty, and it was colder than minus twenty as far south as West Virginia. In her letters of the 1850s and early 1860s, Dickinson often referred to snow (it's unfortunate that no letters survive from 1857). Among the prose fragments Dickinson left was a phrase from Emerson's "The Snow Storm," in which he had written of the cheery privacy a storm afforded: "the housemates sit / Around the radiant fireplace, enclosed / In a tumultuous privacy of storm." "Tumultuous privacy of storm" was what Dickinson plucked out.[276] That contains a hint of the character that embraced the ending of "After great pain."

We are presented, considering these two very different poets, with a life too opaque and a life not opaque enough. Which was which remains an open question. Frost's poetry grows deeper the less we impose constricted meaning upon it. His poems are not so shifty symbolically as Dickinson's, but pinning him down amid his contraries and contrariness can be almost as difficult. We tend to read the nods and winks as defining whatever went on behind the facts. Just as we have too many facts in Frost's poems, we have too few in Dickinson's; yet, in all the volumes about Frost, we learn little of the inner man. Though Dickinson has left fewer traces in the factual record, at least of many things a reader would like to know, sometimes she seems entirely present on the surface of her letters, her poems.

As for the lack of passion in this "recluse," fifty years after the poet's death, her editor Millicent Todd Bingham interviewed a cousin of the niece of Judge Otis Lord, with whom Dickinson may have had an affair, probably in the later 1870s. "Little hussy—didn't I know her?" the niece had said of Dickinson, so the cousin reported. "I should say I did. Loose morals. She was crazy about men."[277] That's another way of saying that in the evasions of their different heats both Frost and Dickinson contributed to a poetics of cold.

Permissions

Emily Dickinson, "After great pain, a formal feeling comes" and "I felt a Funeral in my Brain" from *The Poems of Emily Dickinson: Variorum Edition*, ed. Ralph W. Franklin (Cambridge, Mass.: The Belknap Press of Harvard University Press), copyright © 1998 by the President and Fellows of Harvard College. Copyright © 1951, 1955 by the President and Fellows of Harvard College. Copyright © renewed 1979, 1983 by the President and Fellows of Harvard College. Copyright © 1914, 1918, 1919, 1924, 1929, 1930, 1932, 1935, 1937, 1942 by Martha Dickinson Bianchi. Copyright © 1952, 1957, 1958, 1963, 1965 by Mary L. Hampson.

Robert Frost, "The Draft Horse" and "Stopping by Woods on a Snowy Evening," from *The Poetry of Robert Frost*, ed. Edward Connery Lathem. Copyright © 1923, 1969 by Henry Holt and Company, copyright © 1951, 1962 by Robert Frost. Reprinted by arrangement with Henry Holt and Company. All rights reserved.

Seamus Heaney, "The Skunk," from *Opened Ground: Selected Poems, 1966–1996*. Copyright © 1998 by Seamus Heaney. Reprinted by permission of Farrar, Straus and Giroux and Faber and Faber Ltd.

Donald Justice, "Epilogue: Coronado Beach, California," from *Collected Poems*, copyright © 2004 by Donald Justice. Used by permission of Alfred A. Knopf, an imprint of the Knopf Doubleday Publishing Group, a division of Penguin Random House LLC. All rights reserved. Also by courtesy of Carcanet Press, publishers of *Collected Poems* in the United Kingdom.

Robert Lowell, "Skunk Hour," from *Collected Poems*. Copyright © 2003 by Harriet Lowell and Sheridan Lowell. Reprinted by permission of Farrar, Straus and Giroux and Faber and Faber Ltd.

Richard Wilbur, "The Ride," from *Collected Poems, 1943–2004*. Copyright © 2004 by Richard Wilbur. Reprinted by permission of Houghton Mifflin Harcourt Publishing Company. All rights reserved.

William Carlos Williams, "The Red Wheelbarrow" and "One day in Paradise," reprinted by permission of New Directions Publishing Corp.

Note on the Notes

In a book devoted to returning poems to the world in which they were made, the essay on Shakespeare has retained original spelling for all quotations, limiting modernization to reducing the long "s." References there to Shakespeare's plays have been given doubly, first, the line number from William Shakespeare, *The Complete Works: Original-Spelling Edition*, ed. Stanley Wells and Gary Taylor (Oxford: Clarendon Press, 1986); then, in the familiar act, scene, and line form, from *The Riverside Shakespeare*, ed. G. Blakemore Evans, 2nd ed. (Boston: Houghton Mifflin, 1997). Biblical quotes have been taken from the first edition of the King James Version. One or two other essays required a bout of old spelling (in the snippets from Chapman's Homer, for instance). At the risk of inconsistency, I have otherwise used *The Riverside Shakespeare* and a modernized version of the King James, as those would be closer to what later poets knew.

The notes include very few online sources, as such links, even after a short period, are often worthless. Where it could not be helped, it was not helped.

Notes

Notes Toward an Introduction

1. Emily Dickinson, *The Poems of Emily Dickinson: Variorum Edition*, ed. R. W. Franklin (Cambridge, Mass.: Harvard University Press, 1998), 1:408–9 (#383).

2. Richard B. Sewall, *The Life of Emily Dickinson* (New York: Farrar, Straus and Giroux, 1974), 1:54, 56, 2:436–37.

3. J. Leslie Hotson, *The Death of Christopher Marlowe* (Cambridge, Mass.: Harvard University Press, 1925).

4. Justin Steinberg, *Dante and the Limits of Law* (Chicago: University of Chicago Press, 2013).

5. Eve Kosofsky Sedgwick, *Tendencies* (Durham, N.C.: Duke University Press, 1993), 176. Joan Acocella pointed out this embarrassing bit of lower criticism and identified the Cunard liner in *Willa Cather and the Politics of Criticism* (Lincoln: University of Nebraska Press, 2000), 55–56.

6. Michael Cooper, "Gershwin's ABC's Might Not Be What They Seem," *New York Times*, March 2, 2016.

7. Jonathan Sawday, "A Kinder Isle?" *TLS* (January 13, 2017): 15–17.

8. The directory is now at the Frost Place in Derry, New Hampshire. It was discovered by Richard Holmes, the town historian.

9. Richard Brooks, "Who's Sleeping in Van Gogh's Bed?" [London] *Sunday Times*, October 30, 2016.

10. Katy Jennison, "No Hares Were Harmed" (letter to the editor), *London Review of Books* 38 (November 3, 2016): 5.

11. T. W. Baldwin, *Shakspere's Love's Labor's Won: New Evidence from the Account Books of an Elizabethan Bookseller* (Carbondale: Southern Illinois University Press, 1957). The manuscript leaf on which the title "Loves Labor Won" was inscribed, originally part of the daybook of the Elizabethan stationer Christopher Hunt, was discovered in the binding of a book of seventeenth-century sermons. This leaf recorded some titles of his stock in 1603.

12. Cedric C. Brown, "Milton, the Attentive Mr. Skinner, and the Acts and Discourses of Friendship," in *A Concise Companion to the Study of Manuscripts, Printed Books, and the Production of Early Modern Texts: A Festschrift for Gordon Campbell*, ed. Edward Jones (Chichester: Wiley-Blackwell, 2015), 106–28.

13. Ferris Jabr, "Dickinson's Inspirations Grow Anew," *New York Times*, May 17, 2016.

1. Shelley's Wrinkled Lip, Smith's Gigantic Leg

1. Ruins play their part in, among other poems, Wordsworth's "The Prelude," "Suggested by a Beautiful Ruin Upon One of the Islands of Loch Lomond," "Yarrow Visited," "At Bala-Sala, Isle of Man," and "At Furness Abbey." For Coleridge, the list would include "Melancholy," "Love," and "Love's Apparition and Evanishment."

2. W[illiam]. Wordsworth, *Lyrical Ballads, with Pastoral and Other Poems*, 3rd ed. (London, 1802), 1:xi, vii. The preface first appeared in this edition.

3. For one account of events worldwide, as well as at Lake Geneva, see William K. Klingaman and Nicholas P. Klingaman, *The Year Without Summer: 1816 and the Volcano That Darkened the World and Changed History* (New York: St. Martin's, 2013). Mary Shelley recalled, in her introduction to the 1831 edition of *Frankenstein*, that "it proved a wet, ungenial summer, and incessant rain often confined us for days to the house. Some volumes of ghost stories, translated from the German into French, fell into our hands. . . .'We will each write a ghost story,' said Lord Byron; and his proposition was acceded to." Mary W. Shelley, *Frankenstein* (London, 1831), vii–viii. The usual date for Byron's challenge is June 16, but astronomers have suggested that, based on Mary Shelley's description of the moon, it occurred between June 10 and 13. See Donald W. Olson et al., "The Moon and the Origin of *Frankenstein*," *Sky and Telescope* 122 (November 2011): 68–74.

4. "Poor Polidori had some terrible idea about a skull-headed lady." Mary Shelley, *Frankenstein*, viii. There seems little evidence of this, however. See James Rieger, "Dr. Polidori and the Genesis of *Frankenstein*," *Studies in English Literature, 1500–1900* 3 (Autumn 1963): 464–69.

5. "On the Grasshopper and Cricket," "On Receiving a Laurel Crown from Leigh Hunt," "On Seeing a Lock of Milton's Hair," and "To the Nile." All but the Milton ode were sonnets. We have the testimony of Woodhouse and Cowden Clarke about the quarter-hour deadline, at least for the contests that produced "On the Grasshopper and Cricket" and "To the Nile." See the headnotes to these poems in John Keats, *The Poems of John Keats*, ed. Miriam Allott (London: Longman, 1970), 97–98, 109, 292, 307–8.

6. Percy Bysshe Shelley, "To the Nile," in *The Poems of Shelley*, ed. Kelvin Everest and Geoffrey Matthews (Harlow: Longman, 2000), 2:349–50. The contest and the rediscovery of the poem decades later are detailed in the headnote.

7. Leigh Hunt, "The Nile," in *The Poetical Works of Leigh Hunt*, ed. Thornton Hunt (London, 1860), 235.

8. Shelley, *Poems of Shelley*, 2:307–11. The text is largely that of Shelley's fair copy, though I have adopted his apparent verbal revisions for the *Examiner* as well as the newspaper's capitalization of "Two" in line 2, the punctuation in line 3 (where the fair copy has an ellipsis between "desart" and "near"), and the quotation marks around the words on the pedestal. The fair copy's ampersands have been spelled out.

9. John Keats, *The Letters of John Keats*, ed. Hyder Edward Rollins (Cambridge, Mass.: Harvard University Press, 1958), 1:223–24.

10. Percy Bysshe Shelley, "The Colosseum," in *Shelley's Prose*, ed. David Lee Clark (New York: New Amsterdam, 1988), 226–27. The portrait of the Colosseum was still accurate when Dickens visited the site more than a quarter-century later.

11. If such a traveler detected a sneer, he may have been mistaken. William Empson, in *The Face of the Buddha* (Oxford: Oxford University Press, 2016), 1, remarks, "There are two common misunderstandings about Buddhist sculpture; that the faces have no expression at all . . . or else they all sneer." Though Empson (123n1) was perhaps misremembering remarks by G. K. Chesterton, what is complacent to many may be sneering to some. This temptation to read emotion into the Egyptian sculptures was perhaps common in the nineteenth century. The Reverend John Weiss recalled Thoreau, his fellow student at Harvard, "as looking very much like some Egyptian sculptures of faces, large-featured, but brooding, immobile, fixed in a mystic egotism." *Christian Examiner* 79 (July 1865): 98.

12. [Ralph Beilby], *History of British Birds: The Figures Engraven on Wood by T. Bewick*, vol. 1, *Containing the History and Description of Land Birds* (Newcastle, 1797), 87, 42.

13. The remark may be found in a copy of [Ralph Beilby], *A History of British Birds* (London, 1821), 1:138, annotated by Thomas and Jane Bewick, the latter his daughter. Bewick signed his initials beneath the statement. The volume is held in the National Art Library at the Victoria and Albert Museum in London, shelfmark RC.N.2.

14. [Beilby], *History of British Birds* (1797), 1:42.

15. Percy Bysshe Shelley, *Hellas* (London, 1822), 49 (lines 1002–3).

16. *Examiner* no. 524 (January 11, 1818): 24.

17. *Examiner* no. 524 (January 11, 1818): 17, 24, 26, 31, 31, 29.

18. Shelley, *Poems of Shelley*, 2:307. Frederick A. Pottle, however, in "The Meaning of Shelley's 'Glirastes,'" *Keats-Shelley Journal* 7 (Winter 1958): 6–7, believes the name might have meant "one who behaves like a dormouse." He thought it possibly Shelley's

own pet name, noting Thomas Hogg's recollection of the poet's terrible drowsiness during evenings at Oxford. Shelley's and Mary's nickname for their boy Will was Willmouse.

19. Shelley, *Poems of Shelley*, 2:306. The fair copy is held at the Bodleian, MS. Shelley e. 4, folio 85v. A transcription is provided in *The Complete Poetry of Percy Bysshe Shelley*, ed. Donald H. Reiman, Neil Fraistat, and Nora Crook, vol. 3 (Baltimore, Md.: Johns Hopkins University Press, 2012), 327. See pp. 950–51 for a discussion of the problems of choosing a copy text for the poem.

20. It was hoped that hieroglyphics would reveal the secrets of those antique dynasties. Some of the earliest detective work had required the genius of a Thomas Young, who made important scientific contributions to the wave theory of light and to the concepts of elasticity and capillary action. Even he could not fully break the code.

21. Leigh Hunt, *Lord Byron and Some of His Contemporaries* (London, 1828), 285.

22. *Examiner* no. 527 (February 1, 1818): 73.

23. Horace Smith, *Amarynthus the Nympholept* (London, 1821), 213. "Nympholept" means exactly what one might think—a lover of young girls or, rather, of classical nymphs, whose beauty drove men mad. Smith wrote in his preface that he was "not aware that Nympholepsy has been made the subject of poetical experiment" (ix). Perhaps he had not only himself but Shelley in mind—Harriet Westbrook (Shelley's first wife) and Mary Godwin had each been sixteen when the poet met them.

24. Émile Zola, *Rome*, trans. Ernest Alfred Vizetelly (London, 1898), 1:228.

25. *Henry IV, Part II*, 4.5.133, 136–37.

26. Anna Laeticia Barbauld, *Eighteen Hundred and Eleven* (London, 1812), 10, 16–17.

27. Percy Bysshe Shelley, *The Letters of Percy Bysshe Shelley*, ed. Frederick L. Jones (Oxford: Clarendon, 1940), 2:469.

28. *Edinburgh Review* 72 (October, 1840): 228.

29. Keats, *Poems of John Keats*, 60–62.

30. "In the autumn of 1817 the British Museum had taken receipt of . . . sculptures from the Empire of the Ramases. . . . Among these were the celebrated Rosetta Stone, and the massive figure of Ramases II taken from the King's Funerary Temple at Thebes." Richard Holmes, *Shelley: The Pursuit* (New York: Dutton, 1975), 410. The counterevidence is laid out in Shelley, *Poems of Shelley*, 2:309.

31. Samuel Taylor Coleridge, *The Complete Poems*, ed. William Keach (London: Penguin, 1997), 292.

32. Shelley, *Letters*, 1:548.

33. See, for example, Neville Rogers, *Shelley at Work: A Critical Inquiry*, 2nd ed. (Oxford: Clarendon, 1967), 110–14.

34. The best summary of this complicated matter may be found in *Poems of Shelley*, 2:307–10. I have relied on this discussion, especially for Shelley's sources.

35. G[eorge]. Booth, trans., *The Historical Library of Diodorus the Sicilian in Fifteen Books* (London, 1814), 1:53.

36. *Quarterly Review* 16 (October 1816): 1–27. See also *Poems of Shelley*, 2:309.

37. Richard Pococke, *A Description of the East and Some Other Countries* (London, 1743), 1:106–7, and plates opp. 104, 105, 107. See also H. M. Richmond, "Ozymandias and the Travelers," *Keats-Shelley Journal* 11 (1962): 65–71. Richmond points out (70) that the engraving opposite p. 96 in Pococke shows ruins in an empty desert. He makes a strong case for Shelley's use of *A Description* but thinks the engraving there of the head and torso of the colossus shows a face "cold and brutal" (69). I would call it peaceful and impersonal, almost Buddhist. See note 11, this chapter.

38. Vivant Denon, *Travels in Upper and Lower Egypt*, trans. Arthur Aikin (London, 1803), 2:89–90, 92–93. I have borrowed this point, as well as the quotation, from Johnstone Parr, "Shelley's *Ozymandias*," *Keats-Shelley Journal* 6 (Winter 1957): 33–34. The italics in the quotation, all but one, were Parr's before they were mine.

39. Shelley, *Poems of Shelley*, 2:309, states that the spelling Ozymandias is otherwise unknown; but *Complete Poetry of Percy Bysshe Shelley*, 3:947, shows that the spelling was common at this date.

40. "Ode on a Grecian Urn," *Poems of John Keats*, 537.

41. E. M. W. Tillyard, *Essays Literary and Educational* (London: Chatto and Windus, 1962), 110–11.

42. James Bieri, *Percy Bysshe Shelley: A Biography: Exile of Unfulfilled Renown, 1816–1822* (Newark: University of Delaware Press, 2005), 57; Holmes, *Shelley: The Pursuit*, 407.

43. [Mary Shelley], *Frankenstein; or, the Modern Prometheus* (London, 1818), 1:98, 101.

44. The original film *The Mummy* (1932) appeared in the wake of Howard Carter's excavation of the tomb of Tutankhamun a decade before. The plot is almost certainly indebted to Arthur Conan Doyle's story "The Ring of Thoth" (1890), where an Egyptian cursed with everlasting life wants to join his beloved by drinking an elixir buried with her mummy. Whether Mary Shelley's stray remark had any influence on the writers of the film is unknown.

45. Shelley, *Shelley's Prose*, 297.

46. "Ramses II, Pronounced Cured of All Infection, Goes Home from Paris," *New York Times*, May 11, 1977.

47. Cairo's Egyptian Museum.

2. Frost's Horse, Wilbur's Ride

1. Think of the mysterious stranger who in "Young Goodman Brown" accompanies Brown through the forest, or the fountain-of-youth tale "Dr. Heidegger's Experiment."

2. [Washington Irving], "The Legend of Sleepy Hollow," in *The Sketch Book of Geoffrey Crayon, Gent.*, new ed. (London, 1821), 2:259–60.

3. "Dawes" could have been rhymed on, among other words, "cause," "flaws," "jaws," "laws," and "pause."

4. Putnam may have been the officer who said to his men at Bunker Hill (actually Breed's Hill, but we have printed the myth too long to care much for the history), "Don't fire until you see the whites of their eyes."

5. Thomas Buchanan Read, "Sheridan's Ride."

6. Robert Frost, *Collected Poems, Prose, and Plays*, ed. Richard Poirier and Mark Richardson (New York: Library of America, 1995), 454.

7. "The Fear," "The Wood-Pile," "The Code," in Frost, *Collected Poems, Prose, and Plays*, 89, 100, 71.

8. The most important nineteenth-century American draft horses were the Percheron and the Belgian. The Clydesdale, though well known, was used mostly in cities, the long feathery hair on its lower legs often considered unsuitable to the farm, as it became clotted with dirt and muck. See, for example, Charles S. Plumb, *Types and Breeds of Farm Animals*, rev. ed. (New York: Ginn and Co., 1920), 140.

9. Robert Browning, "'How They Brought the Good News from Ghent to Aix'"; Alfred Tennyson, "The Charge of the Light Brigade."

10. Melody Simmons, "After Shooting, Amish School Embodies Effort to Heal," *New York Times*, January 31, 2007.

11. The notebook probably dates "as early as 1920," according to Robert Frost, *The Notebooks of Robert Frost*, ed. Robert Faggen (Cambridge, Mass.: Harvard University Press, 2007), 629, 633–34. Unfortunately, the transcriptions in this edition cannot be relied upon. See James Sitar, "Frost's Great Misgiving," *Essays in Criticism* 57 (2007): 364–72; and William Logan, "Frost at Midnight," in *The Undiscovered Country* (New York: Columbia University Press, 2009), 300–26. A revised edition of *Notebooks*, not mentioned as such, was issued in paperback in 2010. Though many errors were corrected, hundreds, perhaps thousands, were left untouched. See William Logan, "Frost's Notebooks: A Disaster Revisited," in *Guilty Knowledge, Guilty Pleasure* (New York: Columbia University Press, 2014), 114–29. The poem's inspiration seems to lie in a different and also undated notebook: "As through the woods we drove for fifty miles in the dark a man came out of the trees and stabbed our horse dead." Frost, *Notebooks of Robert Frost*, 358.

12. Lawrance Thompson, *Robert Frost: The Years of Triumph, 1915–1938* (New York: Holt, Rinehart and Winston, 1970), 673n4.

13. Lawrance Thompson, *Robert Frost: The Early Years, 1874–1915* (New York: Holt, Rinehart and Winston, 1966), 263–64, 314–15.

14. "New York Loses Its Last Horse Car," *New York Times*, July 27, 1917.

15. Manny Fernandez, "A Vestige of the Past Shutters Its Stalls," *New York Times*, April 30, 2007.

16. G. S. Kirk, *The Songs of Homer* (Cambridge: Cambridge University Press, 1962), 124.

17. Richard Wilbur, *Collected Poems, 1943–2004* (Orlando, Fla.: Harcourt, 2004), 79.

18. Browning, "'How They Brought the Good News from Ghent to Aix.'"

19. See chapter 5 for further discussion of Milton's sonnet.

3. Lowell's Skunk, Heaney's Skunk

1. $16,500 (2010).

2. Harriett Winslow, having suffered a stroke, offered the house to Lowell and his wife Elizabeth Hardwick "as a summer retreat." Ian Hamilton, *Robert Lowell: A Biography* (New York: Random House, 1982), 223.

3. Robert Lowell, *Collected Poems*, ed. Frank Bidart and David Gewanter (New York: Farrar, Straus and Giroux, 2003), 191–92.

4. "On 'Skunk Hour,'" in Robert Lowell, *Collected Prose*, ed. Robert Giroux (New York: Farrar, Straus and Giroux, 1987), 226–27.

5. Lowell, *Collected Prose*, 226.

6. "Historians' best estimates put the proportion of adult white male loyalists somewhere between 15 and 20 percent. Approximately half the colonists of European ancestry tried to avoid involvement in the struggle." Robert M. Calhoon, "Loyalism and Neutrality," in *A Companion to the American Revolution*, ed. Jack P. Greene and J. R. Pole (Malden, Mass.: Blackwell, 2000), 235.

7. These were, respectively, the Rhinelander Mansion and the earlier of the two Morton F. Plant houses.

8. Lowell, *Collected Prose*, 229.

9. T. Westcott, "Yankee and Yankee Doodle," *Notes and Queries* 6 (July 17, 1852): 56–58. This includes references to previous articles on the subject.

10. Lowell, *Collected Prose*, 228.

11. Lowell, *Collected Prose*, 312; Daniel Hoffman, "Afternoons with Robert Lowell," *Gettysburg Review* 6 (Summer 1993), 481–82. Hoffman mailed Lowell a Christmas present of lead soldiers the younger poet had sought out in Dijon, soldiers Lowell had mentioned in his memoir "91 Revere Street." Lowell graciously replied, "I stuck the Dijon in blindly, on the Flaubertian principle of always being particular."

12. Lowell, *Collected Poems*, 1046n5.3; Logan Pearsall Smith, *Unforgotten Years* (Boston: Little, Brown, 1939), 96, 99.

13. Jean Stafford, Carley Dawson, and Sandra Hochman. See Hamilton, *Robert Lowell*, 80, 132; Sandra Hochman, *Loving Robert Lowell* (Nashville, Tenn.: Turner, 2017), 213.

14. Folder 2206, Robert Lowell Papers, Houghton Library, Harvard.

15. John Milton, *Paradise Lost*, book 4, line 75.

16. Thomas Browne, *Religio Medici*, I, sect. 51; Christopher Marlowe, *Marlowe's Doctor Faustus: 1604–1616*, ed. W. W. Greg (Oxford: Clarendon, 1950), 191, lines 514–15.

17. Milton, *Paradise Lost*, book 4, line 78.

18. Milton, *Paradise Lost*, book 4, lines 105–10.

19. Lowell, *Collected Poems*, 175, 57.

20. Hamilton, *Robert Lowell*, 60.

21. Robert Lowell, *The Letters of Robert Lowell*, ed. Saskia Hamilton (New York: Farrar, Straus and Giroux, 2005), 306.

22. *Merriam-Webster's Collegiate Dictionary*, 11th ed. (2004), s.v. "Skunk," 1.

23. Hamilton, *Robert Lowell*, 224.

24. Hamilton, *Robert Lowell*, 40.

25. Lowell, *Letters*, 597; Paul Mariani, *Lost Puritan: A Life of Robert Lowell* (New York: Norton, 1994), 507n33. Though Lowell was not bequeathed an interest in the house, by Maine law he was entitled to half his wife's inheritance.

26. Lowell, *Letters*, 288, 316.

27. Lowell, *Letters*, 289.

28. "I visited Lowell in Castine, Maine[,] in 1957 when I was up from Brazil with a Brazilian friend of mine. The skunk business was going on then at the back door, where we saw it with a flashlight": Eileen McMahon, "Elizabeth Bishop Speaks About Her Poetry," in *Conversations with Elizabeth Bishop*, ed. George Monteiro (Jackson, Miss.: University of Mississippi Press, 1996), 109.

29. Elizabeth Bishop and Robert Lowell, *Words in Air: The Complete Correspondence Between Elizabeth Bishop and Robert Lowell*, ed. Thomas Travisano (New York: Farrar, Straus and Giroux, 2008), 213.

30. Bishop and Lowell, *Words in Air*, 204.

31. Bishop and Lowell, *Words in Air*, 230.

32. Bishop and Lowell, *Words in Air*, 258.

33. Bishop and Lowell, *Words in Air*, 583.

34. Bishop and Lowell, *Words in Air*, 324.

35. Folder 2238, Robert Lowell Papers, Houghton Library, Harvard.

36. "In March of the same year [1957], I had been giving readings on the West Coast. . . . I became sorely aware of how few poems I had written, and that these few had been finished at the latest three or four years earlier. Their style seemed distant,

symbol-ridden, and willfully difficult. I began to paraphrase my Latin quotations, and to add extra syllables to a line to make it clearer and more colloquial." Lowell, *Collected Prose*, 226–27.

37. Steven Axelrod, *Robert Lowell: Life and Art* (Princeton, N.J.: Princeton University Press, 1978), 250.

38. Charles Darwin, *Journal of Researches Into the Natural History and Geology of the Countries Visited During the Voyage of H.M.S.* Beagle (New York, 1846), 1:103. Darwin also wrote, "If a dog is urged to the attack, its courage is instantly checked by a few drops of the fetid oil, which brings on violent sickness and running at the nose."

39. Telephone conversation, September 12, 2010. Mr. Erhard said that the skunks in Castine come in three-year cycles; after a heavy year, they're killed off by some disease, perhaps distemper. He also mentioned that when he answers a phone call on a Sunday afternoon and is asked whether he's the animal-control officer, he thinks, "I shouldn't have answered the phone."

40. Bishop based the poem on an incident observed from her Rio balcony in April 1963. Brett C. Millier, *Elizabeth Bishop: Life and the Memory of It* (Berkeley: University of California Press, 1993), 345.

41. Hamilton, *Robert Lowell*, 267.

42. Milton, *Paradise Lost*, book 1, lines 254–55.

43. Seamus Heaney, *Field Work* (New York: Farrar, Straus and Giroux, 1979), 48.

44. Ben Jonson, *Epicoene; or, The Silent Woman*, 3.2.66–68. Mistress Otter: "I doe but dreame o' the city. It staynd me a damasque table-cloth, cost me eighteen pound at one time." Ben Jonson, *The Oxford Jonson*, ed. C. H. Herford and Percy Simpson, corr. ed. (Oxford: Clarendon, 1965), 5:203.

45. According to a 1644 contract for building Syon House in Middlesex, "John Hawkes of Hounslow was to have . . . £5 15s. at the end of working half a million bricks, and finally 6s. 8d. for each 10,000 'well and sufficiently burnt and delivered out of the kiln.'" M. W. Barley, *English Farmhouse and Cottage* (London: Routledge and Kegan Paul, 1961), 206. By my reckoning, eighteen pounds would have purchased 375,000 bricks. The face of Elizabethan statute bricks was 9" x 2½". Adding a little for mortar, every foot of a wall six feet high would require about thirty-four bricks, so for the price of a good chasuble a wall of over two miles could be built, enough to enclose Lowell's Nautilus Island. As a statute brick was 4½" broad, a stout wall two bricks deep would have cost as much as two chasubles.

46. "I've looked on a lot of women with lust. I've committed adultery in my heart many times": "Playboy Interview: Jimmy Carter," *Playboy* 23 (November 1976): 86.

47. Dennis O'Driscoll, *Stepping Stones: Interviews with Seamus Heaney* (New York: Farrar, Straus and Giroux, 2008), xxii–xxiv, 62.

48. The airmail-letter rate from the United States to Ireland, as of January 3, 1976, was 31¢ per half-ounce, up to two ounces. *Statistical Abstract of the United States, 1990*, 110th ed. (Washington, D.C.: U.S. Government Printing Office, 1990), 549.

49. "I just returned from reviewing the microfilm of the *New York City Telephone Directory, 1975–1976*. . . . It indicates that calls to Europe run at 3-minute rates of $9.60 or $12.00. However, I was unable to locate rates to specific countries." Email from Stephen Shepard, General Research Division, New York Public Library, September 16, 2010.

50. French: *Dépuceler une fille*, A. Boyer, *The Royal Dictionary, French and English* . . . (London, 1764). Spanish: *Ò desflorár una virgen*, Joseph Giral Delpino, *A Dictionary, Spanish and English* . . . (London, 1763). Swedish: *Kranka a mö*, Jacob Serenius, *An English and Swedish Dictionary* . . . , 2nd ed. (Harg and Stenbro, 1767). Each entry s.v. "Broach." English: Pierce Egan, *Grose's Classical Dictionary of the Vulgar Tongue*, rev. ed. (London, 1823), s.v. "Tap": "To tap a girl; to be the first seducer."

51. J. E. Lighter, *Random House Historical Dictionary of American Slang*, vol. 1: *A–G* (New York: Random House, 1994), s.v. "Bunghole." The earliest use was 1611.

52. O'Driscoll, *Stepping Stones*, 205.

53. Richard Feynman, *Surely You're Joking, Mr. Feynman*, ed. Edward Hutchings (New York: Norton, 1984), 104–6.

54. Titian claimed he wanted to provide variety for King Philip II, his patron.

55. Titian, *Venus and Adonis*, c. 1540–1560; Lucas Cranach the Elder, *The Judgment of Paris*, c. 1528.

56. Lowell began to "speed up" in early December and was eventually committed to Boston Psychopathic Hospital, where he stayed a week or more. By the end of January he had been committed again, this time to McLean Hospital (Hamilton, *Robert Lowell*, 238–43).

57. Stanley Kunitz, "The Sense of a Life," reprinted in *Robert Lowell: Interviews and Memoirs*, ed. Jeffrey Meyers (Ann Arbor: University of Michigan Press, 1988), 234. Referring to this incident in a review collected in *Our Savage Art: Poetry and the Civil Tongue* (New York: Columbia University Press, 2009), 216, I mistakenly recalled that Lowell was revising *Paradise Lost*. In fact it was "Lycidas."

4. Longfellow's Hiawatha, Carroll's Hiawatha: The Name and Nature of Parody

1. [London] *Critic* 15 (April 1, 1856): 170–71.

2. *Chambers's Journal* 45 (July 4, 1868): 420.

3. Henry Wadsworth Longfellow, *Poems and Other Writings*, ed. J. D. McClatchy (New York: Library of America, 2000). See, for example, "The Wreck of the Hesperus" (12), "The Slave's Dream" (24), and "The Haunted Chamber" (615).

4. Longfellow, *Poems*, 347.

5. Vincent O'Sullivan, *Aspects of Wilde* (New York: Henry Holt, 1936), 197.

6. Longfellow, *Poems*, 3.

7. Walter Hamilton, *Parodies of the Works of English and American Authors* (London, 1884–1889), 1:63.

8. Hamilton, *Parodies*, 2:11.

9. Longfellow, *Poems*, 4.

10. Hamilton, *Parodies*, 2:11.

11. A. E. Housman, *The Poems of A. E. Housman*, ed. Archie Burnett (Oxford, 1997), 210–11.

12. See, for example, "Mrs. Winslow's Soothing Syrup," *The Practitioner: A Monthly Journal of Therapeutics* 2 (January 1870): 58–59; "Mrs. Winslow's Soothing Syrup—Another Baby Sacrificed," *New England Medical Monthly* 29 (May 1910): 180–81.

13. Longfellow, *Poems*, 15.

14. Unsigned review of Henry Wadsworth Longfellow, *Ballads and Other Poems*, *Graham's Magazine* 20 (April 1842): 248.

15. Unsigned review of Henry Wadsworth Longfellow, *Voices of the Night*, *Burton's Gentleman's Magazine* 6 (February 1840): 102–3.

16. Hamilton, *Parodies*, 2:10. It's not clear what sort of game the village schoolboy is playing; but Celia Thaxter, a contributor to an anthology edited by John Greenleaf Whittier, *Child Life in Prose* (Boston: James R. Osgood, 1875), 60, recalls that as a girl she and the children in her family "launched fleets of purple mussel-shells on the still pools in the rocks, left by the tide."

17. Hamilton, *Parodies*, 2:10.

18. See, for example, Corey Kilgannon, "Washington Crosses the Delaware, This Time More Accurately," *New York Times*, December 24, 2011.

19. Longfellow, *Poems*, 337, 335, 335.

20. Hamilton, *Parodies*, 1:68.

21. W. S. Gilbert, *Songs of a Savoyard* (London, 1891), 16.

22. Hamilton, *Parodies*, 1:70.

23. Thomas Hardy, *Jude the Obscure* (New York, 1896), 399.

24. I have traced this anecdote only as far as Channing Pollock, *The Adventures of a Happy Man* (New York: Thomas Y. Crowell, 1939), 122, but he writes as if it were commonly known. Edgar Johnson, *Charles Dickens: His Tragedy and Triumph* (Boston: Little, Brown, 1952), 1:304, repeats the tale but gives no source. Peter Ackroyd, *Dickens* (London: Sinclair-Stevenson, 1990), 319, thinks the story "not at all unlikely" though introduces it with "It is always said."

25. Johnson, *Dickens*, 1:304.

26. Ada Leverson, *Letters to the Sphinx from Oscar Wilde* (London: Duckworth, 1930), 42.

27. Longfellow, *Poems*, 135–36.

28. Longfellow, *Poems*, 135–36.

29. Elizabeth Akers Allen [Florence Percy, pseud.], *Forest Buds, from the Woods of Maine* (Boston, 1856), 108.

30. Longfellow, *Poems*, 135.

31. Allen, *Forest Buds*, 108.

32. Longfellow, *Poems*, 135.

33. Allen, *Forest Buds*, 109.

34. Longfellow, *Poems*, 136; Allen, *Forest Buds*, 110; Longfellow, *Poems*, 135; Allen, *Forest Buds*, 109.

35. R[alph]. W[aldo]. Emerson, *Essays*, 2nd ser. (Boston, 1844), 40–41.

36. Newton Arvin, *Longfellow: His Life and Work* (Boston: Atlantic Monthly Press, 1963), 11; Samuel Longfellow, *Life of Henry Wadsworth Longfellow*, 3rd ed. (Boston: Ticknor, 1886), 1:17.

37. Edward Wagenknecht, *Longfellow: A Full-Length Portrait* (New York: Longmans, Green, 1955), 12, 39; Charles C. Calhoun, *Longfellow: A Rediscovered Life* (Boston: Beacon, 2004), 41–42, 68–69, 108, 112, 114; Lawrance Thompson, *Young Longfellow* (Macmillan, 1938), 205–6.

38. For a broader perspective, see, for example, Chase S. Osborn and Stellanova Osborn, *Schoolcraft—Longfellow—Hiawatha* (Lancaster, Pa.: Jaques Cattell, 1942), 38–40. Andrew Hilen, *Longfellow and Scandinavia* (New Haven, Conn.: Yale University Press, 1947), 43n7, suggests that, as Longfellow could not read Finnish, he perhaps read the *Kalevala* in Swedish (he owned a copy), though he also read the German version with a friend.

39. Thomas Percy, *The Reliques of Ancient English Poetry*, 3 vols. (London, 1765); Francis James Child, *The English and Scottish Popular Ballads*, 5 vols. (Boston, 1882–1898).

40. Longfellow, *Poems*, 831n141.1.

41. Thomas Wentworth Higginson, *Henry Wadsworth Longfellow* (Boston: Houghton, Mifflin, 1902), 33.

42. [Henry Wadsworth Longfellow], "Defence of Poetry," *North American Review* 34 (January 1832): 75, 69.

43. Ralph Waldo Emerson, *Letters of Ralph Waldo Emerson*, vol. 8: *1845–1859*, ed. Eleanor M. Tilton (New York: Columbia University Press, 1991), 464.

44. Emerson, *Letters*, 8:446.

45. Emerson, *Letters*, 8:464.

46. J. Rogers Rees, *The Brotherhood of Letters* (London, 1889), 82n.

47. Longfellow, *Poems*, 157.

48. *New York Daily Times*, November 24, 1855.

49. John Brougham, *Po-Ca-Hon-Tas; or, The Gentle Savage* (New York, [1855]), 3. The review appeared in the *New York Daily Times*, December 24, 1855.

50. [Walter Scott], *St. Ronan's Well* (Boston, 1824), 221.

51. [Walt Whitman], *Leaves of Grass* (Brooklyn, 1855), 20.

52. *New York Daily Times*, December 28, 1855.

53. Henry Rowe Schoolcraft, geologist and Indian agent, learned the Ojibwe language from his wife, the daughter of a fur trader and an Ojibwe woman. Schoolcraft's works, which despite their flaws helped open Indian legend to study, included *Algic Researches* (New York, 1839), 2 vols.; *Oneóta; or, Characteristics of the Red Race of America* (New York, 1847); *Historical and Statistical Information, Respecting the History, Condition and Prospects of the Indian Tribes of the United States* (Philadelphia, 1851–1857), 6 vols.; and *The Myth of Hiawatha* (London, 1856). For Longfellow's debts, see Osborn, *Schoolcraft—Longfellow—Hiawatha*; and *Schoolcraft's Indian Legends*, ed. Mentor L. Williams (East Lansing: Michigan State University Press, 1991).

54. Whitman, *Leaves of Grass*, 18.

55. Caroline Ticknor, *Hawthorne and His Publisher* (Boston: Houghton Mifflin, 1913), 158.

56. Nathaniel Hawthorne, *The Letters, 1853–1856*, vol. 17, ed. Thomas Woodson et al. (Columbus: Ohio State University Press, 1987), 429.

57. Julian Hawthorne, *Nathaniel Hawthorne and His Wife: A Biography*, 2nd ed. (Boston, 1885), 2:78.

58. *The Song of Milgenwater*, trans. George A. Strong [Marc Antony Henderson, pseud.] (Cincinnati, 1856). In *The Song of Milkanwatha*, the retitled second edition, also of 1856, the hero's name was styled thus throughout. Strong expanded the section of additional poems, but otherwise the texts are identical.

59. Longfellow, *Poems*, 198.

60. *Song of Milkanwatha* [2nd ed.], 40.

61. *Song of Milkanwatha* [2nd ed.], 79.

62. *Song of Milkanwatha* [2nd ed.], 74–75.

63. Henry Wadsworth Longfellow, *The Letters of Henry Wadsworth Longfellow*, vol. 4, *1857–1865*, ed. Andrew Hilen (Cambridge, Mass.: Harvard University Press, 1972), 91.

64. *Song of Milkanwatha* [2nd ed.], 20.

65. *The Song of Milkanwatha*, trans. George A. Strong [Marc Antony Henderson, pseud.], 3rd ed. (Albany, 1883), 11.

66. *Song of Milkanwatha* [2nd ed.], 12, 77n.

67. *Song of Milkanwatha* [2nd ed.], 37–38.

68. Longfellow, *Poems*, 162.

69. *Song of Milkanwatha* [2nd ed.], 27.

70. Herbert G. Ponting, *The Great White South* (London: Duckworth, 1921), 140–41.

71. Mortimer Q. Thomson [Q. K. Philander Doesticks, pseud.], *Plu-ri-bus-tah: A Song That's-By-No-Author* (New York, 1856).

72. *Perth Gazette and Independent Journal of Politics and News*, September 5, 1856. I have changed the question mark at the end of the passage, probably a typo, to an exclamation point.

73. Franklin Buck, *A Yankee Trader in the Gold Rush*, ed. Katharine A. White (Boston: Houghton Mifflin, 1930), 158.

74. "The smylere with the knyf under the cloke": Chaucer, "The Knight's Tale," line 1999.

75. The parodist apparently wishes to remain anonymous.

76. Lewis Carroll, "Hiawatha's Photographing," *The Train* 4 (December, 1857), 332–33. The last three stanzas of this extract were dropped when Carroll collected the poem in *Rhyme? And Reason?* (London, 1883). By then the technique described was out of date.

77. "The Song of Hiawatha," *Punch* 30 (January 12, 1856), 17.

78. Carroll, "Hiawatha's Photographing," 333.

79. Lewis Carroll, *Sylvie and Bruno* (London, 1889).

80. Carroll, "Hiawatha's Photographing," 334. A missing hyphen has been provided for "right-eye."

81. William Wordsworth, "Address to My Infant Daughter," in *Poems*, 2 vols. (London, 1815), 1:292.

82. Carroll, "Hiawatha's Photographing," 335.

83. Longfellow, *Letters*, 5:376.

5. Keats's Chapman's Homer, Justice's Henry James

1. John Keats, *The Letters of John Keats*, ed. Hyder Edward Rollins (Cambridge, Mass.: Harvard University Press, 1958), 1:114.

2. Charles Dickens, *The Posthumous Papers of the Pickwick Club* (London, 1837), 328.

3. John Middleton Murry made this observation in *Studies in Keats* (London: Oxford University Press, 1930), 21.

4. Keats, *Letters*, 1:114n7.

5. Nicholas Roe, *John Keats: A New Life* (New Haven, Conn.: Yale University Press, 2012), 10. Browne thought Keats's birthday the twenty-ninth (though he has the year wrong), but most modern scholars have chosen the thirty-first. At least one recent

biographer sees the date as still arguable. See R. S. White, *John Keats: A Literary Life* (London: Palgrave Macmillan, 2010), 1–2. Jack Stillinger reviewed the book, approving of this skepticism, in the online journal *Review 19* (October 28, 2010), http://www.NBOL-19.org.

6. "Meteorological Journal," *Philosophical Transactions of the Royal Society of London* 107 (January 1, 1817): 20–21. Temperatures were taken at 7 a.m. For the Year Without a Summer, see chapter 1, note 3.

7. Charles Cowden Clarke and Mary Cowden Clarke, *Recollections of Writers* (London, 1878), 121; Leigh Hunt, *Lord Byron and Some of His Contemporaries* (London, 1828), 246.

8. Clarke and Clarke, *Recollections of Writers*, 130.

9. John Keats, *Poems* (London, 1817), 89.

10. Clarke and Clarke, *Recollections of Writers*, 130, wrote "by ten o'clock." In an article some years before, Charles Cowden Clarke recalled it as "before 10, A.M." See Charles Cowden Clarke [An Old School-Fellow, pseud.], "Recollections of Keats," *Atlantic Monthly* 7 (January, 1861): 90.

11. "I found upon my table a letter with no other enclosure than his famous sonnet": Clarke and Clarke, *Recollections of Writers*, 130.

12. "We have MSS known to be drafts that are cleanly written (where the words flower readily or where Keats composed in his head before setting anything down on paper)": Jack Stillinger, *The Poems of John Keats* (Cambridge, Mass.: Harvard University Press, 1978), 745. See also Jack Stillinger, *The Texts of Keats's Poems* (Cambridge, Mass.: Harvard University Press, 1974), 116–17.

13. Clarke, "Recollections of Keats," 90.

14. W. Cooke Taylor edited Chapman's *Iliad* in 1843, but Richard Hooper's edition of both books did not appear until 1857.

15. Clarke and Clarke, *Recollections of Writers*, 130; William Cowper, trans., *The Iliad of Homer*, 5th ed. (London, 1820), 15.

16. Clarke and Clarke, *Recollections of Writers*, 128.

17. Clarke and Clarke, *Recollections of Writers*, 130.

18. "Just at that time I was installed housekeeper, and was solitary": Clarke, "Recollections of Keats," 89.

19. Edward Pugh [David Hughson, *pseud.*], *London; Being an Accurate History and Description of the British Metropolis and Its Neighbourhood* (London, 1807), 4:454.

20. See the postmark on the letter to Clarke: Keats, *Letters*, 1:114.

21. John Feltham, *The Picture of London for 1809*, 10th ed. (London, n.d.), 155–57, 366. Tooley Street may be found on the list of receiving houses for the two-penny post. The pagination of this book is irregular. After p. 373, the pagination starts over as p. 338. The receiving-house list is in this latter sequence.

22. *The Poems of John Keats*, ed. Miriam Allott (London: Longman, 1970), 63–64; Murry, *Studies in Keats*, 22–23.

23. Critchett and Woods, *The Post Office London Directory for 1817*, 18th ed. (London, n.d.), 413.

24. See note 12, this chapter.

25. "To the Great Variety of Readers," *Mr. William Shakespeares Comedies, Histories, & Tragedies*, ed. John Heminge and Henrie Condell (London, 1623), sig. A3. Hereafter, Shakespeare, *First Folio*.

26. Robert Gittings, *John Keats* (Boston: Atlantic Monthly Press, 1968), 81.

27. Critchett and Woods, *Post Office London Directory for 1817*, 413.

28. The detailed map of the area reproduced here may also be found in Timothy Hilton, *Keats and His World* (New York: Viking, 1971), 15. See also 134n15. In his caption, Hilton misunderstands the map's house-numbering system and misidentifies the site of Keats's lodging—it's across from the chapel at No. 8, not next to it at No. [2]8.

29. On October 9, Keats had invited Clarke to his lodgings in Dean Street. Keats, *Letters*, 1:113–14. This letter, Clarke later recalled, "preceded our first symposium," the night they read Chapman together. Clarke and Clarke, *Recollections of Writers*, 128.

30. For what it is worth, and it's not worth much, on the 13th the weather at 8 a.m. was "gloomy and hazy"; on the 20th, "fine"; and on the 27th, "cloudy, lower," with "wind & rain." See *Gentleman's Magazine: and Historical Chronicle* 86, 2nd pt. (n.s., 9) (December 1816): 482.

31. Leigh Hunt, *The Autobiography of Leigh Hunt* (New York, 1850), 1:295. For the invitation to Hunt's birthday dinner, see his letter to Clarke, October 17, 1816: John Barnard, "Leigh Hunt and Charles Cowden Clarke, 1812–18," in *Leigh Hunt: Life, Poetics, Politics*, ed. Nicholas Roe (London: Routledge, 2003), 46.

32. The facts of even this small anecdote from Keats's life can be hard to get right. In *The Age of Wonder* (New York: Pantheon, 2008), 206–7, Richard Holmes reports that Keats had been to Cowden Clarke's house (it was his brother-in-law's house), where the young poets had read Chapman's translation of the *Iliad* (they read in both the *Iliad* and *Odyssey*), reciting passages to each other (probable but not certain), Keats having "'sometimes shouted' with delight" ("sometimes shouted" is from Clarke; the delight is Holmes's contribution). On the walk home, he says, Keats noticed the planet Jupiter setting over the Thames (pure imagination—and impossible to say, as we do not know the exact date of the walk and thus not the weather, which may have been foggy or cloudy), the same planet to which Homer refers in his simile about the fiery helmet and shield of Diomedes. (Homeric commentators say the simile refers to Sirius, not Jupiter, which, like all planets, seems to travel from constellation to

constellation. Because its orbital period is different from Earth's, it can't be associated with a particular season, as Homer's description requires.) Last, Holmes remarks that the speed with which the poem reached Clarke was a "credit also to the postal system" (we don't know how the poem traveled, but it was probably not by post). Even Keats had difficulty getting things right—he'd told Clarke that Dean Street was the first turning to the right along Tooley, but maps show half-a-dozen streets or alleys intervening.

33. Walter Jackson Bate, *John Keats* (Cambridge, Mass.: Harvard University Press, 1963), 30–31, 703–4. Whether Keats left at fourteen or fifteen is disputed.

34. Charles Armitage Brown, *Shakespeare's Autobiographical Poems: His Sonnets Clearly Developed* (London, 1838), 133–34.

35. "Sleep and Poetry," *Poems of John Keats*, 77, lines 185–87.

36. Samuel Johnson, *The Works of Samuel Johnson, L.L.D.* (London, 1787), 4:126n.

37. Clarke and Clarke, *Recollections of Writers*, 129.

38. George Chapman, trans., *The Iliads of Homer* (London, c. 1614), 42 (book 3, line 243). Line numbers in this and subsequent notes for Chapman's translation have been taken from *Chapman's Homer*, 2 vols., ed. Allardyce Nicoll, Bollingen Series 41, 2nd ed. (Princeton, N.J.: Princeton University Press, 1967).

39. Alexander Pope, *The Iliad of Homer: Books I–IX*, ed. Maynard Mack, Twickenham Edition of the Works of Alexander Pope 7 (New Haven, Conn.: Yale University Press, 1967), 207 (book 3, lines 283–86).

40. Clarke and Clarke, *Recollections of Writers*, 129.

41. Chapman, *Iliads*, 40 (book 3, lines 160–61).

42. Pope, *Iliad: Books I–IX*, 200–1 (book 3, lines 201–2).

43. Pope, *Iliad: Books I–IX*, 200n.

44. Chapman, *Iliads*, 41 (book 3, lines 183–84); *The Iliad of Homer*, trans. Richmond Lattimore (Chicago: University of Chicago Press, 1951), book 3, line 168.

45. Clarke and Clarke, *Recollections of Writers*, 126.

46. Clarke, "Recollections of Keats," 90. (In *Recollections of Writers*, 129, Clarke mistakenly writes the "opening of the third book.")

47. Chapman, *Iliads*, 63 (book 5, lines 6–8).

48. Pope, *Iliad: Books I–IX*, 266 (book 5, lines 7–10).

49. Cp. *The Iliad of Homer*, trans. A[lexander]. Pope (London, 1715); and Alexander Pope, *The Works of Alexander Pope, Esq.*, ed. William Lisle Bowles (London, 1806), where the long "s" is still used, with *The Iliad of Homer*, trans. A[lexander]. Pope, new ed. (London, 1813), where it has been dropped. Curiously, Pope's *Odyssey* (London, 1725–1726) is less given to Augustan capitals than his *Iliad*.

50. Chapman, *Iliads*, 169 (book 13, lines 19–21).

51. Alexander Pope, *The Iliad of Homer: Books X–XXIV*, ed. Maynard Mack, Twick-enham Edition of the Works of Alexander Pope 8 (New Haven, Conn.: Yale University Press, 1967), 105 (book 13, lines 29–31).

52. Clarke and Clarke, *Recollections of Writers*, 130.

53. George Chapman, trans., *Homer's Odysses* (London, c. 1614), 84 (book 5, lines 608–14).

54. Alexander Pope, *The Odyssey of Homer: Books I–VII*, ed. Maynard Mack, Twick-enham Edition of the Works of Alexander Pope 9 (New Haven, Conn.: Yale University Press, 1967), 200 (book 5, lines 584–85). Pope had two collaborators on the *Odyssey*, whose work he revised; but he translated half the books himself, including book 5 (cxciv, cxcvi.)

55. Clarke and Clarke, *Recollections of Writers*, 130.

56. "The poet traveller—his bread is thought": Alphonse de Lamartine, *A Pilgrimage to the Holy Land* (Philadelphia, 1835), 1:14; trans. of *Voyage en Orient* (Paris, 1835). An earlier use of the term in English, however, may be found in E. C. S., "The Hanging of the Spy," *Atkinson's Casket* 8 (September 1833): 386, where a reference to the "poet-traveler" introduces some altered lines of Goldsmith's poem "The Traveler." This likely passed from notice.

57. "When I die I'll have my Shakespeare placed on my heart, with Homer in my right hand & . . . Dante under my head": Keats, *Poems of John Keats*, 14–17; Keats, *Letters*, 1:258.

58. Keats, *Poems of John Keats*, 59–60.

59. Bate, *John Keats*, 25–26, 32; Clarke and Clarke, *Recollections of Writers*, 125.

60. Chapman was sensitive to accusations that he was merely paraphrasing, a slander later aimed at Pope. The former felt that literal versions, whether in prose or verse, were without enough art—and that sometimes such versions did more paraphrasing than he. See Chapman, *Iliads*, "To the Reader," sig. Ar-v (lines 93–134); "The Preface to the Reader," sig. A3v-4r (lines 95–137). Ezra Pound, who called himself "very ill-taught" in Greek, used the Latin translation of the *Odyssey* by Andreas Divus. See Ezra Pound, *Literary Essays of Ezra Pound*, ed. T. S. Eliot (New York: New Directions, 1954), 249, 259.

61. Keats, *Letters*, 1:354n1, 1:404n1, 2:205n9.

62. Keats, *Letters*, 1:141.

63. Percy Bysshe Shelley, *Shelley's Prose*, ed. David Lee Clark (New York: New Amsterdam, 1988), 297.

64. *The Tempest*, lines 1701–3; 4.1.247–49.

65. John Ash, *The New and Complete Dictionary of the English Language* (London, 1795), vol. 1, s.v. "Lowbrowed."

66. Milton, *L'Allegro*, line 8; Pope, *Eloisa to Abelard*, line 244.

67. *Piers Plowman*, A, book 5, line 109; B, book 5, line 190.

68. "Noctes Ambrosiae, No. XLVII," *Blackwood's Edinburgh Magazine* 26 (December 1829), 857; "Letter to the Editor," *Spectator* 14 (February 13, 1841): 159.

69. Chapman, *Iliads*, 239 (book 17, line 108).

70. "Hymn Before Sun-Rise, in the Vale of Chamouni," in Coleridge, *Complete Poems*, 325, line 72; Dante Alighieri, *The Vision; or, Hell, Purgatory, and Paradise*, trans. Henry Francis Cary (London, [1814]), 261 (canto 15, line 11), 274 (canto 19, line 60). See Keats, *Letters*, 1:294, 343n. In 1818, he took the edition of three 32° volumes on his northern tour.

71. Stephen Hales, *Statical Essays: Containing Haemastatics*, 2nd ed. (London, 1740), 2:285.

72. Keats, *Poems of John Keats*, 45.

73. Keats, *Poems of John Keats*, 48 ("To My Brother George").

74. Clarke and Clarke, *Recollections of Writers*, 130.

75. Clarke and Clarke, *Recollections of Writers*, 130.

76. Helen Vendler, *Coming of Age as a Poet* (Cambridge, Mass.: Harvard University Press, 2003), 53, five lines below the inset quote. The mistake was made early and late. See *Classical Journal* 34 (September 1826): 52; *Fraser's Magazine* 14 (December 1836): 679; *Dublin University Magazine* 21 (June 1843): 693; as well as Bate, *John Keats*, 88n.

77. *Examiner* no. 466 (December 1, 1816): 761–62. The *Examiner* was a "Sunday paper," but Hunt also published a Monday edition, identical apart from an update on the London markets. Some copies of the issue with Keats's poem are therefore dated Monday, December 2.

78. *Keats: The Critical Heritage*, G. M. Matthews, ed. (London: Routledge and Kegan Paul, 1971), 42.

79. *Keats: The Critical Heritage*, 68–69, 112. Cf. 324, where a critic as late as 1848 complained that Keats "compelled his subject to bend obsequiously to his rhymes."

80. Chapman, *Iliads*, 42 (book 3, lines 238–44).

81. Clarke and Clarke, *Recollections of Writers*, 125, 126.

82. "He used to spend many evenings in reading to me": *The Keats Circle*, ed. Hyder Edward Rollins, 2nd ed. (Cambridge, Mass.: Harvard University Press, 1969), 2:185.

83. *The Keats Circle*, 2:143–44.

84. *The Keats Circle*, 2:148.

85. *Keats: The Critical Heritage*, 51–53.

86. *Keats: The Critical Heritage*, 54.

87. "Realms of gold": N. Sloan, "Elegy," *European Magazine and London Review* 53 (May 1808): 377. "Wild surmise": I[saac] Watts, *Horae Lyricae: Poems, Chiefly of the Lyric Kind*, 8th ed., corr. (London, 1743), 200.

88. *Keats: The Critical Heritage*, 306.

89. Leigh Hunt, "Harry Brown's Letters to His Friends. Letter VII. To C[harles]. L[amb].," *Examiner* no. 452 (August 26, 1816): 537.

90. John Bonnycastle, *An Introduction to Astronomy*, 5th ed., corr. and improved (London, 1807). See Bate, *John Keats*, 26; and *Poems of John Keats*, 57n67. A listing for Keats's copy, identifying it as the fifth edition, may be found in *American Book-Prices Current*, ed. Victor Hugo Paltsits (New York: Richard H. Dodd, 1915), 354. It was sold in 1914 for $275.

91. "Since the time of its first publication, four additional planets, belonging to our system, have been discovered": John Bonnycastle, *An Introduction to Astronomy*, 7th ed., corrected and greatly improved (London, 1816), ix, 400–1. The fifth edition had mentioned only two new planets in addition to Uranus. Keats presented a copy of that edition to his brother George: *Bulletin of the Keats-Shelley Memorial, Rome* 2 (London, 1913): 149.

92. John S. Martin, "Keats's New Planet," *Notes and Queries* 206, n.s., 8 (January 1961): 23.

93. William Newman, *Rylandiana: Reminiscences Relating to the Rev. John Ryland, A.M.* (London, 1835), 117–22.

94. Bonnycastle, *Introduction*, 5th ed., 371.

95. "To one who has been long in city pent," *Poems of John Keats*, 46.

96. Chapman, *Iliads*, 63 (book 5, lines 6, 8). Richmond Lattimore renders the Greek, "She made weariless fire blaze from his shield and helmet / like that star of the waning summer who beyond all stars / rises bathed in the ocean stream to glitter in brilliance": Homer, *Iliad*, trans. Lattimore, book 5, lines 4–6.

97. Keats, *Letters*, 2:133.

98. Bate, *John Keats*, 67–83.

99. Keats's longings were often frustrated. Keats, *Letters*, 1:147, 268 (Europe); 1:172 (Lisbon); 1:325, 343 (America); 2:114 (South America, India); 2:138 (Switzerland).

100. Clarke and Clarke, *Recollections of Writers*, 123–24.

101. Clarke and Clarke, *Recollections of Writers*, 124; Aileen Ward, *John Keats: The Making of a Poet* (New York: Viking, 1965), 19. Ward, giving no source, says he won the volume at Enfield, but Clarke only that it was one of the volumes the poet read when "he must in those last months have exhausted the school library." Keats was reading it again in the spring of 1819. Keats, *Letters*, 2:100.

102. William Robertson, *The History of America* (London, 1777), 1:204.

103. Richard Garnett, "Notes on Some Poets Connected with Hampstead," in *Hampstead Annual, 1899* (London, n.d.), 21–23.

104. William Wordsworth, *The Excursion, Being a Portion of the Recluse: A Poem* (London, 1814), 427.

105. Wordsworth, *The Excursion*, 428.

106. Keats, *Letters*, 1:203.

107. Robertson, *America*, 2:49–50.

108. Robertson, *America*, 1:204.

109. Robertson, *America*, 1:200.

110. Clarke and Clarke, *Recollections of Writers*, 123.

111. Francis Turner Palgrave, *The Golden Treasury* (Cambridge, 1861), 320n. "A.T." is Alfred Tennyson.

112. Anon., "Leigh Hunt's Imagination and Fancy," *British Quarterly Review* 1 (1845): 576–77.

113. Charles Rzepka contends that Cortez was not an error, an idea that has been floated from time to time. Rzepka believes that Keats was declaring himself only a belated discoverer, and that Homer : Chapman : Keats :: Pacific : Balboa : Cortez. The argument depends on (1) Keats, though remembering his schoolboy conquistadors, having misread a rather jumbled sentence in Robertson, (2) the reference to Darien being the result, and (3) the watcher of the skies being, not Herschel, but any watcher seeing Mars or Venus, say, for the first time, so the planet would be new to him. In other words, Keats did make a grave mistake, only a lesser one. Rzepka has a number of telling points (e.g., that no one caught the error before Tennyson, though Rzepka is mistaken there), but his reasoning is strained and oversubtle. He suggests at one point that Keats may have been unconcerned by readers who could be misled. Rzepka's logic depends on readers of the day understanding Keats's subtlety (or being indifferent to the error) and virtually all readers afterward thinking that Keats got his history wrong. Charles Rzepka, "'Cortez—or Balboa, or Somebody Like That': Form, Fact, and Forgetting in Keats's 'Chapman's Homer' Sonnet," *Keats-Shelley Journal* 51 (2002): 35–75. Before Tennyson's correction, Hartley Coleridge wrote, in "To a Red Herring," *Poems*, 2nd ed. (London, 1851), 2:231, "and none had burst / Into that ocean which first Cortez view'd / From Darien's heights." (The meter seems to confirm the pronunciation COR-tez.) The son of S. T. Coleridge may have been influenced by Keats, but the mistake suggests that the general knowledge wasn't general.

114. Clarke and Clarke, *Recollections of Writers*, 126, 125.

115. Hunt, *Lord Byron*, 249; Keats, *Poems of John Keats*, 62n.

116. Robertson, *America*, 1:204.

117. Robertson, *America*, 1:204.

118. Clarke and Clarke, *Recollections of Writers*, 130. Though the wording is ambiguous, it seems fairly clear that Clarke meant Keats's wonderment.

119. Vendler, *Coming of Age*, 54–55.

120. In what is probably the manuscript Keats sent Clarke, line 12 has a comma after "Pacific," not the comma-dash of the *Examiner* or the simple dash of *Poems* (1817). The dash might have suggested that only Cortez was silent, had "wild surmise" not implied silence among the men as well.

121. Hunt, *Lord Byron*, 248.

122. Ward, *John Keats*, 74. See, however, *The Odyssey of Homer*, trans. Richmond Lattimore (New York: Harper and Row, 1967), book 5, line 454: "His very heart was sick with salt water." Chapman's dense and complex image is not Homeric.

123. Henry James, *The American Scene* (London: Chapman and Hall, 1907), 460. The first English edition ends with five pages not present in the first American edition, published the same year.

124. James, *The American Scene*, 464.

125. James, *The American Scene*, 463.

126. James, *The American Scene*, 463.

127. Sheldon M. Novick, *Henry James: The Mature Master* (New York: Random House, 2004), 423.

128. Donald Justice, *Collected Poems* (New York: Knopf, 2004), 200–1.

129. Donald Justice, *The Sunset Maker* (New York: Atheneum, 1987), 8.

130. Donald Justice, "Henry James at the Pacific," *Atlantic Monthly* 257 (January 1986): 78. Note the variant title.

131. Donald Justice, *A Donald Justice Reader* (Hanover, N.H.: Middlebury College Press, 1991), 5.

132. James, *The American Scene*, 102.

133. Edgar Poe, *Annabel Lee*, music by E. F. Falconnet (Boston, 1859).

134. Henry James, *Letters*, vol. 4, *1895–1916*, ed. Leon Edel (Cambridge, Mass.: Harvard University Press, 1984), 357.

135. Milton, *Paradise Lost*, book 2, line 620.

136. Henry James, *Letters*, 4:328.

137. James, *The American Scene*, 229.

138. James, *Letters*, 4:355.

139. James, *Letters*, 4:357.

140. Novick, *Henry James*, 398.

141. Frederick Jackson Turner, "The Significance of the Frontier in American History," in *Annual Report of the American Historical Association for 1893* (Washington, D.C.: Government Printing Office, 1894), 197–227.

142. Milton's sonnet was discussed earlier, in chapter 2.

143. Mark Twain, *Huck Finn and Tom Sawyer Among the Indians, and Other Unfinished Stories* (Berkeley: University of California Press, 1989), 33–81.

144. Henry James, *The Complete Notebooks of Henry James*, ed. Leon Edel and Lyall H. Powers (New York: Oxford University Press, 1987), 237.

145. Justice, *Collected Poems*, 200.

146. James, *Complete Notebooks*, 242.

147. James, *Complete Notebooks*, 237.

148. Henry James, *The Middle Years* (New York: Charles Scribner's Sons, 1917), 1.

149. Robertson, *America*, 1:203.

150. James, *Letters*, 4:355.

151. James, *Letters*, 4:355.

152. Robertson, *America*, 1:204.

153. Henry James, "George Sand: The New Life," *North American Review* 174 (April 1902): 543.

6. Shakespeare's Rotten Weeds, Shakespeare's Deep Trenches

1. [William Shakespeare], *Shake-speares Sonnets. Never before Imprinted* (London, 1609), leaf Br-v. See note 5, this chapter, for publishing information. All quotations from other sonnets are taken from this edition, referred to in short as Q. The Quarto ends sonnet 2 with a comma, a typo corrected here. A modernized version:

When forty winters shall besiege thy brow
And dig deep trenches in thy beauty's field,
Thy youth's proud livery, so gazed on now,
Will be a tottered weed of small worth held.
Then being asked where all thy beauty lies,
Where all the treasure of thy lusty days,
To say within thine own deep-sunken eyes
Were an all-eating shame, and thriftless praise.
How much more praise deserved thy beauty's use
If thou couldst answer, "This fair child of mine
Shall sum my count and make my old excuse,"
Proving his beauty by succession thine.
    This were to be new made when thou art old
    And see thy blood warm when thou feel'st it cold.

2. Francis Meres, *Palladis Tamia. Wits Treasury.* (London, 1598), 282r; E. K. Chambers, *William Shakespeare* (Oxford: Clarendon, 1930), 2:193–94.

3. [William Shakespeare], *Venus and Adonis* (London, 1593); *The Rape of Lucrece* (London, 1594). Though the title page of the latter reads *Lucrece*, the running heads say *The Rape of Lucrece*.

4. Meres, *Palladis Tamia*, 281v–282r.

5. *Shake-speares Sonnets. Never before Imprinted*. (London, 1609), published by Thomas Thorpe, who entered the volume in the Stationers' Register on May 20 of that year. The printer was George Eld, and the copies were divided between the bookshops of William Apsley and John Wright, for whom separate title pages were printed. Apsley's shop was in St. Paul's Churchyard, under the sign of the Parrot, and Wright's at Christ Church Gate. See *Shakespeare's Sonnets*, ed. Katherine Duncan-Jones, rev. ed. (London: Bloomsbury, 2010), 36–37.

6. Daniel Starza Smith, *John Donne and the Conway Papers* (Oxford: Oxford University Press, 2014), 296.

7. *Catalogue of English Literary Manuscripts, 1450–1700* [*CELM*]: http://www.celm-ms.org.uk/authors/shakespearewilliam.html#folger-v-a-100_id695234. See entries ShW 6–30, including 14.5.

8. Shakespeare, *All's Well That Ends Well*, line 2142; 4.3.200.

9. Gary Taylor, "Some Manuscripts of Shakespeare's Sonnets," *Bulletin of the John Rylands Library* 68 (1985–1986): 220. Facsimiles of the Hand D ms. are available in *The Riverside Shakespeare*, ed. G. Blakemore Evans, 2nd ed. (Boston: Houghton Mifflin, 1997), 1780–92 (transcription included).

10. W[illiam]. Shakespeare, *The Passionate Pilgrime* (London, 1599).

11. Shakespeare, *Sonnets*, ed. Duncan-Jones, 1.

12. Shakespeare, *Sonnets*, ed. Duncan-Jones, 14–15; William Shakespeare, *The Complete Sonnets and Poems*, ed. Colin Burrow (Oxford: Oxford University Press, 2002), 106.

13. Shakespeare, *Sonnets*, ed. Duncan-Jones, 453–62.

14. Taylor, "Some Manuscripts," 211. One of his mss. has since been dropped (a Folger ms. that contained only one quatrain, copied from Q), and another, related to the Spes Altera group, added by Peter Beals, numbered 14.5 in *CELM* (see note 7, this chapter).

15. *Mr. William Shakespeares Comedies, Histories, & Tragedies*, ed. John Heminge and Henrie Condell (London, 1623), sig. A3. Hereafter, Shakespeare, *First Folio*.

16. Ben Jonson, *Timber: or, Discoveries* (London, 1641), in *The Workes of Benjamin Jonson* (London, 1640), 2:97 (pagination starts over numerous times). The disparity in publication dates reflects various disputes over rights during the printing of this edition.

17. John Kerrigan, *On Shakespeare and Early Modern Literature* (Oxford: Oxford University Press, 2001), 4.

18. Jonson, "To the Reader," in Shakespeare, *First Folio*, sig. A3.

19. *Riverside Shakespeare*, 2nd ed., 1780–1788. There are about sixteen blots attributable to Hand D. John Jones, in *Shakespeare at Work* (Oxford: Clarendon, 1995), 18–27, discusses a number of these revisions or corrections.

20. Taylor, "Some Manuscripts," 210–46.

21. Shakespeare, *Sonnets*, ed. Duncan-Jones, 453–7; William Shakespeare, *The Sonnets and A Lover's Complaint*, ed. John Kerrigan (London: Penguin, 1999), 441–43; Shakespeare, *The Sonnets*, ed. G. Blakemore Evans, updated ed. (Cambridge: Cambridge University Press, 2006), 268–70; Shakespeare, *Complete Sonnets and Poems*, ed. Burrow, 690.

22. Taylor, "Some Manuscripts," 212. The manuscript version, modernized, with differences from the Quarto version marked in bold:

When forty winters shall besiege thy brow
And **trench** deep **furrows** in **that lovely** field,
Thy youth's **fair** livery, so **accounted** now,
Shall be **like rotten weeds** of **no** worth held.
Then being asked where all thy beauty lies,
Where all the **luster** of thy **youthful** days,
To say, "Within **these hollow** sunken eyes,"
Were an all-**eaten truth**, and **worthless** praise.
O how much **better were** thy beauty's use
If thou couldst **say,** "This **pretty** child of mine
Saves my account and **makes** my old excuse,"
Making his beauty by succession thine.
   This were to be new **born** when thou art old
   And see thy blood warm when thou feel'st it cold.

23. Taylor, "Some Manuscripts," 215.

24. Taylor, "Some Manuscripts," 233, 215.

25. Shakespeare, *Sonnets*, ed. Duncan-Jones, 453–57.

26. Shakespeare, *Venus and Adonis*, line 1052.

27. Shakespeare, *The Two Gentlemen of Verona*, lines 1399–1400; 3.2.6–7.

28. Shakespeare, *Titus Andronicus*, line 2120; 5.2.23.

29. Robert Armin, *The Works of Robert Armin, Actor (1605–1609)*, ed. Alexander B. Grosart (Manchester: Charles E. Simms, 1880), 24.

30. Shakespeare, *Sonnets*, ed. Duncan-Jones, 456.

31. Email from John Kerrigan, March 3, 2016.

32. Shakespeare, *Love's Labour's Lost*, line 2406; 5.2.660.

33. "Extracts from a Sermon, Preached 1388, and Strongly Presumed to Be Wickliffe's," *Literary Magazine and British Review* 12 (February 1794): 129. See, however, "A Godly and Famous Sermon. Preached in the Yeere of Our Lord 1388, . . . and Found Out Hidde in a Wall," in Richard Wimbledon, *The Regal, Clerical, and Laical Bayliffs . . . : A Sermon in Two Parts*, 14th ed. (London, 1738), 19.

34. Shakespeare, *As You Like It*, line 1261; 3.2.119–20.

35. William Shakespeare, *The Sonnets*, ed. John Dover Wilson (Cambridge: Cambridge University Press, 1966), 89.

36. Shakespeare, *The Sonnets*, ed. Kerrigan, 173.

37. Shakespeare, *The Sonnets*, ed. Kerrigan, 173.

38. Shakespeare, *Sonnets*, ed. Duncan-Jones, 457.

39. Eric Partridge, *Shakespeare's Bawdy*, rev. ed. (London: Routledge and Kegan Paul, 1955), s.v. "Treasure," 2. semen, referring to quote at "Fall" (*Othello*, lines 2747–49; 4.3.86–88).

40. Shakespeare, *King Lear*, line 1985; 3.7.84.

41. Shakespeare, *Henry V*, lines 296–8; 1.2.163–65.

42. Shakespeare, *The Rape of Lucrece*, line 280.

43. Shakespeare, *Sonnets*, ed. Duncan-Jones, 114n8 (cf. sonnet 19, line 1).

44. Shakespeare, *Othello*, line 1843; 3.3.391.

45. Shakespeare, *Titus Andronicus*, line 2417; 5.3.117.

46. John Gower, "Confessio Amantis," in *The English Works of John Gower*, ed. G. C. Macauley (London: Kegan Paul, Trench, Trübner, 1900), 1:176 (book 2, line 1715).

47. Shakespeare, *Twelfth Night*, line 670; 2.2.39.

48. Shakespeare, *Richard II*, lines 2440–1; 5.3.68–69.

49. Shakespeare, *The Sonnets*, ed. Dover Wilson, xcix–c.

50. Shakespeare, *Sonnets*, ed. Duncan-Jones, 453–54.

51. Thomas Wilson, *The Arte of Rhetorique (1553)*, ed. Robert Hood Bowers (Gainesville, Fla.: Scholars' Facsimiles and Reprints, 1962), 73 (fol. 31). Cf. T. W. Baldwin, *On the Literary Genetics of Shakspere's Poems and Sonnets* (Urbana: University of Illinois Press, 1950), 183–85. Baldwin's extensive quotation of Wilson's translation of Erasmus's letter catches most of the passage here but oddly misses the "new born" line. The first scholar to notice Shakespeare's use of Wilson was Edgar I. Fripp, *Shakespeare, Man and Artist* (London: Oxford University Press, 1938), 1:267n5.

52. Taylor, "Some Manuscripts," 244, though Wilson's lines are quoted in the wrong order. In Shakespeare, *The Sonnets*, ed. Kerrigan, 442, the quotations are modernized but again placed in the wrong order.

53. Wilson, *Arte of Rhetorique*, 70 (fol. 29); Shakespeare, *The Sonnets*, ed. Kerrigan, 174n5–6.

54. Shakespeare, *Henry IV, Part II*, line 206; 1.1.167.

55. Gabriel Harvey, *Pierces Supererogation; or, A New Prayse of the Old Asse* (London, 1593), 66.

56. *Shakespeare's Sonnets*, ed. Stephen Booth (New Haven, Conn.: Yale University Press, 1977), 137n11.

57. Shakespeare, *Complete Sonnets and Poems*, ed. Burrow, 384n11.

58. Shakespeare, *Sonnets*, ed. Duncan-Jones, 13–14.

59. Taylor, "Some Manuscripts," 230–32.

60. Shakespeare, *Complete Sonnets and Poems*, ed. Burrow, 92–93. Some defense of the last anomaly has been made on the grounds that fifteen-line sonnets were not unknown. The poem's first or fifth line, critics have argued, must be extraneous, if any line is—but losing the fifth would make the syntax impossible. The first line, however ("The forward violet thus did I chide:"), could have been written above the sonnet as an explanatory title of sorts, like a stage direction. The compositor might have taken it as the opening line and set it into the text—the information it conveys, important but not crucial, has confused matters ever since because the line is metrical and linked by rhyme. It's also possible that the first line was marked for deletion—there are passages in the plays that suggest the compositors did not always see or obey such marks.

61. Shakespeare, *Sonnets*, ed. Duncan-Jones, 456.

7. Pound's Métro, Williams's Wheelbarrow

1. Ezra Pound, "How I Began," *T.P.'s Weekly* 21 (June 6, 1913): 707. Reprinted in Ezra Pound, *Early Writings*, ed. Ira B. Nadel (New York: Penguin, 2005), 214–15.

2. Letter to Harriet Monroe, October 13, 1912, in *The Letters of Ezra Pound, 1907–1941*, ed. D. D. Paige (London: Faber and Faber, 1951), 46.

3. *Poetry* 2 (April 1913): 12.

4. Ezra Pound, "Silet" and "Apparuit," in *Ripostes of Ezra Pound* (London: Stephen Swift, 1912), 9, 12.

5. Pound, *Ripostes of Ezra Pound*, 59. See also Ezra Pound, *Literary Essays of Ezra Pound*, ed. T. S. Eliot (New York: New Directions, 1954), 4 ("The first use of the word . . .").

6. Humphrey Carpenter, *A Serious Character: The Life of Ezra Pound* (Boston: Houghton Mifflin, 1988), 114–17; F. S. Flint, "The History of Imagism," *Egoist* 2 (May 1, 1915): 71.

7. Ezra Pound and Ford Madox Ford, *Pound/Ford, The Story of a Literary Friendship: The Correspondence Between Ezra Pound and Ford Madox Ford*, ed. Brita Lindberg-Seyersted (London: Faber and Faber, 1982), 172. Hugh Kenner, in *The Pound Era*

(Berkeley: University of California Press, 1971), 184, dates the roll to August 1911. Pound was counting *Personae of Ezra Pound* (London: Elkin Mathews, 1909) as his first book. His taste for arcane euphemism made another reader almost violent. William Carlos Williams, *Kora in Hell: Improvisations* (Boston: Four Seas, 1920), 13, remembers that his father, finding a reference to "jewels" in some verse of Pound's, wondered what they could be: "These jewels,—rubies, sapphires, amethysts and what not, Pound went on to explain with great determination and care, were the backs of books as they stood on a man's shelf. 'But why in heaven's name don't you say so then?' was my father's triumphant and crushing rejoinder."

8. F. S. F[lint]., untitled review of Ezra Pound, *Canzoni*, *Poetry Review* 1 (January 1912): 28.

9. Rupert Richard Arrowsmith, *Modernism and the Museum: Asian, African, and Pacific Art and the London Avant-Garde* (Oxford: Oxford University Press, 2011), 105–7, 111–12, 122. Given that there is no proof Pound examined *ukiyo-e* prints, Arrowsmith at times overstates his case (e.g., 126–27); but the conjunction and consequence are striking.

10. F. S. Flint, "Imagisme," *Poetry* 1 (March 1913): 199.

11. Ezra Pound, "A Few Don'ts by an Imagiste," *Poetry* 1 (March 1913): 201–2.

12. Ezra Pound, "Mesmerism," "A Villonaud: Ballad of the Gibbet," in *Personae: The Collected Poems of Ezra Pound* (New York: Boni and Liveright, 1926), 13, 11.

13. Ezra Pound, "Grace Before Song," "Comraderie," in *Collected Early Poems of Ezra Pound*, ed. Michael John King (London: Faber and Faber, 1977), 7, 31.

14. Harriet Monroe to Ezra Pound, August 7, 1912, University of Chicago Library, *Poetry: A Magazine of Verse* Records, 1895–1961, box 38, folder 23.

15. Pound, *Letters*, 43; Noel Stock, *The Life of Ezra Pound* (New York: Pantheon, 1970), 121.

16. "It has announced that it is not edited for the old lady in Dubuque": "Of All Things," *New Yorker* 1 (February 21, 1925): 2. The policy had been "announced" in the magazine's prospectus.

17. "No it wont do," he replied to his own suggestion, written on the back of one of the canceled draft copies of "In a Station of the Metro." University of Chicago Library, *Poetry: A Magazine of Verse* Records, 1895–1961, box 39, folder 29.

18. Ezra Pound, "The Garret," "The Garden," "Commission," in *Lustra* (New York: Knopf, 1917), 15, 16, 22. The English edition had dropped a number of poems after objections by the printer and publisher. See note 76, this chapter.

19. Pound, "The Garden," in *Lustra*, 16.

20. Pound, "Salutation the Second," in *Lustra*, 18.

21. Carpenter, *A Serious Character*, 189–91; Pound, *Letters*, 45.

22. [Ezra Pound, ed.], *Catholic Anthology, 1914–1915* (London: Elkin Mathews, 1915); Ezra Pound, *Lustra* (London: Elkin Mathews, 1916).

23. Homer, *Iliad*, trans. Lattimore, book 11, lines 207–8.

24. Ezra Pound, "Vorticism," *Fortnightly Review*, n.s., 96 (September 1, 1914): 465. Reprinted in Ezra Pound, *Gaudier-Brzeska: A Memoir* (London: John Lane, 1916).

25. Mark Ovenden, *Paris Underground* (New York: Penguin, 2009), 26.

26. Ovenden, *Paris Underground*, 23; "Rapid Transit in London," [*Pennsylvania*] *School Journal* 41 (April 1893): 441; John L. Stoddard, *John L. Stoddard's Lectures*, vol. 9: *Scotland. England. London.* (Boston, 1899), 24; "London's Underground Roads," *Western Electrician* 17 (November 16, 1895): 243.

27. "Electric lighting was described as 'brilliant,' though by modern standards this would be a somewhat grandiose claim": Ovenden, *Paris Underground*, 24. The 1900 photo in *Paris Underground* (a larger version has been reproduced here) shows one enclosed bulb and a series of smaller bulbs under shades, the effect very gloomy indeed; such bulbs would have been incapable of casting a strong light on the surroundings. The whole may have seemed like a shadowy closet.

28. Franz Kafka, *The Diaries of Franz Kafka, 1910–1923*, ed. Max Brod (New York: Schocken, 1976), 460.

29. William Wordsworth, *The Prelude; or, Growth of a Poet's Mind: An Autobiographical Poem* (London, 1850), 197 [book 7, lines 626–29].

30. T. S. Eliot, *The Waste Land* (New York: Boni and Liveright, 1922), 15.

31. Ovenden, *Paris Underground*, 23–24.

32. Undated note to Monroe on back of a canceled draft of "In a Station of the Metro." This is part of a marked-up manuscript of some of the poems in "Contemporania," c. October 1912 (University of Chicago Library, *Poetry: A Magazine of Verse* Records, 1895–1961, box 38, folder 29).

33. Pound, "Vorticism," 465.

34. Ezra Pound, *Exultations* (London: Elkin Mathews, 1909), 30.

35. "My remains have arrived at 3 Rue de l'Odéon" [postscript], in *Ezra Pound and Margaret Cravens: A Tragic Friendship, 1910–1912*, ed. Omar Pound and Robert Spoo (Durham, N.C.: Duke University Press, 1988), 66. Pound wrote the letter on February 25, 1911, while aboard the *Mauretania*, sailing from New York to London; but the postscript cannot have been written before March 2, when he arrived in Paris. The catacombs lay about a mile south of his pension, through the Luxembourg Gardens.

36. Pound, "A Few Don'ts," 201–2.

37. Ezra Pound, *Polite Essays* (London: Faber and Faber, 1937), 170. Pound puts the definition of *logopoeia* in quotes, but he may simply be quoting himself from a source unknown. Cf. note 52, this chapter.

38. Ezra Pound, "How to Read, or Why," *New York Herald Tribune Books*, January 13, 20, 27, 1929; noted in Donald Gallup, *Ezra Pound, A Bibliography* (Charlottesville: University of Virginia Press, 1983), 49. Pound had almost a decade earlier used *melopoeia* and *logopoeia* in a review of Jean Cocteau's *Poésies, Dial* 70 (January 1921): 110.

39. E.g., Hokusai's *Mt. Fuji with Cherry Trees in Bloom* and Hiroshige's *Plum Garden at Kameido*.

40. Online climate records for March 1911: http://meteo-climat-bzh.dyndns.org/relevmois-1-3-1911-1971-2000-1-1675-2017.php; and April 1911: http://meteo-climat-bzh.dyndns.org/relevmois-1-4-1911.php.

41. Email from Melanie Brkich, April 8, 2014, translating a conversation with Julian Pepinster. Smoking was allowed on the Métro until the early 1990s.

42. Emails from Melanie Brkich, March 24 and April 8, 2014, translating a conversation with Julian Pepinster. The original wooden carriages were varnished brown; the first metal cars, which started appearing on the lines in 1908, were painted brown to match. The motor cars and second-class carriages were painted dark green, probably by 1910. (First-class cars were painted red.) On the line Pound was traveling, he probably saw metal cars painted dark green.

43. Kafka, *Diaries of Franz Kafka, 1910–23*, 460.

44. "The cavern was profound, wide-mouthed, and huge": Virgil, *The Aeneid*, trans. Robert Fitzgerald (New York: Random House, 1983), 168.

45. Ovenden, *Paris Underground*, 25; photographs of the Art Deco entrances: 3, 25.

46. Email from Melanie Brkich, April 8, 2014, translating a conversation with Julian Pepinster. This now serves as an exit from the station.

47. Pound, *Fortnightly Review*, 467.

48. "The only way of expressing emotion in the form of art is by finding an 'objective correlative'; in other words, a set of objects, a situation, a chain of events which shall be the formula of that *particular* emotion; such that when the external facts, which must terminate in sensory experience, are given, the emotion is immediately evoked." T. S. Eliot, *Selected Essays*, 2nd ed., rev. and enlarged (London: Faber and Faber, 1934), 145. The relevant essay was originally published as "Hamlet and His Problems," *Athenaeum* no. 4665 (September 26, 1919): 940–41.

49. Carpenter, *A Serious Character*, 296. The friend was John Gould Fletcher. Whistler had died in 1903, so Pound was paying homage to the dandies of an earlier generation.

50. Ezra Pound, "To Whistler, American," *Poetry* 1 (October 1912): 7.

51. Pound, *Fortnightly Review*, 465.

52. "'Great literature is simply language charged with meaning to the utmost possible degree.'" Ezra Pound, *ABC of Reading* (New Haven, Conn.: Yale University Press,

1934), 22, 49. (In the later New Directions edition, 36, 63.) Pound marks this dictum as a quotation, but he is quoting himself ("How to Read," *Polite Essays*, 167).

53. Pound, *Fortnightly Review*, 465.

54. *Poetry* 2 (April 1913): 12.

55. Pound, *Letters*, 53. In a letter that accompanied his return of proofs for "Contemporania," he carefully typed out the way he wanted "In a Station of the Metro" to appear: *Dear Editor: A History of* Poetry *in Letters*, ed. Joseph Parisi and Stephen Young (New York: Norton, 2002), 58. Unfortunately, the editors of this volume have misunderstood Pound's directions, missing the space called for between "black" and "bough." In the *Poetry* archive at the University of Chicago, Pound's two-page note that accompanies some of the poems considered for the series, ranked in red grease-pencil **XX** or **X** or √ , is written on the back of a pair of typescripts of "In a Station"— one with and one without the phrasal spacing. Both have been scored through. University of Chicago Library, *Poetry: A Magazine of Verse* Records, 1895–1961, box 38, folder 29.

56. The *Poetry* manuscripts may be disordered. As mentioned in the previous note, on the back of the letter to Monroe, beginning "I've marked the following poems XX . . . ," are two drafts of "In a Station of the Metro" that Pound has scored through with his usual wavy pencil line. These may have been scrap pages picked up from his desk. University of Chicago Library, *Poetry: A Magazine of Verse* Records, 1895–1961, box 38, folder 29. Elsewhere there's a handwritten and typescript manuscript of poems also considered for "Contemporania," three poems of which were used and two withdrawn (box 39, folder 31).

57. Pound, *Letters*, 53.

58. [Pound, ed.], *Catholic Anthology*, 88. The colon was still present.

59. Pound, *Lustra* (1916), 45.

60. Ezra Pound, *Personae*, ed. Lea Baechler and A. Walton Litz, rev. ed. (New York: New Directions, 1990), 111.

61. Pound, *Fortnightly Review*, 467.

62. Pound, *Fortnightly Review*, 467.

63. Pound, *Fortnightly Review*, 465.

64. Ezra Pound, trans., *Cathay* (London: Elkin Mathews, 1915), 13.

65. Wai-lim Yip, *Ezra Pound's* Cathay (Princeton, N.J.: Princeton University Press, 1969), 7.

66. Pound, *Cathay*, 13.

67. "Chinese Poetry," in Pound, *Early Writings*, 298; *To-Day* 3 (April 1918): 56.

68. Yip, *Ezra Pound's* Cathay, 66–67.

69. Pound, *Polite Essays*, 170.

70. Pound, *Personae* (1926), 112. In *Lustra* (1916), 49, and (1917), 55, the three words are each followed by three dots with no space before the first. I have used the *Personae* text.

71. Michael Silk, Ingo Gildenhard, and Rosemary Barrow, *The Classical Tradition: Art, Literature, Thought* (Chichester: Wiley Blackwell, 2014), 92. Cf. Hugh Kenner, *The Pound Era* (Berkeley: University of California Press, 1971), 5–6, 54–55.

72. Silk, *The Classical Tradition*, 92n33.

73. Pound, *Personae* (1909), 56.

74. Pound, "How I Began," 707; *Early Writings*, 214.

75. Pound, *Lustra* (1917), 109.

76. Gallup, *Ezra Pound*, 21. After the book was in type, the printer and publisher balked. Two hundred copies were printed after four poems (including "Pagani's, November 8") had been dropped, and a further nine poems were dropped from the second impression.

77. Pound and Cravens, *A Tragic Friendship*, 5–6.

78. Pound and Cravens, *A Tragic Friendship*, 136–37.

79. Pound and Cravens, *A Tragic Friendship*, 141. Pound originally submitted the elegy to *Poetry* with the poems that became "Contemporania." The poem then had the title "Madonna e desiata in sommo cielo" (Pound's recollection of a line from *La Vita Nuova*, "Madonna è disiata in sommo cielo"). After he marked the poem "XX" as unnecessary to the sequence (see note 55, this chapter), someone wrote "Withdrawn" on the verso. Pound published the poem as "His Vision of a Certain Lady Post Mortem," *Blast* 1 (June 20, 1914): 48. Under the title "Post Mortem Conspectu," it appeared in *Personae* (1926), 147. Apart from making minor changes in punctuation, Pound dropped the opening line in the manuscript, "They call you dead, but I saw you." University of Chicago Library, *Poetry: A Magazine of Verse* Records, 1895–1961, box 38, folder 29.

80. Writing "In a Station of the Metro" could have taken as long as nineteen months, from the incident in March or April 1911 to his submission of the poem as part of "Contemporania" in October 1912. When he says "six months later" and "a year later" in *Fortnightly Review* (September 1, 1914): 467, he could mean twelve or eighteen months. In *T.P.'s Weekly* (June 6, 1913): 707, "Then only the other night . . ." can't be literal, as he had dispatched the poem to *Poetry* in October the year before. He also says in *T.P.'s Weekly*, "For well over a year I have been trying." By then the poem had been finished for eight months. It's hard to know what to make of all this, unless Pound wrote the essay and either he or the publisher let it sit.

81. Homer, *Odyssey*, trans. Lattimore, book 11, lines 563–64.

82. Kafka, *Diaries of Franz Kafka, 1910–23*, 460.

83. Ezra Pound, *The Cantos of Ezra Pound* (New York: New Directions, 1970), 471, 472.

84. The most thorough history of the incident is contained in Jean Tricoire, *Un siècle de Métro en 14 lignes: De Bienveniie à Météor*, 3rd ed. (Paris: Éditions La Vie du Rail, 2004).

85. Pound, *Early Writings*, 213–14.

86. William Rose Benét, ed., *Fifty Poets: An American Auto-Anthology* (New York: Duffield and Green, 1933), 60.

87. Benét, ed., *Fifty Poets*, vii.

88. William Carlos Williams, *Spring and All* ([Paris]: Contact Publishing, [1923]), 74.

89. John Henry Barrow, ed., *The Mirror of Parliament for the Second Session of the Tenth Parliament . . . in the Second Year of the Reign of King William IV* (London, 1832), 4:3007; *Gentleman's Magazine: and Historical Chronicle* 67, pt. 1 (January 1797), 15; *Kimball's Dairy Farmer* 14 (March 1, 1916): 136; Gilbert, Late Lord Bishop of Sarum, *An Exposition of the Thirty-nine Articles of the Church of England*, 4th ed., corr. (London, 1720), 263; *Proceedings of the Friends' General Conference* (Asbury Park, N.J.: Pennypacker Press, 1902), 99; *American Farmer* 10 (April 25, 1828): 44; Thomas Gill, *The Technical Repository* (London, 1823), 4:307; Joseph Priestley, *Lectures on History*, ed. J. T. Rutt, new ed. (London, 1826), 340; *Report of the Superintendant of Public Instruction of the Commonwealth of Pennsylvania for the Year Ending June 2, 1884* (Harrisburg: Lane S. Hart, 1884), xv; *Lancet* 6 (February 12, 1825): 177; *Analectic Magazine* 5 (January 1815): 60.

90. *Report from the Select Committee on the Extinction of Slavery Throughout the British Dominions* (London, 1833), 364.

91. Hugh Kenner, *A Homemade World: The American Modernist Writers* (New York: Knopf, 1975), 58.

92. Charles Altieri, *Painterly Abstraction in Modernist American Poetry: The Contemporaneity of Modernism* (Cambridge: Cambridge University Press, 1989), 233.

93. Tacitus had no firsthand knowledge of Germany when he wrote *Germania*. He probably borrowed from Pliny the Elder's lost *Bella Germaniae*, but he could have learned some German in Rome by talking to traders or German mercenaries. The city was awash with languages.

94. [Jacob Abbott], *Rollo at Work*, 5th ed. (Philadelphia and Boston, 1841), 62; *Leslie's Monthly Magazine* 59 (April 1905): 685; *Scribner's Magazine* 5 (January 1889): 126.

95. *Garden* 66 (December 31, 1904), 438; [Susan Warner], *The Flag of Truce* (New York, 1878), 75; *Arthur's Illustrated Home Magazine* 43 (March 1875): 183; *Geyer's Stationer* 43 (July 11, 1907): 6.

96. *National Magazine* 27 (February 1908): 534; *New-Church Messenger* 114 (February 13, 1918): 131; *Saturday Evening Post* 192 (April 10, 1920): 19.

97. Emelyne Godfrey, "Victoriana" [review of Charlotte Eliza Humphry, *How to Be Pretty Though Plain*], *TLS* no. 5817 (September 26, 2014): 27.

98. *Sears, Roebuck and Co. Consumers Guide, No. 104* (Chicago: Sears, Roebuck, 1897), 164.

99. *Sears, Roebuck and Co. Consumers Guide, No. 104*, 164. The Handsome Lawn Wheelbarrow cost $2.10, the miners' barrow $5.82.

100. *Sears, Roebuck and Co., Catalogue, No. 124* (Chicago: Sears, Roebuck, 1912), 1039.

101. *Montgomery Ward and Co., Catalogue No. 97, Fall and Winter, 1922–23* (Chicago: Montgomery Ward, [1922]), 601. This was Montgomery Ward's Golden Jubilee year.

102. Charles Ludwig Uebele, *Paint Making and Color Grinding* (New York: Painters Magazine, 1913), 205, 222. For the difference between American and English vermilion, see *739 Paint Questions Answered* (London: Painters Magazine, 1904), 106–7.

103. A[rthur]. C[arlton]. Smith, *The Plymouth Rock Standard and Breed Book*, 2nd ed. (n.p.: American Poultry Association, 1921), 196–98.

104. Smith, *The Plymouth Rock Standard and Breed Book*, 196.

105. *The American Standard of Excellence* (n.p.: American Poultry Association, 1874), 19, 30, 32–34, 58, 63, 75. Between the meetings of 1883 and 1888, the title was changed to *The American Standard of Perfection*.

106. Smith, *Plymouth Rock Standard*, 199.

107. *The American Standard of Perfection* (n.p.: American Poultry Association, 1926), 122.

108. "No one breed or variety ever gains unchallenged supremacy." Smith, *Plymouth Rock Standard*, 199.

109. N. W. Chittenden, "A Life of the Author," in Isaac Newton, *Newton's Principia: The Mathematical Principles of Natural Philosophy*, trans. Andrew Motte, rev. and corrected (New York, 1848), 58.

110. Arturo Schwarz, *The Complete Works of Marcel Duchamp*, 2nd rev. ed. (New York: Harry N. Abrams, 1970), 468. The coat rack nailed to the floor of Duchamp's studio and a hat rack dangling from the ceiling (469) are from the same period. Neither survives.

111. J[ohn]. L. B[ishop]. and G[len]. W. B[axter]., "Chinese Poetry," in *Princeton Encyclopedia of Poetry and Poetics*, enlarged ed. (Princeton, N.J.: Princeton University Press, 1974), 118.

112. Eliot Weinberger, ed., *The New Directions Anthology of Classical Chinese Poetry* (New York: New Directions, 2003), xxv.

113. Calvin Tomkins, *Duchamp: A Biography* (New York: Henry Holt, 1996), 163; William Carlos Williams, *The Autobiography of William Carlos Williams* (New York:

Random House, 1951), 152–53; Herbert Leibowitz, *"Something Urgent I Have to Say to You": The Life and Works of William Carlos Williams* (New York: Farrar, Straus and Giroux, 2011), photograph of the meeting at Williams's home following p. 256. Though Williams never met Juan Gris, he had seen a reproduction of the painting: Paul Mariani, *William Carlos Williams: A New World Naked* (New York: McGraw-Hill, 1981), 313; Leibowitz, *"Something Urgent,"* 77–78, 195–97. Williams may have seen Duchamp's *Nude Descending* at Walter Arensberg's apartment after Arensberg bought the painting in 1919, but it's possible that the poet knew it earlier in reproduction.

114. Ben Jonson, "To the Immortal Memory and Friendship of That Noble Pair, Sir Lucius Cary and Sir H. Morison"; John Milton, "Sonnet XI ('A book was writ of late called *Tetrachordon*')"; Gerard Manley Hopkins, "No worst, there is none" and "Spelt from Sibyl's Leaves"; Lewis Carroll, "Turtle Soup"; Elizabeth Bishop, "Arrival at Santos"; Robert Lowell, "For Delmore Schwartz."

115. Williams, "XVII ['Our orchestra']," in *Spring and All*, 63.

116. Milton, *Paradise Lost*, book 1, lines 62–63.

117. Williams, *Autobiography*, 279; William Carlos Williams, *The Knife of the Times and Other Stories* (Ithaca, N.Y.: Dragon Press, 1932), 92; William Carlos Williams, *Make Light of It: Collected Stories* (New York: Random House, 1950), 59.

118. William Carlos Williams, *Collected Poems, 1921–1931* (New York: Objectivist Press, 1934), 95. Decades later, in *I Wanted to Write a Poem: The Autobiography of the Works of a Poet*, ed. Edith Heal (Boston: Beacon, 1958), 51, Williams refers to it as "The Red Wheel Barrow"; but as this book was produced from interview transcripts it cannot serve as evidence.

119. Barry Ahearn, *William Carlos Williams and Alterity: The Early Poetry* (Cambridge: Cambridge University Press, 1994), 145–46.

120. Lewis Carroll, *Alice's Adventures in Wonderland* (Boston, 1869), chap. 9, "The Mock Turtle's Story," 133.

121. William Carlos Williams, *The Collected Poems of William Carlos Williams*, vol. 1, *1909–1939*, ed. A. Walton Litz and Christopher MacGowan (New York: New Directions, 1986), 547. This is another instance of a remark transcribed from Williams's conversation. See note 118, this chapter.

122. Marion Strobel, "Tarnished Talent," *Poetry* (November 1923): 103–4.

123. Ahearn, *William Carlos Williams*, 4–5.

124. Hugh Kenner arranged it thus to make a different point (*A Homemade World*, 60).

125. Kenneth Lincoln, *Sing with the Heart of a Bear: Fusions of Native and American Poetry, 1890–1999* (Berkeley: University of California Press, 2000), 187.

126. Williams's reading of the poem at Columbia University on January 9, 1942, which takes nine seconds, may be found online.

127. Williams, *Autobiography*, 174.

128. Williams, *I Wanted to Write a Poem*, 36–37. For all the helter-skelter disruption of the chapter titles, the page numbers are in the usual order.

129. Williams, *Spring and All*, 39; *Collected Poems* (1986), 1:200.

130. Williams, *Spring and All*, 11–12, 64–67, 74; *Collected Poems* (1986), 1:183, 217–19, 224.

131. Williams, *Spring and All*, 76; *Collected Poems* (1986), 1:225.

132. Williams, *I Wanted to Write a Poem*, 37.

133. Williams, *Spring and All*, 78; *Collected Poems* (1986), 1:226.

134. Williams, *Spring and All*, 74; *Collected Poems* (1986), 1:223.

135. Williams, *Collected Poems, 1921–1931*, 50; *Collected Poems* (1986), 1:372.

136. Williams, *Collected Poems* (1986), 1:382, 453. See also "Nantucket" (1:372), "A Chinese Toy" (1:407), "Breakfast" (1:457).

137. Paul Engle and Joseph Langland, eds., *Poet's Choice* (New York: Dial Press, 1962), 4.

138. Zhaoming Qian, *Orientalism and Modernism: The Legacy of China in Pound and Williams* (Durham, N.C.: Duke University Press, 1995), is a thorough investigation of the influence of the Orient on the two poets and includes a descriptive list (179–80) of books Williams owned on Oriental literature, history, and philosophy. For Williams's opinion of *Cathay*, see Mariani, *Williams*, 122.

139. Williams, *Collected Poems* (1986), 1:158–60.

140. Mariani, *Williams*, 216.

141. R[alph]. W[aldo]. Emerson, *Essays*, 2nd ser. (Boston, 1844), 40–41.

142. Williams, *Autobiography*, 131; Mariani, *Williams*, 106–7.

143. Mariani, *Williams*, 273. See also Williams, *Collected Poems* (1986), 1:499–501, notes to "The Great Figure," the dedication of *Spring and All*, and "Poem II."

144. Williams, *Autobiography*, 134.

145. Floss Williams, the poet's wife, said years later, "Bill did not attend the first Armory Show, though he always insisted he did. He went to the second one" (Mariani, *Williams*, 785n100). Biographers have frequently taken Williams at his word. Mariani does make a case for Williams's memory (106); but the poet was certainly wrong about the Duchamp painting, which was not at the exhibition.

146. "Mutt comes from Mott Works, the name of a large sanitary equipment manufacturer. But Mott was too close, so I altered it to Mutt, after the daily strip cartoon 'Mutt and Jeff' which appeared at the time": Interview in Otto Hahn, "Passport No. G255300," *Art and Artists* 1 (July 1966): 10. The particular model, whether by Mott or some other dealer in sanitary ware, has not been identified, despite much scholarly investigation. See *Mott's Plumbing Fixtures, Catalogue "A"* (New York: J. L. Mott Iron

Works, 1908), 410 (description of imperial and colonial porcelain), 418. The Bedford-shire model, on the latter page, is the closest to that in the Stieglitz photograph.

147. Stieglitz's photo may be found in *Blind Man* no. 2 (May 1917): 4. For the mis-spellings, see Williams, *Kora in Hell*, 11–12.

148. It's not clear why Williams thought the urinal enameled (that is, porcelain-lined) cast-iron rather than glazed solid porcelain—Duchamp simply called it porce-lain. J. L. Mott, the ironworks from whose New York showroom he claimed to have bought the piece, sold both—but the model closest to the urinal Duchamp exhibited would have been all porcelain. To judge from the single existing photograph of *Foun-tain* (see notes 146 and 147, this chapter), it appears to be imperial porcelain, which was highly glazed.

149. Williams, *Autobiography*, 136, 138.

150. William Carlos Williams, "America, Whitman, and the Art of Poetry," *Poetry Journal* 8 (November 1917): 34.

151. *Blind Man* no. 2 (May 1917): 5.

152. William Carlos Williams, *Paterson*, ed. Christopher MacGowan, rev. ed. (New York: New Directions, 1992), 9.

153. *Hamlet*, 1.2.129: "solid" in the Folio was "sallied," possibly a variant of "sul-lied," in the quartos. *Henry V*, 2.3.16–17: "a' babbl'd," Lewis Theobald's ingenious emendation of "and a Table," has mostly been accepted. *Winter's Tale* 3.3 opens after a ship has landed on the coast of Bohemia, a landlocked country. Jonson made fun of this lapse, though Shakespeare probably took the notion from his source, Robert Greene's *Pandosto*. See *Ben Jonson's Conversations with William Drummond of Hawthorn-den*, ed. R. F. Patterson (London: Blackie and Son, 1923), 20 ("Sheakspear, in a play, brought in a number of men saying they had suffered Shipwrack in Bohemia, wher ther is no sea neer by some 100 miles"). Some have argued that at various times Bohe-mia did have a small seacoast on the Adriatic.

154. Williams, *Collected Poems* (1986), 1:500.

155. John Hollander, *Vision and Resonance: Two Senses of Poetic Form* (New York: Oxford University Press, 1975), 111.

156. William Carlos Williams, "Seventy Years Deep," *Holiday Magazine* 16 (Novem-ber 1954): 78.

157. *United States Census, 1920*, Rutherford, Bergen County, N.J.: district 106, sheet 15a, line 35.

158. *United States Census, 1930*, Passaic City, Passaic County, N.J.: district 16–157, sheet 3b, line 53.

159. *Insurance Maps of Rutherford and East Rutherford, Bergen County, New Jersey* (New York: Sanborn Map Company, 1917), sheet 40. The map marks Marshall's house

"13/11," as if it were a duplex. Two house numbers may have been assigned because the house was occupied by two families, possibly with separate entrances, though the 1920 census taker marked both families as living at no. 11. A copy of this map is available online from Princeton University Library. (The use of "duplex house" goes back at least to 1906; the *OED* entry is inaccurate.)

160. *United States Census, 1880*, Atlantic City, Atlantic County, N.J.: district 1, p. 12, line 49; *United States Census, 1900*, Rutherford, Bergen Country, N.J.: district 38, sheet 18b, line 63.

161. *Insurance Maps of Rutherford* (1917), sheet 40.

162. *Insurance Maps of Rutherford and East Rutherford, Bergen County, New Jersey* (New York: Sanborn Map Company, 1909), sheet 14. Curiously, the 1909 Sanborn map has the house as "13." In the southern corner of the property stands a large structure marked "13½." The Sanborn key identifies this building as a stable, so perhaps Marshall kept a horse or horses. No coop is in evidence. The one problem with using Sanborn maps for historical research is that they were updated by pasting new bits of map over the old. The relevant Rutherford maps for 1909 and 1917, now at Princeton, do not seem to possess any of these revisions; but physical inspection would be necessary to be certain.

163. Williams, *Collected Poems* (1986), 1:132. Williams also refers to Thaddeus Marshall and his son Milton in his essay "Advent of the Slaves" (William Carlos Williams, *In the American Grain* [New York: Albert and Charles Boni, 1925], 210–11), where he provides some details about the elder Marshall's days as a fisherman. The poet was very friendly with these men; but, though he talked in the essay about the "colored men and women whom I have known intimately" (210), he used nearby the racist slur (209, 210) to which he was apparently deaf.

164. *United States Census, 1910*, Rutherford, Bergen Country, N.J.: district 50, sheet 14b, line 91. The census taker wrote "huskster" (*sic*) under "trade or profession," and "street" under "general nature of industry, business, or establishment." The occupation code is 3-6-3, the 1910 Census code for "huckster." See *Thirteenth Census of the United States, Index to Occupations*, rev. ed. (Washington, D.C.: Bureau of the Census, [1910]), 117.

165. "Roy Zelner takes a small wheelbarrow to gather his eggs," *Michigan Poultry Breeder* 20 (February 1905): [9]; "He . . . was living on what he could scrape out of ash barrels, and an occasional dime for kindling-wood which he sold from a wheelbarrow," Jacob A. Riis, *A Ten Years' War: An Account of the Battle with the Slum in New York* (Boston: Houghton, Mifflin, 1900), 166; "You know something about the peculiarities of the Wheelbarrow salesman if you are experienced in the style of acrobatic stunts necessary to the navigation of that unwieldy contrivance from which he derives his

cognomen," Walter Dwight Moody, *Men Who Sell Things* (Chicago: A. C. McGlurg, 1912), 95.

166. *Proceedings of the Board of Public Works, Elizabeth, N.J., 1920* (Elizabeth, N.J., 1920), 36. See also 106–7, 122–23.

167. *Proceedings of the Board of Public Works, Elizabeth, N.J., 1920*, 36.

168. Rutherford, N.J., ordinance 260, enacted July 20, 1897. Information provided by Rod Leith, Rutherford Borough Historian.

169. Williams, *I Wanted to Write a Poem*, vii.

170. Gary Bachlund, "The Red Wheelbarrow," 2008. The score may be found online: http://www.bachlund.org/The_Red_Wheelbarrow.htm.

171. "XI ['In passing with my mind']," in *Spring and All*, 48; *Collected Poems* (1986), 1:206.

172. Reed Whittemore, *William Carlos Williams, Poet from Jersey* (Boston: Houghton Mifflin, 1975), 102–5.

173. "XV ['The decay of cathedrals']," in *Spring and All*, 60; *Collected Poems* (1986), 1:214.

174. *Historical Statistics of the United States, Millennial Edition*, ed. Susan B. Carter et al. (Cambridge: Cambridge University Press, 2006), II, table Ba 814–830: The labor force, by industry: 1800–1960, 2–110; IV, table Da 14–27: Farms—number, population, land, and value of property: 1850–1997, 4–43.

175. "England," in *The Complete Poems of Marianne Moore* (New York: Macmillan/Viking, 1967), 46.

176. Benét, ed., *Fifty Poets*, vii.

177. Benét, ed., *Fifty Poets*, 92.

178. Benét, ed., *Fifty Poets*, ix–x.

179. Williams, *Collected Poems* (1986), 1:372. Williams's wife wrote a reply, published posthumously in *Atlantic Monthly* 250 (November 1982): 145. See *Collected Poems* (1986), 1:536.

8. Dickinson's Nerves, Frost's Woods

1. Emily Dickinson, *The Poems of Emily Dickinson: Variorum Edition*, ed. R. W. Franklin (Cambridge, Mass.: Harvard University Press, 1998), 1:396 (#372).

2. Shakespeare, *The Winter's Tale*, 3.1.5–7.

3. Mark Twain, *Adventures of Huckleberry Finn (Tom Sawyer's Comrade)* (New York: Charles L. Webster, 1885), 230.

4. Anonymous review of W. L. Stone, *Matthias and His Impostures* (New York, 1835), *North American Review* 41 (October 1835): 310.

5. Thomas H. Johnson, ed., *The Letters of Emily Dickinson* (Cambridge, Mass.: Harvard University Press, 1960), 2:319. Hereafter, Dickinson, *Letters* (1960).

6. Jay Leyda, *The Years and Hours of Emily Dickinson* (New Haven, Conn.: Yale University Press, 1960), II, 475.

7. Dickinson, *Poems of Emily Dickinson* (1998), 2:658 (#684).

8. Dickinson, *Poems of Emily Dickinson* (1998), 1:159 (#124A).

9. There's a mild bit of absurdist wordplay here, perhaps explained as a reaction to an event so depressing that the seeming is all but being—that is, the nerves sit like tombs inside the house, as if the house were itself a cemetery for lost hopes. Had the death been real, the tomb would be yet unvisited or only recently visited, since following interment the mourners would gather at the house for refreshment. The solemnity of "sitting ceremonious," however, suggests that this is the mourning that precedes burial. The critic William R. Sherwood, *Circumference and Circumstance: Stages in the Mind and Art of Emily Dickinson* (New York: Columbia University Press, 1968), 112, compares the scene to the "mourner's bench" on which repentant sinners slumped at the front of a revival meeting, their tears the evidence they were mourning their sins. Dickinson refused to attend revivals, but she might have heard of such furniture from members of her family. Alas, the idea is irrelevant.

10. Dickinson, *Letters* (1960), 2:583.

11. John Russell Bartlett, *Dictionary of Americanisms*, 2nd ed. (Boston, 1859), s.v. "Stiff."

12. Shakespeare, *Venus and Adonis*, line 1073.

13. A member of the Shakespeare Club later recalled that, when one of the men suggested inking out suggestive passages, the women replied, "'We shall read everything.' I remember the lofty air with which Emily took her departure saying 'There's nothing wicked in Shakespeare and if there is I don't want to know it'": Leyda, *Years and Hours*, 2:478. This may have meant that Dickinson didn't want to be told what she could decide for herself, or that she didn't want to hear that certain passages were considered obscene. A generation before, Dr. Thomas Bowdler and his sister had dirtied their thumbs on the text. In their *The Family Shakspeare* (London, 1807), 4 vols., reprinted in many editions through the following decades, "those words and expressions are omitted which cannot with propriety be read aloud in a family." Miss Bowdler's contributions went uncredited at the time.

14. *Understanding Poetry: An Anthology for College Students*, ed. Cleanth Brooks and Robert Penn Warren (New York: Henry Holt, 1939), 470.

15. Emily Dickinson, *The Poems of Emily Dickinson: Including Variant Readings Critically Compared with All Known Manuscripts*, ed. Thomas Johnson (Cambridge, Mass.: Harvard University Press, 1955), 1:272; Emily Dickinson, *The Complete Poems of Emily Dickinson*, ed. Thomas H. Johnson (Boston: Little, Brown, 1960), 162.

16. William Empson, *Seven Types of Ambiguity*, 3rd ed., rev. (London: Chatto and Windus, 1953), 81.

17. Richard B. Sewall, *The Life of Emily Dickinson* (New York: Farrar, Straus and Giroux, 1974), 2:357–61; Alfred Habegger, *My Wars Are Laid Away in Books: The Life of Emily Dickinson* (New York: Random House, 2001), 193–95, 199–203, 212.

18. Habegger, *My Wars*, 80, 242.

19. Dickinson, *Letters* (1960), 1:94.

20. Habegger, *My Wars*, 336.

21. Dickinson, *Letters* (1960), 1:67.

22. Habegger, *My Wars*, 398.

23. [Thomas Wentworth Higginson], "Letter to a Young Contributor," *Atlantic Monthly* 9 (April 1862): 401–11.

24. Dickinson, *Letters* (1960), 2:403.

25. Thomas Wentworth Higginson, "Emily Dickinson's Letters," *Atlantic Monthly* 68 (October 1891): 444.

26. Higginson, "Emily Dickinson's Letters," 444.

27. Higginson, "Emily Dickinson's Letters," 445.

28. Dickinson, *Letters* (1960), 2:404.

29. Dickinson, *Poems of Emily Dickinson* (1998), 3:1533 (Appendix 2. Distribution by Year).

30. Dickinson, *Letters* (1960), 2:404.

31. Higginson, "Emily Dickinson's Letters," 445.

32. Polly Longsworth, *The World of Emily Dickinson* (New York: Norton, 1990), 21.

33. Sewall, *Life*, 2:536–37, 632.

34. Dickinson, *Letters* (1960), 2:404.

35. Dickinson, *Letters* (1960), 2:404.

36. Dickinson, *Letters* (1960), 2:405.

37. Sewall, *Life*, 2:415.

38. Sewall, *Life*, 2:420.

39. Sewall, *Life*, 2:419. The phrase "run frolic through the veins" was an allusion to a line from *The Mountaineers*, a long-forgotten play by George Colman the Younger that debuted in 1793. The original line read, "When the high blood ran frolic through thy veins," and in various versions through the next century it became a catchphrase. See Mrs. [Elizabeth] Inchbald, ed., *The British Theatre; or, A Collection of Plays* (London, 1808), 21:39.

40. Habegger, *My Wars*, 235.

41. Sewall, *Life*, 2:419, 421–22.

42. Sewall, *Life*, 2:400–4, 410–15, 418–19.

43. Dickinson, *Letters* (1960), 1:282.

44. Dickinson, *Letters* (1960), 2:408.

45. Sewall, *Life*, 2:445. Dickinson was visiting the Colemans. Reverend Lyman Coleman had been her German teacher at Amherst Academy. His wife, Maria, was a cousin of Mrs. Dickinson; and Emily, their surviving daughter, one of Dickinson's best friends.

46. Sewall, *Life*, 2:447–48. See also Cynthia Griffin Wolff, *Emily Dickinson* (New York: Knopf, 1986), 389, where the letter is quoted in full.

47. Habegger, *My Wars*, 443, 572–73, 636, 731n572; Sewall, *Life*, 2:452–53, 593 and n.

48. Richard Sewall, "In Search of Emily Dickinson," *Michigan Quarterly Review* 23 (Fall 1984): 524–25.

49. Sewall, *Life*, 2:449–50. There are photos of Wadsworth, young and old, opposite pp. 450 and 451.

50. Brenda Wineapple, *White Heat: The Friendship of Emily Dickinson and Thomas Wentworth Higginson* (New York: Knopf, 2008), 71.

51. Sewall, *Life*, 2:448–50, 452–54, 459–62.

52. Sewall, *Life*, 2:452n10, 729–36; Leyda, *Years and Hours*, 2:7–8, 327.

53. Dickinson, *Letters* (1960), 3:727, 737, 744, 745.

54. Martha Dickinson Bianchi, *The Life and Letters of Emily Dickinson* (Boston: Houghton Mifflin, 1924), 46–47. See also Leyda, *Years and Hours*, 2:34.

55. Bianchi, *Life and Letters*, 47; Wineapple, *White Heat*, 334n71 ["the affliction . . ."]. Bianchi melodramatically reported that the poet urged a friend "to name a new little son by the name never like any other to her ears," and later wrote to the mother, "Love for the child of the bravest name alive." The letter was to Mrs. Bowles—and Dickinson asked that she name the boy not Charles but Robert, after Robert Browning: "Will you call him Robert—for me. He is the bravest man—alive—but *his* Boy—has no mama." Dickinson, *Letters* [1960], 2:385. This was shortly after the death of Elizabeth Barrett Browning. Bianchi's notion that Dickinson always called the boy Charles, "whether the family adopted the suggestion or not" is certainly true, but only because the Bowleses named him Charles. Dickinson, *Letters* [1960], 2:383n.

56. Dickinson, *Letters* (1960), 3:901.

57. Sewall, *Life*, 2:449–50; Habegger, *My Wars*, 330. Sherwood, *Circumference*, 81, argues the case for Dickinson having known beforehand.

58. Thomas H. Johnson, editor of Dickinson's letters, suggests the friendship commenced in 1858. Dickinson, *Letters* [1960], 2:335n. Sewall says the beginning of Bowles's regular visits is "difficult to determine" but probably dated to Austin's marriage in 1856 or possibly as late as 1858. Sue later claimed that Bowles had been their first visitor. Sewall, *Life*, 2:468.

59. *Poems of Emily Dickinson* (1998), 3:1531–32 (Appendix 1. Poems Published in Emily Dickinson's Lifetime).

60. Sewall, *Life*, 2:472; Habegger, *My Wars*, 378, 381; Leyda, *Years and Hours*, 1:xxxiii.

61. Habegger, *My Wars*, 378, 578–79; Judith Farr, *The Passions of Emily Dickinson* (Cambridge, Mass.: Harvard University Press, 1992), 206–9.

62. Dickinson, *Letters* (1960), 2:358.

63. Sewall, *Life*, 2:470, 472, 479, 481–83; Habegger, *My Wars*, 426, 444.

64. Sewall, *Life*, 2:483; Dickinson, *Letters* (1960), 2:402–3. Bowles visited Amherst on April 5, four days before he sailed.

65. Farr, *The Passions*, 216, says Bowles had decided the previous September to go abroad.

66. Dickinson, *Letters* (1960), 2:419–20; Habegger, *My Wars*, 446–48, 720n448 (noting letters misdated in Johnson's edition).

67. Sewall, *Life*, 2:472. The warm feelings for Bowles did not end. Some years after his death, Sue bought George Merriam's two-volume *Life and Times of Samuel Bowles* (New York, 1885). The books were inscribed "Austin from Sue / Xmas—1885." They are now in the Periodicals and Books from the Evergreens Collection, Brown University Library.

68. Sewall, *Life*, 2:510; Dickinson, *Letters* (1960), 2:589–90 and n.

69. Sewall, *Life*, 2:473.

70. See note 55, this chapter.

71. Dickinson, *Letters* (1960), 2:404; Jack L. Capps, *Emily Dickinson's Reading, 1836–1886* (Cambridge, Mass.: Harvard University Press, 1966), 86–91. Martha Bianchi recalled the portrait of Mrs. Browning. For Dickinson's taste for drivel, see Capps, *Emily Dickinson's Reading*, 121–22, 125, 135–37.

72. Habegger, *My Wars*, 603–4, 736n604 ["would burn"].

73. "'Swiveller' may be sure of the 'Marchioness'": Dickinson, *Letters* (1960), 2:382.

74. Johnson, in the standard edition of the letters, dates them "about 1858," "about 1861," and "early 1862?" Dickinson, *Letters* (1960), 2:333, 373, 391. "Accurate dating," Johnson admits, "is impossible" (392n). Leyda (*Years and Hours*, 1:352; 2:22, 24) dates them "early spring," 1858; "January?," 1861; "February?," 1861. Emily Dickinson, *The Master Letters of Emily Dickinson*, ed. R. W. Franklin (Amherst: Amherst College Press, 1986), 11, 21, 31, dates them "spring 1858," "early 1861," "summer 1861" but has reversed the previous order of letters 2 and 3. Franklin's introduction lays out the evidence clearly (7–9). For his considerations in dating Dickinson's work, see *Poems of Emily Dickinson* (1998), 1:37–40.

75. Adapted from Dickinson, *Master Letters of Emily Dickinson*, 22. Angle brackets show second thoughts without deleting the original. Franklin's transcription is in error here—there is an apostrophe, not a dash, after "Oh," and a deliberate space between "can" and "not."

76. Dickinson, *Poems of Emily Dickinson* (1998), 1:218 (#184). Habegger, *My Wars*, 380, believes the poem most likely written for Mary Bowles, not her husband. The childlike usage of "its" may have been a commonplace between sweethearts. General Custer, having apologized to his wife for his peremptory manner, wrote her, "It didn't want to be a soldier[,] did it?" Lawrence Frost, *General Custer's Libbie* (Seattle: Superior Publishing, 1976), 122. This was also the practice of Isabella Bird in the 1870s and 1880s, when writing to her sister. See Isabella Bird, *Letters to Henrietta*, ed. Kay Chubbuck (London: John Murray, 2002), 33 and n.

77. Dickinson, *Poems of Emily Dickinson* (1998), 1:454–55 (#431).

78. Adapted from Dickinson, *Master Letters of Emily Dickinson*, 40.

79. For Wadsworth photos, see Sewall, *Life*, opposite 2:450, 451; Habegger, *My Wars*, following 366; Wolff, *Emily Dickinson*, following 370. For Bowles, see Sewall, *Life*, opp. 474.

80. Adapted from Dickinson, *Master Letters of Emily Dickinson*, 36.

81. Lord Byron, *The Works of Lord Byron* (London, 1823), 4:172.

82. Dickinson, *Letters* (1960), 2:393.

83. Dickinson, *Letters* (1960), 2:433.

84. Dickinson, *Letters* (1960), 2:393; Sewall, *Life*, 2:488.

85. Dickinson, *Poems of Emily Dickinson* (1998), 1:218 (#184).

86. Jonathon Green, ed., *Green's Dictionary of Slang* (London: Chambers, 2010), vol. 3, s.v. "Pluck," v.1: "to have sexual intercourse." Not in *OED* in this sense.

87. Dickinson, *Master Letters of Emily Dickinson*, 43; Dickinson, *Letters* (1960), 2:383n (Bowles accompanied his pregnant wife to New York in early December 1861).

88. Dickinson, *Poems of Emily Dickinson* (1998), 1:228 (#194A). Despite the Christian trappings, it's hard not to read this as a very earthly betrothal, one without a ring as an outward sign—a betrothal, perhaps, to someone already betrothed.

89. Dickinson, *Master Letters of Emily Dickinson*, 22.

90. Sewall, *Life*, 1:170–85; Polly Longsworth, *Austin and Mabel: The Amherst Affair and Love Letters of Austin Dickinson and Mabel Loomis Todd* (New York: Farrar, Straus and Giroux, 1984).

91. In her 1894 edition of Dickinson's letters, Mabel Loomis Todd printed only a few sentences from the first Master Letter, with, according to R. W. Franklin, the "deliberately misleading" date of 1885: Todd, ed., *Letters of Emily Dickinson* (Boston, 1894), 2:422–23; Dickinson, *Master Letters of Emily Dickinson*, 6.

92. Martha Dickinson Bianchi and Alfred Leete Hampson, eds., *Further Poems of Emily Dickinson, Withheld from Publication by Her Sister Lavinia* (Boston: Little, Brown, 1929). According to Bianchi's introduction, these were poems Lavinia "saw fit never to publish" (v).

93. Dickinson, *Poems of Emily Dickinson* (1998), 1:218–19 (#185A).

94. Richard B. Sewall, *The Lyman Letters: New Light on Emily Dickinson and Her Family* (Amherst: University of Massachusetts Press, 1965), 76; Habegger, *My Wars*, 483–84.

95. Dickinson, *Letters* (1960), 2:404.

96. Dickinson, *Poems of Emily Dickinson* (1998), 1:497 (#484).

97. Alfred, Lord Tennyson, *In Memoriam A. H. H.*, LIV, 5, 1–2. Dickinson once wrote her sister-in-law, "Dreamed of your meeting Tennyson in Ticknor and Fields": Dickinson, *Letters* (1960), 2:455.

98. Vicesimus Knox, *Essays Moral and Literary* (Basil, 1800), 1:354.

99. Charles Dickens, *Bleak House* (London, 1853), 301; Charles Dickens, *Dombey and Son* (London, 1848), 49.

100. Hubert Howe Bancroft, *The Works of Hubert Howe Bancroft*, vol. 35, *California Inter Pocula* (San Francisco: History Company, 1888), 260; Madeline Vaughan Abbott, "Bryn Mawr College," *Godey's Magazine* 130 (May 1895): 491; Emmons Clark, *History of the Second Company of the Seventh Regiment (National Guard) N. Y. S. Militia* (New York, 1864), 1:251.

101. Dickinson, *Poems of Emily Dickinson* (1998), 2:853 (#926).

102. Dickinson, *The Poems . . . Including Variant Readings* (1955), 1:273.

103. Dickinson, *Further Poems*, 175; Emily Dickinson, *The Poems of Emily Dickinson*, ed. Martha Dickinson Bianchi and Alfred Leete Hampson (Boston: Little, Brown, 1937), 365. In later reprints, the book's title was changed to *Poems by Emily Dickinson*.

104. Dickinson, *The Poems . . . Including Variant Readings* (1955), 1:272–73.

105. Dickinson, *The Complete Poems* (1960), 162. Among the many volumes using the corrupt stanza: James Dickey, *Classes on Modern Poets and the Art of Poetry*, ed. Donald J. Greiner (Columbia: University of South Carolina Press, 2004), 14; Annie Finch, *The Ghost of Meter: Culture and Prosody in American Free Verse* (Ann Arbor: University of Michigan Press, 1993), 29; Harvey Gross, *Sound and Form in Modern Poetry* (Ann Arbor: University of Michigan Press, 1964), 15; David Lehman, ed., *The Oxford Book of American Poetry* (Oxford: Oxford University Press, 2006), 168; and Judy Jo Small, *Positive as Sound: Emily Dickinson's Rhyme* (Athens: University of Georgia Press, 1990), 106.

106. "Here was already manifest that defiance of form, never through carelessness, and never precisely from whim, which so marked her": Higginson, "Emily Dickinson's Letters," 446.

107. Dickinson, *Letters* (1960), 2:451 and n.; Dickinson, *Poems of Emily Dickinson* (1998), 1:27.

108. I have not found a previous example where critics recast the lines thus. A slightly different reordering, in an obscure textbook by Jerome Beaty and William H. Matchett, *Poetry: From Statement to Meaning* (New York: Oxford University Press, 1965), 28, merely reprints the quatrain in the Bianchi and Hampson edition of *The Poems of Emily Dickinson* (1937). The lines are not arranged to reveal the initial pair of rhymes.

109. Dickinson, *Poems of Emily Dickinson* (1998), 1:276 (#257), 2:805 (#857).

110. Nicholas Wood, *A Practical Treatise on Rail-Roads, and Interior Communication in General*, 2nd ed. (London, 1832), 49, 79.

111. Francis Manley, "An Explication of Dickinson's 'After Great Pain,'" *Modern Language Notes* 73 (April 1958): 263; Kamilla Denham, "Emily Dickinson's Volcanic Punctuation," *Emily Dickinson Journal* 2 (Spring 1993): 28.

112. Helen Vendler, *Dickinson: Selected Poems and Commentaries* (Cambridge, Mass.: Harvard University Press, 2010), 170–71.

113. Dickinson, *Poems of Emily Dickinson* (1998), 3:1547–57 (Appendix 7. Recipients). Those who received more than a dozen poems were Samuel Bowles (40), Thomas Wentworth Higginson (103), Elizabeth Holland (31), Louise and Frances Norcross (71), Mabel Todd (13), Sarah Tuckerman (16), and, far the most important, Sue Dickinson, who received over 250 poems.

114. Dickinson, *Poems of Emily Dickinson* (1998), 1:338–41 (#321A,B,C).

115. Sewall, *Life*, 2:337–39, 342–49. For somewhat sarcastic praise of the intellectual and conversational gifts of young Yankee women, see George Augustus Sala, *My Diary in America in the Midst of War* (London, 1865), 2:296–97, 299–300. Sala believed their talents had been fostered in female seminaries.

116. Sewall, *Life*, 2:346. The Dickinson copy of Hitchcock's *Elementary Geology*, 3rd ed., rev. (New York, 1842), is held in the Houghton Library of Harvard University, shelfmark EDR 499. According to the library, when sold the books were "physically located at the Evergreens," Austin's home, but many had "originally been shelved at the Homestead," Emily's home. *Elementary Geology* bears no ownership signature.

117. Dickinson, *Letters* (1960), 1:62.

118. Dickinson, *Poems of Emily Dickinson* (1998), 2:702 (#740).

119. [Josiah Conder], *A Popular Description, Geographical, Historical and Topographical, of Brazil and Buenos Ayres* (Boston, 1830), 1:258; John Hawkshaw, *Reminiscences of South America: From Two and a Half Years' Residence in Venezuela* (London, 1838), 174. For Hitchcock's use of the term, see *Elementary Geology*, 3rd ed., rev., 41, 58, 64, 65 [main entry], etc.

120. Hitchcock, *Elementary Geology*, 3rd ed., rev., 45.

121. Dickinson, *Poems of Emily Dickinson* (1998), 1:388 (#363), "about autumn 1862."

122. Dickinson, *Poems of Emily Dickinson* (1998), 1:263 (#240A); 2:724 (#767), 779–80 (#824).

123. "One thinkes himself a giant, another a dwarfe; one is heavie as lead, another is as light as a feather." Richard Burton [Democritus Junior, pseud.], *The Anatomy of Melancholy* (Oxford, 1638), 193.

124. Shakespeare, *Henry IV, Part II*, 1.1.118; *Love's Labour's Lost*, 3.1.59.

125. Dickinson, *Poems of Emily Dickinson* (1998), 2:722 (#764).

126. Dickinson, *Poems of Emily Dickinson* (1998), 1:365 (#340).

127. For the basic work on Shakespeare's image clusters, see Caroline F. E. Spurgeon, *Shakespeare's Imagery* (New York: Macmillan, 1936); and Edward A. Armstrong, *Shakespeare's Imagination* (London: Lindsay Drummond, 1946). Their work was anticipated by Walter Whiter in *A Specimen of a Commentary on Shakspeare* (London, 1794).

128. William Drummond, *The Poetical Works of William Drummond of Hawthornden*, ed. William B. Turnbull (London, 1856), 328.

129. Dickinson, *Poems of Emily Dickinson* (1998), 1:476–77 (#456).

130. Dickinson, *Letters* (1960), 2:398 ("late March 1862").

131. Thomas S. Myrick, *The Gold Rush* (Cumming Press, 1971), 9.

132. "Miss. [shuddering] Lord! there's somebody walking over my grave": Jonathan Swift, *Polite Conversation* (London, 1783), 68.

133. Dickinson, *Letters* (1960), 2:649.

134. Nathaniel Hawthorne, *Twice-Told Tales*, new ed. (Boston, 1865), 1:47. The Dickinsons owned three of Hawthorne's novels in early editions and the complete works in an 1881 edition, the latter containing *Twice-Told Tales*. All the volumes are now at Harvard (shelfmarks EDR 374–77). There may of course have been volumes that have not survived.

135. Dickinson, *Poems of Emily Dickinson* (1998), 1:454 (#430B).

136. Wolff, *Emily Dickinson*, 230–31. The emblem is drawn from William Holmes and John W. Barber, *Religious Allegories: Being a Series of Emblematic Engravings* (Cincinnati, 1851), 10–11.

137. Dickinson, *Poems of Emily Dickinson* (1998), 1:366 (#340).

138. Sewall, *Life*, 2:481; Habegger, *My Wars*, 426 and n. ["His crisis"].

139. "The Christmas Letter," *Godey's Lady's Book* 53 (December 1856): 533.

140. Elisha Kent Kane, *The United States Grinnell Expedition in Search of Sir John Franklin: A Personal Narrative* (New York, 1854), 262.

141. [Mary Shelley], *Frankenstein* (1818); [Anonymous, poss. John Cleve Symmes], *Symzonia, a Voyage of Discovery* (London, 1820); [Edgar Allan Poe], *The Narrative of Arthur Gordon Pym, of Nantucket* (New York, 1838).

142. Samuel Taylor Coleridge, *The Rime of the Ancient Mariner*, in *The Poetical Works of S. T. Coleridge* (London, 1834), 2:3 (lines 59–60), 9 (line 193), 13 (line 295), 14 (lines 305–8). The poem first appeared in Coleridge's collaboration with Wordsworth, *Lyrical Ballads* (London, 1798), and was revised for the various editions of that volume, for Coleridge's own *Sibylline Leaves* (London, 1817), and for editions of his collected poems, ending in 1834.

143. James Fenimore Cooper, *The Sea Lions; or, the Lost Sealers*, new ed. (New York, 1852), 2:151–52.

144. Elisha Kent Kane, *Arctic Explorations: The Second Grinnell Expedition in Search of Sir John Franklin, 1853, '54, '55* (Philadelphia, 1856), 1:194.

145. Kane, *Arctic Explorations*, 1:194–95.

146. The two-volume edition is now at Harvard (shelfmark EDR 451). Martha Dickinson Bianchi, in an unpublished biography of the poet, reports that *Arctic Explorations* was Mr. Dickinson's "prime favorite" volume of travels. See Barton Levi St. Armand, *Emily Dickinson and Her Culture* (Cambridge: Cambridge University Press, 1984), 338n18. Edward Dickinson also owned a copy of William Elder's *Biography of Elisha Kent Kane* (Philadelphia, 1858), now in the Periodicals and Books from the Evergreens Collection, Brown University Library.

147. Michael F. Robinson, *The Coldest Crucible: Arctic Exploration and American Culture* (Chicago: University of Chicago Press, 2006), 54. It had sold 60,000 copies by 1859: Nicolas Trübner, ed., *Trübner's Bibliographical Guide to American Literature* (London, 1859), lxxxviii–lxxxix.

148. Charles Francis Hall, *Arctic Researches and Life Among the Esquimaux* (New York, 1865), 234. Instances where the "Feet, mechanical, go round" are common in anecdotes of those lost on ice, in desert, in woods. "With what uniformity a lost man travels in circles . . . was exemplified in two gentlemen of the Hudson's Bay Company but a short time ago. . . . They strolled into the woods, and after a time commenced their return. . . . They continued on until, reaching a fallen tree rather more remarkable than the rest, one of the two expressed an opinion that he had passed it but a few moments before. . . . A third time they reached the tree, yet not thoroughly convinced of the fact; so they engraved a mark, and a few moments more actually brought them to the very same spot again": Richard King, *Narrative of a Journey to the Shores of the Arctic Ocean in 1833* (London, 1836), 2:194–95. Beneath the circuits of such lost travelers lies stark terror.

149. Dickinson, *Poems of Emily Dickinson* (1998), 2:874 (#957).

150. Dickinson, *Poems of Emily Dickinson* (1998), 1:221–22 (#187B).

151. Dickinson, *Letters* (1960), 2:394–95 and n. Johnson dated the poem 1863 in his variorum edition (1955) but later assigned the poem and letter to early 1862, without much assurance. Franklin (*Poems of Emily Dickinson* [1998], I, 221n) redated the poem and letter to 1861. See also "In the Northern Zones— / Icicles—crawl from polar Caverns" ("Safe in their Alabaster chambers," 1:162 [#124E]); "Some Polar Expiation—An Omen in the Bone" ("I tried to think a lonelier Thing," 2:567 [#570]); "Then— Diamonds—which the Snow // From Polar Caskets—fetched me" ("The Angle of a Landscape," 2:578 [#578]). This complex of polar ice and death is scattered in poems through this period.

152. Robert Herrick, "To Elektra," lines 1–2.

153. The house is pictured in Habegger, *My Wars*, 121. Emily and her family lived there from 1840 to 1855.

154. Robert Frost, *Collected Poems, Prose, and Plays*, ed. Richard Poirier and Mark Richardson (New York: Library of America, 1995), 143.

155. Letter to Thomas Poole, January 28, 1810, *Collected Letters of Samuel Taylor Coleridge*, vol. 3, *1807–1814*, ed. Earl Leslie Griggs (Oxford: Clarendon, 1959), 282.

156. Dickinson, *Poems of Emily Dickinson* (1998), 1:367 (#341), 464 (#441); 2:736 (#782).

157. "The death did not appear painful; the vital powers, and with them the sensibility, being extinguished by degrees." Stephen H. Ward, *The Science of Health* (London, n.d. [1853?]), 72. Ward is translating from Du Baron D. J. Larrey, *Mémoires de chirurgie militaire et campagnes* (Paris, 1817), 4:127–28, in which he recalls the deaths by freezing of Napoleon's diminished army as it returned from Moscow.

158. John Keats, "Ode to a Nightingale," in *The Poems of John Keats*, ed. Miriam Allott (London: Longman, 1970), 525.

159. Frost, *Collected Poems* (1995), 207.

160. Lawrance Thompson, *Robert Frost: The Early Years, 1874–1915* (New York: Holt, Rinehart and Winston, 1966), 145–46, 246–48, 250–53.

161. Thompson, *Early Years*, 257–61, 263.

162. Thompson, *Early Years*, 62, 85–86, 95–96, 135.

163. Thompson, *Early Years*, 150–51, 153–55.

164. Thompson, *Early Years*, 263–64, 547n12.

165. Thompson, *Early Years*, 261–62, 284; Jay Parini, *Robert Frost: A Life* (New York: Henry Holt, 1999), 71. Maps of the vicinity and of the Derry farm may be found on the front and rear endpapers of Lesley Frost, *New Hampshire's Child: The Derry Journals of Lesley Frost*, ed. Lawrance Thompson and Arnold Grade (Albany: State University of New York Press, 1969).

166. Thompson, *Early Years*, 49–50, 261, 275–76; Louis Mertins, *Robert Frost: Life and Talks—Walking* (Norman: University of Oklahoma Press, 1965), 64–65.

167. Thompson, *Early Years*, 277–78, 280; Mertins, *Robert Frost*, 78.

168. Thompson, *Early Years*, 276, 282, 285, 314–15.

169. E.g., *Derry Enterprise*, October 20, 1908: "WED. and THURS. October 21 and 22 / TALKING PICTURES / MOVING PICTURES THAT TALK / AND IN ADDITION A SPLENDID PROGRAM OF / Moving Pictures and Illustrated SONG HITS" [advertisement]. "Talking pictures" of the period used a gramophone in sync with a film. "Cinematograph and gramophone are made to act together,—in other words, the movements of animated photographs are synchronized with the time of sounds, and this is done with such exactitude that the illusion is perfect": *British Trade Journal* 42 (May 1, 1904): 202.

170. N. Arthur Bleau, "Robert Frost's Favorite Poem," in *Frost: Centennial Essays III*, ed. Jac Tharpe (Jackson: University Press of Mississippi, 1978), 174–75.

171. Bleau, "Robert Frost's Favorite Poem," 175–76.

172. "A Note by Lesley Frost," in Bleau, "Robert Frost's Favorite Poem," 177.

173. Sir Philip Sidney, *Astrophil and Stella*, "Seventh Song," lines 1–2.

174. *Derry News*, December 14, 1906.

175. W. H. Auden, *The Enchafèd Flood* (New York: Random House, 1950), 7.

176. Charles W. Cooper, *Preface to Poetry* (New York: Harcourt, Brace, 1946), 604.

177. Richard Holmes, "19th Century Survey Documents the Decline of Local Farming," *Derry News*, November 26, 2015; William K. Stevens, "The Forest Primeval Isn't What It Used to Be," *New York Times*, September 24, 1995. See also *Report of the Forestry Commission of New Hampshire, June Session, 1885* (Concord: Parsons B. Cogswell, 1885), 74: "There are many large, cleared tracts which should be returned to woodland. . . . These lands are mostly either the sandy or gravelly plains, which form the highest terraces of the rivers, high hill and mountain pastures, or farms which have been abandoned because of impoverished and cold, sterile soil. . . . The thin soil gathered from the debris of centuries of forest vegetation is now gone—either burned up, washed away by the rains, or exhausted by cropping and pasturage." David R. Foster and John F. O'Keefe, in *New England Forests Through Time: Insights from the Harvard Forest Dioramas* (Cambridge, Mass.: Harvard University Press, 2000), 8, report that throughout New England, except in the mountains, by the 1840s "60 to 80 percent of the land was cleared for pasturage, tillage, orchards and buildings."

178. The U.S. Department of Agriculture has published a convenient spreadsheet with the relevant data on wheat prices since 1866–67: http://www.ers.usda.gov/data -products/wheat-data.aspx. See "Wheat Data—All Years" and "Table 1—Wheat: Planted acreage, harvested acreage, production, yield, and farm price." The prices are not in

constant dollars. The comparison here, made using USDA figures (constant dollars in parentheses), is $2.06 per bushel in 1866/67 ($32.70), $.49 in 1894/95 ($14.10), and $.99 in 1909/10 ($26.90). Calculations were made using https://www.measuringworth.com/uscompare/. Wheat is now far cheaper, under $4 per bushel.

179. Holmes, "19th Century Survey." In addition, "By 1900, local shoe factories were paying men $1.85 and women $1.45 for a 12-hour workday. Staying on the family farm meant working longer hours for less money; hired male farm workers might earn a dollar a day."

180. *New England Farmer*, n.s., 5 (June 1871): 299; *Fourth Annual Report of the Bureau of Industrial and Labor Statistics for the State of Maine, 1890* (Augusta, 1891), 131; *Country Life in America*, n.s., 1 (November 1901): 4.

181. Frost, *Collected Poems* (1995), 74, 100, 341.

182. Holmes, "19th Century Survey." See James, *American Scene*, 14–15: "The history was there in its degree, and one came upon it, on sunny afternoons, in the form of the classic abandoned farm. . . . These scenes of old, hard New England effort, defeated by the soil and the climate and reclaimed by nature and time—the crumbled, lonely chimney-stack, the overgrown threshold, the dried-up well, the cart-track vague and lost—these seemed the only notes to interfere, in their meagreness, with the queer *other*, the larger, eloquence that one kept reading into the picture."

183. Richard Holmes, town historian of Derry, said in a telephone call (January 13, 2016) that a dozen places locally still collected sap.

184. There are many ways to calculate the value of currency over time. The relative standard of living, perhaps the most effective method for the purposes here, suggests that because of deflation $100 in 1865 would have been worth only $49.90 in 1898 and $54 in 1905. In 2015 that same $100 would be worth $1250. See http://www.measuringworth.com/uscompare/.

185. Kenneth Libbrecht, "Snow Crystal Structure," in *Encyclopedia of Snow, Ice and Glaciers*, ed. Vijay P. Singh, Pratap Singh, and Umesh K. Haritashya (Dordrecht: Springer, 2011), 1040.

186. Thompson, *Early Years*, 264, 266, 314, 336; Frost, *Collected Poems* (1995), 63.

187. Frost reproached himself for having failed to call a doctor when Elliott fell ill. Frost, *Letters*, 1:532; Thompson, *Early Years*, 258; Lawrance Thompson, *Robert Frost: The Years of Triumph, 1915–1938* (New York: Holt, Rinehart and Winston, 1970), 623n26.

188. William Wordsworth, *The Prelude* (1850), 40–41 (book 2, lines 164–88).

189. Frost, *Collected Poems* (1995), 506. See also Thompson, *Early Years*, 267–68, 548n19.

190. Thompson, *Early Years*, 267, 548n18; Elizabeth Shepley Sergeant, *Robert Frost: The Trial by Existence* (New York: Holt, Rinehart and Winston), 58.

191. "Books and Kitchens," *Atlantic Monthly* 126 (July 1920): 137.

192. Alexander Smith, *City Poems* (Cambridge, 1857), 168.

193. The old tales were often set in an enchanted forest. For refuge, see "Snow White" and "The Girl Without Hands"; for danger, "Hansel and Gretel" and "Babes in the Wood."

194. Smith, *City Poems*, 170.

195. Arthur Quiller-Couch, ed., *The Oxford Book of English Verse, 1250–1900* (Oxford: Clarendon, 1900); Arthur Quiller-Couch, ed., *The Oxford Book of Victorian Verse* (Oxford: Clarendon, 1912). See Frost, *Letters*, 1:11, 55 and n67, 145, 154, 167 and n233.

196. For jiggery-pokery, see, for example, *Pearson's* 14 (November 1905): 529–30. Frost sold the *Youth's Companion*, a magazine for children. See Jonathan N. Barron, "Robert Frost in the Magazines," in *Robert Frost in Context*, ed. Mark Richardson (New York: Cambridge University Press, 2014), 313.

197. The cost of a year's subscription to the *Derry News* was stated beneath the nameplate.

198. Frost, *Collected Poems* (1995), 54.

199. Emails from Trudy Van Houten, June 19 and 21, 2016; and Suzanne Stillman, June 26, 2016.

200. "In these times of good sleighing, the law providing that horses travelling in sleighs, shall wear bells, ought to be rigorously followed up. The accidents happening from this neglect, are numerous": *Exeter News-Letter*, February 26, 1833, reprinting an item from the [Nashua] *New-Hampshire Telegraph*. Courtesy of the Exeter Historical Society.

201. Mertins, *Robert Frost*, 197.

202. *Poems of Emily Dickinson* (1998), 2:965 (#1107).

203. William Cowper, "The Task," in *The Poetical Works of William Cowper* (Philadelphia, 1806), 2:113; Thomas Moore, "The Loves of the Angels," in *The Works of Thomas Moore* (New York, n.d.), 6:56; *Oppian's Halieuticks: Of the Nature of Fishes and Fishing of the Ancients*, trans. John Jones (Oxford, 1722), 67.

204. *Derry News*, December 7, 1900.

205. *The Journal of Horticulture, Cottage Gardener, and Home Farmer*, n.s., 38 (March 4, 1880): 200; *The New-York Mirror, and Ladies' Literary Gazette* 5 (October 20, 1827): 120; Robert Southey, *Madoc* (London, 1807), 1:47.

206. Walter Scott, *Rokeby: A Poem* (1813), 222, 42, 56, 62, 63, 160, 229, 250, 290.

207. Milton, *Paradise Lost*, book 3, line 11.

208. Thomas Cole, *The Garden of Eden*.

209. Robert Frost, *The Poetry of Robert Frost*, ed. Edward Connery Lathem (New York: Holt, Rinehart and Winston, 1969), 224.

210. Frost, *Collected Poems* (1995), 209, 211.

211. Frost, *Collected Poems* (1995), 207. Who inserted the comma is not known, according to Mark Richardson, one of the editors of the Library of America edition.

212. *New Republic* 34 (March 7, 1923): 47; *Chapbook (A Monthly Miscellany)* no. 36 (April 1923): 3.

213. There's evidence of later dithering or sloppiness when Frost provided a holograph version of the poem for a calendric anthology of his poems: *From Snow to Snow* (New York: Henry Holt, 1936), frontispiece. There, as George Monteiro notes in *Robert Frost's Poetry of Rural Life* (Jefferson, N.C.: McFarland, 2015), 104, the handwritten "Stopping by Woods" has no internal punctuation in the thirteenth line, while the printed text (*Snow to Snow*, 20), among small changes in punctuation elsewhere, has the comma after "lovely." It's not unusual for a poet to have multiple versions of lines in his head—to have settled on one but under pressure find memory providing another. With no sign of considered intention, little weight can be put on such evidence.

214. Edwin Arlington Robinson, *The Three Taverns* (New York: Macmillan, 1920), 12.

215. Henry D[avid]. Thoreau, *Walden; or, Life in the Woods* (Boston, 1854), 185.

216. Frost, *Collected Poems* (1995), 15. See also "A Dream Pang" (25).

217. John Ciardi, "Robert Frost, the Way to the Poem," *Saturday Review* 41 (April 12, 1958): 13–15, 65; reprinted in John Ciardi, *Dialogue with an Audience* (New York: J. B. Lippincott, 1963), 147–57.

218. Mertins, *Robert Frost*, 371–72.

219. Lawrance Thompson and R. H. Winnick, *Robert Frost: The Later Years, 1938–1963* (New York: Holt, Rinehart and Winston), 267.

220. Vladimir Nabokov, *Pale Fire* (New York: G. P. Putnam's Sons, 1962), 203–4.

221. Thompson, *Years of Triumph*, 231, 236.

222. Frost, *Collected Poems* (1995), 160.

223. Elizabeth Shepley Sergeant, *Fire Under the Andes* (New York: Knopf, 1927), 300.

224. Thompson, *Early Years*, 597n7. Thompson first heard the tale in 1940.

225. Ciardi, *Dialogues*, 156–57.

226. Frost, *Collected Poems* (1995), 504.

227. *The Rubáiyát of Omar Khayyám*, [trans. Edward FitzGerald] (London, 1859).

228. Cooper, *Preface to Poetry*, 605.

229. The word seems to have an initial descender and to be four or five letters long, but the descender may be just an ink blot. It can't be "bay" or "gray," as it has no terminal descender.

230. Cooper, *Preface to Poetry*, 605.

231. Thompson, *Early Years*, 282, 336. Dr. Bricault bought Billy after Carl Burell left the farm in March 1902. Frost purchased Eunice shortly afterward.

232. Letter to Charles Madison, February 26, 1950, in *Understanding Poetry: An Anthology for College Students*, ed. Cleanth Brooks and Robert Penn Warren, rev. ed. (New York: Henry Holt, 1950), 603n.

233. Cooper, *Preface to Poetry*, 607.

234. R. C. Townsend, "In Defense of Form: A Letter from Robert Frost to Sylvester Baxter, 1923," *New England Quarterly* 36 (June 1963): 243. By "four of a kind" Frost meant keeping the *deep/keep* rhyme through the whole stanza. He may have felt that the rhetorical drama of the repeated line capitalized on rather than succumbed to the monotony—or call it single-mindedness.

235. Monteiro, *Robert Frost's Poetry*, 106, referring to letters to *Saturday Review* and *New Republic*.

236. "A Prayer in Spring," in Frost, *Collected Poems* (1995), 22.

237. [Edmund Burke], *A Philosophical Enquiry Into the Origins of Our Ideas of the Sublime and Beautiful*, 2nd ed. (London, 1759), 107. The first edition of 1757 had the ambiguous "than those which." Though even the revision is troublesome, he meant, "than those [images] have which."

238. Thompson, *Early Years*, 2, 49–50, 275–76.

239. Victor Emanuel Reichert, *Out for Stars: An Appreciation of Robert Frost* (Cincinnati: Hirschfeld Printing, 1969), 13.

240. David Hamilton, "The Echo of Frost's Woods," in *Roads Not Taken: Rereading Robert Frost*, ed. Earl J. Wilcox and Jonathan N. Barron (Columbia: University of Missouri Press, 2000), 130. Hamilton heard this at a reading in May 1961.

241. "Real estate agent H. G. Shute has sold the Magoon place for E. Y. Harwood of Manchester, to R. Frost of Lawrence, Mass., who will take immediate possession." *Derry News*, September 28, 1900. Frost moved in October 1, according to Parini, *Robert Frost*, 72.

242. Thompson, *Early Years*, 263–64.

243. Conversation with Richard Holmes, Frost Place, Derry, N.H., May 21, 2016.

244. Thompson, *Early Years*, 276.

245. The birthdays of the Frost children are conveniently recorded in Lesley Frost, *New Hampshire's Child*, note to book 1, 22 (the volume is unfortunately unpaginated beyond the child's numbering within her journals).

246. Thompson, *Early Years*, 280–81, 552n14.

247. Thompson, *Early Years*, 285, 314–15.

248. Thompson, *Early Years*, 323; Parini, *Robert Frost*, 94–95.

249. Thompson, *Early Years*, 339.

250. The weather records may be found in the National Oceanic and Atmospheric Administration (NOAA) online database: https://www.ncdc.noaa.gov/cdo-web/search ?datasetid=GHCND.

251. Lesley Frost, *New Hampshire's Child*, book 2, 45–46.

252. Thompson, *Early Years*, 252, 315. Dr. Charlemagne Bricault, to whom Frost sold the eggs, had decided to return to his veterinary practice in late 1905 or early 1906. Richard Holmes, the Derry historian, thinks the contract was canceled before Christmas because Bricault shows up as a veterinarian in the 1906 Lawrence city directory (email from Richard Holmes, January 13, 2016). There's no convincing evidence either way—Bricault might have placed his name in the directory before winding up the egg business. Frost could still have sold eggs to the Hoods, though at wholesale rates.

253. John Evangelist Walsh, *Into My Own: The English Years of Robert Frost, 1912–1915* (New York: Grove, 1988), 130, 251n130.

254. Lesley Frost, *New Hampshire's Child*, book 2, 45.

255. Lesley Frost, *New Hampshire's Child*, foreword to book 3.

256. Lesley Frost, *New Hampshire's Child*, book 3, 62–63.

257. Thompson, *Early Years*, 339, 341–42, 566n5, 567n8; Frost, *Collected Poems* (1995), 937. Frost took the family to the White Mountains in New Hampshire from 1906–1908 and to Lake Willoughby in Vermont in 1909, after which he sold the chickens and moved into Derry Village.

258. Lesley Frost, *New Hampshire's Child*, book 5, 36–37.

259. Tharpe, *Frost: Centennial Essays III*, 177.

260. Thompson, *Early Years*, 336, says that Frost had sold Eunice "before summer vacation" the year he started teaching part-time at Pinkerton Academy; that is, 1906. See also Lesley Frost, *New Hampshire's Child*, book 4, 54–55.

261. Lesley Frost, "Our Family Christmas," *Redbook* 122 (December 1963): 45.

262. *Derry, Rockingham Co. Seabrook, Rockingham Co. Rye . . .* (Boston: D. H. Hurd, 1892), 174. The corner where Frost stopped is at the crossroads south-south-east of Derry P.O. The poet, who would have been traveling from the west, after stopping turned south toward home, noted on the map as then the property of S. Magoon. See illustration.

263. *Derry News*, December issues, 1900–1906. The weather is usually reported in the "Derry Doings" column, when reported at all. The Nashua temperatures come from the NOAA online database: https://www.ncdc.noaa.gov/cdo-web/search ?datasetid=GHCND.

264. *The New Hampshire Register, Farmer's Almanac, and Business Directory for 1901* (Concord: New Hampshire Register, 1901), 93.

265. Thompson, *Early Years*, 548.

266. Email from Richard Holmes, October 22, 2015, and in conversation at the Frost Place, Derry, N.H., May 21, 2016.

267. Conversation with Richard Holmes, Frost Place, Derry, N.H., May 21, 2016. See also the Frost Place website: http://www.robertfrostfarm.org/historyproperty .html.

268. Thompson, *Early Years*, 339.

269. Thompson, *Early Years*, 260.

270. Thompson, *Early Years*, 266.

271. It may be hard to believe that Frost took seven hours to drive the wagon the ten miles or so from Pelham to Derry, though he did mention getting lost. Traveling on bad roads in heavy snow can be lethal.

272. NOAA online database: https://www.ncdc.noaa.gov/cdo-web/search ?datasetid=GHCND.

273. Louis Untermeyer, ed., *Letters of Robert Frost to Louis Untermeyer* (New York: Macmillan, 1963), 163; Reginald L. Cook, "Robert Frost's Asides on His Poetry," *American Literature* 19 (1948): 357.

274. Mertins, *Robert Frost*, 72.

275. Frost, *Collected Poems* (1995), 931.

276. R[alph]. W[aldo]. Emerson, *Poems* (Boston, 1849), 65; Dickinson, *Letters* (1960), 3:928.

277. Millicent Todd Bingham, *A Revelation* (New York: Harper and Brothers, 1954), 23. Lord's papers went to his sister's daughter (13–14) and after her death to a cousin, Mrs. Stockton (19, 21).

Index

In the crowded tenement of an index, there is never enough space. The main poems each have a separate entry here. With rare exceptions, other books and poems by the same author appear in the author entry, though in greater or lesser ways they are relevant to the main poem. Minor references have been discarded, like unhappy children—usually books and authors mentioned only in notes; insignificant figures who dash in once or twice; and any gods, biblical figures, Homeric heroes, and Shakespearean characters relegated to bit parts they no doubt resent.

CPSIA information can be obtained
at www.ICGtesting.com
Printed in the USA
LVHW01*2219030818
585887LV00002B/3/P